The Spanish Civil Wars

The Spanish Civil Wars

A Comparative History of the First Carlist War and the Conflict of the 1930s

Mark Lawrence

Bloomsbury Academic
An imprint of Bloomsbury Publishing Plc

B L O O M S B U R Y
LONDON · OXFORD · NEW YORK · NEW DELHI · SYDNEY

Bloomsbury Academic
An imprint of Bloomsbury Publishing Plc

50 Bedford Square
London
WC1B 3DP
UK

1385 Broadway
New York
NY 10018
USA

www.bloomsbury.com

BLOOMSBURY and the Diana logo are trademarks of Bloomsbury Publishing Plc

First published 2017

British Library Cataloguing-in-Publication Data
A catalogue record for this book is available from the British Library.

ISBN: HB: 978-1-4742-2940-1
PB: 978-1-4742-2939-5
ePDF: 978-1-4742-2941-8
ePub: 978-1-4742-2942-5

Library of Congress Cataloging-in-Publication Data
A catalog record for this book is available from the Library of Congress.

Cover design: Simon Levy
Cover images: (top) Pronouncement by the monarch, 1834, Madrid © Museo Zumalakarregi
Museoa. (bottom) The Karl Marx Battalion hailed by the populace, Spanish Civil War,
Barcelona © Photos 12 / Alamy Stock Photo

Typeset by Newgen Knowledge Works (P) Ltd., Chennai, India.
Printed and bound in India

CONTENTS

ILLUSTRATIONS

ACKNOWLEDGEMENTS

This book is the product of my past years of research and teaching in modern Spanish history. My project coincided with a move from Newcastle University to the University of Kent, and I have colleagues past and present to thank for being so accommodating in various ways. I owe particular thanks to a number of fellow Hispanists whose help, encouragement and corrections have proved invaluable. My particular thanks go to Adrian Shubert, Paul Preston, Charles Esdaile, Diego Palacios Cerezales, Seb Browne and the late Christopher Schmidt-Nowara. Any errors or weaknesses surviving in this script are entirely my own.

Some of my archival research in Spain and Mexico was funded by a Santander Mobility Grant and by a Newcastle University Faculty Research Grant. I am grateful for the permissions for citing material granted by the National Archives (UK), the Archivo Histórico Nacional (Madrid), Archivo General del Palacio (Madrid), the Real Academía de la Historia (Madrid), the archive of the Centro de Estudios sobre la Universidad of the Universidad Autónoma Nacional de México (Mexico City) as well as the Arxiu Històric de la Ciutat de Barcelona, the archive of the Biblioteca Universitaria de Zaragoza, the Archivo Municipal de San Sebastián and the Archivo Municipal de Málaga.[1] I owe particular thanks to the Museo Zumalakarregi (Ormáiztegui) for allowing me to reproduce images from its archive in this book.

Above all I thank my wife, Susana, and my daughter, Nicole, for making my efforts worthwhile. Our family odyssey over the past three years has taken us back and forth between Mexico and Europe, and finally from one extreme of England to another. It has been an exciting and challenging time for all of us, and we have extended family in Mexico and the United Kingdom to thank for their love and support. Neither this book, nor our new life in Kent, would have been possible without my wife's love and commitment. *Este libro está dedicado a Susana y Nicole.*

Canterbury, May 2016

Introduction

Why a comparative study?

The popularity of the Spanish Civil War (1936–39) invites a new comparative study. A war which legend has cast as an epic and tragic struggle between right and wrong was actually a complex and multifaceted civil war whose fault lines stretched back at least a century in Spanish history. As Romero Salvadó remarked, the Spanish Civil War pitted 'Republicans against Monarchists, centralists against devolutionists or regionalists, Catholics against anti-clericals, modernists against landowners, farmers against workers, and towns against villages'.[1] Helen Graham remarked, '[The] Spanish Civil War was not one civil war but several fought simultaneously'.[2] This book will show that it was also a civil war that read like a drawn-out episode of history played out one hundred years earlier. Spanish protagonists were polarized about the nineteenth-century origins of their tragic struggle. For General Franco's Nationalist side, all Spanish history since the first liberal constitution of 1812 had been an unmitigated disaster of lost empires, 'foreign' assaults on Church and Tradition, and of civil wars provoked by liberals in the name of godless rationalism. For the Republican side, the nineteenth century was full of tragic missed opportunities to uproot feudalism and modernize Spain along European lines, even though in 1839 and again in 1876 the liberals vanquished the most defiant strand of the old order, Carlism. The tragedy of a divided Spain loomed large on both sides as another chapter of civil war unfolded in 1936.

This book compares the two bloodiest civil wars in modern Spanish history, the First Carlist War (1833–40) and the Spanish Civil War (1936–39). Whereas the First Carlist War is barely studied outside of Spain, the Spanish Civil War is one of the most studied conflicts in history. Yet these two conflicts show striking similarities with respect to militancies, politics, regions, ideologies and their international context. The heartlands of right-wing insurrection in 1936 were the same as those of 1833. The ideological conflict was similar, only the outcomes were different. The battlefronts and rearguard of both conflicts show similar tensions with regard to mobilization, centralization and discontents. Both conflicts had origins in the collapse of Spanish imperialism at both extremes of Spain's 'short' nineteenth century, and imperial veterans dictated the nature and outcome of both civil wars. In 1840 the leftist American veteran (*ayacucho*) and Carlist War hero Espartero became the regent of Spain, and one hundred years later, the rightist (*africanista*) 'crusader' Franco followed suit. Above all, the international diplomatic environment with regard to Spain showed similarities. Foreign intervention proved decisive in both conflicts, albeit with opposing results. Both wars were also fought out in the opinions and consciences of other societies, the 1830s ushering in a 'First Great Cause' of international volunteering, pre-empting the famous International Brigades one hundred years later.

Naively we might wonder why these two civil wars have not been subjected to comparative study in a single monograph. Bookshelves across the world groan under the weight of books related to the Spanish Civil War, but outside of Spain they are bereft of First Carlist War titles, and nowhere do we find any study linking the two wars. But in fact the reasons for this omission are not at all baffling. As one of the leading authorities on Carlism, Jordi Canal, has commented, 'The centrality of "our" war of 1936–39 makes us forget that civil wars were the backbone of Spain's nineteenth century and leads us to underestimate their significance and impact.'[3] The First Carlist War seems irretrievably northern and old-fashioned, being the world's last major conflict before the advent of the photograph and the 'revolution in military affairs' produced by the rifle, railway and telegraph. The Spanish Civil War, by contrast, seems precociously modern. A correspondent in Spain called it 'the most photogenic war anyone has ever seen'.[4]

Two Spains?

Any study of the *longue durée* of the Civil War in Spain invites serious engagement with the somewhat discredited stereotype of the 'Two Spains' (the dichotomy of a secular and progressive Spain frustrated by the forces of traditionalism and clericalism). Even though the Two Spains have endured in the popular imagination, since the 1990s they have been critiqued by three significant developments in the historiography. First, a kind of 'normalization' school of historians has argued that Spain's nineteenth century marched much more in step with other European nation-states in terms of political and economic modernity. In part, this trend was a product of Spain's economic prosperity in the 1990s.[5] Second, Spanish Civil War historians have couched their analysis in the different comparative (and transnational) paradigm of the 1919–39 'European Civil War'.[6] This paradigm argues that the insoluble diplomatic and economic problems of the 1919 peace meant that interwar Europe effectively remained at war, and Spain acted as a vector linking the 1917 revolution with the Second World War. In the words of the 1930s Soviet foreign minister, peace in Europe had to be 'indivisible' or it was no peace at all.[7] Third, Spanish Civil War historians have stressed that the conflict's outcome was really decided not by indigenous factors but by international involvement in a context of impending world war, and that Spain as such was the fulcrum of the 1914–45 Thirty Years' War.[8] Foreign intervention certainly did dictate the outcome of the Spanish Civil War. But foreign intervention also dictated the outcome of the First Carlist War, yet no 'hundred years' comparative has been attempted.

In other ways the three Europeanizing trends have been welcome in that they have rescued Spain's history from the margins of 'core' Europe, and the comparative method has done most of this rescuing.[9] Marxian historians established a European path to modernity for which Britain and France provided the norm.[10] Spain, Germany, Russia and even Italy were found wanting because they failed to experience proper 'bourgeois revolutions', which were the key drivers of modernity. 'Peculiarities' were found in German history, 'backwardness' in Russian history and 'failure' in Spain.[11] These countries were too German, Russian or Spanish to be British or French. But from the 1970s, the failure-finding Marxian model was itself criticized, and this critique accelerated with the ending of the Cold War. The 'old order' was shown to have persisted across Europe, not least because the bourgeoisie merged with the old nobility instead of displacing it, thereby perpetuating the cultural as well as the economic hegemony of traditional elites.[12] Alexis de Tocqueville once likened the ancien régime to those rivers which 'after going underground, re-emerge at another point'.[13] Peculiarities were discovered even in advanced Western Europe which cast Spain's apparently patchy historical modernization in a new light. The idea of a European 'norm' lost ground. As Adrian Shubert observed, 'When everyone is "peculiar" peculiarity itself becomes a common ground.'[14]

This was ironic because Franco's regime itself accepted its 'difference'. 'Spain is different' was the slogan coined by the 1960s tourism ministry, and behind its exotic appeal to Northern European holidaymakers lay Franco's resolve to keep Spaniards in a state of perpetual political adolescence, with dogmatic claims that any liberalization along Western European lines would reopen the Civil War. Given the rebarbative dictatorship, historians felt an ethical as well as an intellectual interest in rejecting the Two Spains stereotype which pessimistically explained Franco's regime as a natural (to some even a necessary) victory of one Spain over the other. A comparative aspect to modern Spanish history therefore gathered pace. While Franco still ruled, Jordi Nadal and Josep Fontana compared the social and economic burden posed by Spain's large landowners – the *latifundistas* – with the endurance of Prussian agrarianism.[15] Andalucían landowners were compared to Prussia's Junker class, as political and military hegemons bereft of economic dynamism.[16] Helen Graham in 2012 drew comparisons between two 'Republics without Republicans', namely Spain's Second Republic and Germany's Weimar Republic, and also between the 1990s Balkan wars and the 1930s war in Spain.[17] Carlism itself has been compared to the irredentist Catholicism driving Polish nationalism.[18] The social and political history of the Spanish Civil War has attracted comparisons, especially from North American scholars for whom the remoteness of Spain created practical as well as intellectual reasons for subjecting the country to comparative analysis. Michael Seidman contrasted the success of Franco's counter-revolution with the failure of counter-revolutionary Whites in the Russian, Chinese and English civil wars.[19] Stanley Payne and Philip Minehan have systematically compared Spain's war with other European civil wars in the first half of the twentieth century.[20]

Placing the origins and course of the Spanish Civil War in the context of other civil wars is the business of the comparative method. This variety of history, after all, compares continuity in one context with change in another, thereby helping to identify the problems and peculiarities of case studies. To a large extent, comparative history existed even before the term was coined, above all because of the importance placed on the comparative method by the nineteenth-century founders of sociology, Emile Durkheim, Karl Marx and Max Weber. Weber's *Protestant Ethic and the Spirit of Capitalism* compared regions and continents and included sociological analyses. James Frazer's *Golden Bough*, written around the same time as Weber's *Protestant Ethic and the Spirit of Capitalism*, was a cornerstone of comparative anthropology and religious history. But the real father of comparative history in its own right was Marc Bloch, a medieval historian and co-founder during the 1920s of the Annales School, who was murdered by the Gestapo in 1944. Bloch developed what he termed a contrast-oriented chronological analysis. This analysis aimed to combine the strengths of narrative and comparative history by integrating the best parts of the former (i.e. the simultaneous analysis of factors that shape reality at any given instance) with the best parts of the latter (i.e. a thematic organization that shows contrasting patterns of continuity and change). Complex social questions are commonly explained by comparing local studies with global trends.

In other words, comparative approaches are implicit to a range of studies. They are particularly useful in new military histories.[21] Perhaps their greatest potential lies in the study of civil wars. Such studies have been increasing since the end of the Cold War. Internal, rather than interstate, conflict has dominated the post–Cold War world, informing strategic, social and ethical studies.[22] Comparative history interests not just historians and Hispanists, but also political scientists and sociologists. It is also relevant to current events as proxy wars, and their study, are coming back into fashion. The boom in the study of civil wars, as Stathis N. Kalyvas explains, comes from three sources: development economists, international relations experts and comparativists. The comparativists are mainly political scientists interested in state capacity, or the interface between economic inequalities and the inability of the repressive regimes to police their violent manifestations.[23]

Admittedly, comparative history has been criticized for its chronological determinism, for sacrificing analysis at the altar of 'telling the story' and, at worst, for smuggling preconceived and uncritical concepts into narrative analysis whose questionable validity must inevitably go unchallenged.[24] A common charge levied against comparative history is that it tries to compare unique and unrepeatable events. Two more charges relate to works which end up analysing different case studies in *parallel* rather than comparatively, or end up forcing similarities where they do not really exist.[25] Nineteenth-century historians were generally sceptical of historical comparisons. Instead, historicism in its Hegelian sense revered the individual traits and events that forged nations, and celebrated their intrinsic value as endowers of identity. This nationalist schema presupposed that nations predated all other political considerations, and, usually, that some golden age had existed which deserved to be revived. The architect of late-nineteenth-century Spanish conservatism Cánovas del Castillo said that nations were 'natural' and 'God-given'. Conservative historians well into the twentieth century rejected comparative perspectives as unwelcome intrusions from other disciplines, and even as an affront to national identity.[26] But the national identity of Spain was perhaps the most conflicted of all major states in modern Europe. The challenge posed to absolutism by the Constitution of 1812, along with the traditionalist Manifesto of 1814, polarized debate about the legitimate nature of the state and made recourse to armed force more habitual than anywhere else in Western Europe. The insurgents of 1833 and 1936 saw their cause as legitimate just as vehemently as the government forces opposing them. Given the irreconcilability of the Two Spains as demonstrated in both civil wars, we may reasonably state that a comparison of the two conflicts would be welcome.

A comparative study of two civil wars in the same state separated by one hundred years is at once both less controversial for its lack of Second World War reference and less likely to succumb to the major drawback of the comparative method. Comparative histories have often been criticized for failing to define clearly different times, regions and cultures, and for unbalancing transnational comparisons via a dearth of primary research in one case study.[27] But given that my case studies cover the same geography, state and evolving culture, the continuities and ruptures are inherently plain to see. There is far less risk of the sort of bias and preconception that might affect disparate case studies. The success of the Spanish government in 1839 and its defeat in 1939, or equally, the failure of the rebels in 1839 compared with their success in 1939, would appear a productive comparative study, given the background similarities.

By keeping the comparisons Spanish, this study avoids the tendency of the 'normalization' school to extrude Spanish history into a European framework, which ultimately proves inadequate. The philosopher Miguel de Unamuno judged cultivated Spaniards to be similar to cultivated Europeans across the continent, but 'there is an enormous difference between the Spanish social body and that of any other European country'.[28] Unamuno's generation was shaped by the 'Disaster' year of 1898 when Spain lost its remaining colonies of Cuba, Philippines and Puerto Rico in the war with the United States. The 1898 generation dominated early twentieth-century Spanish culture and its abiding anxiety concerned Spanish backwardness compared with the rest of Europe. Spaniards' perception of their country's 'difference' was a source of shame, which meant that any comparison of Spanish history to the rest of Europe was emotionally taxing, especially when the victors of 1939 flaunted Spanish 'difference' for partisan ends.[29]

After all, even though latent civil war is a common feature of modern European history, formal civil war dominates modern Spain more than any other Western European country. However much Spain conforms to a European norm, even if a European norm really exists, Spanish historians since the nineteenth century have been more polarized about their country's history than have the historians of any other Western European country. Spain had fewer symbols of national unity, and even today its national anthem lacks words.

Spanish contemporaries of the civil wars bestowed Manichean meaning on their tragedy. The poet and pessimist Mariano José de Larra (1809–37) surveyed the carnage of the First Carlist War: 'Here lies half of Spain. It died of the other half.' Liberal intellectuals in the 1830s showed a brutal intolerance towards the Carlist 'faction': the words of Espronceda in 1835 called for war to the knife. Pascual Madoz called three times for the Carlists to be sent to the scaffold.[30] Works of fiction, such as Galdós's *Maestrazgo*, did not need artistic licence in detailing gruesome atrocities. One hundred years of history did not dim the polarized Spanish imagination. The 1930s Catholic possibilist José María Gil Robles excoriated the Republic's anticlericalism as 'a battle-cry between the two Spains'.[31]

Spanish culture under Franco showed repeated allegorical references linking the 'Crusade' of 1936–39 with the earlier struggle of 1833–40. The historical Carlist movement, steeped in Romantic ideals and battles as it was, was a safer object for reflection than its troublesome modern successor. The Carlist movement itself obliged by remaining the most exclusive 'family' of the victors of 1939, as their creed, especially as far as northerners were concerned, was 'in the blood' and handed down through generations, symbols, rituals and fantastical stories that baffled outsiders. The twentieth-century doyen of mainstream Carlism Jaime del Burgo, in 1942, published a novel called *The Lost Valley* (*El valle perdido*). A Civil War pilot shot down over Navarra descends into a hidden valley inhabited by supercentenarian veterans of the First Carlist War who have aged in isolation and remained faithful to the pure values of the 1830s.[32] The Franco-era film *La Reina del Chantecler* (1962) depicts a Madrid actress of the Great War who is mistaken by her tragic suitor as a Margarita. Meeting his ultra-traditionalist family circle of Margarita maiden-aunts and matriarchs in Navarra, the actress indulges the misconception that she is descended from an insurgent family of the 1830s. She is praised to come from a line from the First Carlist War, the *purest* of the struggles. One of the official 'Saturday novels' of 1939 contrasted the pure and 'fair and square' nineteenth-century wars between Carlists and Liberals with the degenerate 'reds' of the 1930s.[33] Sometimes works of fiction linked the 1830s and 1930s wars in a manner less than supportive of the Victory of 1939. The best-selling novel by Gaspar Gómez de la Serna, *Cartas a mi Hijo*, won the Francoist '18 July' prize for fiction in 1961, even though the author offered a critical analysis of the violence of civil wars and of why modern Spain had been so prone to them. The novel made pointed reference to the 1839 Vergara Accord that ended the First Carlist War as an allegory to the failure of the victors of 1939 to attempt any reconciliation with the vanquished.[34]

The Two Spains thus haunted the culture of Francoism. Yet they have also haunted academic history. The baton of polarization was passed by such contemporaries as Larra and Gil Robles to historians. Right-wing historians liked to exaggerate the international (especially French) origins of Spain's liberal tradition, casting the left as essentially un-Spanish,[35] while others on the extremes celebrated the organic 'Spanishness' of Carlism in both civil wars.[36] Left-wing historians, for their part, wrote historicist tomes anchoring nineteenth-century reforms in precedents found in early modern Spain.[37] And while partisanship is a dominant feature of nineteenth-century history writing, it pales in significance to the partisan Spanish Civil War scholarship. Even today historians who revise our understanding of Spain's fateful 1930s are accused of being either unreconstructed Marxists or apologists for Franco.[38] The Two Spains have never really gone away; in fact, they are in rude health.

By anchoring this comparison in Spain itself, this study adds two new comparative perspectives to the Spanish Civil War. First, the role of foreign intervention will be placed not in the unhelpfully teleological context of the Second World War, but in the context of similarly decisive foreign intervention in Spain one hundred years earlier. Second, by keeping the comparisons Spanish, it avoids some of the complications of transnational civil war studies. Stanley Payne found revolutionary political violence in the Spanish Civil War to have been 'middling': proportionately greater in degree than Hungary in 1919, less than Russia during the 1917–22 civil war and about the same as Finland during its 1918 civil war.[39] But the violence was also proportionately the same as Spain's own civil war one hundred years earlier. Unlike in the case of Hungary and Finland, neither the First Carlist War nor the Spanish Civil War was shaped by linguistic exclaves of foreign powers or existing foreign garrisons. Both civil wars took place in an established nation-state with the same national borders.

Modern Spain is Western Europe's most conflicted state. The Spanish state failed to convince all Spaniards of its legitimacy between the collapse of the Bourbon monarchy in 1808 and the death of Franco in 1975. Periods of apparent stability, such as the 'Restoration' of 1876–1923, barely concealed tensions under the surface. Formal civil war afflicted Spain during 1820–23, 1827–28, 1833–40, 1846–48, 1872–76 and 1936–39. Even the national war of 1808–14 and the imperial wars of 1810–24 and 1895–98 were to some degree civil in nature, owing to their revolutionary and counter-revolutionary impact. The Peninsular War of 1808–14 in particular has attracted comparative attention. Foreign volunteers saw 1936 as a rerun of 1808, as foreign armies invaded Spain in both conflicts.[40] Both Nationalists and Republicans exaggerated the foreign backing of their internal enemies, harped on the 'popular resistance' lesson of the Peninsular War, and the ghost of the Peninsular War heroine Agustina de Aragón apparently fought on both sides in the 1930s.[41] The origins of modern Catalanism have even been dated by some historians to the Peninsular War.[42] The most complete Peninsular War comparison was delivered by the late Ronald Fraser, whose study is one of two major histories comparing the Peninsular and Spanish Civil Wars.[43] Of course, neither the liberal challenge of 1812 nor the traditionalist challenge of 1814 can be properly understood without reference to the Peninsular War. But the Peninsular War remains a 'national war', hence its Spanish name 'War of Independence', even if the summer of 1808 was racked by social conflict and a collaborationist *afrancesado* element existed under French occupation. In fact, the Two Spains of 1812 and 1814 did not come to blows under Napoleon but only later, briefly during the 1821–23 Royalist War, and substantially during the 1833–40 Carlist War. In so many ways the same Spains came to blows again in 1936, and not just in terms of ideology, but also in similar terms of soldiering, radicalization, civil–military relations, exile and international participation.

If a comparative study might thus seem justified, it must confront a major imbalance in sources. The 1930s civil war enjoys a veritable galaxy of literature, and until the 1980s consolidation of democracy in Spain its best examples were written abroad.[44] The 1830s civil war, by contrast, has attracted very little non-Spanish literature beyond memoirs and travel narratives. Even though the Spanish scholarship is substantial, and innovative in respect of the Carlism side, links between the 1830s and 1930s wars have only been made thematically and only in terms of the Carlist movement itself.[45] Martin Blinkhorn presented the Spanish Civil War from a Carlist perspective ('Fourth Carlist War'), but without substantial comparison to its 1830s predecessor.[46] The significant role played by Carlism in securing the rebel victory of 1939 was deliberately downplayed by official Francoist histories. At best, the Francoist state saw Carlism as a medievalist quaintness adrift in the regime's ethos of urbanization and industrialization. At worst, Carlism from the 1960s spawned its own left-wing 'heresy' (neo-Carlism) associated with the Pretender Carlos Hugo and socialist 'self-management', and a historical reinterpretation of 1830s Carlism as 'objectively revolutionary'. After Franco's death, historical Carlism experienced a boom in scholarship led by Pedro Rújula, Josep Carles Clemente, Alfonso Bullón de Mendoza, Antonio Caridad Salvador, Jordi Canal and Julio Aróstegui, to name only some of the most distinguished historians. But Carlism still lacked appeal when compared with the vindicatory studies of Spain's vanquished Second Republic, even when compared with such other 'catastrophist' right-wing forces as the Falange.

Therefore, navigating two such historiographically and internationally mismatched conflicts in the space of a medium-sized monograph presents challenges in terms of integrating primary and secondary sources. The uneven historiographical base prevents a systematic and equal comparison in each paragraph; rather comparisons are frequently made between rather than within paragraphs. Given that the Spanish Civil War has already been unusually well researched in Spanish archives, and given that my international comparison of the two conflicts forms a discreet chapter, my study draws substantially on less-explored international archives (the National Archives of London and Mexico City) in the case of the 1930s. Two particularly useful archives I have used for internationalizing both wars are the letters of the all-powerful British ambassador during the Carlist War, George Villiers, and one of the leading Latin American advocates of the rebels in the 1930s, Aurelio Acevedo. My reflections of the 1830s conflict are substantially informed by primary research undertaken both at Spanish archives and at the National Archives of London, as well as by contemporary Spanish and European newspapers. This privileging of primary sources relating to the First Carlist War helps to augment the minor corpus of English-language scholarship and to cast the Spanish Civil War in a new light.

The book is divided into two sections (Domestic and International Aspects of the Spanish Civil Wars), each containing three thematic chapters. The domestic section divides into battlefronts, home fronts and memory and legacy. As battles are the business of wars, including civil wars, the need for military history would appear self-evident. According to Carl von Clausewitz, the military theorist whose readership peaked during the Spanish Civil War, 'battle is for war what cash payment is for trade'.[47] But instead of adopting the 'bird's eye' view of Clausewitzian military strategy, this study joins the flourishing field of new military history in its exposition of the 'worm's eye' view of soldiering, embracing such everyday anxieties as food, sex, hospitals, desertion, morale and family. There is no dwelling on battles from a purely strategic point of view, and some famous battles are left out for this reason. Some of these themes are civil–military in nature and are discussed in Chapter 2, which explains the similar patterns of political fragmentation and radicalization which each war produced. While these two chapters follow a broadly chronological approach to each conflict, their main emphasis is thematic. I admit that the battles of 1937–38 were fought in a much more modern way than those of 1936, but my main interest remains in the surprisingly primitive battle conditions which continued in the 1937–38 Battle of Teruel and, to a lesser extent, the 1938 Battle of the Ebro. The first section concludes with a comparative study of the legacies and memories of each conflict. The second section opens with a short chapter comparing the imperial origins of both civil wars, relating to Spanish America and Morocco, respectively. The study then develops two chapters comparing the diplomatic and military interventions of foreign powers, the experiences of foreign volunteers and the experiences of defeat and exile.

Context of the Spanish Civil Wars

The context of the Spanish Civil Wars includes a longer history of the Spanish armed forces and more irregular armed combatants effecting revolutionary and counter-revolutionary change. The cause of Isabella and her mother in the First Carlist War opened up a period of praetorianism in Spanish history that culminated in the war one hundred years later. Victory over Carlism in 1840 undermined civilian supremacy in the liberal state. Just like her father during the Peninsular War, Isabella could not live up to her propaganda image forged during the Carlist War. The 'innocent' princess turned worldly soon after coming of age in 1843. Her crown was the lynchpin of a dysfunctional party system which rendered both 'restrained' liberals (*moderados*) and, to an even greater extent, 'advanced' liberals (*progresistas*) beholden to military champions to get them into power. The veteran generals of the Carlist War became handmaidens of politics, discarding their sashes for prime ministerial frock coats, and performing this clothes-change in reverse whenever the queen called upon a rival general to form a government. All officer ranks were understandably eager to enrich themselves in this post-war praetorianism system, as whichever military faction that successfully 'pronounced' to form a new government was showered with pensions, decorations, promotions and, best of all, a title of nobility.[48] Even though the civil war against the Carlists had been waged in the name of liberalism, the victors, beginning with the queen herself, retained remarkably illiberal political and social values. A British obituary of the queen, coming from the country which had done the most to ensure her victory in the 1830s, captured this situation perfectly, as the leading generals of her day, 'Whatever their mutual dissensions … were always interested in keeping her on the throne as an instrument of their own power.'[49]

Isabeline liberalism came to an end in the 'Glorious Revolution' of 1868, which opened up six years of disintegration and reintegration amid Cantonalist revolts, another Carlist War and the reassertion of the army's role in political life from 1874, now as the spearhead of counter-revolution and adopting an insular, corporate ideology. The Second Carlist War of 1872–76 marks a milestone between the two civil wars analysed in this study. The Second Carlist War, after all, not only stemmed from the first;

it also anticipated the 1930s. The post-war Canovine Restoration of 1876 entrenched the socio-economic power of the large landowners (*latifundistas*), bestowing the Republic of 1931 with its most dangerous social crisis. The Second Carlist War was the product of a monarchical crisis in 1868 just as surely as the Spanish Second Republic would be in 1931. The Carlist and ultra-Catholic press of 1931 compared the calamity of revolution in 1931 with that of 1868. Similar Republican programmes of 'religious freedom' provoked violent anticlericalism in both these wars, and Carlists in both were quick to see this in apocalyptic terms, ironically drawing strength from the decadence of liberal revolution, oblivious to the fact that both the preceding Isabeline and Alfonsine liberal monarchies had in fact been strongly supportive of the Church.[50] The Republic's heavy-handed suppression of the Carlist press in 1931 was provoked by fears of what happened after 1868 and not (yet) of fascist entryism into the traditionalist movement.[51] And even international comparators were drawn. The Paris Commune shaped the way that Spanish Republicans, Monarchists and Carlists – along with their foreign backers – viewed their struggle just as surely as the Bolshevik Revolution shaped the militancies of the 1930s. The centrifugal tensions between the Cantonalists of 1873 and the Republican regime are analogous to the breakdown of the Republican state in 1936, as was the ensuing counter-revolution brought about by the government armed forces (Pavía's coup of January 1874 and the Communist-backed counter-revolution of 1937). There were even traditions linking the war of the 1870s with that of the 1930s. The humanitarian attentions of the Pretender's wife, Doña Margarita, led to the eponymous Carlist women's organization that tended to welfare and the wounded during the 1930s. There were countless examples of elderly veterans of the 1870s being feted during the Carlists' preparations for war after 1931.

If the Second Carlist War must await its own comparative historian, for our purposes there are compelling reasons to compare the 1830s and 1930s. As we shall see, both these wars separated by one hundred years were fundamentally distorted by international intervention. Harsh peaces linked the experience of 1839 with 1939, and Franco-era repression can in many instances be explained by the events of the 1830s. The Carlists' beloved *fueros* (devolved rights under the Spanish Crown) were undermined in 1841 by the definitive removal of the Spanish customs frontier to the Pyrenees. This move rewarded the liberal victors of San Sebastián and Bilbao and punished the Carlist hinterland.[52] Franco's victory one hundred years later reversed these advantages, as the provinces of Alava and Navarra, which had been defeated in 1839, now found themselves on the winning side and under Franco would experience significant industrialization and modernization for the first time.[53]

There are also compelling socio-political factors linking the 1830s with the 1930s. The Republican coalition of 1930 comprised a majority of parties which thought that the historical problem of the Spanish left had been its timid readiness to compromise with the forces of reaction.[54] Underlying this view was an ideological dispute born out of the 1830s liberal revolution, namely whether Spain had yet undergone a 'bourgeois revolution'. However arcane this point of Marxist ideology may appear, it retains relevance for comparativists. The revolutionary of 1835–37 who abolished the feudal order and instituted capitalism, Juan Alvarez Mendizábal, was that rarest of creatures in nineteenth-century Spain, a bourgeois genuinely committed to bourgeois revolution.[55] But the bespectacled intellectuals of the Republican Pact of San Sebastián missed this indigenous precedent out of fascination for the apparently more cogent models of other countries, especially France. In their lack of wonder at the Carlist War revolution they appeared vindicated by the behaviour of Spain's bourgeoisie after 1931. Far from consolidating the bourgeois Republic, Spain's bourgeoisie was alienated by its egregious anticlericalism and the power of its working-class allies. Most of the middle classes voted not for the secular centre-left Republic of Manuel Azaña, but for the Catholic umbrella party, the Acción Popular (from 1933 known as the CEDA), which vowed to protect property and the 'natural' hierarchies of society.

Given the absence of a revolutionary bourgeoisie in 1931, the key role played by the Socialists in the first Republican government was misfired from the start. This was expressed in an unworkable conflict between revolutionary and parliamentary legitimacies once the Republic was established in 1931. Whereas the political leader of the Socialists, Indalecio Prieto, embraced a parliamentary evolution towards socialism, his great rival, the trade union leader, Largo Caballero, became increasingly prone to revolutionary solutions to the social crisis. Outlying this rivalry was the great intellect of Spanish Socialism, Julián Besteiro, who opposed the Pact establishing the Second Republic in his ideologically purist belief that the bourgeoisie must first make their revolution. Besteiro was blamed for the failure of the Socialist general strike of December 1930 and the failed army rising in its support, which meant that the initiative passed to the pro-Pact wings of the party.[56] Besteiro's view that Spanish feudalism survived unchecked, that the liberal reforms of the First Carlist War had not produced a middle-class breakthrough, was shared by the vast majority of foreign observers. The liberal Catholic expert on the Second Republic, Henry Buckley, dubbed the Army, Bishops and the Crown the 'ABC of Spanish politics'.[57]

In fact, both Besteiro and Buckley were right but for the wrong reasons. The old order survived in Spain precisely because its nineteenth-century middle classes had merged with the old feudal order, intermarrying economic with cultural hegemony. Spain's generally non-existent revolutionary bourgeois class would appear to have been in good company. Twenty-first-century historians are highly sceptical about whether the Marxian model of bourgeois revolution is of any use at all, as studies of even such hallmark revolutions as 1640s England and 1790s France have shown their respective bourgeoisie to have been anything but dynamic in displacing feudalism.

Even though the advent of the Republic in 1931 marked a rupture significant enough as to require comparison with similar ruptures in history, the candidates for comparison lie not with France, England or Russia, but within Spain itself. Feudalism was formally abolished during the Carlist War of the 1830s, sustaining the triumph of a liberal constitutional tradition in Spain which endured with a few exceptions until the Spanish Civil War. The 1830s civil war began a liberal hegemony and the 1930s civil war ended it. In other words, one Spain was defeated in 1839, and in 1939 that Spain had its revenge.

Placing the Spanish Civil War in an indigenous context requires us to re-engage with the timeworn paradigm of the Two Spains. Cleary, the Two Spains are in reality hermetic and rigid in simplifying the nature of Spain's division in both conflicts. Although both civil wars demonstrate two visions of Spain in the broadest sense, leftist Liberals and Republicans against rightist Carlists and Nationalists, both wars also show ideological and sectarian divisions within 'both Spains' which cannot be easily straitjacketed into either one vision of Spain or the other. The 1830s right was divided between an absolutist wing, exemplified by the late Ferdinand VII, and a traditionalist, theocratic wing which wanted to turn back the clock in respect of eighteenth-century Enlightened Absolutism and to restore the medieval rights of the Church, nobility and decentralized political structures.[58] These *ultras* grew alarmed at Ferdinand's policy of limited amnesties and his gradual revival of the most moderate economic and administrative reforms trialled during the Liberal Triennium. Even though Ferdinand defeated an armed royalist rising in Catalonia in 1827, the 'Carlists' took heart that the ultra Crown Prince, Don Carlos, might still succeed the now ailing Ferdinand as the king had no son. Yet the healthy birth in 1830 of the king's daughter, Princess Isabella, changed everything. The 'Salic Law' that had regulated Spain's Bourbon monarchy since the early eighteenth century reserved the throne for male heirs (even though this law had been abolished, albeit secretly, in 1789). Yet in a complicated series of events the king and his last wife, the Neapolitan María Cristina, ensured that their daughter, Isabella, would succeed under her mother's regency once Ferdinand was dead.

One hundred years later found the Carlist rebels just one faction among as many as five (Catholics, Alfonsine Monarchists, the Army and the Falange) fighting the Republican government. All of these comprise the right-wing variety of the Two Spains, yet complexities can still be found in respect of the extremist movement which had not (nor could have) existed in the 1830s: the Falange, or Spanish Fascist party. Carlists charged that the totalitarianism and industrialism of the Falange invited Bolshevism by the back door. Significantly, the more moderate Catholic middle classes, largely former supporters of the authoritarian reformist movement known as *maurismo*, shared Carlist fears of the Falange, especially its propaganda attempts to 'redeem' the Spanish worker.[59]

Rebels in the 1930s were thus as split as their 1830s forebears. What they shared was their rebelliousness against broadly left-wing governments (the 'other Spain') which they thought lacked legitimacy. They were therefore rebels, and throughout this monograph I shall describe them as such rather than get bogged down in other plausible descriptors (e.g. reactionaries, Carlists, Nationalists or White Spain). My rationale for doing so is neither to cast value judgements nor to sacrifice differentiation on the altar of readability. Francoists spurned rebellion. The first Francoist history of the Spanish Civil War insisted that the rising of July 1936 was no mere rebellion but a 'war of liberation'.[60] With possibly more justification the Carlists of 1833 insisted that the government side were the real rebels and the insurgents the 'liberators'. But in fact both the Carlists of 1833 and the Nationalists of 1936 may be termed rebels because they militated against constituted governments. In 1832 Pope Gregory XVI condemned all rebellion or sedition against constituted powers.[61] This matters because the Carlists made far greater claim to religious justification than the government, even though Gregory XVI was bound by his own doctrine against open support for their cause. Equally, the Vatican in 1931 had been conciliatory to the Republic, removing the inflammatory monarchist, Cardinal Segura, from the role of nuncio and replacing him with the apparently more amenable Tedeschinio and Vidal i Barraquer and issuing only modest condemnation of the church burnings committed by anarchists that year.[62] When the rebels of 1936 launched civil war, they claimed clerical blessing, but in fact no substantial Vatican support for the rebellion against the constituted power arrived until a year into the war.

By the same rationale I describe both the triumphant Liberal side of the 1830s and the vanquished Republican side of the 1930s as 'the government'. Whereas 'National' Spain in the 1830s was the Cristino government, the *Nacionales* of the 1930s were the rebels. The 'Two Spains' paradigm is equally as problematic for describing the left-wing Spain as it is for the right. The 1830s war, after all, produced the definitive division of the Liberal movement into 'moderate' and 'progressive' wings, each with different ideologies about political participation, local government and the Crown. The 1830s civil war witnessed sectarian divisions behind government lines pitting the periphery against the centre, the revolution against moderation and militias against the army, constituting a spectrum of politics ranging from the centre to the radical left. Equally, the 1930s civil war found the political elements constituting the government radically divided between revolutionary and moderate wings, the major difference being that unlike in the 1830s these divisions proved fatal. Only a minority of the Republicans waging war were actually 'Republicans' in the image of 1931, owing to the mobilization of anarchism and the more ambiguous role of communism. The Republic's General Monck, Colonel Casado, was sanguine about the forces serving the government: 'All the political parties and the syndicalist organisations of the Popular Front began to recruit volunteers to repel the aggression. The masses, both of workmen and peasants, came out in their thousands. Groups and battalions of militiamen were formed rapidly, and this was the basis of the People's Republican Army.'[63] But in practice the Republican forces were only partially Republican. The Basque government controlled its own forces, many of the militias in the Aragón front supported the workers' and peasants' revolution and not the bourgeois democratic Republic. Those that did – such as the Communist brigades – are best understood as 'the People's' only in the sense that Stalin's Congress of Soviets by 1936 was 'the People's'. What united these disparate forces was their defence of the government, even if they differed as to what form the present and future government should take.

Pre-war political crises

The downfall in April 1931 of Alfonso XIII and the implantation of a Republic caught the Carlist movement at perhaps its lowest ebb ever. Yet Carlists greeted the advent of the Republic with undisguised joy. The answer to this mystery is twofold. First, the dynastic dispute between the two branches of the Bourbon dynasty was largely settled and, second, popular foreboding that a Republic was bound to assault clericalism promised to rouse hitherto despondent militants into a new Carlist crusade.[64] The advent of an unambiguously secularizing government promised to heal the Carlist movement of a century of debilitating infighting that was basically caused by the fact that a legitimate movement is tied to its legitimate king. Whereas Carlos V of the first civil war had shown himself bigoted, militarily mediocre and lacking in vision, all his successors except Carlos VII of the 1870s war had proved even worse. Admittedly, matters improved during the last third of the nineteenth century thanks to the legacy of the 'Neo-Catholic' intellects, Jaime Balmes and Donoso Cortés, and the ongoing influence of Cándido Nocedal whose neo-Catholic homilies were entirely concerned with traditionalism as a whole and entirely detached from the dynastic dispute of 1833. Above all, the publications of Vázquez de Mella offered an ideological canon which had been largely absent in the 1830s and which, crucially, established the overriding principle of legitimacy as a set of values and actions and not merely a question of the rightful succession. Even though Carlists in the twentieth century could not seriously hope for the military strength of their 1830s forbears, they were nonetheless liberated from the prospect of their future war effort being held hostage to the whims of their king.[65]

Spanish Civil War protagonists utilized indigenous precedents. July 1936 found the Carlists in Navarra as the only military force among the rebels possessing a preconfigured and consistent worldview of religious monarchy stretching back to their first great war of the 1830s.[66] Both contemporaries and subsequent Marxists were engaged by the controversial march of Spanish liberalism which triumphed in the 1830s and succumbed in the 1930s. As Carlists prepared for renewed war in the 1930s, their initial reluctance to side with Falangists (on account of the Falangists' 'heretical' statism and secularism borne of a 'socialist deviation' of Hegelianism) was overcome when both radical right-wing forces underlined their common rejection of the entire nineteenth-century legacy of liberalism.[67] As one Falangist ideologue put it, 'The Latin sees that liberalism involves something *against nature*.'[68] The traditionalist historian, Jesús Casariego, in 1938 rejoiced that 'twice in the nineteenth century Liberals enlisted foreign help to crush Spanish tradition, but in this third war we are back. Let them suffer.'[69]

During the 1830s Spain was still seen as important enough in itself to occupy the diplomacy and political agendas of Europe's Great Powers. By contrast, by the 1870s, Spain had become a sideshow, and would have remained even more so in the 1930s had not Europe's proxy war between left and right supervened. Moreover, the greater reach and brutality of the 1830s war bears comparison with the 1930s. Foreign volunteers fought in both wars, inspired by similar motives and under comparable banners of propaganda. The Spanish Civil War may have been the first modern European war in which propaganda played a key role in shaping both war aims and the conflict's international appeal. But a large degree of this Manichaean propaganda, of 'liberty' *versus* 'religion', reads like a page out of the booming newspapers of the 1830s war which were devoured in pulpits and cafes across Spain. The 'pure' Carlist insurgency model of 1833 was heralded as the national model for defending God, King and Tradition by later generations of Carlists who could no longer dream of the support enjoyed by their predecessors in the 1830s. Carlists in the 1870s and again in the 1930s were at pains to stress the examples of the first struggle: the memory of the 'Great Man' (Zumalacárregui), Red Cross interventions drawing precedents from the 1835 Eliot Treaty, even the loan-seeking entreaties of the 1870s 'Carlist Committee of England' trying to learn from the mistakes of their 1830s forbears.[70]

The Navarra *requetés* (Carlist militia) who rose in July 1936 repeated the heady mix of penitence, festivity and above all memory that linked their rising with their forbears in 1872 and, especially, 1833.[71] The 1930s Carlist press gave particular publicity to surviving veterans of the 1870s,[72] just as the 1870s press had honoured veterans of the 1830s.[73] Civilians coming under fire in the 1930s remembered how similar experiences befell their grandparents in the 1870s,[74] just as their grandparents in the 1870s had remembered their own grandparents' experiences in the 1830s. Oral history testimonies remained all the more resilient because no Spanish involvement in the recent Great War had displaced them.[75] Carlist insurgents in 1936 saw the conflict as a 'third Carlist War', their offensive towards Bilbao as a 'third Carlist siege' and the treasuring of martial and religious phenomena handed down since the 1830s was proof of the survival of bygone ways.[76]

The Cristino transition of 1830–33 was markedly different from the Republican takeover of 1931–36. A year elapsed between the Cristino 'coup' at La Granja and the outbreak of civil war in October 1833. The last pre-war prime minister, Cea Bermúdez, purged organizations prone to rebel. Most of the 200 officers of the palace guard purged in 1832 appeared as armed Carlists a year later, whereas the two new regiments of household cavalry that replaced them were resolutely Cristino. Most importantly, a misfired Carlist revolt in Leon in March 1833 enabled Cea to banish to Portugal both Don Carlos and his entourage.[77] Given both the poor infrastructure in Spain and the fact that 1833, unlike 1936, was a dynastic war, this banishment of the rebel figurehead was a masterstroke. It ensured that the rebels of 1833 had to ignite their insurgency in the country, for, barring the fleeting exception of Bilbao, all attempts to seize control of the cities failed. The rebels of 1936, by contrast, hoped and planned for a coup: a frantic telephone call between Prime Minister Giral and rebel leader Mola forty-eight hours after the revolt revealed that Mola planned to 'pacify Spain' within a week in the style of Primo de Rivera in 1923.[78] What thwarted the rebel coup in 1936 was the loyalty of about half of the Republic's military and paramilitary forces, egged on by the radicalized working classes. The 1936 war, even more than the war of 1833, was the product of a polarized and radicalized society. In order to set this in context, we should explain the events of the pre-war 1931–36 Second Republic, offering comparisons to the pre-1833 period where appropriate.

Spain's 1920s were generally characterized by an economic boom caused by the repatriation of the colonial capital since the lost war with the United States in 1898 and Spain's profitable neutrality during the First World War. Generally, economic growth was concentrated in areas where Spanish industry had been concentrated to begin with, especially Barcelona (which diversified its economy) and Bilbao. The population of major cities doubled between 1900 and 1930.[79] The revenues generated by the boom led to a huge investment in public infrastructure, including schools and hospitals, much greater than anything that would be accomplished during the Republic. But an economic crisis underlay the last years of the Primo de Rivera regime, marked by a structural trade deficit despite an aggressively protectionist government policy. Foreign investors were frustrated by the oil monopoly, and the peseta, which was already weak in 1926, soon fell to 39 to the pound sterling, and then 58 to the pound sterling a few weeks after the Republic had been proclaimed, while the same standard of living cost 4 pesetas in 1920 but 7.20 in 1931.[80]

The Republic of April 1931 thus inherited a deepening economic crisis set amid the world's Great Depression. Spain's Socialist movement had been divided by the Primo dictatorship which fell from power in 1930. The majority part, the trade union confederation (UGT) led by Largo Caballero, a pragmatic, then ideologically uncommitted organizer, and, to a less obvious extent, the pro-Fabian professor, Besteiro, collaborated with the dictatorship. Thus they were rewarded with seats on the Council of State in return for a no-strike policy. But the democratic socialists, Indalecio Prieto and Fernando de los Ríos, both resisted collaboration. The anarcho–syndicalist union (CNT), along with the tiny Communist Party (PCE), had been weakened by Primo's repression. This situation meant that when Primo de Rivera resigned in January 1930, little initiative came from the political centre or right as the late-nineteenth century Liberal and Conservative parties were decrepit and the dictator's 'single party', the Patriotic Union (UP), was fast disintegrating. But if the Republicans and Socialists possessed a rare window of opportunity during 1930–31, the deteriorating economy robbed them of a solid base of support. The economy was being pulled down by the Depression, which was accompanied by strikes, poor harvests and an ensuing explosion in membership for the rival CNT as a result of General Berenguer's legalization of the organization (as a product of his less hard-line dictatorship called a *dictablanda*). Caballero feared the rise of the rival CNT and therefore kept faith with the demands for social revolution emanating from the UGT membership. An agriculture union, the FNTT (National Federation of Workers on the Land), was set up in 1930. But most Spanish farm labourers faced a bleak 1930s of depressed prices, underemployment and starvation wages, much like their counterparts on the eve of the First Carlist War who battled against a comparable depression in world agriculture.

The other pillar of the 1930s Pact were the Republicans themselves. A Republican alliance had already existed in 1926, led by Lerroux's old Radical Party, and joined by Azaña's Acción Republicana. But a creed which had previously been based on small discussion groups became rapidly modern, organized and popular. The Pactists knew that the old intellectual republicanism of elites would no longer suffice. Gabriel Jackson explained that they would have to take 'quick action on behalf of the rural masses if the new regime were to take root outside the urban middle classes and the aristocracy or organised labour'.[81] Yet republicanism was no longer the preserve of the left. Even the centre-right founded the Derecha Liberal Republicana in July 1930, led by Alcalá Zamora and Miguel Maura.[82]

The Spanish right thus faced an acute crisis. The last caretaker dictator, Admiral Aznar, faced unstoppable momentum to reconvene the Cortes. In the meantime municipal elections were convened for 14 April 1931 and these turned into an effective referendum on the monarchy. Republican candidates swept the boards in most towns and large cities; only in the cacique-ridden countryside did the monarchists keep their grip. Alfonso XIII temporized by proposing to abdicate in favour of his heir Don Carlos. A year before this gesture might have worked, but now it was too late. He left Spain in order to 'avoid a civil war', a grandiloquent statement as a civil war needs two sides, and hardly anyone was about to raise a finger to defend the king.[83] Even the most conservative of political elites, such as the *regeneracionista*, Miguel Maura, refused to have to do anything with the monarchy (Maura said the monarchy had committed suicide).

The right was in such disarray that the new Republican authorities did not need to undertake the same level of purges as had the Cristinos of 1832–33. Most of the leftist socio-economic and political reforms were enacted before the civil war erupted in 1936, unlike in the 1830s when these were carried out under the duress of war. For this reason, the pre-war Republican period continues to polarize historians. Whereas leftists have claimed the governments of 1931–33 and 1936 as high points of Spanish culture, rightists have called them intolerant and anti-pluralistic,[84] which in trying to undertake drastic reforms in old order Spain produced 'an impossible Republic',[85] or a 'Republic without republicans'.[86] It is clear that the first Republican government attempted to correct the abuses that had festered under a century of constitutional politics. The war minister Manuel Azaña endeavoured to 'republicanize' the army, thereby curing it of a legacy of praetorianism dating back to the 1830s, in the knowledge that the army was a 'matter of life and death'.[87]

Preparing for war

Both civil wars were preceded by localized civil wars which acted as dress rehearsals for prolonged conflict. During 1827–28 this took the form of the rising of the Aggrieved, or Malcontents, in Catalonia, which was a Carlist rising in all but name. The ultra clerics and aristocrats who rose against the liberalizing reforms of King Ferdinand were crushed, but the same figures and ideas inevitably rose again once the king died in 1833. Ideologically, the Carlist faction demanded the restoration of the traditional monarchy of the feudal orders and a privileged role for the Church. Such was the promise, they claimed, of King Ferdinand, who in 1814 acknowledged the traditionalist 'Manifesto of the Persians' as his justification for ousting the Peninsular War liberals from office. But Ferdinand did not convene the traditional Cortes as the 1814 signatories had hoped, not even in 1823 when the king had the real armed support of traditionalists to thank for restoring him to his full powers. By 1827 the gloves were truly off. Traditionalists launched a rising in Catalonia aiming to replace Ferdinand with his more reactionary younger brother, Don Carlos (hence the term 'Carlist'). They failed, but the Cristino 'coup' at La Granja in 1832 energized their attempts once more.

The split in the ruling classes upon the king's death foreshadowed the more dynamic split of 1936. Just as the First Carlist War was pre-empted by the reactionary rising known as the Agraviados in 1827–28, so was the Spanish Civil War pre-empted by a revolutionary rising in October 1934. The Socialist rising in Asturias in October 1934 was as much a product of Socialism's frustrated engagement with the Republic as the Agraviados revolt was a product of Traditionalism's frustrated engagement with

Fernandine absolutism. The insurrectionary 'Manifesto of Pure Royalists' of 1826 was the first 'legitimist' rebellion against a legitimate king. As the conservative historian, Carlos Seco Serrano, put it, 'The manifesto launched a revolt which ignored the legitimate *origins* of absolutism in favour of the legitimate *practice* of absolutism.'[88] Another conservative historian, Stanley Payne, makes similar critique of the pre-war Socialists of the 1930s for whom the Republican system of bourgeois elections could be supported only if it led to Socialism.[89]

The political leaders of both revolts planned for a restrained show of strength in order to move government policy in their direction, which meant, respectively, the abdication of Ferdinand VII or at least a timetable for his succession by his younger brother, and the retraction of the right-wing CEDA members from the government in order to prevent a Dolfuss-style fascist takeover of Spain. Both Carlist and Socialist rebellions were localized to Catalonia and Asturias, respectively, but the limited geographical range did not make for easier planning, as militants escaped the control of their leaders. But the violence of the insurgents, and the even greater violence of the successful government counter-insurgencies, turned both the Agraviados and the Socialist revolts into dress rehearsals for the real civil wars which followed. Militants in both risings presented a pattern which distinguished the military history of both civil wars that followed, namely, their reluctance to submit to militarization under the direction of Carlist and Communist authorities, respectively.[90]

Military force crushed Reaction in 1828 and Revolution in 1934 but not the ideas behind them. It has been a central shibboleth of Francoist and neo-Francoist literature that the Popular Front regime of 1936 against which the rebellious officers revolted was not democratic but a leftist regime controlled by revolutionaries.[91] So powerful was this trope that in 1939, even the leader of the Republican forces in Madrid, Segismundo Casado, delivered the defeated Republic to Franco in order to 'save Spain from Communist takeover'.[92] A similar shibboleth pertained to the 1832–33 period following the events in 1832 at the royal palace of La Granja, which both Carlist and mainstream conservative historians have described as a coup d'etat. The 'events of La Granja' in September and October in 1832 saw the fall of the pro-Carlist prime minister Calomarde and his replacement by Cea Bermúdez. On 16 September, when King Ferdinand appeared to be at death's door, Calomarde persuaded María Cristina to revoke the 'Pragmatic Sanction' of 1830 and restore the succession to Don Carlos. Calomarde held that neither the army nor the Carlist-dominated militia, the Royalist Volunteers, would accept the infant Isabella as the successor to the throne. But the recovery of the king's health two weeks later emboldened the royal couple to reinstate the Pragmatic Sanction in short order, and to conduct a purge of Carlists from the army, militia and administration. The path to civil war was now set. The Carlists called the purges tyrannical, and the female succession illegal both in terms of Bourbon custom and of the Pretender's

God-given birthright (Don Carlos had been born in 1788, one year before the Cortes secretly abolished the Salic Law for the first time). The Cristinos, an exiled Carlist propagandist proclaimed, 'are liberal in word and tyrannical in deed', who despite their rhetoric of representative government refuse to convene a Cortes to resolve the dynastic dispute: 'We Carlists are neither scared nor disgusted by the convening of the Cortes … as long as it meets in the traditional manner promised in 1814 … why did no-one advise Cristina to mend this broken promise and break the impasse?'[93] Carlists, along with Alfonsine monarchists, rallied to reject the 'illegitimate' Republic of 1931. Barely weeks into the Republic's anticlerical programme, one ultra-Catholic deputy from Navarra threatened to repeat his forefathers' resistance to the revolution, 'taking refuge in the mountains to seek counsel of our despair and of our dignity as free men against tyranny'.[94] The years 1823 and 1931 made a right-wing revolt a possibility, 1827 and 1934 made it a probability and 1832 and February 1936 made it a certainty. The only question was whether these revolts would succeed, fail or do neither (and instead lead to civil war).

PART ONE

The domestic aspect of the Spanish Civil Wars

Carlos V, 'King of Spain', to his subjects (Abrantes, Portugal):

Spaniards! Now I am your king, and in introducing myself to you for the first time under my royal title, I have no doubt that you will follow the example of obedience that I showed to my brother, the late King Ferdinand, and that you will all fly to join me under my banner, making yourselves worthy of my fond and sovereign good will. Obedience is owed to princes who have legitimate claim to the throne, and you will know that the full weight of justice will come down on those disobedient and disloyal fellows who do not wish to heed their Sovereign and Father who wishes only to bring them happiness.[1]

Francisco Franco Bahamonde, divisional general in chief and high commissioner of Morocco:

Once more the Army, united with the other forces of the nation, has found itself obliged to respond to the wishes of the great majority of Spaniards who, with infinite bitterness, have seen disappear that which unites us in a common ideal: SPAIN. At stake is the need to restore the empire of ORDER within the REPUBLIC, not only in its external appearances but in its very essence; to achieve this, it will be necessary to labour with justice, taking no account of classes or social categories, to end the division of the country into two groups: those who dispose of power and those whose rights are trampled underfoot ... The re-establishment of AUTHORITY, forgotten in these past years, implacably demands that punishments be exemplary and are seen to be so by the seriousness and rapidity by with which they are carried out.

To execute these tasks rapidly, I order and command:

Article 1. Martial law is declared in the whole territory and all armed forces in consequence are militarised.[2]

1

The battlefronts in the
Spanish Civil Wars

Overview

Both the First Carlist War and the Spanish Civil War shared battlefield similarities in terms of tactics, morale, technological backwardness, foreign soldiers and terror, and in terms of the human geography of the fighting. But whereas the 1930s war took less than three years to reach its military denouement, the 1830s war took more than twice as long. The 1930s witnessed formal front lines criss-cross Andalucía, Extremadura, Castile and Aragón, and before the last government resistance in the north was crushed in Asturias in October 1937 a front line also divided the Basque country and encircled Cantabria and Asturias. Unlike in the 1830s there was comparatively little guerrilla warfare behind front lines. The 1830s, by contrast, witnessed Carlist guerrilla activity – some persistent, some fleeting – afflict most of the forty-two newly designated provinces of Spain. A front line similar to that of 1936 encircled the Basque country from 1834, but the only other areas of Spain where Carlists became established enough to defy government territorial control was the Maestrazgo area from 1835, expanding after 1837 to include parts of Valencia and other parts of Aragón, and some of the mountain fastnesses of Catalonia (and here largely only from 1837). Barring the Basque country, military campaigns thus experienced greater degrees of chronological and territorial unevenness than in the 1930s, as well as a much greater insurgency and counter-insurgency dimension.

Whereas the rebels of 1936 managed in the first forty-eight hours of their revolt to seize control of about one-third of Spain, their predecessors in 1833 failed to achieve anything like this success. The only real military genius of the 1830s was the Carlist general Tomás de Zumalacárregui, who by the end of 1834 established a regular army to expand control over rural Navarra and the three Basque provinces proper. Rebel expansion was halted in the summer of 1835 by government defensive victories at Mendigorría and the first siege of Bilbao. But revolution in government cities weakened the ability of the army to do much more thereafter than defend the Basque coastal ports and a series of forts encircling the Carlist-held Basque country. The permeability of this northern front allowed the Carlists to mount expeditions into government-held areas of Spain beyond the River Ebro, on a limited scale into Catalonia in 1835, and on a much greater scale in 1836 and 1837, but the Carlists failed to take Bilbao or to conquer sizeable cities.

The 'deep war' of 1836–37 produced a radicalization of the government rearguard comparable to the Spanish Revolution one hundred years later. A centralized military and political structure from November 1837 helped to defeat the last serious rebel expeditions and gradually to suppress both guerrilla activity and to blockade the rebel Basque country. When the northern Carlists sued for peace in August 1839, the eastern zones of General Cabrera could not withstand overwhelming government superiority and all national territory was in government hands by June 1840. The complex history of the 1830s contrasts with the conventional trajectory of the Spanish Civil War. The rebels of 1936 planned for a successful coup but the fact that government resistance proved neither so weak as to succumb nor strong enough to suppress the coup meant that civil war was the result. Terror and superior tactics brought most of Andalucía and Extremadura under rebel control in the summer and autumn of 1936, but the rebels failed to take Madrid. Government defensive victories followed early in 1937 around the capital at the Jarama, the Coruña road and Guadalajara, aided as at Bilbao in the 1830s by significant foreign intervention. But the rebels regained their initiative in 1937 conquering the Basque country, Cantabria and Asturias, ending the war on the northern front and allowing superior reconcentration of forces against the main front. Despite initial government success in offensives at Teruel and on the Ebro, the rebels held the upper hand, dividing Catalonia from the rest of the government zone in April 1938, and rapidly conquering Catalonia over the winter of 1938–39. Although Madrid held out unbeaten, a coup from within in March 1939 sealed the fate of the Republic and Franco's Nationalists occupied all national territory by 1 April 1939.

Whereas the start of First Carlist War found the army on one side of the struggle (Cristino), the start of the Spanish Civil War found the army divided. The Cristino purges of 1832–33 were both ruthless and thorough: upon the death of Ferdinand VII in September 1833 virtually the entire establishment was Cristino. In July 1936, by contrast, Spanish society was divided from top to bottom, as the Popular Front government had been unable to purge potential rebels effectively. But the Cristino establishment did not have everything its own way. Once hostilities began, the Cristino army was wasteful, poorly supplied and ineffective in its operations against the smaller enemy forces which, for their part, maximised their advantages, especially in terms of guerrilla warfare. By contrast, the Spanish Civil war was exceptional in seeing conflict from the outset as being waged between two conventional armies.[1] One continuity qualifies this observation: Carlist Navarra, which, uniquely in July 1936, saw armed civilian uprising in support of Nationalist rebellion.

Government ability to prevail in both 1833 and 1936 was compromised by the limited, and sometimes counter-productive, effect of pre-war military reforms. Cea Bermúdez, the prime minister summoned to office in the wake of the La Granja coup of September 1832, purged the army and Royalist Volunteers of Carlists, but this crackdown involved reducing the standing army to a mere 40,000 effectives at the time of the Carlist rising. Recent history had taught Cea of the dangers of army coups, and while he made the army safe from subversion, he also made it too small to nip the rising in the bud (and the best part of the army upon Ferdinand's death was deployed not in the restive north but along the Portuguese frontier). The government army was poorly prepared not just in terms of numbers, but also in doctrine. Even though academies had gradually professionalized their training since the Peninsular War, they remained remarkably slow to digest the lessons of a generation of civil and imperial wars. Conventional war doctrine was emphasized in manuals instead of the more relevant question of irregular war, and government officers had to wait until 1834, a full year into the Carlist War, for a manual concerning vital mountain warfare to be made available.[2] The first Spanish translation of Antoine-Henri Jomini's *Treatise on Grand Military Operations* was published at the start of the First Carlist War. But Jomini's stress on the importance of internal lines of communication – the key source of Carlist strength in the Basque country – was not studied in advance by government officers, and General Fernández de Córdova, commander of the army of the north between the revolutions of 1835 and 1836, had to learn Jomini's lessons the hard way.[3] At the height of military disasters in 1837, radical journalists urged imitation of the apparently successful Prussian military model.[4] But the key to the success of Prussia's system, the marriage of civil and military society via universal conscription into the part-time reserve (*Landwehr*), was unrepeatable in Spain. The Spanish *Landwehr*, the National Militia, was no ally of the regular army as in Prussia, and still less a buttress to authoritarianism.

One hundred years later found the government equally ill-prepared to confront the rising. The official infantry training manual, which dated from 1914, was already four decades out of date, and yet it was reissued in 1937 unedited, despite the fact that the tactics were proving very different in the Civil War. Whereas Spanish infantry tactics in the 1930s as in 1830s remained second-to-none, there was very little theoretical instruction in the great military innovations of the 1880s – artillery and engineers – and the lessons of failure in the Cuban War of 1898 went unlearned.[5] General Franco's prestigious Zaragoza military academy (Academia General Militar) was staffed by instructors who had been chosen purely on the basis of battlefield merit in Morocco rather than their theoretical or pedagogical abilities.[6]

These military shortcomings had provided ample work for Manuel Azaña, the war minister in the first Republican government of 1931–33. Azaña, however, was more concerned by the political rather than military dangers in the Spanish Army. He vowed to civilianize an army which since the Disaster of 1898 had been the backstop for social and political counter-revolution. Azaña tried to impose effective civil supremacy over the Spanish army by closing the africanista-dominated military academy at Zaragoza, offering retirement on full pay to officers unwilling to serve the Republic, abolishing the army's authoritarian regional structure (the Captancies-General) and reducing the army's ability to administer its own promotion and discipline.

In one way, this Republican civilianization of the army struck the greatest contrast to the decade before 1833. Even though Ferdinand VII in 1823 reduced the revolution-prone Spanish army to a skeleton force, its praetorian powers were restored at least on paper, which meant that the army during 1832–33 had carte blanche to purge Spain of Carlists and to ride roughshod over civilian authority. Yet in another way pre-war Spain in the 1930s remained just as dependent on military power for domestic order as during the era of Calomarde. Azaña, who was anxious to defend the Republican centre-left against violence from both the right and the extreme left, did not fully revise the 1906 'Law of Jurisdictions' legislation which shielded the army from civilian jurisdiction. In June 1933, the centre-left government tightened up public order legislation by declaring three escalating states of exception. The first 'state of prevention' allowed Civil Guard and army forces to ban meetings, publications and travel, and allowed intervention in commerce and industry. The second 'state of alarm' empowered authorities to arrest suspects without trial, entry into private homes and temporary exile of troublemakers up to 250 kilometres from their homes. The third 'state of war', or martial law, handed over all power and responsibility to the military. Emergency courts could dispense summary justice in all three states.[7] Rebels in July 1936 could thus legally proclaim a state of war 'in defence of the Republic', even though this legislation had ironically been designed to quash rebellions. Equally, the rebels of 1833 exploited the draconican legislation of 1824 which allowed for the summary execution of 'rebels' in the name of the king.[8]

Ironically, the Azaña reforms had the potential to improve the military effectiveness of the army, being inspired as they were by the post-Dreyfus French army model. But they failed to remake the army in the Republic's image. Of the 8,000 of Spain's 21,000 officers who accepted the generous retirement terms, some 5,000 to 6,000 were of the army's Republican minority, which produced an even more reactionary army in 1936 than had been the case in 1931.[9] To some extent, the beleaguered Popular Front government elected in February 1936 followed the example of the Cristino faction of La Granja: instead of shrinking the army it extended soldiers' summer leave as the best means of defusing a coup attempt. Yet, unlike the Cristinos of 1832–33, who dismissed, imprisoned and exiled Carlist officers on the simple grounds of lèse-majesté, the Popular Front of 1936 faced a harder task of neutralizing officers who remained outwardly 'Republican'. Basically, Spain was more polarized in 1936. The forebodings of the liberal poet Mariano José de Larra, in 1833, that 'it only takes one word to raise a mob, inflame passions, and cause a revolution,'[10] were doubly true in 1936, especially as suspect generals retained their commands. The government dispatched suspect generals to remote garrisons, in the Canaries, Balearics and the peripheries of mainland Spain, all the while fearing a backlash from the revolutionary left as much as an overthrow by a rightist coup. But the rebels' access to aircraft, first liaison and then transport, transformed their chances to a degree unimaginable in 1833.[11]

Strategies of war

Despite the modernity of international propaganda and military intervention, both conflicts were waged by the Spaniards themselves using obsolescent strategies of warfare. The First Carlist War was the last great conflict before the mid-nineteenth-century military revolution, and the Spanish Civil War a strategic 'swan song' of Great War (and earlier) styles of combat before the onset of the mechanization revolution. Siege warfare characterized the two most iconic international causes of each war, Bilbao and Madrid, respectively. But both involved offensive strategies as if from a bygone era. No great or rapid concentration of guns was mounted against Bilbao in the Napoleonic warfare style of the previous generation. Equally, even though developments in artillery stretching back to the 1880s were supposed to have made the fortification of cities an irrelevance in twentieth-century warfare, sieges during the Spanish Civil War accounted for two of the greatest propaganda campaigns of the entire conflict. General Franco's relief of the besieged Alcázar at Toledo in September 1936 made no sense from a purely military perspective, as it delayed what might have been a decisive assault on Madrid. But it served the dual propaganda purpose of increasing Franco's fame and stiffening the resolve of the rebel garrison besieged for fifteen months at Oviedo (Asturias), and of the troops encircled by the winter 1937–38 government offensive at Teruel (Aragón).[12] The siege of the Alcázar had been a virtual parody of the militia offensive. The worst the rebel defenders had to endure was potshot rifle fire and the occasional light artillery round. Franco's media-catching delay at Toledo gave the government defenders time to prepare rudimentary defences outside Madrid. The capital was not taken, and it became an international symbol of liberty just as assuredly as Bilbao during 1836–37. But the capital, much to the bafflement of foreign observers, was neither surrounded by the rebels nor subjected to a truly intense combination of artillery and aerial bombardment.

The major military innovation on the government side in the 1930s concerned the Mixed Brigade, a unit between 3,400 and 4,200 strong containing all necessary arms of service (artillery, medical, supply, veterinarian) with the intention of allowing independent actions. But these units, which formed the basis of the Popular Army, have been criticized for being unwieldy and containing too many non-combatants.[13] In other respects, the fact that no Spanish innovation in warfare could expedite either the 1830s or 1930s war rendered foreign military intervention all the more decisive. As we shall see in a later chapter, in the first war intervention was decisive not so much regarding British, French and Portuguese troops on land, but regarding British naval intervention along the northern coast. On land, Spain lacked modern communications, railways and electric telegraphs, localizing the experience of war to a remarkable degree, but at sea British naval support, especially the advent of the steamboat, denied victory to the rebels. In May 1835 the British government transferred two large steamboats to Cristino service and these were rechristened the *Reina Gobernadora* and *Isabel II*.[14] Anglo-Cristino naval cooperation across the northern Spanish coast was vital in protecting Bilbao and repelling repeated seaward offensives by Carlist forces intent on securing access to seaborne foreign aid. Government troops, sometimes supported directly by British Royal Marines, in turn could be transported swiftly over comparatively long distances and yet retain their full fighting strength. The First Carlist War was the first conflict in which steam vessels played a decisive role. Equally, the Spanish Civil War witnessed the advent of a new weapon for transporting troops, but from the air. The Nazis' 'Operation Magic Fire' dispatched Ju-52 transport aircraft to sustain the rebel Army of Africa's fragile offensive in Andalucía. The modernity of steamship and aircraft rescued their respective sides from defeat. But they could not alter the low-intensity and attritional nature of each war.

The wars are decided in the north

From September 1834 the rebels' growing strength in the Basque country was answered by the erection of government 'blockhouses' on commanding peaks.[15] Thereafter the pattern of the northern war involved increasing militarization by both sides resulting in local sieges, offensives and counter-offensives. The rebel insurgency of the Basque country reached regular dimensions by the spring of 1835. Yet formal (though still porous) front lines now encircled the Basque country, even as rebel guerrilla activity persisted in

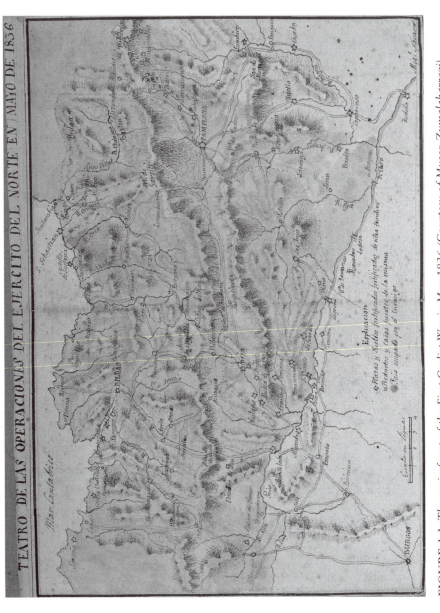

FIGURE 1.1 *The main front of the First Carlist War in May 1836 (Courtesy of Museo Zumalakarregi).*

other regions of Spain. From early 1937, the 'war of the columns' was over as regular armies dominated militia and vigilantes, carving out formal (yet still porous) front lines across Spain. Rebel advances on the Basque front were halted by government defensive victories at Bilbao and Mendigorría in the summer of 1835. Similarly, rebel advances on and around Madrid were halted by government defensive victories at the Battles of Madrid (1936), followed by three rebel encircling attempts at Coruña road, Jarama and Guadalajara (1937). All these rebel attempts failed and led to a stalemate.[16] Thereafter both wars would be decided by the fronts in northern Spain, either directly or indirectly. Government pressure forced the northern rebels to sue for peace in 1839, ending the war on its main front. Over the summer and autumn of 1937 the rebels conquered all of the government-held north, thereby gaining economic and demographic superiority over the government, and gaining the ability to concentrate forces on the main front, and so win a war of attrition.

From 1835 Carlist Spain remained strategically secure in its redoubt north of the River Ebro (see Figure 1.1). Over the summer of 1835 the government Army of the North amounted to 120,000 effectives, including 30,000 held in reserve, but sickness and supplies rendered only one-third in war-fighting readiness, which meant that local victories (such as Los Arcos in August 1835) could not be exploited.[17] The militarization drive was immense by 1830s standards: by the end of 1835, the government army had been doubled to 200,000, not including the same number of paramilitary militia, and the addition of some 22,000 foreign auxiliary troops and 25,000 Basque 'free corps' totalled the government regular forces at a quarter of a million.[18] But as in the Spanish Civil War this high militarization did not always equate to actual fighting. Service was accompanied by long spells of inactivity, and just as in respect of quiet fronts in the Spanish Civil War, quiet fronts in the 1830s bred everyday patterns of resilience, live-and-let-live with the enemy, camaraderie and the distractions of involvement in civilian social and economic activities. The rebel army, too, from the summer of 1835 was now normalized, large and often spent days without seeing action. One hundred years later found Spain once more the scene of a 'pauper's war', in which both sides could only deploy one significant operational army at any time. Even though the battles of 1937 and 1938 were far more modern than those waged by the columns of 1936, throughout the Spanish Civil War important military activity only occurred on comparatively small sectors of the front.[19]

Rebel resourcefulness

Pauper's war was a natural result of ill-preparedness. Spain had worse military infrastructure than other European powers in both the 1830s and 1930s. Also, pre-war governments in both epochs, with the possible exception of the 1935 Gil Robles war ministry, were concerned not with the military abilities of their armed forces, but with the political danger they presented. Even though the government kept the loyalty of all its preserved officers in 1833, the army itself had been reduced to a mere 45,000 men as a safeguard against a Carlist coup. Equally the anguished Popular Front government deliberately extended conscripts' summer leave in 1936 as a safeguard against a coup. In 1833 the government was successful to the extent that the rebels were forced to mount their insurgency from the countryside. Purged officers rallied those Royalist Volunteers who had not yet been disbanded, as well as villagers alive to the religious and economic advantages offered by armed rebellion. If the government army over the winter of 1833–34 had been large enough to suppress the rebellion before it had become established in the Basque country, then there may have been no Carlist 'war' at all but perhaps another localized counter-insurgency like the suppression of the *Agraviados*.

The situation facing the government in July 1936 was more acute in terms of time and resources. Certainly, the government possessed most of the 145,000 serving soldiers, along with most artillery and arms depots, whereas the only obvious initial gain by the rebels was the highly defensible Castilian plateau (*meseta*) and its wheatlands.[20] The government also possessed most and the best aircraft. Only twenty-four aircraft were available to the rebels at the start of the rising, and these were both outnumbered and outclassed by the 120 machines available to government.[21] The government possessed most of the navy, and at least two-thirds of the population, including Madrid and Barcelona. However, the forces available to the government were inferior in quality, and outwardly loyal officers and the paramilitary Civil Guard proved more prone to defect to the rebels than was the case in reverse. There was less chance of defection from the paramilitary militias under the control of political parties and their trade union affiliations. But, as Michael Alpert has shown, these forces were militarily less effective than their actual numbers would suggest. During the first weeks they lacked unified command and coordination. Even though the government tried to call up reservists, it never intended to send these to the militias as this would have compounded the problem of military ineffectiveness. As the Spanish Revolution gripped the government zone, the militias' sectarian politics proved deleterious to the war effort. Despite revolutionary propaganda, the 'people in arms' proved to comprise neither the majority of the male population of military age nor necessarily its best fighters. Even though anarchist and socialist propaganda proclaimed that a few lorry-loads of manly volunteers would suffice to defeat the fascist attack-dogs, the results were mostly negative for the government side. Equally, loyal government officers were often demoralized by their dealings with the militias, and it is little surprise that most middle-class officers, Catholics and Liberals alike, joined the pro-militarization Communist Party for protection.[22]

An analogous military inferiority beset the government side in the 1830s, as the desperate expansion of regular and militia forces from 1835 failed to halt the surge of Carlism. Restrained liberal (moderado) army officers were at loggerheads with revolutionary liberal (exaltado, later progresista) militias on their own side, who, like their 1930s descendants, differed as to whether militarization or people's militias were the best prescription to defeat the enemy. The exaltado-progresista regimes of 1835–37 were accompanied by a heightened civil–military crisis, and several civil and military governors were hounded from office or assassinated.

The rebels in both wars were militarily effective not just because of the sectarianism of their enemy. Rather they also showed success in a country where Napoleon famously observed 'large armies starve and small armies are swallowed up'. Carlism's greatest warlord, General Tomás de Zumalacárregui, presided over a brilliantly parsimonious expansion of guerrilla forces in Navarra from 1833 until 1835, seldom wasting scarce food or munitions. A British Carlist volunteer rejoiced that Zumalacárregui had improved Carlist forces from 'a guerrilla band into an army threatening the conquest of Spain'.[23]

The second-best warlord was the commander-in-chief of Carlism's eastern zone after 1835, Ramón Cabrera, who demonstrated similar resourcefulness. Cabrera spoke of war 'having innate secrets' which could 'outweigh the technical superiority of the enemy'.[24] The British ambassador George Villiers derided the antiquated order of battle deployed by the 'Tiger of the Maestrazgo' and his '1200 indifferent cavalrymen and three or four thousand vagabonds armed with pikes and sticks and knives … including officers whose only care is to steal and who leave the countryside a scene of desolation'.[25] But Villiers failed to appreciate the operational effectiveness of Cabrera's foco-style strategy. Cabrera attracted so many recruits that he had to keep groups of them armed only with pikes in the rearguard, where they could be readied to pounce on arms left by retreating government forces. On occasion he even confounded his enemies by using flocks of sheep to leave false footprints which distracted pursuing government troops. Cabrera regularly formed testudo formations from surrounding carts and used them as a battering-ram in localized sieges. Rebel soldiers used to itinerant and irregular fighting did not balk at taking shoes from dead soldiers on the battlefield, something which government soldiers were comparatively reluctant to do.[26] One hundred years later, Carlists drew inspiration from the historical example of the shoestring war effort of Carlos V, as if the austerity of the rural campaign could negate the godless materialism of the 1830s Urban Militia and the 1930s Popular Front.[27] Even on their most militarized front (the Basque country), where the Carlists from 1835 possessed advanced armaments foundries, demands on production always outstripped supply, and various voluntary measures were encouraged, such as the making of saltpetre and the turning in of old iron and even antiquated Peninsular War–era weapons, including artillery and shot. Carlism was 'ruralized' not just by its reactionary world view but also by its war effort.

The strains of insurrection in 1936 made great demands of the rebels once again, albeit in a context of powered flight and the internal combustion engine. Rebel officers in the crucial first weeks of the war exhausted necessary zeal in the knowledge that failure would result in disaster. Rebel fighter ace García-Morato used his obsolete fighter to great effect during the summer 1936 advance into the province of Córdoba. Imitating a one-man combined arms operation, García flew in close support of advancing rebels, dropping hand-held bombs on government militia and strafing machine-gun posts.[28] Navarra Carlists in the first days of the 1936 rebellion updated Cabrera's tactics by placing sheet-metal on cars, turning them into makeshift armoured vehicles and using them to great effect in bolstering the rebel drive north to seal the French frontier.[29]

Securing the frontier with France

The neighbouring Great Power to the north shaped the calculations of both sides and of foreign interventions in both wars. The Nazi ambassador to the rebels at the end of 1936 was already foretelling the strategic calamity Franco's victory would pose to France: 'The French would need three army corps along their border with Spain, and it would be rendered difficult, if not impossible, for them to transport their North African forces by sea to France.'[30] Very much with this hope in mind, Germany supplied the rebels with artillery, light tanks, naval firepower and even aircraft, to spearhead the offensive to seize control of Irún on the French-Basque frontier in September, even as the bulk of the Spanish forces involved remained with their obsolescent and, in many cases, improvised weapons. Makeshift armoured cars of sheet-metal were also employed by the 2,000 assorted government militia defending the border city of Irún, a product of factories in the government zone which were busy manufacturing primitive armoured cars called 'tanks'. But the defenders were outnumbered by the rebel General Mola's 3,000 soldiers and Carlist militia, and the city fell in early September 1936.[31] Even so, the truly twentieth-century weapons which cleared their path came from foreign instead of Spanish arsenals, and the first rebels actually to storm Irún were Carlist militiamen.[32]

One hundred years earlier, the Carlist control of Irún had stymied Franco-Spanish efforts to halt supplies reaching the rebels from France. In May 1837 the government committed some 20,000 government soldiers in an offensive to reopen communications between San Sebastián and the French frontier. The outnumbered rebels yielded most positions in the path

FIGURE 1.2 *Anglo-Cristino assault against Irún on 17 May 1837. On the far left is Hondarribia. On the right is Hendaye in France (Courtesy of Museo Zumalakarregi).*

of the offensive but made a firm stand at Irún. The British-led forces secured a bloody victory in house-to-house fighting which destroyed much of the city, anticipating the 'scorched earth' committed in Irún by the retreating anarchists in 1936. General Evans was honoured by the Cortes and British Radicals alike, and he used the fame of his victory to increase his majority in the 1837 parliamentary elections for his Westminster seat. The government had secured the most important sector of the French frontier, obliging the rebels to resort to remote smuggling from their agents and sympathisers in France.[33] Irún in the summer of 1936 had a decisive political impact once more, albeit in favour of the rebels. The fall of this border-city (along with Talavera on the approaches to Madrid) caused the fall of the middle-class government of Prime Minister Giral and its replacement by a left-wing administration led by Largo Caballero. Unlike in the 1830s, the city was never retaken.[34]

The protracted nature of fighting near the French border during the 1830s made the First Carlist War in some ways an even greater international conflict than the 1930s. The newly appointed commander-in-chief, Fernández de Córdova, was unable to exploit either the death of Zumalacárregui or the subsequent government victories at Bilbao and Mendigorría in the summer of 1835. Zumalacárregui was dead, yet his rebels consolidated all his hard-won conquests. Virtually all of the Basque country north of the river Ebro minus the provincial capitals was in the hands of the rebels and they were even able to send expeditions tearing into government-held Spain during 1835–37. Fernández de Córdova responded by waging a war of containment, seldom committing his reserves centred on Miranda del Ebro and Bilbao, and instead pressing the French to seal their border with the now-substantial Carlist state on the other side of the Bidasoa. But various difficulties conspired to topple Córdova from his command during the revolution of 1836. His three-to-one superiority over the Carlist Royal Army existed really only on paper as the enemy skilfully exploited its advantages of internal lines and superior espionage networks at sensitive areas of the front. His own extended lines led Córdova to despair how ten government soldiers were needed to transport one battle casualty to safety, and hyperbolically, that 'nineteen out of every twenty messengers I send out surrender their intelligence to the Carlists, the brave twentieth man perishing instead.'[35] The British ambassador sympathized with Córdova's plight. Villiers thought the government army's task was even harder than that faced by the French against the Patriots in the same area a quarter of a century earlier: 'The French war was a foreign war – the present is one of principles, privileges and dynasty, and now even of religion according to the turn given to it by the priests, its great and most important supporters.'[36]

Córdova realized that only a rigorous French blockade could defeat the Carlists in these circumstances. His offensive against the mountains of Arlabán between Alava and Guipúzcoa in January 1836 underlined this in his mind. The offensive got bogged down in blizzards and not even the support of French and British auxiliaries was sufficient to score a decisive victory. Córdova's faulty intelligence had led him to attack the head of the enemy salient rather than its vulnerable flanks. Relations worsened with Prime Minister Mendizábal, who demanded revolutionary élan against the 'enemies of humanity'. Córdova, for his part, demanded that Madrid exercise the utmost pressure on France to keep its border sealed, and, ideally, that France commit its regular army to attack the rebels (this being a wish shared by most moderados, the party with which the commander-in-chief identified).[37] But as we shall explain in Chapter 5, the French were wary of supporting the radical liberals, and a cabinet crisis at the Tuilleries in March 1836 derailed Córdova's strategy. French ambassador Rayneval, protesting the disruption caused to the economy of French border departments, announced the reopening of its frontier with the Carlists to allow the transit of all 'non-military' supplies (mainly food).[38] Even though he assured a continued embargo on military supplies, an infuriated Mendizábal replied that the most valuable commodity in the blockaded Carlist Spain was not arms but food. The crisis in Franco–Spanish relations was partially resolved by an undertaking by Paris to allow Spanish government troops to transit French territory.[39] But as in the 1930s, piecemeal concessions to the government side did not alter the overall pattern. In both wars, French policy objectively aided the rebels more than the government, despite France's constitutional system.

International intervention intensifies the civil wars

The resourcefulness shown by the rebels ultimately exhausted Spain's limited stocks of military supplies during the frantic fighting of summer 1936. Foreign arms supplies of the kind witnessed at Irún thus became a military necessity far more rapidly than in the 1830s. In response to early German and Italian intervention, Communist-organized 'International Brigade' volunteers arrived in Spain from November 1936. Unlike Nazi and Fascist interventionists, who enjoyed weapons supplied by the German and Italian governments, some of them state-of-the-art, the volunteers for the Republic were armed with the obsolescent vagaries of depleted government stocks and whatever could be sourced from the international arms market. The volunteers were shocked to be fighting a war which in their mind could hardly be more modern with weapons dating from the turn of the century.[40] A British Communist recoiled at his 'appalling, foul, rusty, worn, and cracked' rifle which 'had been made in Austria, exported to Afghanistan in 1913, and ended up being used in the Great War by the Turks'.[41] The saga of the elderly, overpriced and non-standardized weapons available to the government side has been well explained.[42] Although there was no virtue in using obsolescent weapons as such, the conditions in Spain (the fact that both sides were poorly armed and the front lines quite primitive) rendered their use less disadvantageous than would otherwise have been the case. An Irish volunteer was impressed by the Spanish government's ageing light artillery. The quick-firing 75mm gun, which had proved unequal to the modern defences of the Great War,[43] was 'the best for this kind of war' and was 'always used to great effect'.[44] A British Carlist recalled during the 1937–38 Battle of Teruel that the enemy's 75mm artillery was most damaging 'because our dugouts were only thinly covered with earth'.[45] Obsolescent artillery was more than a match for obsolete defences. By contrast, the scattered nature of government bombing was less effective. The same Carlist later remembered having no difficulty sleeping through government nocturnal air raids 'which of course were not comparable to those of the last (Second World) war'.[46] The 1930s battlefronts seldom exhibited combats in which both sides employed state-of-the-art weapons.

The antiquated state of armaments matched an antiquated code of honour and bravery which impressed foreign observers in both wars. Spain's moral code in the 1830s placed great importance on personal and collective honour, as is consistent with a 'Romantic' pre-industrial society. Real or imagined transgressions of honour tended to produce a cycle of violence that was elaborated and justified by the existence of the war. The machismo and honour-based culture of Spain in both conflicts placed a premium on demonstrating fearlessness and shaming cowardice. Deep-rooted Latin military values of panache and ostentatious glory must account for some of the reluctance to drill and to dig.[47] The rest may be explained by highly contemporary cultural values which privileged self-sacrificial heroics in the name of a political cause. The 1830s breakthrough of romanticism in Spain fused personal behaviour with demanding political causes, which meant that officers who in an eighteenth-century 'cabinet war' might have behaved with non-ideological circumspection instead showed reckless pretensions to glory. Even though this honour code diminished over the course of the war, the tragic heroism of the 'Pardiñas affair' of 1838 proved its enduring appeal. Europe, which was captivated by the cruel war waged in Spain between the two most romantic extremes of 'Restoration' politics, reaction and radicalism, became a willing accomplice in exaggerating their character and exploits in literature and press.

In the 1830s the Spanish *guerrillero* fascinated European readers and travellers, and visits to the seat of war became a rustic antidote to the *juste milieu* of bourgeois society enveloping the rest of Europe. The Carlist *guerrillero* was celebrated for his plebeian origins which subverted the claim of his liberal enemy to govern in the interests of the 'people'. A Polish aristocrat touring Old Castile commented: 'The *faccioso* is the personification of the democratic genius of Navarra and Aragón, regions which wage war in their own way, steeped in glory … In Spain one becomes a guerrillero as in France one becomes a doctor, lawyer or journalist.'[48] Similarly, the image of plebeian insurgency captivated foreign onlookers of the Spanish Civil War, the only difference being that the romantic 'people' were now fighting for the left. It was no coincidence that the first images to dominate the global media showed a modernized version of 1830s romanticism, namely self-sacrificial popular resistance in defence of the Republic, sustained by photographs of barricades, armed militiawomen and crowds giving the clench-fisted salute.[49]

Such romanticised representations, which were nourished by both Spanish and international demands, of course bore little relation to the actual nature of each war. The proliferation in Republican Spain of posters depicting heroic volunteers fighting fascism was not a reflection of war enthusiasm but a reflection of the lack of it.[50] In a manner little understood by foreigners, the excessive propaganda served a didactic function. The modernity of 1930s imagery, influenced by socialist realism, belied the anti-modernity of combat. Both conflicts produced patterns of behaviour which frustrated military tacticians and baffled foreign observers used to the 'sober' military culture of Northern Europe. The German Carlists participating in the rebels' 1837 March on Madrid were outraged by the king's 'armed pilgrimage', his slow advance of 'liberators' who would hear Mass in every village that crossed their path.[51] The Nazis' frustration with Franco's failure to use 'Blitzkrieg' strategies one hundred years later is well documented.[52] Franco might have been speaking the words of Don Carlos when he claimed that 'success is found where there is the intelligent expertise of the commander, the bravery of the troops and faith'.[53] Even though Madrid in many ways anticipated the Battle of Stalingrad, foreign observers were baffled by the now *Generalísimo* Franco's failure to wage truly modern warfare. The British air attaché judged that rebel bombing was sufficient enough only to stiffen the resolve of the *madrileños* instead of demoralizing them and that aircraft had missed the most obvious target of interdiction, namely the fragile supply roads linking Madrid with the Eastern Mediterranean along which all supplies to the capital had to pass and yet were within easy range of the rebel air force.[54]

At tactical levels, too, foreign fighters expressed emotions ranging from disgust to wonder at the Spaniards' failure to modernize defences. Time and again Republican militiamen failed to dig trenches to maximize their defensive power. It was not just the often hard, sun-scorched earth that turned them against this, but also the dishonourable trappings this had in a culture of machismo and ostentatious bravery.[55] Spaniards had had no combat experience of Great War trench warfare, and Paul Preston credited General Franco with too much modernity when he described his tactics as 'fixed in the strategic world of the Great War'.[56] George Orwell recalled the Aragonese trenches where 'the Spanish machine-gunners disdained to take cover, in fact exposed themselves deliberately, so I had to do likewise'.[57] During her speechifying visit to the front in August 1936, the communist leader La Pasionaria rejected the pleas of militiamen to duck in the face of incoming enemy fire, thereby demonstrating the bravery of local heroines in the 1830s.[58] Such theatrical bravado naturally did not last very long once the war became more organized, but its romantic appeal endured. The prolonged rebel siege of Madrid resulted in the most sophisticated trenches of the conflict, but the outer lines of defence broken through during the last stage of the rebel offensive had been amateurishly dug up by the people, not by soldiers, and foreign veterans of the Great War were astonished at their simplicity. One veteran was asked whether their dugouts resembled those of 1914–18, which produced mirth in his reply: 'If you had the trenches dug properly, and if you had three miles of communications trenches, a mass of saps running out, firing steps, pillar-boxes … (then perhaps).'[59] According to a British Carlist volunteer, 'Spanish troops could not be induced to dig proper trenches, this applied even to the Foreign Legion. They seemed to think it indicated cowardice to dig themselves in securely.'[60]

The ostentatious disdain for defensive measures was also in evidence in the more primitive conflict of the 1830s. To some extent, this attitude was more justified one hundred years earlier as the use of artillery was far less concentrated in pitched battles than had been the norm in the Napoleonic Wars, even among the government armies which for the first year of war enjoyed a complete monopoly of field guns. Artillery was the weak link in the government order of battle. Even though horse and field artillery pieces had doubled in size by 1835, these guns could only make an impact when concentrated for siege warfare, very much according to Early Modern norms, such as the counterbattery fire during the failed rebel attempts to capture Bilbao. Given the mountainous inaccessibility of the main Navarra front, what really counted was pack artillery. Pack artillery was expanded from sixteen guns to over eighty by August 1838, and this expansion was supplemented by British-supplied Congreve rockets which could easily be transported by mule.[61] Early Modern attitudes persisted during sieges, such as in the employment of civilians for ancillary duties of transporting guns and digging trenches. Carlists paid civilians to dig trenches during their climactic second siege of Bilbao.[62] On several occasions, women and children performed the mundane tasks of digging trenches in frontline communities facing Carlists in the east. Government military authorities throughout 1834 were locked in a dispute with the civilian authorities of Puente la Reina (Navarra) over the latter's failure to fortify this key communications and hospital centre properly.[63] Military glory, it seemed, did not come from sound defences. General Córdova's 1835–36 strategy of blockade attracted criticism for cultural as well as military reasons. In the later civil war, too, positions were frequently lost in the early months because of militiamen's refusal to dig trenches. The greatest reluctance was found among urban militiamen recruited from workplaces: they were both unfamiliar with rural life and had an urban code of honour, alienated from any affinity with the rural earth. Military geography, by contrast, dictated that proportionately more Nationalist conscripts came from rural communities and therefore did not feel as vulnerable as Republican militiamen who instinctively envisaged battle in terms of street fighting or, at least, garrisoning towns and villages.[64]

Such anti-modern attitudes were challenged by the concerted employment of new weaponry. At the height of the 1836 siege of Bilbao, an eccentric Spanish inventor offered to sell the British government, the 'leader of the civilised world', his blueprint to construct 'an aeronautical machine which could destroy an army of 200,000 men within two hours'.[65] Once aircraft actually appeared one hundred years later, they subverted the bravado of their victims whom greater rebel skill dictated were disproportionately on the government side. With the exception of the Soviet-supplied fighters over the skies of Madrid, the rebels achieved air superiority using German and Italian machines. The pro-Basque *Times* correspondent, George Steer, claimed the unique mystique of aerial bombing and strafing which seemed to seek out victims personally. Those on the receiving end felt no compunction to withstand this 'unnatural terror' and often fled before it.[66] Steer reported three decisive effects of rebel air superiority during the 1937 collapse of the northern front: the morale boost offered to advancing Nationalist troops seeing their planes overhead, the demoralization of the enemy by bombing and strafing, and the suppression of counter-battery fire.[67]

Unlike in the 1830s, when government forces defending Bilbao could always rely on British naval supremacy for reinforcements, supporting fire and even amphibious landings behind rebel lines, no such technological backstop existed in 1937. German technological superiority in 1937 gifted the rebels with victory just as surely as British technological superiority in the 1830s denied it to them. But even beyond the decisive northern front, rebel aircraft had a demoralizing impact. Whereas government soldiers remained steadfast against rebel artillery assaults, the strafing and bombing of the Luftwaffe proved to have offensive effects out of all proportion to their numbers.[68] Rebel soldiers were just as terrified of aircraft, of course, but the government side, despite its slight superiority in aircraft numbers until late 1937, generally did not concentrate its airpower like the nationalists. A teenage militiaman sheltering from a rebel air raid on Madrid was consoled by an officer when a slammed door made him cry: 'It's only a door, man!'[69] Rebel aircraft often terrorized the government militias in the first weeks of the war, sending them into disorderly retreats, or *desbandadas*. Matters were complicated by the trade union–led organization of militiamen into revolutionary 'pals' battalions' which fought only by day and returned to home comforts in the evening, as if they were performing a shift at a factory.[70] Militarily, the lack of a cadre of Great War veterans in 1936 distinguished the Spanish Civil War from the persistent wars and mobilizations that predated 1833. Unlike the Cristino conscripts and Carlist guerrillas of 1833, the Republican militiamen of 1936 had had no experience of contemporary warfare. There had been no mass Spanish baptism of fire in the Great War and accordingly no widespread use of new military technology or training.[71] Veterans of recent Moroccan wars – Africanistas – were a minority who sided disproportionately with the insurgent Nationalists. The socialist Arturo Barea had served as a conscript in the Moroccan wars, and he suddenly found that his unusually thorough military experience commanded him respect and authority in his desperate attempts to prepare Madrid militia volunteers facing the onslaught of the summer of 1936:[72]

> Well, look! You all want a gun to go and you all want to go to the front as soon as possible to shoot at fascists. But none of you wants the slightest military training. Let's suppose I gave you all a rifle and put you on a lorry to take you up to the sierra. How would you fight Mola's army there, with its trained officers and soldiers used to obeying orders and understanding what each order meant? What would you do? I bet all of you will manage your guns whichever way you see fit. But do you really think shooting these fascists is like shooting rabbits?

Just as Zumalacárregui's guerrillas in the 1830s had to be drilled into the Royal Army, so did the Republican militia in terms of the Popular Army.[73] Yet government militarization was at once both controversial and necessary. Modern work patterns did not equate to familiarity with modern warfare. Working-class militants defended their barricades, the urban and revolutionary variety of the rural trench, retaining the largest cities for the government, just as their 1830s militia forbears had held Bilbao and other urban centres. But 1930s militants resented being deployed on manoeuvres in the unfamiliar countryside from which they had lost all family links, being often second- or third-generation migrants. Moreover, the enemy was still rife in the cities, they thought. The 'baroque' oppression of bourgeois clericalism had to be reversed. Priests were humiliated or killed in gruesome ways and religious buildings profaned in revenge for generations of class oppression.[74] Anarchist leader, Buenaventura Durruti, proclaimed, 'No compromise! No surrender of the streets. The revolution before everything!'[75]

Furthermore, distant front lines exposed soldiers to their ignorance of local geography and their lack of access to intelligence networks. This was particularly a feature of the 1830s given the greater importance of counter-insurgency. The arrest and imprisonment of the alderman of Salva (Navarra) who had failed to supply rations and intelligence to the government forces at Puente la Reina is one of countless examples of local authorities fearing the omnipresent rebels in the Basque country more than they feared the garrison-bound government forces.[76] The lack of local intelligence added to the bewilderment of government forces which were usually ignorant of local geography to begin with. The brief 1835 occupation of the rebel capital of Estella (Navarra) was delayed by a night-time firefight on the outskirts between two government columns which, under the strain of the offensive, thought they were engaging the enemy.[77] A government army battalion conscripted in Málaga was in action against Carlists in distant Catalonia in April 1836. Ignorant of the local language, surroundings and the uniforms of the pro-government Catalan militia (*migueletes*), the Andalucíans fired on their Catalan allies in the fog of war.[78] The month before, disaster had befallen a detachment of Belgian auxiliaries at Bruch (Catalonia) who were unable to distinguish local accents. The rebel chieftain Tristany answered 'Isabel II' to the question of '*¿quién vive?*' ('Who lives?') put by the Belgians defending fortifications at Bruch. Thinking the approaching column comprised allies, the foreigners were unprepared for a bayonet charge which led to the capture of fifty Belgian prisoners.[79]

Instances also abounded one hundred years later of fear and unfamiliarity leading to fratricidal casualties. The militiamen of Madrid were estranged from their own city during the winter of 1936–37, as rebel shelling, the paranoid search for 'fifth columnists' and blacked-out nocturnal streets led to phantom firefights. Panicked government militia fired their weapons against suspicious movements and noises, often hitting targets which turned out to be militia on the same side.[80] Both government and rebel aircraft possessed either primitive or non-existent radio communications, which led to repeated instances of poor weather or fuel exhaustion causing pilots to land in the wrong zone.[81] The 600 Irish 'Blueshirt' volunteers for the rebels were deployed in February 1937 to the Jarama section of the front. The only action they saw was a 'friendly fire' shoot-out in which four Irishmen and thirteen Falangists were killed. The Blueshirts lapsed into alcohol abuse and indiscipline and their commander, Eoin O'Duffy, secured Franco's agreement in April to withdraw the volunteers from Spain. Speaking to the United Press, O'Duffy put a political spin on his alienation, claiming to be leaving Spain 'because White Spain did not live up to the Catholic image motivating the Blueshirts'. The Nationalist propaganda minister Luis Bolín suppressed this report in the need to maintain the important fiction that the rebels lacked armed assistance from abroad.[82]

The dark side of honour

The fog of war increased the likelihood of falling into enemy hands and being subjected to atrocities. Atrocities, part real and part imagined, horrified Europe and explained outside efforts at humanitarian intervention in both wars. Self-preservation, perverted braggadocio, honour, prestige, gain and irresponsibility, all have some bearing on the decision to kill or not to kill captives. The polarization of hatred in 1936 in some ways predisposed both sides to bloodletting. The government officer Rafael Miralles recalled, 'We were possessed of the most ardent warlike spirit ... aware of the brutal reality of civil war in which nobody gave or asked for quarter.'[83] Yet Miralles's view describes the condition of officers and volunteers much more than conscripts, for whom the sheer accident of geography dictated on which side they fought. In fact, the killing of captives in Spain tended to obey predictable patterns. Volunteers and officers captured by the enemy in both civil wars could expect to be executed whereas conscripts' lives were generally respected (and they might even be recycled into service on the other side).[84] This pattern required time to have elapsed in order for something approaching geographical areas of control to become established and for internal enemies, real or imagined, to have been punished. In this respect, Stathis Kalyvas's model of 'logical violence' in civil wars also applies to Spain. According to this model, combatants commit violence against civilians for the purpose of gaining information about the enemy, and non-combatants participate in violence, and sometimes even instigate it, in order to obtain security.[85] This model explains the panoply of denunciations and rearguard killings in both wars. Even when eliminating 'enemies', notions of honour still shaped the attitudes of perpetrators. Rebel insurgents in Burgos in August 1936 were shamed by incidents surrounding the summary execution of leftist prisoners who had been told that they would be 'released' from captivity – shamed not by the killing of these unfortunate innocents, but by the discovery that their captors had stolen the victims' belongings and even raided their corpses for credit-notes.[86]

Honour in both conflicts was understood both as a protective and an acquisitive commodity. Personal insults against enemy commanders wounded honour in both wars, but especially in the 1830s given the sway of romanticism and the limited ability of the media to deploy counter-narratives. A barely literate rebel commander regretted the terms he had offered to the government garrison he was besieging at Lucena (Castellón) over the autumn of 1835. The better-educated government militia publicly ridiculed

José Miralles's grammar as the incomprehensible twaddle of a bandit, and a timely government counter-attack robbed the Carlist of a chance to avenge his outraged honour.[87] The military pretensions of Carlist irregulars conflicted with those of the government 'people in arms' militia. Government forces were outraged to meet rebel civilian vigilantism. Martín Zurbano (aka Martín Varea) commanded a free corps of mounted infantry on *chevuachée*-style long-range raiding missions against supplies and depots in the rebel-held Basque country. Carlist civilians dubbed them the 'death riders' on account of their propensity to violence against non-combatants. While Zurbano respected the internationally convened Eliot Treaty by offering quarter to surrendering Carlist soldiers, his military honour was outraged when he encountered civilian vigilantism in his path, and frequently ordered reprisals against the lives and property of priests and their parishioners.[88] The protection of military honour could prove costly to civilians.

The demands of militarization also provided opportunities to the undistinguished to achieve honour. Early nineteenth-century Spain was plagued by rural banditry provoked by the post-Napoleonic depression in agriculture and by the opportunities apparent to men on the margins of Spain's remote communities to desert from the repeated *quintas* and to prey on vulnerable muleteers and travellers. After 1833 these wrongdoers joined Carlist bands thereby becoming self-styled warriors who nonetheless continued to commit crimes 'in the name of the king'. The government side despised these barbarous fellow travellers and refused time and again to extend the humanitarian Eliot Treaty to their protection. This treaty, convened by both sides in April 1835 at the instigation of British mediators sent by Lord Wellington, respected the lives only of regular soldiers surrendering in the Basque-Navarra front and stipulated their imprisonment in designated depots where they would await exchange for an equal number of prisoners of war held by the other side. This restriction was controversial among beleaguered government communities on the eastern front. Three Aragonese notables decried Madrid's metropolitan calculations: 'Not extending the Eliot Treaty to the rebels of Aragón and Valencia was to consider as national the opinions of those who shouted slogans in cafés far from the dangers of the war.'[89] But the British ambassador, for once approving of his ally's conduct of the war, echoed the reasons for the government's refusal to bind the treaty to the expanded front:

> The guerrillas operating in Galicia, Aragón, Catalonia and Valencia may ride under the flag of Don Carlos but they are really a law unto themselves, so agreement with one group would not be binding on the other ... Besides, this country is infested with bandits and upon being caught miscreants would plead 'Carlism'.[90]

Comparable opportunities to cloak wrongdoing existed one hundred years later. Anarchist *incontrolats* settled personal scores in the name of the 'revolution'. The town of Puigcerdà commanded Catalonia's border with France. During the Carlist War it was frequently abandoned in the face of persistent rebel guerrilla assaults, but from July 1936 it became a bastion of anarchist control in Catalonia. Its key customs revenues and the devolution of control of the border to the Catalan Generalitat allowed the anarchist mayor to enrich himself on the back of extortion. Mayor Antonio Martín went by the name of the *Cojo de Málaga,* 'lame man of Málaga', in honour of a plebeian radical of the Peninsular War. When he was shot by communists in the May 1937 counter-revolution, the middle classes sighed with relief and the anarchist movement had another martyr.[91] On the rebel side, too, the proclamation of martial law permitted undistinguished men to achieve 'honour'. Railway workers who went on strike to derail the Nationalist rising of July 1936 were broken by blackleg railway engineers who were rewarded with military rank.[92] At the end of the war, the Francoist 'fifth column' organization in Madrid (the SIE) flaunted military uniforms to welcome the entry of the Nationalists into the capital. Nationalist officers protested the underground's claim to a share in the victory and Franco disbanded the organization the following day, citing victory as making it unnecessary.[93]

Membership of the government militia in the 1830s offered pseudo-military rank and higher pay without, in many instances, incurring the risks of real soldiering. Much interservice rivalry ensued between the army and militia regarding pay and honour. The militia rioted at the deterioration of their conditions after 1835 when Madrid detailed some militia battalions for obligatory service under army regulations and outside their home provinces. Eastern rebels serving under Cabrera chanced the absence of any right to quarter in return for daily wages four times those of their comrades serving in the Basque country.[94] Equally, the 1936 government militia were drawn by a wage of ten pesetas per day, a sum far in excess of comparable working-class jobs, making them the best-paid soldiers in the world. Wages were lower in the rebel army but control was maintained by stricter discipline as well as the creation of promotion-friendly provisional second lieutenancies (*alfereces provisionales*). A Francoist historian remembered fondly that 'the Nationalist army was, to a high degree, a popular army'.[95] Yet casualties were so high among the provisional officers that the men were dubbed 'provisional coffins' (*ataúdes provisionales*).

Honouring and dishonouring the dead

Honour could transcend an individual's life to become collectively owned after death. The death of prominent militants produced collective displays of honour. Fallen street fighters fighting Falangists in 1936 and military insurgents in July 1936 were immortalized by their comrades in banners, posters and ostentatious funeral processions.[96] The honouring of dead comrades' bodies distinguished both conflicts. In the First Carlist War, the first great liberal martyr, Espoz y Mina, died a natural death at the end of 1836, his terminal cancer having been aggravated by commanding the Army of the North and Catalonia. Espoz's corpse was transported on a catafalque on a patriotic tour of government-held provincial capitals. His corpse became a focus for radical protest when municipal authorities in Málaga refused to render homage. Threats of violence by the militia forced them to stage an elaborate funeral procession.[97] One hundred years later, some half a million Barcelona workers lined the streets to witness the funeral cortege of the 'son of the city', and the first great anarchist martyr of the Spanish Civil War, Buenaventura Durruti.[98] In late 1937, in a context of growing communist–socialist ascendancy, George Orwell returned to Barcelona where he witnessed a public funeral full of political stagecraft and undercurrents of sectarian violence:

> Roldán, a prominent member of the U.G.T., was murdered, presumably by someone in the C.N.T. The Government ordered all shops to close and staged an enormous funeral procession, largely of Popular Army troops, which took two hours to pass a given point. From the hotel window I watched it without enthusiasm. It was obvious that the so-called funeral was merely a display of strength; a little more of this kind of thing and there might be bloodshed.[99]

The honouring of dead bodies was the counterpoint to their more common use in the Spanish Civil Wars: their humiliation. When Gómez's Carlist expedition occupied Córdoba in 1836, their public display of executed Cristino authority figures showed an ancien régime desire to intimidate (and entertain) the population with the spectacle of death. In 1837 disaster befell an off-duty infantry battalion at Liria (Valencia), which was captured by Cabrera before it even knew it was in action. As was custom in the east, most of the captured officers were shot. But these victims acquired a ghoulish afterlife. According to legend, the officers' corpses were stacked in pyramids amid an orgy of drunkenness.[100] In fact, as John Keegan argued, the stacking of enemy corpses in wartime was a grim but practical response to the onset of rigor mortis, and the indulgence of alcohol was a common resort for anguished victors and vanquished alike.[101] Yet the rumours of this ghoulish fete of corpse pyramids certainly served an intimidating function, and Cabrera – much like the Moorish shock troops of the 1930s – did not mind his satanic propaganda image because of the advantages it gave him in intimidating the enemy. One hundred years later, the Nationalists of Burgos showed their power of intimidation as no one dared come forward to identify the bodies of executed leftists.[102] Rebels in the 1830s, implementing the king's 'Durango decree' (the denial of quarter to captured foreign fighters), left the bodies of executed British auxiliaries to decompose, dangling from the walls of Guevara castle.[103] The spectacle of disturbed corpses made great psychological demands on witnesses. The sieges of the 1930s sometimes placed municipal cemeteries in the firing line, and foreign observers used black humour to cope with the grotesque spectacle of rebel shell impacts disinterring corpses. A foreign volunteer at the Battle for Madrid witnessed corpses raised at a cemetery on the front near the Extremadura highway: 'Is it possible that the fascist motto "Spain, Awake!" is meant for them, too?'[104] George Steer witnessed a ghoulish 'resurrection day' following the rebel shelling of the cemetery at Derio (Bilbao), the demoralizing impact of which for the Catholic Basques 'was more serious than the loss of the line before the *cinturón* (Iron Ring)'.[105]

Atrocities

Between the 1830s and 1930s Spain evolved from a rural, honour-based society into a half-urbanized society of the masses. Propaganda, especially images, saturated the 1930s home fronts. Whereas the 1830s honour-based society meant that atrocities were usually the result of personal vendettas or reprisals, by the 1930s, mass society and its hatreds would predetermine the nature and scale of atrocities. In the 1830s Maestrazgo, where the economic conflict was fierce, it was the local militia which committed counter-atrocities against local Carlists rather than the army whose conscripts came from all over Spain.[106] In the Spanish Civil War, by contrast, there was a tendency for atrocities by outside insurgents to be worse than those committed by locals.[107] The old order, priests and aristocrats in the first conflict, caciques in the second, often aided perpetrators, but local attachments sometimes drove them to mitigate reprisals. The mitigation of atrocities in the Nationalist zone tended to come from local quarters. A few Galician caciques intervened to protect workers.[108] The Bishop of Pamplona condemned killings in Navarra of 'rojillos' snatched from neighbouring villages in reprisal for the deaths of comrades in battle.[109] Even during the half-modernized 1930s, local interests dominated Republican responses to the Civil War, too, as most people still identified with their village before the nation.[110]

Yet civilians were still targeted from afar because advances in military technology created a civilian 'investment' in fighting in the most hideous terms. Firefights made useful human shields of civilians. Colonial warfare experience had taught the Africanistas not to distinguish between military and civilian targets, and Moroccan rebels had responded in kind by tying Spanish prisoners to guns in order to dissuade air strikes.[111] Queipo de Llano's outnumbered forces managed to conquer the working-class Triana district of Seville in part thanks to his soldiers' use of women and children as human shields.[112] This colonial practice, which Nationalists employed in rural assaults, too, helped them to intimidate the masses.[113] Research into the 1990s Balkan civil wars has revealed that population centres could be held by armed fanatics comprising as little as 10 per cent of the local population, as long as they controlled defensible points and could rely on at least 60 per cent of the urban population being unswayed in its allegiance.[114] These proportions were similar to Queipo de Llano's 1936 campaign in Andalucía, as elite Moroccan-based forces supplemented by Falangist and Carlist vigilantes were vastly outnumbered by the civilian population in their path. But the resort to extreme terror, including mass executions and hostage-taking, cowed enough of the population in order to impede effective support for the working-class militants who did resist with arms. In areas where the 1936 military rebellion failed, by contrast, leftist atrocities were often unleashed as a form of revenge in response to gruesome news and indiscriminate bombing.[115] Much pre-war class and factional sectarianism was re-baptized as anti-fascist activism. Barcelona's *incontrolats*, the criminal element in the FAI-CNT, now became revolutionaries who helped to defeat General Goded's failed rising and, in the following weeks, performed revolutionary justice against class and factional enemies.[116]

Urban and rural terrain

The battlefronts in both wars revealed a general rural–urban divide in partisanship. Whereas the rebels drew more support from the countryside, the government side did so from the larger cities. Some of this divide was circumstantial. The Nationalist capital of Burgos expanded its population of 40,000 in 1936 to 115,000 three years later in a desperate attempt to accommodate functionaries.[117] Also the government countermeasures of 1832–33 were more successful than those of February–July 1936, so the fact that rebels had to launch their insurrection from the countryside rather than the cities was partly a reflection of effective purges and policing. The displacement of rebel strength into certain regions is not always a reflection of commensurate regional support, as was demonstrated by Cabrera's terror in the liberal Levante and Queipo de Llano's grip on working-class Andalucía.[118] Defeated Republican guerrillas, unlike the French resistance during 1940–42, were forced to sustain their very urban values of revolution in some of the remotest countryside of the Pyrenees, ironically establishing their spatial sovereignty only in the most inaccessible wilderness.[119] But the fact that Old Castile rose with the rebels in 1936 whereas Andalucía did not can be explained by the 1830s. The disentailment process begun by Mendizábal during the First Carlist War informed the geographical differences in Republican and Nationalist areas of control. Whereas modest land purchases by modest landowners in Old Castile had created a culture of rural pro-Franco conservatism, the failure of the yeomanry to break through in most parts of Andalucía and Extremadura polarized politics, obliging the rebels here to use brute force against the Republicans.[120]

The urban values of the government side were reinforced in both wars by the higher degrees of success enjoyed by government militia in defending towns, where fewer demands for manoeuvre and proximity to supplies eased the lot of the 'people in arms'. But the ruralism of the rebels was also cultural and economic in nature. The 1830s government side drew distinctions between 'enlightened' urban populations and quaint countrywide dwellers. Antonio Pirala condescended: 'The higher educational levels of the cities made people consider liberty as the greatest happiness, whereas in the small towns people treasured what was ancient, and especially the clergy.'[121] Government officers, who noticed that they were capturing the same insurgents more than once, were convinced that they were being forced to fight by their priests and insurgent officers, and were mostly oblivious to the economic motives of impoverished villagers.[122] The towns, according to the 1830s rebels, were full of godless liberals, and the militia were derided as playboy revolutionaries. In the 1930s, Spain's proletarian cities were diabolical in rebel eyes. Several Nationalists urged heavy bombing of Barcelona's reddest districts as a form of 'social hygiene' and to spare Franco the need to shoot thousands of reds once he conquered the city.[123] After his victory, Franco expressed to a confidant his desire to construct new towns of industry and harmony which would eliminate the 'monstrous' dangers of the large cities.[124]

Rural Spain provided the springboard for rebel offensives against Madrid. In 1833 the sexagenarian priest and Peninsular War veteran Gerónimo Merino was made Carlist captain-general of Old Castile. His call to arms in 1833 was laced with the militantly Catholic imagery of El Cid, the traditionalist idol of Merino's native medieval Burgos. When Merino in 1833 marched south towards Madrid, he did so in the name of God and King: 'The declared enemies and captors of the late King Ferdinand cannot be trusted to defend our monarchical institutions.'[125] Mola, 103 years later, was pulled in one direction by his own Republican background and in the other by the Carlist monarchism of his men, so his address avoided the question of monarchism. But his verbal assault on Madrid shared Merino's vituperation of the left all the same: 'The government that was the wretched offspring of Liberal and Socialist concubinage is dead … the true Spain has laid the dragon low … and it won't be long before two banners – the sacred emblem of the Cross and our own glorious flag – are waving together in Madrid.'[126]

Despite similar rebel rhetoric, the immediacy of Madrid's war in the 1930s differed markedly from the 1830s. During the 1830s, the capital was subjected to only occasional invasion alarms unleashed by Carlist bands. In April 1835, one band reached the outskirts of Madrid before being repulsed by mobile militia and soldiers.[127] In September 1837, the Carlist invasion known as the 'Royal Expedition' arrived at the city's gates, but unlike Franco's and Mola's offensive in 1936, the Pretender's troops retreated back to the Basque country without a single artillery shot being fired at Madrid. The rebel assault against Madrid in 1837 amounted to some 11,000 infantry and 1,200 cavalry, rather more than the 10,000

FIGURE 1.3 *The siege that never was. In contrast to the Spanish Civil War, the rebel march on Madrid in 1837 was routed with barely a shot fired at the city (Courtesy of Museo Zumalakarregi).*

Nationalists actually committed to the assault on the capital in November 1936. Furthermore, despite pleas for aggression by Cabrera and influential German Carlists, Don Carlos refused to storm the capital. The king's peace feelers had deluded him into believing he would be welcomed through the gates by a war-weary queen-regent and pious population.

In November 1936, by contrast, the rebels were under no illusions that Red Madrid would put up a fight. Some 10,000 assault troops, protected by another 5,000 on their flanks, pushed towards the western outskirts of the capital, supported by the full range of available Spanish army artillery calibres (75mm, 105mm and 155mm), small German and Italian tanks (the Panzer I and L.3, respectively), and some fifty of the one hundred aircraft available to the Nationalists across the rebel zone. Opposing them were some five government militia columns comprising 13,000 men equipped with materiel of comparable quality and quantity to that of the rebels, and even superior quality in the case of the newly arrived Soviet fighter-plane, the Il16 'Mosca'.[128] Even though the government militia lacked training and organization, they retained four key defensive advantages which blunted the military superiority of the rebels: possession of the Madrid plateau, of hastily prepared trenches criss-crossing the old royal hunting ground to the west of the city, of defensible built-up areas along the city's outskirts (especially the new university campus) and the morale-boosting presence of a few foreign fighters imbued both with military training and political commitment. The government's defensive victory in early winter kept the rebels at the gates of the capital until March 1939. In the 1830s, by contrast, Madrid's war was fought out mainly in the press, as news of defeats and massacres in the north and east radicalized the Liberals and intimidated Carlist sympathisers.

The main difference between the civil wars in terms of mobile warfare was the strength of paramilitaries and guerrillas. The 1930s conflict has interested civil war experts for the high degree to which it was waged primarily by conventional armies, very different from the porousness of territorial control besetting both sides in the 1830s.[129] That said, for months after July 1936, both sides suffered from irregular enemy activity, especially in Andalucía where rebel Civil Guard units preyed bandit-like on government communities and some anarchist bands reverted to 'social banditry' in rebel-held areas.[130] Most irregulars in rebel territory were either fugitives from Nationalist conscription or government soldiers cut off behind rebel lines. The government endeavoured to organize dispersed soldiers into guerrilla armies but these existed largely on paper and certainly did not answer closely to government control. The biggest influx of irregulars into the rebel zone came with the collapse of the government's northern zone in the autumn of 1937. Thereafter, Prime Minister Negrín redesignated them to the XIV Corps Guerrilla Army and charged them with waging war against rebel logistics. But Negrín was making a virtue out of a necessity, and in fact political support for guerrilla warfare was equivocal. Even though anarchists relished the guerrilla as at once both Spanish and revolutionary, they were suppressed by the communist counter-revolution of May–August 1937. The communists, by contrast, remained wedded to their doctrine of militarization. Sponsoring irregular war could create a force outside their control, cast the Spanish Republic in an unhelpful revolutionary light, and, as the war deteriorated, communists thought that the organization of stay-behind forces smacked of defeatism.[131] Even if a 'people's war' could have been ignited in rebel-held Spain, none of the government army leaders, neither Casado, nor Rojo, nor Miaja, believed in resistance à la outrance.[132] The matter was really out of their hands. Unlike the Carlists, who up until the Vergara surrender of 1839 could still count on guerrillas plaguing the government zone, the Republicans of 1939 commanded only pinpricks of guerrilla activity behind Franco's lines.

The only Carlist War front which approximated the formalized front lines of the Spanish Civil War was the Cristino ring around the Basque country. The Basque front was decisive in both wars. The rebels' failure to occupy Bilbao and the coast robbed them of any hope of victory in Spain as a whole. Equally the government's failure to hold the north in 1937 tilted the balance in favour of the rebels and virtually guaranteed its eventual defeat. Battlegrounds of the 1830s returned to violence in the 1930s. The Vizcayan market town of Guernica was the traditional seat of the historic parliament of Vizcaya, the spiritual home of Basque liberties (fueros) and a symbol of the wider traditionalism motivating rebels in Spain's civil wars. A Catalan royalist proclaimed, 'We also want a constitution, but one anchored in our ancient laws ... adapted to our times and customs, under the shade of another tree of Guernica.'[133] But Guernica was not just a symbol of ancient liberties, it also commanded a key road junction between Bilbao and the coast and its inhabitants in both wars suffered the attention of contending armies. Zumalacárregui's assault on the town in December 1833 was his first great 'blooding', when he inflicted 300 casualties on government forces for only 100 of his own. In spring 1835 Guernica formed an active front line as rebels seized the town in April, only to be forced out again by Espartero the following month. By then the war-weary civilians had abandoned their town to encamp in nearby hills and government troops were billeted in the abandoned houses.[134] Following the collapse of the government front in June 1835, the battered town once more fell to the rebels, and generally remained in their hands until 1839. Basque Carlists established Vizcaya's deputation in the town and decreed the meeting every two years under Guernica's famous oak-tree of a Junta General tasked with administering the rebel war economy.[135] The 1830s rebel government honoured the ancient symbolism of Guernica even as it ramped up measures against local economic and political autonomy in the name of the war effort. Equally, even though the 1930s rebels flattered neighbouring Navarra as the 'best part of Spain', the emphasis on Spanishness proved a double-edged sword for Navarrese Carlists who secured nothing more than the most token autonomy from the victory of 1939.[136]

Victorious Liberals curtailed Basque fueros in 1839 and again in 1876, but they could not curtail the cultural significance of Guernica or of its famous oak tree, the national symbol of the Basque country. The Basque Nationalist Party (PNV) grew its support from the turn of the twentieth century, mainly among the Catholic middle classes in Vizcaya who rejected both the 'Spanishness' of Carlism and the new growth of socialism among the 'immigrant' working classes arriving from the rest of Spain. But just as Catalanism displaced Carlism in rural Catalonia, the PNV also displaced many traditional Carlist heartlands in the small towns and villages of Vizcaya, Guipúzcoa, and even in some parts of Alava and Navarra, the 'diehard' provinces of 1839.[137] The advent of the Republic in 1931 legalized the possibility of home rule, and the Basque Nationalists' Catholic hostility to the Republic was outweighed by the chance to gain autonomy within it. Yet the Basque country was politically split three ways. Working-class socialists would accept autonomy only on the condition that Carlist Navarra was subjugated (rather than be allowed to exist as an anti-Republican 'Vaticanist Gibraltar'). Carlists had their own vague demands for 'national regionalism' involving the rolling out of the ancient fueros from Navarra across Spain as a whole, and they would only consider 'regional nationalism' (home rule) in return for religious guarantees. The PNV condemned the Carlists for 'betraying the Basque cause', dubbing Navarra the 'Basque Ulster', alluding to Irish Protestants' blocking of home rule in Ireland. The home rule bill (the 1931 Statute of Estella) was put to a plebiscite in November 1933. It was approved in Vizcaya and Guipúzcoa but rejected in Alava and Navarra.[138] Given the impasse, home rule arrived only in October 1936, three months into the Civil War, and only because the Basque Ulster had declared for the rebels. Little love had been lost. The young Carlist Jaime del Burgo was convinced that the Second Republic from its outset was determined to destroy religion.[139] Carlists reserved particular contempt for the 'accidentalism' of Gil Robles's CEDA, the umbrella party which before the war had advanced the interests of landowners and the middle classes under the cover of the Republic.[140] Carlist militia were at the heart of rebel plans, and Navarra in the summer of 1936 experienced greater popular participation in the rebellion than anywhere else in Spain. A Carlist peasant, marching against the 'traitor' provinces of 1839, rejoiced that the uprising 'seemed like the Carlist Wars all over again'.[141]

Once the rebels in March 1937 began their northern offensive, Guernica once more became a seat of war. Lying inside the government zone, Guernica's local strategic importance in terms of its roads and its three arms factories made it a legitimate 'military' target.[142] Even the government side appreciated this. After the rebels had occupied Guernica's ruins, the government spared four of its scarce aircraft to bomb and strafe the abandoned market-town in a bid to interrupt the rebel advance towards Bilbao.[143] But the nature and scale of the infamous Nazi air raid of April 1937 did more damage to lives and property than all the attacks of the First Carlist War combined.

Monday, 26 April 1937, 5.00 pm, was still a normal market day for the people of Guernica. But everything changed at that hour when the first wave of German Condor Legion aircraft attacked the town, followed every twenty minutes for the next three-and-a-half hours by successive waves of bombing and strafing. An unknown number of people died in the flames, and survivors like their forbears in 1835 abandoned the town. The outraged *Times* correspondent, George Steer, wrote: 'Guernica was not a military objective. A factory producing war material lay outside the town and was untouched. The object of the bombardment was seemingly the demoralisation of the civil population and the destruction of the cradle of the Basque race.'[144] The embarrassed rebels spun the lie that Guernica, like Irún, was destroyed by 'retreating Republican arsonists', but the truth prevailed even before Picasso's famous *Guernica* painting was exhibited in Paris in June.[145] The rebel denial of their authorship of an air raid against a military target turned unhappy Guernica into a worldwide propaganda war. The only incident one hundred years earlier approximating Guernica's propaganda impact was the execution of Cabrera's mother, María Griñó, in 1836, a high-profile victim of the 'law of hostages' operated by both sides.[146] The carpet bombing of a small market town thus became indelibly associated abroad with the very modern barbarism of fascism and war,

FIGURE 1.4 *The war reaches Guernica in 1834 (Courtesy of Museo Zumalakarregi).*

pre-empting the atrocities of the Second World War. But contemporaries on the spot mourned not the world that was to come but the world that was lost. Among the buildings destroyed, a Basque Nationalist minister lamented, was the house where Don Carlos had sworn to defend the fueros one hundred years before.[147] Once the rebels occupied the ruins of the town, the ancient oak tree was found intact. A group of Falangists resolved to destroy the tree with axes, but the Carlist Jaime del Burgo hastily organized an armed platoon of *requetés* to protect this ancient symbol of traditionalist liberties. Burgo had already protested against the air raid, and a friend had to intervene to stop a fight when a Falangist officer shouted him down: 'We're going to ruin the whole of the Basque country and Catalonia!' 'And your whore of a mother,' Burgo replied.[148]

The violent success of the rebels in their 1937 northern campaign contrasted with the deadlock of the 1830s. Zumalacárregui's run of victories ended with defeat before Bilbao in the summer of 1835, and his mortal wound in battle. Zumalacárregui's death deprived the rebellion of its only military genius, so it was surprising that Don Carlos and his court rejoiced at the demise of the man whose control of the insurgency had turned him into a 'rebellious subaltern'.[149] The king had succeeded in defeating his best general whereas, one hundred years later, Franco succeeded in defeating both king and general. Franco cunningly rejected the pleas of Don Juan,

FIGURE 1.5 *War returns to Guernica in 1937 (Getty Images). The first corre-spondent to approach the town after the raid was George Steer. He reported: 'Out of the hills we saw Gernika itself, a meccano framework. At every window, pierc-ing eyes of fire; where every roof had stood wild trailing locks of fire. The mec-cano framework was trembling, and a wild red disorder was taking the place of its rid geometry. We drove down the street which led into Gernika from the south carefully, for it was a street no longer. Black or burning beams and tattered tel-ephone wires rolled drunkenly ... across it, and the houses either side streamed fire as vapour rises effortless from Niagara ... In the centre of the town the smaller tongues of fire were turning into a single roar ... We tried to enter, but the streets were a royal carpet of live coals; blocks of wreckage slithered and crashed from the houses, and from their sides ... the polished heat struck at our cheeks and eyes'* (Steer, *Tree of Gernika*, pp. 243–244).

heir to the vacated Spanish throne, to return to Spain in the service of the Nationalists. Franco cited fears for His Majesty's personal safety, but in reality Franco feared the presence of an unimpeachable rival to his supreme power.[150] Six months later saw the death of Franco's only remaining rival and the Carlists' best hope for a new Zumalacárregui, General Mola. Stanley Payne judged Mola 'the only subaltern capable of talking back to Franco'.[151] Mola's command of the Navarra Carlists had increased the odds of the restoration of traditional monarchy, or at least so was the impression he gave. In Mexico, the Cristeros celebrated Emilio Mola as the true spirit behind Spain's 'Crusade': 'Spain gave birth to twenty nations and now it shows us a system which, though old, is still a model for us. Alas we Cristeros lack a figure of the stature of Mola.'[152] A refugee journalist who had escaped from reactionary Burgos was convinced that Mola would have overshadowed Franco and his fascist backers:

> The conquest of Bilbao would have given Mola the chance, as victorious general, to bring out the national character of the rebel cause, but his plans met with the intense hostility from the Berlin-Rome axis, and an open conflict would have broken out if the leader and directing genius of the reactionary elements in the Nationalist camp had not lost his life in the aeroplane accident on the Brújula hill.[153]

Unlike the ill-fated Zumalacárregui in 1835, Mola's death in June 1937 was at least followed by victory over Bilbao. The city which had held out unbeaten in the nineteenth-century Carlist Wars was now symbolically conquered by the 1830s Carlists. In August 1937 an avenue in the city was named after Zumalacárregui, while a bridge named after the child-heroine of the 1830s, Isabel II, was rebranded as 'Victory'.[154] After his death, Mola was generously compared with Zumalacárregui, the romantic man of action whose death in combat offered the Carlist movement its enduring aesthetic.[155] Even Franco flattered his late rival with this comparison, while also making him a posthumous grandee,[156] exceeding in death Don Carlos's live offer to Zumalacárregui of a duchy. The Carlists lost their leaders but got to keep historical 'ownership' of the victory: 'Our men marched upon Bilbao along the same green paths trodden by the lancers of Zumalacárregui and the scouts of Don Carlos.'[157]

Uniquely, there had been no anticlerical terror in the government-held Basque country. Its conquest thus eased the Vatican's formal endorsement of the rebel cause – expressed in the 'Collective Letter' of Spanish bishops – now that international Catholicism no longer had to explain the embarrassing anomaly of 'respectable' Catholics fighting on the side of the Republic. In the 1830s, by contrast, government defensive victories at Bilbao provoked four years of clerical and anticlerical extremism. The government's first victory at Bilbao in 1835 allowed the city governor to captain the upsurge in radicalism that summer. He decreed the banishment from Vizcaya of all monks from monasteries still in government hands, a drastic reduction in numbers of parish clergy, and the confiscation of the property of Carlist families in order to compensate the losses suffered by pro-government families.[158]

Quiet fronts

Both civil wars had generally permeable front lines punctuated by the intense violence of the offensive and counter-offensive. This situation created a strongly irregular dimension to both conflicts, guerrilla warfare in the first war and militias in the early months of the second.[159] Both conflicts uncovered a gulf between theories of warfare and practice, as recent examples of the Napoleonic and Great Wars had only limited lessons to impart on the low-intensity warfare of Spain. In fact, the front line experience of both wars comprised cold, hunger and monotony, and soldiers devised various coping mechanisms, ranging from fraternization with the enemy to desertion, moonlighting, mutiny and defection. Even defection offered little change from the monotony of soldiering. During the 1830s government defectors were frequently disappointed by the spartan Carlist villages to which they were billeted.[160]

Rebel defection to the government side was less common in both wars. Yet the government side captured rebel prisoners, and as many of these in the first war were irregulars without any right to quarter, their disposal was frequently controversial. Irregulars captured could consider themselves lucky to be recycled into the desertion-prone ranks of the government army. Newspapers related the 'demoralising scandal' of this practice.[161] But there was very little else that could be done with them. Depots housing prisoners of war existed only on the main Basque-Navarra theatre of operations. Throughout 1834 the Portuguese government complained of the refusal of the Spanish government to accept the repatriation, and even the subsistence costs, of Carlist officers captured fighting alongside Dom Miguel. Instead these men lingered in fortresses and hulks around Lisbon.[162] Transportation was another option, thanks to the Royal Decree of 21 January 1834, and the ports of Cuba and the Philippines began to fill with indentured rebels. But this presented other risks. In June 1835, some 150 Carlist irregulars captured in fighting in Catalonia and Aragón were scheduled to be transported for indentured garrison duty in Cuba. Yet the transportees under the leadership of Count Romagosa mutinied at sea and sought asylum in Gibraltar. The British eventually sent the vessel to Málaga, where Romagosa was disembarked and executed, and the ship was set on course once more to Cuba. Even so, the captives mutinied again, and docked at Oran, from where the captives managed to reach varied shores, including Gibraltar and France, and many re-entered Spain to fight in the north.[163] Captivity was a 'quiet front' in its own right, and clearly an unacceptable one for some.

For those stuck in inactive front lines, boredom is perhaps the experience which unites both civil wars. The 1930s trenches produced boredom, cold and hunger (the latter especially for the Republican side). Nationalists' pay was less than their Republican counterparts, but the former's rearguard was better provisioned, especially, relatively speaking, as the war progressed. This meant that food parcels were generally sent from home to the front in the

Nationalist zone, but this was less common in the Republican zone where the home front grew increasingly famished. Food and its fair distribution was a vital factor in unit cohesion, and the Nationalists had the better relationship in this regard throughout the war. The material welfare also stretched to the provision of hotels in San Sebastián geared for convalescing Nationalist soldiers. Yet its occupancy was low as most soldiers preferred to spend precious leave with their families.[164]

Fraternization became common as the front lines were very long and relatively undermanned in contrast to, for example, the western front of the First World War. Mutually agreed truces across no-man's land would often see mutual harvesting of food, exchange of shortage items to both zones, swapping of newspapers, chats and enquiries about family members in the other zone. The siesta was usually observed as a truce. Officers, naturally, disapproved, as fraternization gave a human face to the enemy (who comprised, after all, conscripts) and undermined careful propaganda campaigns, as well as potentially threatening fighting cohesion in the event of high-intensity warfare.[165]

The rearguard

Both civil wars saw peacetime spatial relations interrupted, severely affecting economic, social and leisure activities. Spanish wars had always produced measures against the transit of suspicious persons. The Patriot authorities of the Peninsular War in July 1809 ordered the arrest of beggars and other suspicious persons.[166] In the first war, this interruption was caused by irregular warfare; in the second, by the plethora of internal controls set up by rival factions in the Republican zone and by the militarization of the war effort in the Nationalist zone. The pre-war choices facing disaffected right-wingers about whether and when to flee were much more pressing during the days and weeks building up to war in 1936 than had been the case in 1833. Rightists who left things too late and tried to flee 'red' zones of control after 18 July 1936 were impeded by militia roadblocks and checkpoints that sprouted up outside of major urban centres.[167]

Social standing in both 1930s zones of control was measured by the freedom and ability to travel. Unlike in the 1830s, guerrilla operations presented no systematic threat, but no-one could travel far without having to pass through internal passport checkpoints. In Nationalist Spain, the freedom to travel was an exceptional social privilege.[168] Horses were the most desired mobile asset in the 1830s, and cars followed suit in July 1936. The 'sequestration committees' set up behind Nationalist lines to confiscate the property of supposed 'reds' took great pleasure in stealing motor cars for the purposes of ostentation. Even high-level functionaries encountered difficulties obtaining the use of a car even for official purposes, and a military safe conduct was required for driving beyond the locality.[169] The motorization of privilege also featured in the government zone. The initial failure of the rebellion in San Sebastián was followed by the seizure of the cars of holidaying aristocrats.[170] These cars were emblazoned with the acronyms of various left-wing groups and driven by inexperienced drivers. The craze for 'burning gasoline' led to a spike in road accidents and damaged bodywork, often as a consequence of drunk driving.[171] Despite this reality, anarchist propaganda posters emblazoned the walls of Barcelona with sleek images of collectivized public transport, with cars, buses, trams and metro trains painted in the anarchist red and black and all running apparently smoothly and without displaying the remotest sign of damage.[172]

Environmental factors in warfare made travel prohibitive. The world's second cholera pandemic ravaged Iberia during 1833–34. Cholera's worst ravages struck in July 1834 as authorities quarantined outsiders across the south (in accordance with the prevailing 'miasma' theory of transmission) and postal and commercial communications with Portugal were severely delayed by the quarantine on the border.[173] A hundred years of medical advances would end waterborne infections, but an environmental side effect of the mass killings of the summer of 1936 included the rise in stray animals. The prevalence in mass killings, shallow graves and absentee dog owners, led to a rise in dogs occupying public spaces. Recently dug shallow graves of executed leftists in Burgos attracted the unwelcome attention of dogs and a demand from certain Nationalist authorities for more discreet burials.[174] Outside Toledo, government militia columns had no time to bury the corpses of fallen comrades which were dragged to the side of the road 'where they lay for weeks, horrible, worried by dogs at night, stinking in the sunlight'.[175] The *Daily Mail* correspondent Harold Cardozo recalled his kindness towards the many strays produced by the war on the Madrid front in December 1936, and how military authorities prohibited kindness towards these animals for fear of rabies and wild packs:

There were two little dogs running about the place. One black mongrel, very small, very old and frightened, would come out of her hiding-place to take a little food. The other, a yellow puppy with clumsy paws, was a war victim, a fragment of shell having cut her head, blinding the poor animal in one eye. Earlier in the war we had taken dogs back and found them homes, but by now there were strict rules about this, and all dogs found wandering at the front were to be shot on sight, as it was feared they would spread hydrophobia and other diseases. We were only able to save the lives of these two animals by shutting them in the ground of the villa and leaving them sufficient food and water every time we went back to Talavera or Avila.

The dog problem was indeed acute at one time. Abandoned by their owners, they had often formed into savage bands and would roam the country looking for food. They were known to have adopted the habit of disinterring dead bodies, and it became necessary to get rid of them all. I remember one night, walking back to my car in the Casa de Campo, having to chase off half a dozen huge brutes circling round a very frightened donkey which they had evidently picked out as affording the prospect of a good meal.[176]

As each side consolidated control of its respective zones, the feral animal problem of the summer was suppressed with ruthlessness.

The wars disrupt human relations

Families were cruelly divided by accidents of geography and loyalty in both wars. Many hitherto inseparable families were divided in July 1936 by the sheer accident of summer holidays.[177] Perhaps the greatest of the diverse motivations for soldiers to desert was their desire to be reunited with family members in the other zone.[178] Even highly distinguished families were divided by the war. On the Cristino side, the thirty-something Leopoldo O'Donnell, future prime minister of Spain, defied the ultra-Catholic character of his family by fighting on the Liberal side of the civil war, even though he had other family members fighting on the Carlist side. In 1984, the historian Julia Gómez Prieto published a series of private letters in the possession of a family connected to Balmaseda (Vizcaya) but which also corresponded during the Carlist War with relatives in Valladolid and Jerez. During the revolutionary September of 1835, Alejandro Antuñano wrote to his brother in Jerez, complaining of the racketeering of local Carlist forces levying punitive taxes on the transit of civilians and their goods. Owing to this siege, Alejandro 'had to behave like a smuggler, moving on remote roads and by night in order to dodge the ruinous sum (one real per pound of merchandise) demanded by Carlist revenue guards'.[179] At times of acute violence, the penalties on those breaking siege lines were ultimate. In the summer of 1835 Don Carlos decreed the death penalty against Cristino postmen running the blockade to besieged Cristino towns. At the start of August, the defenders of Vitoria were cut off from news from the outside world when their postman was captured and executed by Carlists.[180] In January 1836 a detachment of National Guard and of a line regiment was massacred as it left Barcelona to escort mail to Madrid.[181]

As repeated siege attempts of Bilbao lapsed into general blockades, the Carlists also imposed draconian curfews around known Cristino positions. All communication with Bilbao (which proved a particularly attractive destination for deserters in both wars) was forbidden on pain of death, as was the unauthorized approach to within half-a-league's radius of known Cristino positions. These measures simply exchanged one problem for another, as the gains made punishing desertion were lost with the economic dislocation caused by the ordinance on no-go areas. Equally, the Cristinos ratcheted up their total war by imprisoning the relatives of known Carlist combatants who were in their power, fining them 120 reales per month until their kin laid down their arms. Espartero tempered this harshness with some humanitarian measures, such as loosening up the counter-blockade decree of December 1835 which forbade the export of any goods whatsoever into Bilbao's Carlist hinterland. Knowing the potentially counter-productive devastation armies were causing to civilians, Espartero allowed food and other non-military material through.[182]

The summer of 1835 saw Carlist bands flare up in proportion to the weakening of Cristino counter-insurgency operations during the liberal revolution. The porousness of government territorial control disrupted normal civilian transport by stagecoaches. Even though the young poet Larra boasted about paying off Carlists in order to transit between France and Spain via the Pyrenees, few civilian Cristino officeholders dared do the same as the war progressed.[183] Although Commander-in-Chief Córdova was pleased in January 1836 to declare the key strategic road linking Vitoria with Madrid via Lerma and Aranda reopened for post and stagecoach services, revolution the following summer would disperse security once more.[184] Government efforts to keep road communications open rose in proportion to the importance of the message. When Mendizábal in February 1836 dissolved the Cortes, news of this event was carried to the provinces using 256 couriers dispatched simultaneously in order to avoid both serious interception by rebels and any unwelcome localized rumours or plots from developing.[185]

One hundred years later government territorial control was easier to establish, especially after the communist-led crackdown on anarchist collectives and militias. The main impediments to government control were the severance of the northern territory and, more vitally given the importance of Barcelona, the Nationalists' cutting off of Catalonia from the central zone following their advance to the Mediterranean coastline at Vinaroz in April 1938. Government officials with business in one of the other zones were still permitted to travel on passenger aircraft. But they were restricted to night flights, as rebels' air supremacy over their territory made daytime movements inadmissible.[186]

Authorities in both zones of Spain in both civil wars were profoundly affected by recent historical examples of popular mobilization for war efforts. In both early nineteenth and early twentieth century Europe the unwelcome radical consequences of arming the people anguished political elites traumatized by the French and Russian Revolutions, respectively. The opening of hostilities in 1833 saw the initially restrained liberal authorities in Madrid resist for several months radical calls for a serious mobilization of the revolution-prone militia. In 1936 a similar scenario played out in the space of forty-eight hours. In both civil wars the result of mass mobilization was the radicalization of street violence behind the lines. Once mass mobilization was underway, ideological pretensions obscured debate about the motives of the enemy. The Liberals of the 1830s came from a newly invented tradition which celebrated popular sovereignty and looked askance at the need for militarization. Yet, paradoxically, 'the people' of the 1830s appeared to be more Carlist than Liberal. Equally, in the 1930s leftists failed to see through the mix of ideological wishful thinking that depicted Republican warriors as 'the people' and the Nationalists as mere conscripts. The British communist William Rust was convinced that National conscripts were ready, even eager, to surrender.[187]

In fact, harsh discipline combined with martial law from the start of the rising made surrender or defection from Nationalist ranks far less likely than left-wing commentators imagined. Even the rearguard rebel militia (sometimes and ironically called the 'National Militia' despite the revolutionary example of the 1830s) showed greater cohesion than the Republican militias of the early weeks. The communist Arthur Koestler witnessed recruitment into this militia in poverty-stricken Andalucía, where the low pay of three pesetas per day (30% of the pay awarded to government militia) were offered. Out of thirty miserable men who had been presented for selection by a Nationalist recruitment commission in newly conquered Seville at the end of August 1936, only five (illiterate) candidates were admitted. Any men with 'suspicious characters' or last glimmers of defiance in their eyes were excluded, as was anyone with any definable contact with revolutionary ideas. Koestler charged that such pathos revealed that Franco's rebellion lacked popular support.[188] Yet what was true of the brutalized recruits in newly conquered Andalucia was not true of all areas of Nationalist Spain. A study of the rearguard militia in Galicia (which immediately declared for the rebels in July 1936) shows a gentler picture in which the working classes comprised some 15 per cent of recruits in La Coruña and 35 per cent in Santiago.[189]

The Nationalists helped to maintain the morale of their troops by sponsoring the 'godmother' (*madrina*) scheme of pen pals for single soldiers or soldiers whose families were out of contact in the enemy zone. Some soldiers chose to flirt with single women via mail, a morally justifiable act as the female correspondents were usually out of physical reach, not just in Spain but also sometimes in sympathetic foreign countries like Fascist Italy and, remarkably, Japan, whose embassy was swamped with applicants. The Republicans' enthusiasm for a similar scheme later in the war wore off, as the correspondence was suspected as being a means of espionage (and commissars were supposed to censor these letters).[190] No such scheme appears to have existed in the less-literate times of the 1830s.

Soldiers' moral wellbeing was supposed to be mentored by chaplains in the case of the rebels in both wars and by commissars in the case of the Republicans of the 1930s. The chaplain serving Franco's Foreign Legion in the 1930s, Fernando Huidobro, rejoiced at the nineteenth-century Carlist wars, which he thought were providential in 'keeping a living, ardent faith alive'.[191] Government soldiers in the 1830s were permitted to seek spiritual guidance only from priests who accepted the right of Isabel to reign, but these priests were relatively few in most areas of fighting. Modern anticlericalism deprived the 1930s government army of chaplains, who were substituted by commissars. Some uncertainty persists regarding the commissars' exact role. They were not created by the PCE, but the communists became a majority of their numbers (although there were also socialist, anarchist, Syndicalist and left-Republican commissars), even though they stressed how their work was about defending the Popular Front. Commissars explained to Republican conscripts why the war had to be fought, and were in effect the modern equivalent of chaplains on the other side. The modern and, in many instances, over-intellectualized propaganda of the trench newspapers distributed by commissars appears to have had a negligible effect on maintaining morale, especially in the Republic's 'forgotten army', the Army of Extremadura.[192] In fact, the imageless four-page newspapers of the 1830s appear to have had a greater effect, for good or ill, at influencing soldiers' behaviour than in the more literate times of the Spanish Civil War. The commissars' twentieth-century mission was frequently sidetracked by the conscripts' nineteenth-century problems, such as when they found themselves giving more lessons about basic hygiene than they had bargained for. But in other respects, commissars had an uncontroversially positive impact. The mass education drive for which they were responsible via the *milicianos de cultura* made excellent progress with soldiers' literacy, even among casualties who from May 1937 benefited from a hospital library initiative.[193] From late 1938, however, such efforts went into reverse as an acute shortage of newsprint diminished the availability of newspapers for both soldiers and civilians in the government zone.[194]

Such efforts could not benefit those who could not, or would not, fight. The role of the commissars was not just educational but also coercive in nature, and much of their time was dedicated to disciplining acts of desertion and deciding whether medical incapacitation was real or faked. Draftees, who were seen by friendly doctors (or doctors who were pro-Insurgent), could be pronounced medically 'unfit' for service. Even honest conscripts faced a greater likelihood of poor health because, unlike Nationalist conscripts, who were frequently relieved, government conscripts spent longer periods of time on the line. With the exception of the isolated northern zone of the Republic (the remnants of which fell to the Nationalists in October 1937), Republican conscripts tended to serve at places on the line far from their home areas. Desertion was the other way out. As in the 1830s, desertion became so bad that amnesties were offered on separate occasions as a way of trying to get on top of the backlog of desertion. Military justice in the 1930s included punishment battalions (which involved building fortifications) for misdemeanours like disobeying officers, and the diversion of 90 per cent of a miscreant soldier's pay to his family. Commissars had to agree the decisions of tribunals but were not permitted to make speeches after sentence.[195]

Above all, the commissars were a political issue for the Republican government whose strengthened state apparatus after May 1937 depended upon communist strength. The socialist war minister Indalecio Prieto was not vexed by the institution of the commissariat itself, but by the communist propagandization and domination of it. He thus tried to rebalance their members to represent other Popular Front parties and exploited opportunities to exert state discipline over communist commissars (the most famous case being his demotion of Francisco Antón, the 27-year-old communist lover of La Pasionaria). Yet it remains an open question whether the infighting between communist commissars and other Popular Front groups prolonged the war, even if the answer should incline towards the affirmative with regard to the decisive July 1938 Battle of the Ebro in which the communist commissars' activity was at its most intensive.[196]

Peak militarization

The communist-dominated commissars spearheaded the moral case for militarization, and in so doing became mired in a controversy which divided the left just as during the 1830s. In the 1930s, militias that resisted the Africanista-led Spanish army were merged into a Republican regular army. Both the 1830s Liberal and 1930s Republican left were divided into pro-militarization and anti-militarization camps. Militarization won this internal battle of the left from 1836 and 1937, respectively, but with different outcomes. Hence, the PCE, with its 'Fifth Regiment' model, which it presented as a model for the Republican 'Popular Army', became the vanguard for a militarization policy which the Communists started carrying out as early as November 1936.[197]

Equally the demands made by war obliged both sides to undertake militarization in the 1830s. The proponent of maximum militarization was the moderado General Fernández de Córdova, who commanded the Army of the North between the revolutions of 1835 and 1836. His blockade strategy was matched by the rebel general Nazario Eguía who reorganized Carlist forces into divisions, brigades and operations of reserve and also oversaw the building of defensive lines between the rivers Ebro and Arga. This fortification work increased during the 1835–36 winter lull in fighting.[198] Cristino Spain was never more militarized than during 1836–37; in the wake of the Gómez expedition there were 207,414 men under arms of all classes and nations and some 14,308 cavalry. Losses and desertion had reduced the French Legion to some 857 men, the British Legion to 1,452 men and 222 cavalry and the Portuguese grenadiers (*granaderos*) and Oporto chasseurs (*Caçadores de Oporto*) to some 1,528 men (other Portuguese units having been withdrawn to bolster the Liberal regime at home against its own absolutist faction). But on the other hand, these statistics belied the real war-fighting morale and potential of Liberal Spain: only Espartero commanded real respect and discipline in his ranks.[199] By contrast, Carlist arms peaked at the end of the conflict. By early 1839, Carlist arms totalled some 70,000 across Spain, including perhaps some 15,000 guerrillas.[200]

The attritional warfare that set in close to the northern seaboard underlined the importance of coastal warfare, as the Quadruple Alliance endeavoured to deny the rebels seaborne relief for their blockade. In between their two efforts against Bilbao, Carlists over the winter of 1835–36 tried to capture San Sebastián. But the city held fast thanks to its governor's mobilization of all available manpower and the actions of the Royal Navy.[201] Veteran militia from Bilbao were transported to San Sebastían aboard Royal Navy ships and the British also gave supporting fire to the city's defenders, lobbing shells at a maximum range of 1,600 yards against the attacking rebels.[202] Relations grew frosty with the increasingly lukewarm French after the latter's warships refused Lord Hay's request to 'get out of the way' during his bombardment of rebel-held Pasaia.[203] Cooperation and even solidarity between the Cristino troops and British vessels flowed smoothly in comparison. Such solidarity in local point-defence also characterized the Spanish Civil War. Alas, as in the Spanish Civil War (in the case of the treacherous compromising of Bilbao's 'Iron Ring') this solidarity did not extend to civil–military relations. The reconstruction of Bilbao's defences after the first siege went agonizingly slowly, owing to a financial dispute between the local Cristino authorities and the military.[204] This dispute escalated to the undersupply of food and pay to the defensive garrisons. Two Cristino regiments at Bilbao revolted over the spring of 1836, and this example was followed by units in several other locations.[205]

Ultimately, government militarization concerned not just the main northern front in the 1830s, but also Cabrera's growing eastern insurgency from 1835 and, crucially, the crisis of banditry throughout the government zone. Indeed the lawlessness of bandits, who often claimed to be paramilitaries for one of the sides, appears to have been a factor in hurrying the government to offer the Carlists something better than an unconditional surrender. Evidence from Valencia shows a massive increase in the executions of bandits captured by the authorities after 1836, with the number peaking in the 'peace' of 1840.[206] Local elites despaired at lawlessness. The prefect of Guadix (Granada) demanded army reinforcements against 'deserters and criminals' who were extorting local farmers.[207] Near Málaga, property-owners, municipal authorities and clergymen petitioned Madrid for reinforcements against a similar scourge. Reinforcements met with thanks and a request for even more troops in order 'to finish off the bands'.[208] The signatories criticized the law of 25 April 1821 which allowed criminals to escape military jurisdiction by surrendering themselves to civil authorities who would try them before juries.[209]

After the moderado election victory of November 1837, militarization reached the towns as states of siege were gradually imposed on the provincial capitals. The left-leaning National Militia were either glumly subordinated to army discipline or dissolved altogether, sometimes in response to conspiracies and violence. An Army of the Reserve was created, much to the chagrin of General Espartero who demanded full resources for what he deemed to be the pivotal northern front. Espartero's great rival, General Ramón Narváez, commanded the Reserve. Narváez performed a generally successful pacification of the rebel bands plaguing southern Castile and Andalucía throughout 1838. But the real concentration of fighting remained the task of the Army of the North which continued to wear down the war-weary Carlist Basque country. The northern front's claim to primacy was helped when Narváez himself was forced to flee into exile following his bungled attempt to topple Espartero by raising the Militia of Seville.[210] Espartero's effectiveness and fame rose throughout 1838. Ever since his defeat of the rebel 'Negri expedition' in early 1838, he had been increasing his powerbase. He made very public complaints about government neglect in its duties to supply his army, all in a manner which won him his men's affection (he paid so many of his men out of his own pocket, even tapping up friends and relatives for the same end). He spoke in terms of 'nation', not 'party', and demanded that all future ministers of war be generals, not politicians. The 'Spanish Bonaparte', which was both a term of endearment and abuse, was clearly identifying the cause of the army with that of the nation. Espartero sent a petition to the Cortes and talked about going to Madrid in person (presumably at the head of the army). The terrified government response was to try to buy him off with honours, dignitaries and other diversions. But Espartero, with one experience of the premiership already behind him, had now nailed his colours to the mast of martial liberalism. His petitions were couched in the popular tone and were avidly read by his soldiers.[211] Since the incapacitation and death of Espoz y Mina in 1836, no Liberal caudillo had emerged to rival Espartero. His military prowess (relative though this was), and the coterminous flourishing of Spain's romantic movement, which saw this son of a carter depicted as the incarnation of popular will, placed Espartero at the centre of the public imagination and at the heart of leftist programmes and conspiracies for political change.[212] By the summer of 1839 the main Carlist front would sue for peace, and Espartero became the undisputed Liberal hero of the peace.

The enemy within

One more phenomenon united the domestic battlefronts of the Spanish Civil Wars. The 'enemy within' existed both in reality and in the paranoid imagination of inhabitants of government areas of control. The rebel general Mola popularized the term 'fifth column' in the English language. His promise during the winter of 1936 that a 'fifth column' inside Madrid would open the city to his attacking forces certainly represented the political views if not the bravery of vast swathes of the capital's well-to-do classes. Most of the 'red terror' in the capital happened even before the rebels began their siege of Madrid. Once the rebels began bombarding Madrid in earnest, they did their best to avoid targeting the wealthy Salamanca district on the grounds of the huge number of surviving rebel sympathizers who were presumed to be living there, either in their own homes or in one of the numerous foreign embassies that still dot the area.[213]

Madrid had its own 'enemies within' one hundred years earlier. Jerónimo Merino, like Mola, drew the support of Carlists. Merino's abortive march on Madrid over the winter of 1833–34 drew disaffected royalists out of the capital and into his ranks and led to demands from the revived liberal press that the National Militia of the Triennium be recalled.[214] When the Carlists in September 1837 reached Madrid's walls in force, a Neapolitan agent operating out of a safe house on the Alcalá acted as a go-between for an abortive plan to open the capital to Carlist occupation and to arrange a dynastic reconciliation to end the war.[215] The Carlist Royal Expedition against Madrid in 1837 was predicated in part on the belief that the capital's respectable classes had tired of revolution and would pronounce in favour of the entry into their city of Don Carlos. The foreign correspondent of the pro-Carlist *Morning Herald* present in Madrid in 1836 believed that three-quarters of the capital's 'respectable' population were in favour of Don Carlos.[216] Despite Burke Honan's assessment, Madrid's respectable class did not save him from being hounded out of the capital in the revolutionary atmosphere of 1836 and expelled to Portugal after the British ambassador had refused him any diplomatic protection.[217]

Even though for most of the war there was no external Carlist threat to Madrid, revolutionaries often cast a suspicious eye towards the foreign embassies and legations in their midst. As the Radical prime minister Mendizábal took the ominous step in January 1836 of dissolving the Cortes, the moderado former prime minister, Martínez de la Rosa, took refuge with the Danish chargés d'affaires in response to news of an assassination plot against his person.[218] But whereas the hostility of diplomats in the 1830s was equivocal, in the 1930s it was blatant. After July 1936 almost the entire Spanish diplomatic corps defected to the rebels. The majority of foreign embassies in Madrid provided shelter for rightists fleeing revolutionary violence.[219] Unlike Villiers in the 1830s, British ambassador, Henry Chilston, favoured the rebels. In early 1938 the British Embassy hosted clandestine meetings of the rebels' only official fifth-column organization (the SIE, or Servicio de Información Español), a safe venue at which to execute Franco's demand for the unification of underground right-wing parties into a single party (FET de las JONS).[220] Fifth-column activity increased as defeatism grew in the government zone, and the discovery of subterranean arms caches in Madrid was a frequent subject of the press.[221] The most spectacular act of sabotage occurred in January 1938 when saboteurs detonated an ammunition dump in one of the capital's metro tunnels, causing an explosion which claimed the lives of about 400 people.[222]

Whereas grander diplomatic establishments attracted controversy in the 1930s, in the 1830s, controversy surrounded the consulates. Consuls occupied an invidious position because they were often Spaniards who lacked the security of the grander diplomatic establishments in Madrid. Once Cabrera raided the government seaport of Benicarló (Valencia) he successfully halted a bombardment by a British vessel after signalling that he was holding the local British consul hostage.[223] Spaniards acting as British vice-consuls at Cartagena and Santoña (Santander) during revolutions in 1835 and 1836 needed diplomatic intervention to prevent the local militia from enlisting them into their ranks.[224] Revolutionaries who seized control of Barcelona in January 1836 arrested a certain O'Shea, a British subject serving as consul for pro-Carlist Russia, who was released only after high-level diplomatic intervention.[225] The following year, Málaga's powerful Chamber of Commerce petitioned the Cortes to end the immunity from national law enjoyed by Spaniards serving as foreign consuls, citing examples of individuals who had invoked consul status in order to escape conscription and forced loans.[226] Anxieties about the enemy within underlined how the battlefronts were part of the home fronts, and it is to this subject which we must now turn.

2

The home fronts in the Spanish Civil Wars

This situation of civil war, provoked by an idle and exploitative landowning class that refuses to die, has its direct origins in the barbarism and cruelty of the Carlism of last century … in the descendents of such hyenas in cassocks as Merino.[1]

Constitutional legacies

Both the 1812 and 1931 Constitutions reserved the majority of power in the hands of the legislature, leaving only a weak and dependent judiciary and executive.[2] So wanting was a strong and stable executive power that a cogent argument has been made that support for Carlism in the 1830s was based on a desire for authoritarianism as a formula for stability.[3] The justice minister in the 1835–36 Cristino government, Alvaro Gómez Becerra, complained of the all-powerful legislature overruling judges and magistrates without any real safeguards as in France. It was not just that 'a civil war is devouring us … but that sectarianism on the Liberal side has produced a second war from within' which rode roughshod over theoretical constitutional guarantees. Even worse, untrammelled military power had imposed states of siege by 1839 even in areas where there was no need, with the result that military authorities were overruling the competencies of civil authorities, ordering the execution of some who might be innocent and freeing those who might be guilty.[4] Such military interventionism was made easier by the weak executive power that described both civil wars. The 1812 Constitution was known for restraining the king, and the revolutions of 1835 and 1836 stripped María Cristina of most of her theoretical power. By this stage, the self-exiled critic Blanco White had come to believe that 'Spain was *incurable*', and in desperate need of a Senate which might 'allow the nobles to become servants of the state rather the people its slaves' and, in accordance with the utilitarian British model which so impressed him, allow for 'the condition of stability in political society which is a strong principle of cohesion among the members of the same community'.[5]

Equally, the 1931 Constitution allowed for only a weak executive and blurred the distinctions between legislative and judicial power. This charter resembled no other indigenous Spanish constitution other than that of 1812, and radical arguments for the defence of unicameralism showed striking similarities to those advanced by the 'hotheads' of 1835. Sovereignty was 'indivisible' and an upper chamber, or even an independent executive power, would risk encouraging the monarchical abuses of Alfonso XIII, which were comparable to those of Ferdinand and the pretensions of Don Carlos one hundred years earlier.[6] Alfonso's abdication in 1931 was followed by the Republican government's high-profile prosecution of figures linked to the king and his dictator in a manner exceeding the 1830s persecution of the 'creatures of Calomarde', the effect being the alienation of possibilist right-wingers owing to the inconsistent investigations into 'responsibilities'. Whereas the 1930 Republican army *golpistas*, Galán and Hernández, were celebrated, a 1932 coup attempt by a right-wing general produced a wave of legislative persecution.[7] Equally, the right-wing government of 1933–36 exploited overbearing legislative power to persecute political opponents. While judicial powerlessness repeated the controversies of the Carlist War, in the 1930s it served to polarize politics even before civil war began. In 1933 a CEDA deputy had been sent to prison merely for inciting farmers to restrict wheat cultivation in view of the leftist government's wheat price.[8] Presidents Alcalá Zamora and Manuel Azaña were virtual spectators of politics. The Catholic former was accused by rebels of 'imbecile treachery' in refusing to use his executive power against the Popular Front.[9] José Antonio Primo de Rivera, the photogenic martyr to the Nationalist movement executed in government captivity in November 1936, is remembered as the leader of Spanish fascism. His first forays into politics in the 1930s Unión Monárquica called for the strengthening of executive power.[10] The call for a strong executive was not only the preserve of the rebels. Whereas the anarchist Emma Goldman rejoiced how 'no outstanding leader like Lenin or Trotsky had emerged: the masses themselves have risen from the very bounds of the earth',[11] moderate Republican leaders were far less sanguine. General Miaja regretted that the Second Republic was not presidential, and that most power lay in the Cortes.[12]

Revolutionary similarities between
1835–36 and 1936

The government home fronts in both civil wars experienced political radicalization which changed relations to property and local authority. Whereas the Carlist War produced the first major revolution after almost two years of fighting, the outbreak of the 1930s war was coterminous with the 'Spanish Revolution' in the government zone. At a superficial level, there was no revolution in the summer of 1936, as the Republican government was still in charge. Yet the rebel conspiracy of 1936 justified itself on the grounds that full-blown leftist revolution had to be forestalled, but both the rebel and government side fostered a great irony in their political considerations. Despite rebel claims, full-blown leftist revolution did not precede the rebellion; rather it followed it, mainly in response to the failed rebel coup. Two days into the rebellion, the new Giral government armed the workers.[13] The fact that full-blown revolution in the 1830s began not two days after the start of the war, but *two years* later, reveals that the First Carlist War itself was a motor for radicalization to a greater degree than the Spanish Civil War, whose polarized origins lay long before July 1936.

Yet a comparison of the events of 1835–36 and 1936 reveals a similar pattern of revolutionary politics. The radicalization of the liberal revolution of 1835–37 coincided with the greatest scale and range of war-related violence, just as the period of July 1936–May 1937 did. In the depths of the Carlist War, the Cristino state managed to hold on to its authority and even channel many of the militants' grievances by empowering the juntas and the militia. In contrast, a century later, the people-in-arms were the vanguard of the localized revolutions which unfolded across Spain in the summer of 1936, and operated formally outside of the parameters of state authority. This was reflected in popular attitudes towards private property. Whereas few revolutionary elites in the 1830s civil war promoted or even believed in the socialization of private property, in 1936 virtually every commodity from cigarettes to hotels to private cars, were asserted to be publicly owned.[14] It is unclear the extent to which (if at all), this 'idealism' described 1830s revolutionaries, too. What is clear in both conflicts is how the wars could suddenly give power to the powerless. This was expressed not just in terms of loot and violence, but also in the bureaucratic trimmings designed to humiliate class enemies who before the war had humiliated the perpetrators. Thus we see popular participation in the fleeting Carlist regimes of Córdoba and other conquered Cristino cities in 1836. In 1936, the powerless took great pride confiscating the fineries of the rich, using their cars for 'official' purposes (including extrajudicial killings), and turning the best hotels into soup kitchens. The vengefulness of the powerless was also directed at temporizing governments. Just as the Radicals of the mid-1830s had railed against the crypto-Carlism of elements in the government, so the working-class militants of 1936 vented their fury at the 'legalism' of the Republic under siege.[15]

Much of this radicalism was the result of five years of pre-war failure to address social justice. As one eminent scholar of Republican land reform has observed: 'The magnitude of the threat that the agrarian law posed to the propertied classes did not permit them to tolerate its fulfilment, while the magnitude of the promise offered to the peasantry was equally intolerable.'[16] Even though the implementation of the Agrarian Reform Law was unsuccessful – only some 12,260 labourers had been resettled on some 11,638 hectares of usually poor-quality land by December 1934 – the landowning right felt that its vested privileges and economic supremacy had been mortally threatened by socialists determined with their Constitution to plot the overthrow of capitalism.[17] A cultural mass opinion developed among the landowning right who viewed alienation of land from private ownership as symbolic of a 'red' takeover.[18] Yet instead of attempting to appease the landowners, the Republican coalition's lack of application provoked a rightist response which was already gratuitously fuelled by the assault on the Church, which led to the growth of the CEDA.[19] The right countered that the September 1932 Agrarian Reform Law was revolutionary and ignorant of the complex reality of Spanish agriculture. What was needed, the CEDA argued, was a government policy of gradualism using scarce state funds to buy up the largest *latifundia* for redistribution and to effect long-term modernization to solve the unemployment problem.[20] The right-wing government of 1933–36 frustrated what little progress had been made, and even though five months of peacetime Popular Front government in 1936 resulted in land redistribution by both the government and the masses, little could be done by the summer to thwart a revolutionary response to the army's uprising.

Barcelona in both civil wars became the reddest city in the government zone. Its 1829 nominal population of 113,780 had ballooned owing to the influx of refugees from the Civil War.[21] Government-held towns swelled with hungry refugees. Cortes deputy Castell in April 1836 spoke of 'hundreds of wandering émigrés in towns whose faint and cadaverous aspect bespoke that their sufferings were approaching the last extremity', and railed against rebel clerics.[22] Even though Mendizábal had wanted to abolish tithes altogether, the disastrous state finances dictated that this could not happen until 1841, and could only be halved in the meantime. Yet a radicalized Cristino population was in no mood to fund a Church which was represented as the enemy. During the summer of 1836 tithe-proctors in the province of Toledo were jeered and assaulted, and municipal authorities were powerless to protect them.[23] A state of siege had to be used to collect the tithe in the province of Málaga during the summer of 1838.[24] The following year, citizens in this province mobilized in a mass tithe strike that began in Motril (Granada) before spreading to other pueblos, this general refusal to pay this time rendering futile the intervention of an infantry battalion being deployed to protect the proctors.[25] When authorities in Carataunas (Granada) municipality tried to break the strike, villagers in Cáñar answered with a charivari, publicly burning figurines of past and present mayors.[26]

Catalonia and most of Aragón were the scene of anarchist property revolution in 1936; the same regions had subjected to a form of social war one hundred years earlier. Carlist efforts in the Maestrazgo had suffered from their disparate groups being defeated in detail, but from March 1835 a major rebel effort ensued when Cabrera consolidated the forces of Quílez, Torner, Forcadell and Añón into a 900-strong force. The Cristino captain-general of Aragón, Antonio María Alvarez, on 30 April 1835 responded to this new threat with more condign punishments to be meted out. A 320 reales fine would be levied on each family and, if its members were absent or unable to pay, on the district for each individual who had defected to the Carlists, half of this fine being awarded to the Urban Militia and the other half to the vigilante groups of 'flying columns' (*cuerpos francos*). One hundred years later, it was the rebels rather than the government which funded vigilante groups who terrorized 'red' wage-labourers in the countryside. A thirty-day amnesty was offered for these men to return (but the fine would stand). Alvarez also imposed a draconian ban on the export of war-related material to anywhere in Navarra apart from the Cristino stronghold of Tudela. But if Alvarez thought he could outbid Cabrera in ruthlessness, he was sorely mistaken. On 23 May 1835, Cabrera fell on Caspe, a prosperous liberal town of 7,500 inhabitants 14 leagues from Zaragoza.[27] Five captured urbanos were shot and the town was given over to widespread sacking. News of these outrages reached Zaragoza and fuelled the anticlerical outrages there.[28]

Even far from the front lines, villagers exploited the demands made by the war to assert property rights. For five years, villagers had imbibed propaganda identifying clericalism with Carlism. Fifty miles to the north-west of the tithe riots activism of a different nature struck Íllora (Granada). At Íllora, villagers repeatedly encroached upon the large estate bequeathed by the Cortes in 1814 to the Duke of Wellington for his services in the Peninsular War. The estate manager, General José O'Lawlor, reported that the villagers saw no crime in stealing from the estate of a foreigner. For generations, villagers claimed that O'Lawlor had exploited the chaos of the 1820s and 1830s to expropriate land beyond what had been granted by the Cortes. Given the problem of Tory opposition to the Quadruple Alliance, the Captain-General of Granada wasted no time in securing Wellington's estate personally.[29] Eighty miles east of Wellington's estate, the villagers of Ohanes (Almería) asserted their 'moral economy'. Customary rights to share the scarce water of the River Chico with the neighbouring village of Canjáyar were disrupted in December 1836 when the mayor of Canjáyar exercised the municipal autonomy he enjoyed courtesy of the 1836 revolution by building a dam which parched his neighbours. A lengthy legal dispute was truncated by the actions of the local hero, José Solsona, who destroyed the dam and dared to compare the authorities to Carlists deserving deportation: 'For the money wasted on the case we could have transported all our officials to the Philippines!' An attempt at the end of the war to restore the dam was beaten back by a lynchmob. The people of one village defeated the people of another, showing contempt for law and asserting the sort of community rivalries which distinguished many anarchist collectives in the 1930s. There was no glory in this at all for the mayor of Ohanes, who was thrust completely to one side.[30]

One hundred years later saw the government side suffer a breakdown in its authority in the summer of 1936, which could only be painstakingly re-established. Revolutionary 'People's Courts' were set up on 26 August, and their remit was extended over the army on 15 September, second-guessing officers to an extent far greater than the 'representatives on mission' dispatched by the Cortes to the Cristino armies during 1836–37. On 16 February 1937, Prime Minister Largo Caballero took a major step in reasserting state control by establishing separate courts for military matters, and Negrín expanded state control over military justice with the 9 August 1937 SMI (*Servicio de Investigación Militar*).[31] The recovery of state power in 1937 in many ways resembled that of 1837.

Both civil wars in the government zones witnessed two sources of political oppression, the legislative and the military. Catalonia from the summer of 1835 was subjected to rebel insurgency in the rural west and radical revolution in the cities. Grandees and other wealthy individuals fled to France in droves. The revolutionary authorities confiscated the property of these émigrés, extending in a sectarian direction a practice hitherto reserved for punishing known Carlists.[32] The government lifted the provincial state of siege on 5 November 1836 but summary justice against 'conspiracy' and 'anti-constitutional activities' remained exempt from normal civil jurisdiction. Madrid remained in a state of siege throughout the 1836–37 *progresista* administration. In November 1836 it took the combined opposition of the British ambassador and the more moderate parts of the *progresismo* and the *moderados* to block demands by radicals to expand revolutionary justice. Tribunals were proposed to try Carlists and to pass death sentences without any recourse to appeal. Villiers condemned the bill as 'legalising the gratification of private vengeance which would only boost the ranks of the Pretender and the émigrés'.[33] In the end, the bill was rejected for pragmatic rather than reasons of principle. An amendment to allow a fifteen-day time limit for appeals was deemed inadequate. Dozens of countryside-dwellers captured during the pursuit of the Carlist Gómez expedition claimed to have been abducted by the enemy against their will, and their home parishes sometimes lay more than a hundred miles away from their point of capture, which rendered impracticable the request for witnesses.[34]

Impressive though the radicalization of politics was, it pales in comparison to the combination of revolution and terror which gripped the government zone in 1936. The outbreak of civil war propelled Spain's powerful anarchist movement to avenge itself on its 'oppressors', putting into practice its tenet of literal class war.[35] Even though the 'Red Terror' produced new patterns in violence, it would be an exaggeration to claim that the working classes in the government zone supported the actions of the militants. The social historian Michael Seidman has argued that the outbreak of Civil War did not radically change the ordinary attitudes and behaviours of Spain's million-strong CNT membership. Most people were politically uncommitted, and saw the Civil War as 'an episode of unwelcome public interference into their personal existence'.[36] Catalan engineers during the Revolution were afraid to object to men they called 'anarchist rogues', with the result that output declined.[37] But the Spanish Revolution did have a strongly anarchist dimension to the extent that some 750,000 Spaniards joined agricultural collectives and perhaps a million worked in their industrial equivalent. Moreover, the anarchists had ideological as well as security motivations in leading the terror against suspected fifth columnists, a terror which resulted in perhaps 80,000 killings on the government side.[38] Foreign admirers drawn to the workers' revolution tended not to dwell on this violence. For Hank Rubin, the American communist and International Brigader, workers' control in Barcelona was like a 'party', a festive atmosphere. Anarchists were hailed as the masters of Barcelona, having saved Catalonia from Goded's rebellion and thereby raising their profile as an effective defensive force in both political and military senses of the term.[39]

The strident image of revolution exaggerated the degree of change. Only some 18.5 per cent of all land in the Republican zone was collectivized, and this was farmed in conditions of 'collective selfishness'. Seidman identifies three types of individualistic behaviour: the acquisitive (hoarding), entrepreneurial (politicking for benefits), and subversive (sabotage, desertion, absenteeism). Collectives were bedevilled by the problems of localism and the Republic was unable to achieve a coherent structure in which they could operate. In the Republican zone, the rural population that had seized or been allocated land stockpiled what they had produced, or sold their surplus on the black market at inflated prices. In the Republican zone, over 80 per cent of those who joined a union or political party did so only after the conflict began and this was for such material reasons as jobs, housing and healthcare (all of which increasingly required that a party membership card be produced). The strike wave which had paralysed much of Spanish industry in the wake of the Popular Front victory continued after the onset of hostilities.[40] The fact that anarchist autonomy and collectivization had a very mixed impact made it easier for the 'counter-revolutionary' communists to sustain their drive towards centralizing politics, militarizing the militias and recapitalizing those many businesses which had been collectivized. The communist press prepared the property counter-revolution with months of press coverage calling for 'respect for the property of small businessmen and industrialists, for they are our brothers'.[41]

Regional politics

The 'revolutionary justice' besetting the government zone did not exist in the government-held Basque country, which from 1 October 1936 was under home rule. The Basque Autonomy Statute led to the creation of the first Autonomous Government of Euskadi, with Aguirre as *Lehendakari* (president), leading a cabinet that contained five Basque Nationalist representatives and five representatives of leftist parties. The new Basque government did not make any drastic changes to Vizcaya's industry and no nationalization or collectivization was implemented in either province. This moderation was unpopular with the revolutionary juntas in the Asturias to the west who were increasingly dependent on Vizcaya for economic assistance; many of them saw their Basque Nationalist neighbours as Church-loving reactionaries. By contrast, the communists of the Basque Country were able to escape the control of Comintern with Basque communists cooperating fully with the leadership of Aguirre, who had refused to place the Vizcayan front under the control of the Republic. The Basque Country's industry and military were being controlled independently unlike those of neighbouring Santander and the Asturias; the factories in Bilbao bought coal from England rather than the Asturias. This, in addition to the tendency of Aguirre to give his forces (the *Euzko Gudaroztea*) orders distinct from those of other Republican troops and the presence of Basque priests at the front, led to more disapproval from many of the Basques' leftist allies.[42]

During the war, Aguirre made a speech at a Valencian Cortes session; he claimed that the Civil War was a fight between democracy and fascism and emphasized the complete identity of the Basque Nationalists with the former. After receiving criticism from the Bishop of Pamplona for resisting the Nationalists, Aguirre claimed that Christ came to aid the weak and not the powerful. In his view the Catholic Basque Nationalists were fighting for the Basque people's freedom. At the same time, the PNV barred leftists and non-Basques from joining their militia.[43]

The association made by the Catholic Basque Nationalists with resistance to the rebels' 'Crusade' marked a major contrast to the Basque-Carlist nexus of the 1830s. One of the major reasons for Carlist strength in the Basque country was their defence of the medievalist structure of Spain, and Navarra and to a lesser extent the three Basque provinces proper, were the only places left where the pre-modern fueros had survived. The enemy were the centralizing Castilians, and indeed some contemporaries interpreted the First Carlist War as a struggle for Basque liberty for this reason.[44] But this interpretation is weakened by the fact that analogous processes were at work on the government side, too. The 1835 revolution of the juntas pitted the periphery against the centre, and although the 'sovereignty' proclaimed by provincial juntas in most areas amounted to little more than a power-grab supported by hot air, in other areas of Spain, provincial 'sovereignty' made sense because of more recent traditions of autonomy. The juntas of Valencia, Aragón and Catalonia proposed to form a federation in a conscious imitation of the pre-absolutist Hapsburg model.[45] Elsewhere the juntas had more prosaic motives for proclaiming their autonomy from the central government. In Málaga, a call for volunteers to defend the province fell on deaf ears and instead some 500 convicts were disembarked from galleys for this purpose to be led by a local mobster so notorious that local elites welcomed Prime Minister Mendizábal's centralizing ordinances.[46] Revolution, in 1835 and again in 1936, in respect of the famous Durruti column, provided opportunities for criminals to secure political cover for their nefarious deeds. The periphery thus militated against the government centre during 1835–36 for diverse reasons.

Spain's other economically advanced region, Catalonia, possessed a modern autonomy in the 1930s that was very different from one hundred years earlier, at the dawn of Catalanism as we know it. The First Carlist War began a process of Catalanism which ended in the Spanish Civil War. This phenomenon represents another dimension to the 'First Great Cause' and 'Last Great Cause' linking the Spanish Civil Wars. In fact, as Angel Smith has recently demonstrated, the years 1770–1814 witnessed merely the growth of a 'provincial' Catalan identity which enhanced rather than diminished a nascent pan-Spanish nationalism. Significant Catalanism began with the *Renaixença* of the First Carlist War, associated above all with Victor Balaguer.[47] Even then, Catalanism was truly *españolista* as Catalan Liberals rallied to the central government in the war against Carlism in the Catalan far west. The 'rebirth' of Catalan identity during the first conflict nonetheless led to a more articulate and separate identity which, by the 1890s, would prove irreversible.

The 1930s thus cast Catalonia as the main champion of the periphery (Barcelona) against the centre (Madrid). The advent of the Republic in 1931 was greeted in the CNT stronghold of Barcelona by Republican civil governor and Catalanist Luis Companys with a gesture towards the anarchists. He organized the destruction of district police records.[48] This hurried indulgence of anti-authoritarianism exactly mirrored elite responses to popular radicalism one hundred years earlier. As the civil war radicalized leftist opinion in 1835, Cristino civil governors made public bonfires of police registers.[49] As Mendizábal was swept into power by the juntas, he abolished the notorious internal passports established in 1824 by what was then the first nationwide police force in Spain.[50] But once war began in July 1936, the grip of the central government loosened swiftly. In the Basque country, as we have seen, the Autonomy Statute was passed. In Catalonia, the Generalidad maximized its devolved powers to the fullest extent, and President Companys led an administration dominated by anarchists and left Catalanists, both of whom rejected the centralization of Madrid.

Counter-revolutionary politics

Despite the resurgent regions, counter-revolutions were underway in the government zones of both civil wars many months before they became visible. During the First Carlist War the revolution peaked during the period of the juntas between September 1835 and Prime Minister Mendizábal's gradual reassertion of central control by the spring of 1836. For this reason, the 1835 revolution rather than the La Granja revolution of 1836 has attracted more interest from historians, and interpretations have ranged from the nineteenth-century liberal, the twentieth-century Marxist, and the twenty-first-century revisionist. Liberal historians like Pirala celebrated how the juntas were elected by 'the people', albeit only active citizens (militia members and substantial taxpayers), and he glossed over the actual political violence accompanying their supremacy. But in fact the frequent resort to directionless violence set the tone for the central government to reassert control. The only foreign power in the least sympathetic to the liberal revolution was Britain. But even ambassador Villiers lamented the scale of violence that summer: 'The civil and military governors of Tarragona have been lynched at sea, the people of Badajoz have rounded up and ejected all the monks from their city, seven monks have been murdered in Murcia and the 1812 Constitution proclaimed in Madrid.' Some 150 rural refugees and sailors were killed by Urban Militia suppressing riots in Barcelona in the wake of Bassa's lynching.[51] Just like the May Days of 1937, the junta revolution of September 1835 had the hallmarks of a civil war within a civil war. Government generals recovered their nerve and showed zeal in reducing radical-liberal revolutions in urban centres and, crucially, the Army of the North did not defect to the revolutionaries of September 1835.

María Cristina's attempts in the summer of 1836 to restrain the revolution further, mainly by dismissing Prime Minister Mendizábal, recoiled with the *progresista* revolt of the Sergeants at La Granja in August. General Fernández de Córdova was forced into exile during the ensuing revolution. The 'Revolt of the Sergeants' at the summer palace of La Granja appeared to anticipate the plebeian takeover of the streets almost exactly one hundred years later. Lowly sergeants, radicalized by pay arrears, leftist newspapers detailing the cowardice of government elites in the path of the Carlist Gómez invasion, and supported, unofficially, by ambassador Villiers in cahoots with the recently dismissed Mendizábal, launched a *proununciamiento* which forced the queen-regent to swear allegiance to the Constitution of 1812. This radical charter was a virtual declaration of war on Metternich's Europe. Revolutionary authorities promised a war to the knife against both Carlists and their supposed apologists in the moderado party whose property was seized with the same alacrity as that of the bourgeoisie in the summer of 1936. French revolutionaries were drawn to a neighbouring country where internal passport controls were suspended and the policing of secret societies had been relaxed. The ayacucho governor of the capital proclaimed 'a guillotine must be established in Madrid and every provincial capital in Spain'.[52] Yet behind the scenes the leaders of the revolution resolved to moderate its extremes. As early as October, Prime Minister Calatrava expressed his desire to restrain the Constitution of 1812 by introducing an upper chamber.[53] In January 1837 a suspensive royal veto was introduced, anticipating the Senate established by the Constitution of 1837 six months later.[54] Moreover, crucial British support did not measurably increase in the wake of the La Granja revolution. Ambassador Villiers continued to reject Finance Minister Mendizábal's year-long pleas for a formal British loan. Villiers countered that the Spanish government had already exceeded its credit line for British arms imports and that 'the termination of the war quite as much upon finding generals who were not cowardly and incapable as upon getting money'.[55] In fact, the government of both 1835 and 1836 revolutions strained every nerve to restore central government power and to rein in the street radicals.

The moderating influence of the Constitution of 1837 allowed the government to re-establish control over street radicals. Public officials who had been fired since August 1836 for refusing to swear allegiance to the Constitution of 1812 could now be reinstated as long as they were not Carlists or common criminals and would swear allegiance to the new Constitution of 1837.[56] The 1837 charter was generally progresista in that it recognized substantial town-hall autonomy and gave municipal votes to all householders. But it had moderating features, too: a Senate, a royal suspensive veto and a highly restrictive (albeit direct) franchise. This last feature enabled the moderados to win the November 1837 elections and thereafter to complete a counter-revolution which had been underway in fits and starts since the designation of 'mobile militia' in 1835. In particular, regional governors imposed martial law in the revolution-prone cities.

The moderados did not have things entirely their own way. When the Cádiz National Militia commander, Carlos Azopardo, was imprisoned in December 1837 for his part in trying to sabotage the elections, the men who had been serving under him met in the centre of the town 'shouting subversive cries' and demanding the prisoner's release. A state of siege was declared and loyal troops and militiamen from other battalions managed to contain the riot, after which the third battalion along with a rebellious artillery section was dissolved.[57] The moderados retained their political grip through better organization and by the subordination of the left-leaning National Militia via states of sieges. The French consul in Valencia noted during the 1838 elections that both dynastic parties were bribing beggars and the unemployed for votes to the tune of between 20 and 25 reales per day. Since the Moderates tended to represent larger and more secure landed and business interests, they were generally able to use the stick more than the carrot. The powerful Duke of Alba ordered his dependents to assist the

Moderates during the 1839 campaign, thus contributing to an electoral victory which would be overturned the following year by the progresista 'Duke of Victory', Baldomero Espartero.[58]

May Days in Barcelona

In both wars, the army was most tested suppressing revolutions in Barcelona. The suppression of the juntas of 1835 and the modification of the Constitution of 1812 in 1836 did not suppress popular radicalism in Barcelona. On 4 May 1837 a bloody insurrection swept Barcelona, killing dozens, and inspired by Xaudaró y Fábregas, an agitator skilled in the byways of radical infighting. During exile in 1832 he published his *Bases de una constitución política*, a blueprint for a federal republic elected by a wide franchise and based upon autonomous, bicameral provincial legislatures which would cede sovereignty to Madrid.[59] His supporters were radicalized by Xaudaró's proselytizing in the newspaper *El Vapor*, whose propaganda campaign prepared Barcelona radicals in May 1837 to seize control of town-hall buildings. A secondary rising in Reus was led by local notables and soldiers whose rituals included the planting of liberty trees, in imitation of the French Revolution. Captain-General Meer suppressed both risings, and executed Xaudaró after a summary courts martial. Yet martial law in Barcelona diverted government attention from the encroaching rebels to the west. In the end, the civil governor Pastors was forced to rearm the city's National Militia which Meer had disbanded at gunpoint only weeks before. From their perspective, the authorities ended up with the worst of both worlds. The rearmed militia proved ineffective against the Carlists, but was masterful at agitating in the streets and in the press, obliging Captain-General Meer to retain martial law in the city until the end of the war.[60]

Barcelona's trauma came in the wake of two years of radical agitation in the army itself. In March 1836 General Córdova's aide-de-camp complained of the deleterious effect of revolution on the war effort against the rebels: '*Exaltados* are hated by the army, especially the returned exiles … our sergeants and lieutenants are prey to their revolution,' and 'The Liberals are the Carlists' best friends in terms of war.'[61] One hundred years later found the communist army elites describing the anarchists in a similar fashion, as 'thieves in revolutionary clothing'.[62]

Government army leaders clearly had an interest in suppressing left-wing subversion. The most important counter-revolutionary event during the second war concerns the so-called May Days in Barcelona in 1937. The spark which led to the erection of barricades across the city came on 3 May, when the police chief Rodríguez Salas, under orders from the Generalitat, took the Telephone Exchange in Plaza de Cataluña, which had been under CNT control since July 1936.[63] George Orwell, who was in Barcelona throughout the May Days, describes the events via the aid of friends who were on the

Plaza de Cataluña at the time: 'Several lorry loads of armed Assault guards had driven up to the Telephone Exchange, which was operated mainly by CNT workers, and made a sudden assault upon it.'[64] This attack on the telephone exchange was seen as an aggressive provocation, and barricades went up around the city. The fighting, however, was largely defensive as is highlighted in a radio message from CNT activist García Oliver on 4 May: 'All of you should remain in your respective positions ... but should cease firing.'[65]

Of those involved, the Friends of Durruti were the only group openly to advocate further conflict, as their handbill released on 5 May 1937 indicates: 'We must not surrender the streets. The revolution before all else ... Long live Social Revolution! Down with the counterrevolution!'[66] Crucially this was reprinted by the small but influential non-Stalinist communists (the POUM) in their paper *La Batalla* the following day. The fighting came to an end on the 7 May 1937, when the Republican government sent 5,000 troops into Barcelona, later to be reinforced by several thousand more.[67] This is corroborated by a letter from Lois Orr, an American revolutionary in Barcelona during the May Days: 'Now the Valencian government has stepped in and taken control, restored order, etc. Eight thousand guards ... have come from Valencia and are patrolling the streets.'[68]

The Spanish communists have traditionally been seen as counter-revolutionary in their 'entryism' since 1935 via the Popular Front and, especially, in their May 1937 repression of the anarchists and non-Stalinist communists. Stanley Payne's *The Spanish Civil War, Soviet Union and Communism*, however, presents the Spanish communists in a new light, as revolutionary rather than counter-revolutionary. According to Payne, they stopped the 'bottom-up' revolution of 1936–37, not in order to present a bourgeois face to the world, but in order to start their own 'top-down' creation of a Stalinist people's democracy on the post-1945 model in Eastern Europe. As George Esenwein notes, this thesis, though fresh and stimulating, fails to revise the fact that PCE policies, in the context of the 1930s, could be very legitimately described as counter-revolutionary.[69] Certainly, the ex-communist (and therefore 'in the know') Franz Borkenau reported the frustration felt by the left of the socialist movement: 'Comment on the Communists is especially bitter in the Caballero circle ... The Soviet Union does not help us any more than France or England; all they do is intrigue, strengthening every tendency towards the right wing of the movement, in order not to jeopardise the Franco-Soviet pact by too revolutionary attitude in Spain.'[70] Yet it remains debatable whether there was a high degree of revolutionary fervour in the first place, and no answer can be conclusive because the government's defeat in 1939 robs us of an identifiable outcome like that of 1839. The moderado states of siege, resented though they were by radicals, helped clear the way for Espartero's victory in 1839. The communist-led counter-revolution of 1937, by contrast, led to defeat, and to one of the most contentious debates in Spanish history.

Another 'counter-revolution', or at least centralization, gripped the rebel zone from the period of Franco's appointment to full powers in October 1936 until the last internal rebellion failed in April 1937. As far as Franco was concerned, the Falange had been usefully decapitated by the revolution in the Republican zone, as key figures, including the leader, José Antonio Primo de Rivera, had been caught in the wrong place at the wrong time. The Carlists, however, posed a different obstacle to Franco's supreme authority, as their Navarra heartland had been the only part of Spain where civilians had risen en masse for the rebellion. A civilian junta thrived in Pamplona and by November, under the leadership of the 'maximalist' Manuel Fal Conde, plans were launched to reshape Spain along corporatist lines and to establish an autonomous Carlist military academy. Franco intervened drastically, exiling Fal Conde upon pain of death, and on 20 December 1936 he militarized the hitherto autonomous militias belonging to the Carlist Traditionalist Communion, the Falange and the CEDA.[71] Franco had obtained full militarization even before his political mission was completed. The April 1937 Unification Decree was a masterstroke: on the face of things, the cumbersome FET de las JONS appeared to cater to all right-wing tastes, but in reality, they were all subordinated to Franco.[72] Franco obtained a unity of command of which his 1830s predecessors could only have dreamed. Zumalacárregui's personal command of the Basque war effort had been curtailed by the arrival of the king in July 1834 and then his own death a year later. A rudimentary administration operated in the Maestrazgo from 1836, overseen by a Carlist junta. Even though Cabrera frequently ignored its decisions and retained sole control over his forces, the junta and Cabrera himself still ultimately answered to the dithering Carlist government at Estella.[73] No single authoritarian rebel leader endured during the 1830s war, and still less in the post-war era. Franco, by contrast, enjoyed untrammelled power until his natural death in 1975.

Women

Nineteenth-century mores about the proper role of women in European society certainly discouraged Spanish women from militating in the 1830s conflict. Traditional views of gender appeared to apply doubly in Catholic Spain, leading historians to make strident views of feminine subordination. According to historian Jesús Cruz,

> with the exception of the Peninsular War, women were excluded from the public sphere. Barricades admitted few women, the National Militia, parliament and pronunciamientos none at all. There was no Spanish woman in those times who even came close to matching the feminism years before of Mary Wollstonecraft or Olympia de Gouges. Agustina

de Aragón and Mariana Pineda were converted into universal symbols without even the slightest feminist baggage.[74]

Even when women's suffrage was granted by the Second Republic, it had to overcome formidable obstacles advanced by Republicans – even by some women deputies – that the piety of women (their vulnerability to manipulation by priests) meant that they were not ready to exercise their vote 'responsibly'.[75] Once opposition was overcome, full legal equality between men and women followed. This was a remarkable example of legislative activism in a country with one of Europe's weakest feminist movements.[76] Given the legislative rather than grass-roots nature of these changes, it is unsurprising how little social attitudes changed. The most famous woman of the Spanish Civil War, Dolores Ibárruri, like all communists advocated class, not gender, struggle. Republican propagandists appealed to a better version of masculinity by suggesting that only military victory could protect women and the family from Nationalist rape and violence. Despite legal equality between the sexes, Republican discourse charged men with protecting the family.[77]

Spain would thus seem the least likely European country to spawn a gender revolution. Yet there is another side to the classic land of machismo. The young playwright and writer Antonio García Gutiérrez during the Carlist War produced his first works which placed women as agents of reconciliation between warring brothers. The romantics celebrated Spain's mythology of female militancy in sieges dating back to the Roman sieges of Numancia and the Moorish invasion. Despite nineteenth-century mores, women 'manned' ramparts and barricades in the Carlist War. The protracted and irregular nature of the Carlist War interfered with women's lives all the same, propelling them into masculine roles. The wives and girlfriends of government militiamen played key roles supporting their menfolk during the localized sieges that afflicted government towns in Aragón.[78] Women caught in front lines became targets and responded accordingly. The lengthy Carlist siege of Gandesa was answered by the civilian population, including women, who rallied to its defence. Luisa Bará resembled Zaragoza's famous Agustina de Aragón by delivering arms and food to the defenders while under fire. Turning to terror to subdue the defenders, the rebel Torner seized from adjoining villages the wives and daughters of militiamen and imprisoned them. The liberals replied by imprisoning powerful men and women in Gandesa who were related to the besieging Carlists. Gandesa became a symbol of liberal heroism, with women at its heart. Women in sieges became powerful symbols in both wars. Zaragoza protected its walls from Carlist attack in 1838 with women residents pouring burning oil, anticipating the actions of working-class *sevillanas* defending their streets against Queipo de Llano in the summer of 1936.[79] Civil wars even more than national wars targeted the hearth and home, the traditional sovereignty of women.

The story of the home front in any war is fundamentally a story about women. The appeal of both civil wars, and even their cause, were partly gendered in nature. In the 1830s war this gendering related to what the rebels termed the female 'usurpation' of power. Until his twilight years brought Ferdinand VII to marry María Cristina, he was incapable of performing even the most elementary functions of reproduction, and the issue which resulted in October 1830 was a highly problematic female (Princess Isabella) rather than a male whom the Carlists would have had to accept as the rightful heir. Carlists thus found themselves on the sexist side of the dynastic dispute, the propagandist Luzuriaga proclaiming that Spain had to be ruled by a king rather than a queen, as 'women simply are not designed to govern men, still less nations; on the contrary their physical and intellectual weakness dictates that men should govern them'.[80] The gendered nature of monarchy was more remote in the 1930s, and yet Alfonso XIII's abdication in 1931 was certainly the consequence of his exaggerated masculinity that drove him to flaunt militarism with disastrous effects in Morocco and on the Spanish constitution.

In both civil wars, politically radical Cristinos and Republicans refused to extend their radicalism to the sphere of social and gender relations. Despite misgivings, including by women parliamentarians themselves, the left eventually extended its legal emancipation of Spanish women into the realm of voting rights, too. Their misgivings were well-founded. Women's suffrage being passed in 1933 probably tipped the balance for the CEDA in the November elections: evidently, not all women wanted to be 'liberated'.[81] Helen Graham noted that 'in an astonishingly short time, in one of Europe's most backward societies and polities women became the *legal* equals of men'.[82] But Graham has also shown the persistence of unreconstructed chauvinistic attitudes towards women, even amongst the CNT/FAI, the one leftist organization possessing an unequivocal commitment to the equality of the sexes. Although women participated in anarchism and its trade unions, gender equality utopianism died as soon as they crossed the threshold as male culture and members were dominant in every way. Dolores Ibárruri, a PCE leader, implicitly accepted male dominance when she famously said that it was better to be 'widowed to a hero than married to a coward'. Mass education for children would liberate women from some of the childcare burden, but despite the radical ambitions of leftist Republicans, success on expanding secular education was distinctly limited. Agricultural work lured children away from 'compulsory' education and only some 51.2 per cent of school-age children were actually attending school during 1932–33.[83] Abortion was eventually legalized, but the childcare burden remained the woman's lot and abortion along with other birth control techniques were immediately illegalized under Franco.[84]

Once war had broken out, women in the Republican zone certainly underwent integration into public spheres traditionally reserved for men.

Factory work was added to the more traditionally female roles of social work and education, yet even these 'emancipated' women were paid less than men. Very soon the wartime Republican slogan emerged of 'men to the war front, women to the home front', and PCE leader Dolores Ibárruri explained the place of women as being 'at the rearguard where they would be of more use to the war effort'.[85] In any case, the degree of female militancy in the summer of 1936 had been exaggerated for propaganda purposes. Most pictures of women fighting on the government side were staged in order to recruit men.[86] Not only were they staged; they were also regretted. The 1936 flourish of militiawomen propaganda was seen as being counterproductive because it alienated international opinion and boosted the rebels' own propaganda agenda, and the production and dissemination of such images dropped off markedly from the start of 1937.[87] Even before the government edict ordered women back to the rearguard, militiawomen generally found themselves caught in the 'double burden' traditional to their gender by being obliged to wash and cook for their male comrades.[88] The German émigré volunteer, George Felix, found the militiawomen 'cooking, washing clothes, and performing first aid'.[89]

Thus women generally performed traditional gender roles despite the initial flurry of egalitarian propaganda. Ironically, the inverse became apparent in the rebel zone. The leader of the half-million-strong 'Women's Section' of the Falange, Pilar Primo de Rivera, in February 1938 repeated the sexism of 1830s propaganda when she declared that 'women will never succeed in equalling men; if they try, women will lose the elegance and grace necessary for a life with them'.[90] But the fact that half a million women were mobilized for rearguard activities (hospitals, social care, education) proves that the rebel state relied heavily upon home-front women even when official doctrine was supposed to keep them in the home. A page-long dedication to the Carlist *margaritas* running the Alfonso Carlos veterans' hospital was almost apologetic in the way the war had obliged the women to perform masculine roles. The 'restless bees extract the richest honey of their labour ... accepting with resignation their roles as instructors, pharmacists, office workers and radiologists.'[91] The male director was repeatedly thanked by name even though he did not appear to direct anything. Despite the opposing worldviews of Republican and Traditionalist womanhood, the contingencies of war thrust women into public roles in both zones of Spain. Such state-driven emancipation produced a wider intrusion of the state's power into the private sphere of women's lives: women did not conquer the public sphere, it conquered them. Leftist organizations gave subordinate roles to women consistent with their domestic chores. Rightist organisations mobilized women for conservative, gender-traditional ends. It is ironic that despite all the traditionalist rhetoric concerning womanhood, that the 'nationalization' of Spanish women begun by Republican reformists was continued even in the rebel zone. Women under rebel control had to resort to traditional female roles in order to exercise any sort of influence over men. A Carlist ward matron treating government prisoners averted violence against them when a government air raid drove a sheltering Nationalist soldier to swear reprisals. María Urraca appealed to the soldier's Christian sense of charity, persuading him not only to avert violence but also to share his rations with the government patients.[92]

This feature is all the more significant because a similar pattern can be observed in the 1830s. Despite the reactionary propaganda of their authorities, rebel women sometimes exerted not just influence but outright power. Espartero's final offensive in the east prompted virtually the entire male population in April 1840 to flee from the settlement of Las Cuevas de Castellote (Teruel). Occupying the town, Espartero had no option but to sanction the women to take over the running of the civil administration. The female mayor, one Liberal newspaper asserted, did a better job of governing than the fugitive Carlist mayor she replaced.[93]

Yet for every instance of women exerting power, there were several more of women becoming victims, and it is likely (although impossible to measure) that this denouement was influenced by rebel propaganda. The 1830s Carlists riled against the female 'usurpation' of the throne, producing gender-inflected propaganda to mobilize their 'home front' (the *ojalatero* phenomenon) and to emasculate the enemy (propaganda which led to the moral and sometimes physical emasculation of captives). A Carlist newspaper in 1838 complained how 'even the fair sex has been made unnatural and degraded by the current revolution'.[94] Ironically, leftist elites shared this moral concern. The architect of 1830s anticlericalism, Juan Alvarez Mendizábal, devoutly raised his children as Catholics and condemned the 'immorality' in gender relations produced by the Carlist War.[95]

This immorality was plain to see as battlefronts reached women. Female spies from both sides were routinely shot when uncovered by the enemy, and the Carlists on one occasion executed several tradeswomen who were trying to supply besieged San Sebastián. As during the 1930s conflict, rape was used against 'enemy' women in order to emasculate male adversaries, women's heads were often shaved in order to humiliate their fugitive menfolk and both sides occasionally used civilians, including women, as human shields, especially in the far bloodier fighting in the east.[96] Both sides degenerated into casual or even vindictive violence against women. The case-study identified by the German Carlist von Rahden of the 'madwoman' of Montalbán (Teruel) illustrates the immoral extremes that conflict situations produced. Raped by a government militiaman in 1837, the woman gave birth to the rapist's child and was publicly shunned by the community in rebel-held Montalbán. When a local government offensive tried to conquer Montalbán again in April 1839, the madwoman was carrying her one-year-old child to the market square. Soldiers from both sides identified her as the madwoman and some targeted their firing at her, including, perhaps, her rapist who was holed up in a fort at one end of the square. The madwoman and her child were killed in the market square and their decomposing bodies remained in situ for several weeks after the rebels had repulsed the government attack, victims of men from both sides of the civil war.[97]

Abduction of women was a common tactic of dishonouring the enemy, especially in regions of the Carlist War, such as northern Catalonia, where allegiances divided neighbouring villages and even families. During one Cristino counter-insurgency campaign against irregulars operating near the Cerdaña border area with France, Carlists burnt the village of Montellá Martinet, sacked and pillaged the property of liberals, and abducted the wives of militiamen, demanding hefty ransoms for their release. When news of this assault on their honour reached the pursuing militiamen, it provided a fillip to their campaign as they stole a march on the Carlists, beat them and rescued the women.[98] Other women rescued themselves. The camp-follower of a British sergeant, Mrs Millar, was the sole survivor of a Carlist ambush who mounted a horse 'in regular masculine style' and rode at full gallop towards the safety of government lines.[99] The localized nature of warfare in 1830s Vizcaya resulted in women joining some government National Militia units and in the case of Palencia even forming their own company, complete with uniforms, drums, flags and guns. Their capture by Carlists in February 1836 and subsequent ransoming became an acute source of embarrassment for the Cristinos as well as a coup for the Carlists whose propaganda, after all, vowed to 'correct' revolutionary women in the event of nearby Bilbao falling into their hands.[100] Eguía hastily demobilized them in case his rank-and-file ended up wanting to recruit them for sinister purposes into their own ranks, imprisoning them and bailing them for a 3,000-real fine.[101] Eguía knew that any licensing of sexual assault by his men would undermine discipline as a whole. When the Cristino port of Lequeitio fell to the Carlists in April 1836, female militia were once again captured and ransomed. Most militiawomen had followed their menfolk in a seaborne evacuation to San Sebastián, but thirteen had been left behind.[102] The topic of women combatants in the 1830s remains massively unexplored, in stark contrast to the 1930s, and we may conservatively attribute contingent, economic and family factors to female enlistment in the drawn-out fighting.

The government side proved just as ruthless in targeting the wives, mothers and daughters of absent rebels. Rebels who in autumn 1834 attacked the 'heroic' town of Villarcayo (Burgos) were warned that their families would be identified and dispossessed in order to compensate for the damage inflicted on the property of pro-government civilians.[103] As the war progressed, punitive measures were ratcheted up against the relatives of rebels. Espartero's general offensive in late-1838 was matched by condign measures against Carlist civilians falling under government control. Parents of absentee Carlists in Guipúzcoa were subjected to banishment and dispossession, condemning several to die of exposure, and these harsh measures were rescinded only if their sons handed themselves over to the government military authorities. On 23 December 1838 the alarmed Carlist court called for 'strong, energetic and vigorous measures to prevent the sinister consequences developing in this phenomenon'.[104]

The 1930s Nationalists targeted violence against women to an even greater degree than during the 1830s. By having achieved equal rights under the Republic, Republican women had 'usurped' the moral order more thoroughly than their 1830s forbears. Both 1830s Carlists and 1930s Nationalists treasured irreproachable female symbols of virgins, mothers and nuns, and the Virgin Mary was made Generalísima in both civil wars. A young nun, Sor Patricinio, was a mystic and stigmatic who offered celestial advice to the rebels. Her stigmata were declared fraudulent by a government investigation in 1836, and she was banished to a convent far away from court by a revolutionary regime anguished by her intangible boost to rebel morale.[105] As a propaganda weapon during the first war, Carlist traditionalism appears to have had a mixed impact. Cabrera used sexist propaganda to demoralize the enemy. In February 1839 he fired off an address to the Liberal rank-and-file, appealing to them to abandon their ranks as María Cristina was selling off the Palace silver and getting ready to abandon her followers to their fate.

By contrast, 1830s Cristinos and 1930s Republicans advanced secular female icons. In the former case, this was the battle-cry exalting the innocent Princess Isabella, in the latter, representation of the Republic as the 'beautiful girl' (la niña bonita). The foremost female icon on the left was communist leader, Dolores Ibárurri (aka La Pasionaria), who despite her secular life struggles was conferred a pseudo-religious symbology by the working classes. Women adorned themselves with neck-medallions bearing her image, displacing the Virgin Mary from her traditional domain over the heart, and young communists like Santiago Carrillo could not help but ascribe her saintly characteristics: 'I was moved … There emanated from her a dignity, a majesty that is so often found in the women and men of our people … People came up to touch her as they would a saint.'[106] Even the ex-communist, Franz Borkenau, admitted that 'the masses worship her, not for her intellect, but as a sort of saint who is to lead them in the days of trial and temptation'.[107] The hegemonic cultural values of Spanish Catholicism had not spared even the militant left. For her part, La Pasionaria did better when she condemned a provocative pre-war religious procession with the worst insult a left-wing Basque could utter: 'Carlist'.[108] The nineteenth-century origins of the Spanish Civil War were etched in the mind even of this symbol of modern communist womanhood.

Religion in the Spanish Civil Wars

i. Rebel clericalism

One of the paradoxes of the Spanish Civil Wars was how rebel religious fervour was indifferent to the Church hierarchy. All but one of Spain's forty-two bishops accepted the Cristino transition of 1832–33, albeit by default and without any conviction. For all the Carlist activities across northern Spain, the hugely wealthy dioceses of Toledo and Santiago did not defect to them, even if several impoverished rural clergy did. By contrast, the Basque country, which lacked a bishopric, produced the most Carlist clerics throughout the 1830s. In 1835 a Royal Ecclesiastical Junta was established in the Carlist Basque country under the aegis of Spain's only openly Carlist bishop, Joaquín Abarca, Bishop of Leon. It busied itself with counteracting all anticlerical legislation emanating from Madrid, cloistering refugee religious fleeing the government zone and supporting the king's increasingly desperate overtures for support from the Holy See. On 17 November 1836, when the Carlists were in high spirits during their second siege of Bilbao, Don Carlos issued a proclamation promising to rescind all government anticlerical legislation and to restore both the tithe and the religious orders in all their former glory.[109] Given the height of anticlericalism in the government zone, Don Carlos's proclamation helped to move the Papacy's position on Spain from neutrality to virtual non-belligerence. On 1 February 1837 the Pope gave an encyclical in which he condemned the irreligion and attacks on the Church sown by the Spanish crown, and full relations between the victorious Liberals and the Vatican would not be re-established until twelve years after the war.[110]

In the 1930s the wealth gap between the bishoprics and the parish clergy remained as yawning as ever. Unlike in 1833 most bishops sided with the rebels, but mostly as followers rather than instigators of the politicized 'Crusade'. Most priests sided with the rebellion in July 1936 and almost all of the bishops approved of the Nationalists in their so-called collective letter of July 1937, which led to a papal nuncio being appointed to the Francoist side three months later. The bishops' fence-sitting in the 1830s and subordination in the 1930s did not cause a vacuum in rebel religiosity. Rather rebels in both wars (Carlists in the 1830s and disproportionately Carlists in the 1930s) developed a lay form of religious militancy which took on such diverse extremes as clericalized massacre, mercy and popular iconography. These phenomena were at their most prevalent in Spain's Catholic redoubt, Navarra, and to varying degrees, the surrounding Basque provinces.

Just as 1830s Carlist Basques fashioned their own religious iconography around such heroes as Zumalacárregui, so did Basques one hundred years later. The advent of the Republic spurned a wave of sightings of the Virgin

Mary, dozens having claimed to have seen her in Ezkioga (Guipúzcoa) between April and August 1931.[111] Traditionalists in both conflicts mobilized their own religious symbols for the purpose of morale. Yet, until the 1980s, the importance of religion was either ignored or sidelined by historians, both foreign and Spanish, who instead attributed socio-economic factors and the autonomy of the fueros to the persistence of Carlism.[112] Spain's Marian apparitions inspired Mexico's Cristeros whose own three-year war against the anticlerical federal government had ended in 1929 with their highly embittered conditional surrender (known in Mexico as the 'Arreglos'). Cruz Lete, an eighteen-year-old trainee teacher from Guipúzcoa and one of the dozens of witnesses to the Virgin's visitation at Ezkioga, corresponded with the Cristero leader, Aurelio Acevedo, who was about to launch a second Catholic revolt and whose pro-rebel views concerning the Spanish Civil War led the counter-culture against Mexico's support for the Republic:

It was on 29 October 1931, my fourth visit to Ezkioga, when I saw her. During the Rosary when I was chatting to a friend, I looked towards the ground and saw two feet appear. I fell to my knees and saw the Virgin with her face veiled. Those around me placed rosaries and crosses into my hands and the Virgin unveiled her face. Since then my three subsequent visions of her have seen her unveiled. She seemed about 23 years old but with a seriousness beyond her years. She told me that Jesus Christ was offended by all the outrages in the world and wanted to punish the ungodly but the Virgin, like a good mother, was intervening to tell people to amend their ways. She told me not to go to train in Pamplona, as I would be boarding in the home of some Socialists known by my father who never stepped foot in church. I went to Pamplona all the same. From Ormáiztegui to Ezkioga I saw her twice more. On the 28th she told me that the whole world should dress in black for mourning. Yesterday, on the morning of 29 December, she announced the punishment, and said that the only flag which there will be afterwards will be the one that you have in your hands. I had the Cross in my hand, and now I always have it with me. She didn't return that afternoon.[113]

Such religious conviction motivated rebels in both civil wars. A Catholic newspaper in 1931 urged Catholic–Carlist unity, otherwise what had happened in Mexico could happen in Spain.[114] Improbable religious miracle stories shaped the course of both wars. A rightist woman imprisoned by reds in Avila during the Spanish Revolution miraculously vanished. The story spread in the province of Avila that she was none other than Saint Teresa, come to save the city from red invasion, rapine and pillage.[115] Diplomatic embarrassment followed the Italians' rescue of the mummified arm of Saint Teresa of Avila upon the fall of Málaga in February 1937 (the holy relic had been carried there from Ronda by Republican militiamen). There were few more 'national' religious symbols than this, and even though Franco had the Italians to thank for its rescue, the mummified arm stayed at his side throughout the war.[116]

Rebels in both wars were ostentatious in their claim to religious blessing. Carlists in 1835 made the Virgin Mary celestial commander-in-chief (*Generalísima*) of their forces, and Franco's Nationalists followed suit in 1936. At the local level, rebel-controlled villages flaunted their folk Catholicism. The careful upkeep of shrines served the purpose not just of demarcating village boundaries but also of invoking divine authority for asserting territorial disputes and communicating to outsiders.[117] Rebels who captured population centres sealed their military successes with acts of religious ostentation. When Don Carlos led the 1837 'Royal Expedition' towards Madrid, he measured his success not on his speed in reaching the capital, which was derided as pitifully slow by his foreign allies, but on the number of Masses he held in liberated villages.[118] The expedition marched in the context of two years of legislative and violent anticlericalism in the government zone. In 1936 the rebels revolted against a backdrop of pre-war government anticlericalism. One of the features of this had been the silencing of bells, a major issue in 1930s villages and provincial capitals which lacked the constant din of motor traffic and other modern environmental noises. When the Nationalists rose in the summer of 1936, clerical-traditionalist Burgos re-established its sovereignty over public noise by defiantly ringing its many church bells in honour of the convocation in the city on 25 July 1936 of the National Defence Junta, the provisional government of the newly emerged rebel zone.[119] As one public official recalled:

> The bells of the city were ringing out in a deafening saraband – I don't believe there can be any city in the world where there are so many bells and where their chimes are so insistent as in Burgos. It is a titanic symphony, a continuous clashing of metal invading the whole life of the city. When the bells of Burgos ring out the town become one vast diapason, an immense resonance-chamber of which the air is the sound and the cathedral the echo, and everything else is subordinated to that vibrant litany.[120]

Despite such apparent religious revival, the rebels' doctrine of 'National Catholicism' was just that: national. Time and again from 1936 pro-Nationalist clerics vented their frustration at the Holy See's failure to support their side to the full. Arrogant Nationalist emissaries, the brutal treatment of 'separatist' and left-leaning Catalan and, especially, Basque clerics, and the Vatican's fears of Nazi influence in Spain, all conspired towards a gradual rather than sudden Papal blessing of the insurgents, and embarrassing aftershocks from this tension persisted after the war. Even though the Holy See had issued an encyclical condemning the persecution of the Catholic Church in Mexico, and had even justified the right of Catholics in that country to rebel, no such backing came in respect of Spain. The pro-Axis Serrano Súñer refused to seek an audience with the Pope during his 1940 visit to Rome, a serious snub from the minister of 'Catholic Spain', and Franco only gradually revoked the last vestiges of the Republic's secularizing reforms.[121] Striking comparisons are to be drawn with the Nationalists' forbears one hundred years earlier. In both conflicts, the Spanish Church (despite its vocal minority of reformists during the period 1808–23) was a bastion of reaction. The 1830s saw Carlist clerics defying the Spanish bishops in droves in their support for and even participation in the rebellion. The 1930s saw a Spanish Church which alone in Europe had still not accepted as uncontroversial the 'accidentalist' doctrine of Leo XIII, the result being that fundamentalist (*integrista*) clerics grew in influence from the 1890s.

ii. Government anticlericalism

The 1830s and 1930s civil wars are the only times in modern Spanish history when substantial numbers of religious have been murdered. The occasional killings of priests during the 1820–23 Royalist War, the Democratic Six Years (1868–74), and 'Tragic Week' in Barcelona (1909) amount to so few: slightly more than one hundred over the course of one hundred years, that they cannot bear comparison to the hundreds slain over seven years in the 1830s and the thousands killed in the 1930s. Also, the vast majority of the extra killings (ninety-five) were committed during the 1820–23 Royalist War, which itself was a virtual dress rehearsal for the 1830s.[122] Anticlericalism was the logical government response to the rebels' religiosity. Historians have been routinely perplexed to explain why violent anticlericalism established itself as a tradition during the First Carlist War. Spain, after all, was (along with Italy) the most Catholic of European polities, the sword of the Counter-Reformation and the faith conqueror of the Americas.

Yet the structural power of the Spanish Church began to be undermined two generations before the Carlist War. In response to the economic crisis of the Napoleonic Wars, the royal favourite, Manuel de Godoy, seized the welfare organs of the Church (orphanages, hospitals, poorhouses), and dissolved one-seventh of the Church's entailed properties.[123] During the Peninsular War, the prolonged French occupation of Spain's major cities left an indelible laic stamp, as the Bonapartist regime dissolved the cloistered clergy and friars and nuns disappeared from the streets. Young men, a leading liberal recalled, reacted in wonder to their reappearance in 1814.[124] The Church issued invectives against post-war villagers refusing to pay tithes: 'Their souls will be damned for vile self-interest and their harvests shall wither on the vine.'[125] Once the Spanish Liberal government of the 1820–23 'Triennium' embarked upon its own dissolution of the cloistered clergy, royal opposition was successfully countered by the threat to raise the streets of Madrid if the king did not sign the November 1820 dissolution bill into law.[126] Clerical power appeared to revive in 1823 as the triumphant counter-revolution restored dissolved properties to the Church, ruining buyers who got no compensation. But unlike in 1814, the Inquisition was not revived, infuriating the theocratic 'Carlist' faction that grew around the king's younger brother and heir apparent, Don Carlos. Throughout the 1823–33 'Ominous Decade', episodes abounded of clerical and anticlerical violence, to a degree barely imaginable only a generation before. In May 1826 the Bishop of Barcelona complained that twelve churches in the city had recently been robbed and blamed these misdeeds on the work of liberal secret societies and the density of radical cafés: 'For the past year this city has been suffering sacrilegious robberies, the like of which were unheard-of before the vile period of the constitutional system.'[127] The Church in Spain had become a controversial institution in large towns by the time of the first summer of the First Carlist War, when government agents unleashed violent anticlericalism.

The major difference one hundred years later with the Church question concerned timing and degree. Although the First Carlist War concluded a laicism which had been underway in fits and starts since the 1790s, the Church recovered all its power and more besides over the ensuing ninety years, and the Primo de Rivera regime which preceded the Second Republic actively flaunted its 'National Catholicism', anticipating the regime of Franco. The first government of the Second Republic thus expedited an ambitious programme of secularization (an escalation from the laicism of the nineteenth century), reviving and in many cases exceeding the measures of the First Carlist War. Article 26 of the Constitution of 1931 implemented secularism, which meant the end of state financial support for the clergy, the banning of the 'foreign' Jesuit order, and limits on the Church's right to wealth. Further legislation culminated in the October 1932 'Law on Confessions and Religious Congregations'. A Social Catholic historian condemned these strident reforms as egregiously alienating a middle-class Spain which in 1931 was not yet anti-Republican.[128] But the reforms did not come from nowhere. Since the late nineteenth century a 'muscular' anticlericalism had grown among Spain's working classes which derided sexless priests as neither properly male nor female.[129] Also the reduction of clerical power was one of the few policies which all centre-left and left parties shared.

Despite this, at the outset, the Church had actually called for 'obedience to the new constituted power' and was looking for some kind of accommodation with the new regime.[130] Episodes of anticlerical violence, and what Catholics home and abroad condemned as the inadequate government response to these, quickly soured the atmosphere, even without the regime's radical proclamation of religious freedom, which alienated Rome.[131] The Republican coalition, after all, had been quick to pass laws for the 'defence of the Republic', amounting to full powers and suspension of civil liberties, and this authoritarianism was soon codified in the new Constitution.[132] The

Socialist press of 1931 repeated the language of the 1830s liberals when it condemned Carlist-led protests as 'Reaction descended from Calomarde'.[133] Within 12 days of its promulgation, the Vatican was one of only two foreign powers which had not yet recognised the Spanish Republic (the other being Japan).[134]

Both wars were accompanied by anticlericalism on the government side. In the 1830s this was generated by the war itself. From 1833 thousands of religious were killed, exiled and defrocked as a direct consequence of the war. In response to wartime anticlericalism, increasing numbers of clerics fled into Carlist areas of control, where nuns were put to work nursing the war-wounded, while others even went overseas. During the August–September 1835 revolution, several were welcomed to Buenos Aires from where they occupied vacancies in River Plate monasteries.[135]

The second half of the Carlist War is significant for the liberal social, economic and political reforms it witnessed in both the Mendizábal administration (September 1835–May 1836) which had been hoisted into power by the revolution of the juntas, and the 'revolutionary Cortes' of August 1836 to July 1837 – i.e. first, the *mendizabalista* spoliation of Church property, and, second, the definitive abolition of feudalism under the revived Constitution of 1812. Regarding the former, the mendizabalista assault on the Church had already been pre-empted when anticlerical riots provoked the Toreno administration into abolishing the Jesuit order on 7 July 1835, its assets being used to fund the ballooning National Debt. Most dramatically, all monasteries and convents containing fewer than twelve inmates were suppressed and put up for sale. This amounted to some 900 religious houses, almost half of the total in Spain, and the money gained from their auction was used to pay down the national debt.[136] Mendizábal's anticlericalism both fuelled the Carlist war effort and pushed the Papacy almost to the brink of recognizing Don Carlos. Also, those citizens who had bought Church property during the Triennium, only to see it confiscated in the 1823 crackdown, were now reunited with their purchases courtesy of a July 1837 decree.[137] The unpopular tithe (along with the clerical tax levied in Galician known as the *Voto*) was also abolished and replaced from 1837 by a smaller tax (*culto y clero*) which was collected by the constitutional municipalities in order to pension off monks and nuns made redundant by the disentailment.[138] Religious were forbidden from wearing cassocks and wimples in public spaces, anticipating the Azaña legislation of the 1930s.[139]

Yet while governments conducted secularizing measures, there was a difference in the nature of each. The clericalism of the 1830s was targeted by a gradual ratcheting up of anticlerical ordinances during the civil war itself, alongside a growing wave of localized assaults on church property and religious. The clericalism of the 1930s, by contrast, had already been legislatively targeted by two pre-war leftist governments. Partly because the Church had successfully weathered the Republican storm and given heart to the rebels of 1936 – Shelagh Ellwood argued that the passing of church reform 'hardened the resolve of those who did not support the Republic more than it strengthened the hand of those who did'[140] – the anticlerical violence that erupted in the government zone far exceeded that of the First Carlist War, almost 7,000 religious being murdered in 1936 compared to the hundreds, but certainly not thousands, over the whole 1830s. Yet, surprisingly, there were similarities in government responses to anticlerical violence.

In both civil wars, authorities tried to contain the anticlerical excesses of militants. Espartero's infamous decimation of a battalion that had vandalized a 'Carlist' church in Guetaria was matched by government complaints of the despoliation of nationalized monasteries and convents.[141] Despite Espartero's draconian discipline, he was vilified by the rebel press as the profaner of Basque churches.[142] Once the Carlists in 1835 appropriated the Virgin Mary as their commander-in-chief, there were complaints of militiamen and soldiers using her icons for target practice.[143] This iconoclasm anticipated the photogenic 'execution' by Republican militants in 1936 of the statue atop the Cerro de los Angeles outside Madrid consecrated to the Sacred Heart of Jesus. Countless other anticlerical altercations were mundane in nature, although they too constrained 'respectable' government authorities to intervene. In a holding cell for fifth-columnists at Madrid's War Ministry in 1936, officials had to remove a huge crucifix because it had been visible on the street below to radicalized militiamen who had been making gestures of firing at it.[144]

Episodes of rebels' sacrilege in both wars, by contrast, can be explained entirely by the opportunism offered by looting church treasures in the name of religion. In fact, church-burning has been noted as a peculiarly Spanish form of popular protest throughout the ages, as the wealth and prominence of churches made them obvious targets of protest against the abuses of elites. During the Carlist expedition of La Mancha, invading troops burnt and pillaged churches and their commander, Basilio García, was reprimanded for transporting valuables looted from government churches back to the Basque country.[145] In 1836 the radical government ordered the sequestration of Church valuables across government-held areas of Spain in order to deter Carlist looting.[146] Rebel destruction of church property also served purely military purposes. Benet Tristany was a major-general of Carlist forces in Catalonia and a priest. Yet in retreat before government counter-insurgency operations, he routinely burnt the bell towers of churches and monasteries in order to deny the enemy shelter and fortified buildings. Catalonia's physical war of attrition impacted the church like all others.[147]

Just as clerical Carlists were often guilty of despoiling Church property, the government side was not always guilty of ideological exactions. The cultural impact of both wars was felt in the marketization of artefacts hitherto in the custody of clerical institutions. The Church was the lowest-hanging fruit for revenue in economic as well as political terms. Radicalized militiamen were taking the government law into their own hands, confiscating valuables from monasteries and convents in circumstances barely distinguishable from looting. Even worse, most valuables, including some distinguished artistic property, was auctioned in fire sales which attracted only low prices from Spanish buyers. Other valuables ended up abroad.[148] Equally, in the second war, the artefacts of the Prado and the National Library were evacuated to safety and some were sent abroad at the end of the fighting.

The 1830s disentailment was compounded by the inability of the Cristino government to pay stipends to evicted religious inmates. In April 1836 both the Bishop of Córdova and the last Spanish Archbishop of Mexico City condemned Mendizábal's policy of turning monks into vagabonds.[149] Sometimes clerics resisted disentailment violently. The Dominicans of Manacor (Mallorca) in August 1835 had no intention of being massacred like the religious of Zaragoza and Barcelona and instead raised their god-fearing parishioners against the government militia. An atrocity followed in which captured militiamen were burnt alive. Reinforcements cleared the monasteries but authorities treated the clerics leniently, provoking a rising of 1,400 indignant militiamen in Palma who demanded the ultimate penalty.[150] One hundred years later only 14 per cent of *mallorquínes* now attended Mass, yet Manacor was again subjected to a clericalized massacre. Falangists rounded up dozens of non-attending labourers who were given absolution before being executed and burnt in pyramid pyres.[151]

Galicia saw more brutal and generalized Carlist violence which the liberal counterinsurgency blamed on the Galician church, as the Cristinos decreed that damage caused by Carlist violence would be made good by the Galician Church: one half at the location where the outrage took place, the other half being levied on priests and their flock within a one-league radius; only those with a father or son in the National Guard were exempted from this collective punishment. Relations remained poisonous when local Cristino garrisons frequently stopped villagers from hearing Mass at churches where priests were refusing to bless the throne of Isabella.[152] During the bitter fighting in Aragón, government soldiers deliberately profaned churches they occupied, viewing them as schools of Carlism. In the village of Fórnoles (Teruel), government forces turned the church altar tables into livestock mangers and the sacristy into a gaol.[153] Far from the front in Málaga militia showed more ambivalence towards the government's anticlerical revolution. Nuns evicted from their convents in September 1836 were followed in procession by tearful townswomen. The following day, militia obeyed orders to arrest dissidents but mutinied at orders to remove bells from the cathedral because to do so, they protested, 'would be criminal'. The standoff ended a week later when news from Madrid arrived of the abolition of the tithe and of plans to redistribute church property.[154] The demise of church bells left vivid memories for communities used to their punctuation of silence.[155] As for the nuns of Málaga, their eviction was humane compared to the violence meted out to their male counterparts. Liberals made grudging exception to inmates who performed works in welfare and education. The pastoral work of the women appears to have spared them anticlerical violence during 1834–35, just as they would prove far less likely to fall victim in 1936.

Unlike the predominantly urban nature of the Church's wealth in the 1930s, in the 1830s the Church was still predominantly a rural landowner. The Church presided over complex landownership in Galicia where the growth both in population and a market economy in agriculture during the second half of the eighteenth century had resulted in shrinking plots and higher rents. The nature of land ownership in 'Spain's Ireland' was complicated by the fact that this process of subdivision was accompanied by the long-term leasing to the middle classes and wealthier peasants of rental properties held by the Galician Church. This led to speculation on ever-shrinking plots (known as *minifundismo*). Penalties levied against the Galician Church therefore ended up being levied against village communities.[156] Cristino suppression of Carlist clericalism was not always disproportionate. Eastern Carlists were funded by the Bishop of Lérida who donated supposedly abolished ecclesiastical revenues to the rebel cause.[157] An ecclesiastical schism broke the Holy See's increasingly ambiguous policy of non-Intervention when some priests from Tortosa and the Bishop of Orihuela went to Morella to set up a chapter (*cabildo*) with the blessing of the Carlists and even of some Vatican representatives acting in the name of the Pope.[158]

The non-belligerency, rather than neutrality, of the Spanish Church was answered by a clamour for anticlerical measures, especially during the revolutions of 1835–37. The Jesuits were banned for good from 1835 and, most importantly, all convents and monasteries of fewer than twelve inmates abolished. Effective Papal recognition of the Cristino regime ended with the withdrawal of the nuncio in 1835, but formal relations technically remained in place, even though they were never exercised. In April 1836, a radical deputy pitchforked into the Cortes by the revolution of the juntas demanded a complete secession of relations with Rome, 'given the Pope's encouragement to our enemies'. Prime Minister Mendizábal warned that to do so could prove counter-productive, given the Pope's religious as well as temporal power.[159] In the wake of the La Granja revolution, the Spanish government agent in Rome reported growing hostility from the Holy See, and the Pope's open preference for the Carlists. Ambassador Villiers suggested to Prime Minister Calatrava that a definitive break in relations between Madrid and Rome might be the easiest response. Calatrava would not take this step, but he did concede that 'an absolute break with Rome would be no major step, seeing as ecclesiastical relations have been suspended for three years'.[160] Normal relations would not resume until 1851.

SON ENCONTRADOS LOS FUSILES EN LA IGLESIA DE HUESA.

FIGURE 2.1 *Government soldiers uncover weapons in a church in Huesa (Aragón) (Courtesy of Museo Zumalakarregi).*

Friendly and unfriendly billets

As Carlist armies carried the war into Northern Castile after the summer of 1835, population centres became open towns, leaning towards Carlism, but taking care to show outward neutrality in case of the transit of Cristino troops and campaign militia. Mostly, Cristino officers passed through the same

FIGURE 2.2   *The Church is targeted for its support for the rebels one hundred years later (Getty Images).*

urban centres more than once, and took care to remember friendly billets and to avoid pro-Carlists; conversely Carlist armies also did the same with respect to their adherents. Thus civilians could 'manage' occupations and counter-occupations in a manner which normally avoided conflagrations.[161] In the 1830s soldiers were billeted in public buildings where possible and in private residences where necessary according to the 'baggage and lodging' (*carga y concejil*) regulations which would not begin to be revised until the post-war creation of the Civil Guard led to barracks becoming the norm.[162] Even though 1930s soldiers were thus much more likely to be barracked, the advance of rebel front lines still resulted in the requisitioning of private accommodation, and civilians falling under rebel occupation faced stiff penalties for refusing to accommodate members of the Nationalist Army.[163] Yet the greater insurgency and counter-insurgency features of the 1830s war turned billeting into a greater source of contention in civil-military relations.

The compression of Cristino defensive forces into urban areas in the Basque country over the course of 1834 exacerbated overcrowding as refugees and soldiers competed for accommodation. The satisfactory resolution of disputes rose in proportion to the rank of the complainants. For foreign auxiliaries arriving from the summer of 1835, billets were provided in ex-convents which had either been ruined or emptied by government military authorities which had been expelling monks they considered Carlist or vulnerable to Carlism. Government generals who boasted about how many convents they closed also reminded the government of available accommodation.[164] But British auxiliaries complained of being allocated draughty ex-convents in the Basque country which they claimed were inferior to the lodgings offered to the French and aggravated the typhoid which swept their ranks over the winter of 1835–36.[165] The complaints of the International Brigades of their training conditions at Albacete would appear indulgent by comparison. An American volunteer complained of the lack of decent chocolate and the prevalence of unsatisfyingly strong Spanish cigarettes.[166] Vitoria, under Cristino control throughout the 1830s, was remembered as a dreary garrison town. One hundred years later, in July 1936, the Carlists finally succeeded in capturing Vitoria and billet conditions had improved enough to make the town an 'oasis' in the rustic countryside.[167] British auxiliaries quartered in San Sebastián during the rebel siege of 1836 were remembered as 'uncomfortable but necessary guests', as the city suffered both from overcrowding and shortages.[168] Yet one hundred years later the rebels captured this summer resort early and intact, and it became a became a privileged destination for Nationalist soldiers recovering from injury and illness.

Common soldiers got little redress for grievances of accommodation. Often they lost out to competing claims by prominent civilians. A lawyer fled from the Carlist countryside complained to the Viceroy that his whole family had to accommodate troops on both floors of a house in Puente la Reina. The Viceroy approved Rafael Elisabet's plea that only the first floor be allocated to army billets.[169] The British merchant community secured diplomatic intervention to gain exemption from the *carga y concejil* regulations as early as February 1834. Even though revolutionary authorities in Alicante billeted troops on wealthy British merchant houses in the autumn of 1836, protests to Villiers ended this practice in short order.[170]

During the 1830s war little official effort was made to accommodate the thousands of women and children fleeing rebel-held areas, even when, at the height of Carlist invasions during 1836–37, the revolutionary authorities ordered prominent families to abandon exposed residences.[171] But a century of sentimentalizing childhood combined with an enhanced military ability to target civilians obliged the government in the 1930s to evacuate children from front-line areas whenever possible. The government launched a famous propaganda poster abroad portraying a child killed by a rebel air raid in a bid to mobilize Western opinion against Non-Intervention.[172] By August 1937 a National Council for Child Evacuees had been created, and by December almost 17,000 children had been evacuated to 170 different locations mostly along the eastern seaboard.[173] The largest of these was the seaside sanatorium of La Rabassada at Tarragona, where hundreds of children from Madrid were housed.[174] Other children were evacuated abroad. Sometimes this emigration served convenient political aims, such as was the case of the 1,092-strong 'delegation' of Republican children, teachers and attendants who in September 1937 left for the Soviet Union, where they were housed in Moscow and Leningrad. Soviet hospitality was impeccable, largely on account of the presence of Pablo Miaja, cousin of the Spanish government commander-in-chief of the Army of the Centre, José Miaja. Even so Pablo Miaja complained of the repeated Soviet attempts at communist indoctrination. The Soviets dismissed his complaints as the product of Miaja's 'Spanishness', which they thought meant that he had been 'excessively indoctrinated in religion'.[175] But most international evacuations – to Portugal after the Badajoz massacre and to France in 1939 – were chaotic and devoid of ceremony, even if the integration of children into their host communities fostered an international memory of Republican exile, such as in the famous case of the 4,000 Basque children evacuated to Wales during the fall of Bilbao. Rebel propaganda, for its part, understandably ignored the plight of the growing numbers of civilian victims of Franco's military success and instead targeted its ire at the 'cowardly and selfish' exiles of leading government figures.[176]

Hospitals

Until the second half of the nineteenth century, military surgery remained steeped in the Early Modern practice of brace-and-bit amputations and no understanding or provision either for anaesthetics or infection control. Yet Spanish military hospitals, despite the one hundred years of medical advances separating each conflict, show some surprising similarities. Until January 1836 no dedicated government military hospitals existed, and the same situation prevailed until January 1937 in the second war.[177] Rather, existing institutions were turned over for military casualties as and when required. This lack of any system or systematic planning took its toll as hospitals near the front lines were overburdened by casualties and compromised by lack of supplies. Puente la Reina (Navarra) had a guesthouse dating back to its medieval origins on the pilgrims' route to Santiago, and it was quickly taken over as a hospital by the government Army of the North which was fighting insurgents in the immediate vicinity. As early as May 1834 its director reported that the hospital could no longer cope with demand. The Viceroy intervened to instruct the commander of Puente la Reina to admit only those casualties that had real wounds, to limit their time of convalescence, and to restrict patients' rations to a daily allocation of a pound of meat, 18 ounces of white bread, 2 ounces of chickpeas and a quart of wine.[178] In the month of August, 252 patients were treated for wounds and diseases ranging from venereal diseases to scabies, with a fatality rate of between 15 and 20 per cent and a median hospital stay of about one week.[179]

The crisis in government hospital care peaked over the winter of 1835–36 as a flu epidemic coincided with the overcrowding of patients in besieged towns in the Basque country. The villages of the Baztán valley (Navarra) funded their own hospital, which the government army increasingly filled with war casualties as the war worsened. Before the valley fell to the rebels in April 1835, the casualties were evacuated to Pamplona. While the Carlists adopted the captured hospital, the fate of the government casualties evacuated to Pamplona grew so dire that, by the winter, the Spanish consul at Bayonne pleaded with the government to provide relief.[180] In January 1836 the government placed all military hospitals under the control of the Ministry of War. Even this measure could not manage the casualties crisis arising from the government offensive at Arlabán, when newspapers reported some 6,000 casualties dying in hospitals for lack of food and medicine. By the summer of 1836, matters had become even worse. Córdova was astonished that some 22,000 of his soldiers, or 30 per cent of the Army of the North, were hospitalized. The real figure of incapacity was even worse. Given the fear that rebels would bayonet wounded government soldiers, considerable efforts were made to transport casualties to safety, which meant that some 300 battlefield wounded required some 5,000 fit comrades in their support. Córdova related these shocking statistics to the British ambassador, doubtless in the hope that they might result in greater Allied support.[181] Even though rebel casualties were proportionately similar, interior lines and the proximity of caring hospitals or relatives enabled their faster recovery. Mutilated rebel survivors continued to prove militarily useful. Following the government victory at the second siege of Bilbao, the Carlist court supplemented its fully mobilized total of 32,000 infantry and 1,500 cavalry by raising three battalions of *inválidos* (wounded and other unfit to serve) to streamline the logistics effort.[182]

The preponderance of thermal waters across the Pyrenees allowed for more salubrious recovery for casualties. High-ranking officers, such as the cancer patient Espoz y Mina and the nerve-broken governor of Barcelona Pedro María Pastors were given leave to take the waters at the French spa town of Cauterets. Their safety in exile contrasted with government soldiers who were allocated waters on the Spanish side of the frontier, invariably in Navarra and thus in close proximity to rebel activity. At the end of the war, military authorities at the spa of Fitero (Navarra) complained that the cross-border invasion of Balmaseda's forces posed a security risk as 'Fitero is full of wounded soldiers who are here to take the waters'.[183] Sickness was no guarantee against being subjected to reprisals, especially in hospitals beyond the Basque country where the Eliot Treaty did not apply. In January 1836 government troops massacred in their beds the rebel wounded seized at L'Hort de Sant Cebrià. The perpetrators had been radicalized by propaganda concerning rebel atrocities against government prisoners, and the press went to extraordinary lengths to suppress news of these outrages being committed by the self-styled cause of humanity.[184] In the 1930s patients were frequently the victims of atrocities, especially at the hands of the rebels in their 1936 terror campaign in Andalucía. Violence in both wars was often the product of a distorted expression of fear, and the more that fear was suppressed for the sake of primary group cohesion, the more extreme the result.

Conditions at hospitals were far worse than at spas, and many casualties who could reach their families for care did so. George Borrow was outraged by inadequate hospitals, describing his meeting in Salamanca with a wounded officer and three mutilated soldiers who either could not or would not take their chances in a hospital and instead made the long and painful journey to relatives in Extremadura.[185] Even though a body of military hospitals (*cuerpo de sanidad militar*) was organized from January 1836, government hospitals still suffered from a grim reputation. The Prussian Carlist August von Goeben was wounded and captured in 1837 and sent to a government hospital at Cuenca. Goeben wrote of his four-month bedridden state, suffering the ill will of his captors and sharing a ward with thirty other patients, each taking their turn for subjection to amputation as 'their cries to heaven made us all shudder inside, while corpses lay for hours in our midst without interesting the wardens' while between operations others succumbed to infections or discomfort cause by 'straw mattresses and woollen blankets and a fatty diet consisting of a small piece of mutton and a half-pound of bread for lunch and dinner, and a thin soup of water, garlic and salt with bread for breakfast. Most of the mutton was inedible and even beggars would not eat it. Such was the hospital fare of the Cristinos, the propagators of Enlightenment and Humanity as they like to call themselves.'[186] The pro-Carlist William Walton called Cristino hospitals slaughterhouses.[187]

One hundred years later advances in surgery and infection control had improved hospital treatment. But only the Madrid front in the government zone was well-provisioned with facilities and transport infrastructure, and even here American medical volunteers found themselves sometimes working forty-hour shifts.[188] Elsewhere the rural fronts were faced with a nineteenth-century casualty environment. A British Carlist was shocked to encounter the corpses of comrades frozen solid during the Battle of Teruel, a primordial spectacle far worse than the 'icicles hanging from noses' he had read about in Charles Napier's account of the Peninsular War one hundred years earlier.[189] Battles fought in such poorly accessible regions as the Guadarrama and Teruel required the general use of mules to transport

FIGURE 2.3 *Government mobile hospital (Courtesy of Museo Zumalakarregi).*

wounded soldiers to safety – particularly for Nationalist casualties whose advances set them adrift of infrastructure – which meant that the torturous experience of being transported to dressing stations and hospitals for many soldiers was not markedly different from the 1830s. Once casualties reached hospitals some surprising similarities pertained. Like Goeben one hundred years earlier, George Orwell was wounded on the Aragón front, and like Goeben he complained of the unsatisfying soup in government hospitals. He also recounted undertrained nurses and a severe absence of doctors.[190] This ill-preparedness resulted in part due to the defection to the rebels of most military doctors in 1936. As a result military casualties in the Republican zone were treated in civilian hospitals run by various left-wing organizations until the Ministry of War in January 1937 centralized control over dedicated military hospitals and rationalized their numbers as the war progressed. All hospitals with at least three hundred beds were proclaimed 'military' hospitals.[191] Government hospitals in both wars were regularized in tandem with the general process of militarization, the mass mobilization decreed by Mendizábal in 1835 and the painstaking expansion of the Popular Army from 1936.

Despite government efforts, health and hygiene in fact proved to be generally better in rebel areas of control in both civil wars. This situation had little to do with standards of surgery. The rebels in 1936 may have been favoured by the defection to their ranks of most of the army medical branch, but the medicine academies remained in government hands and civilian practitioners tended to remain where they were.[192] Rather rebel superiority relied upon more reliable logistics and upon the maintenance of more 'blood hospitals' in the field for transfusions.[193] In the first war, wounded rebels tended to face better chances of recovery mainly for the reason of internal lines of communication and proximity to caring family members. But, by the end of the Carlist War, the best hospitals were found in the eastern rebel zone where Cabrera had made a concerted effort to expand provision.[194]

Surgery was far less primitive in the second war. Government medicine excelled in Professor Trueta's pioneering wound treatment research in Barcelona (basically, the use of rest and plaster to heal wounds and of sulphonamide to treat septicaemia whenever this infection set in), and the advent of battlefield blood transfusions via Mobile Army Surgical Hospitals (MASH).[195] But as in the first war government strengths pertained only to large urban centres, as MASH facilities were swamped. Wounded troops at the front had better chances of recovery if they could rely upon logistics to transport them from the battle quickly. In the first war, recovery essentially depended upon internal lines of communications and the proximity of caring family members. On the main front these conditions placed Carlists at an advantage, whereas the Cristino commander-in-chief complained of routinely deploying ten soldiers to litter one battlefield casualty to safety.[196]

International intervention in both civil wars had limited success at easing the management of casualties. The British auxiliaries dispatched to Spain in the summer of 1835 were accompanied by medical equipment deemed sufficient for a maximum of 10,000 men conducting twelve months' campaigning. This amounted to 'thirty-six field sets of medicines and instruments, eighteen spring carts with harnesses, fifty-two sets of Amesbury splints, eighteen blankets for mules, eighteen water-decks, 108 stretchers, eighteen sets of capital instruments and four portable field cases'.[197] But this provision was rendered inadequate by human and environmental factors. Only two-thirds of the British auxiliaries hastily recruited were of the age and fitness required of British Army recruits, and of the remainder, one-eighth comprised recruits who were either too young, old or disabled to be fit for any military service.[198] An unusually cold winter and inadequate billets greeted the British auxiliaries over 1835–36, compounding medical inadequacies. The British commandant at Vitoria, Charles Shaw, despaired at the conditions:

> The hospitals were very bad, but this convalescent depot was terrible. I believe no officer had gone through it; and no wonder, as the filth was shocking. All were lying huddled together on the bare stones of a convent without windows and no blankets … three poor fellows were dead, with their mouths close together to keep each other warm … Entering a small room in a corner, I was nearly knocked down by the effluvials. Here nine

men had been for four days without any surgeon to look after them. I suppose they are now all dead.[199]

Shaw realized that overcrowded hospitals were a blessing in disguise, as casualties barred from entry actually stood better chances of survival in the infection-free cold of the open air. The dreary spectacle of neglected casualties and discarded corpses made him lose his respect for human nature: 'Man is the most brutal and crapulous animal alive.'[200] One hundred years later a young South African volunteer for liberty also despaired at the sight of neglected casualties:

> I found a group of wounded men who had been carried to a non-existent field dressing station and then forgotten. There were about fifty stretchers, but many men had already died and most of the others would be dead by morning ... One little Jewish kid of about eighteen lay on his back with his bowels exposed from his navel to his genitals ... they all called for water and I had none to give. I was filled with such horror at their suffering and my inability to help them that I felt I had suffered some permanent injury to my spirit.[201]

Medical relief came from abroad in both conflicts. The successful Anglo–Cristino offensive at Irún and Hernani in May 1837 reopened government communications with France and encouraged French General Harispe to admit Cristino casualties into French hospitals.[202] The Carlists' best surgeon was a foreign volunteer, Frederick Burgess of Guy's Hospital, London, who was promoted to senior surgeon on Zumalacárregui's staff.[203] In the 1930s medical volunteers from abroad made a greater impact. The British Spanish Medical Aid Committee (SMAC) attracted communist idealists and adventurers and was staffed in Spain by exclusively male doctors and exclusively female nurses. Foreign nurses brought a technical application which was largely lacking among Spanish nurses. Even as late as the 1930s, training for Spanish nurses amounted to little more than housekeeping and hygiene.[204] A British Carlist found the nuns running a hospital in San Sebastián to be 'indifferent to the principles of asepsis'.[205] The Moroccan wars had imparted lessons in wound treatment, but the experience of military nursing as a whole had not changed radically from the 1830s. The ordinary women of San Sebastián who tended the government and British wounded during the 1835–36 rebel siege of their city were nurses in all but name.[206]

Many military casualties arose from sexually transmitted infections spread between soldiers and prostitutes. A suspiciously high proportion of 1830s hospital casualties were treated for scabies, the symptoms of which could easily be confused with sexual infections. Prostitution was traditionally indulged in Spain, despite (or because of) prevailing Catholic patriarchal values. Authorities generally intervened in matters relating to brothels only for pragmatic rather than moralistic reasons. Two-and-a-half years of war had caused the numbers of prostitutes in Barcelona to grow exponentially, and by August 1836 the growth of 'corrupting' illnesses among government soldiers and militia led the authorities to turn a former convent into a 'lock hospital' for infected prostitutes. Military authorities complained that sexual encounters both between troops and women and between men continued at the new location all the same.[207] One hundred years did not dim the Spanish culture of prostitution, even if a noticeable class dimension had grown equal to the polarization of the 1930s. A foreign observer commented that 'common' prostitutes supported the Republic while 'better' prostitutes supported the rebels.[208] Pragmatic responses from military authorities dominated once more. Rebel officers early in 1937 intervened in a brothel in Vitoria popular with Carlist militia only when it emerged that some of the women had been running a desertion network for young men wanting to escape to government-held Bilbao.[209] During the first year of the Spanish Civil War, some 3.5 per cent of reported casualties among government troops were diagnosed with venereal diseases (VD), although the real figure was probably greater. Possibly, the moralizing of the Nationalists, or perhaps the moralizing under-reporting of VD, made it at least seem less of a problem in the rebel zone.[210] Women volunteers, both real fighting milicianas and that uncertain quantity of 'whores' at the front drawn to the presence of well-paid Republican soldiers with little else on which to spend their wages, were an iconic feature of the government's war. An International Brigade volunteer who secured a favour from a militiawoman was cheered by his comrades who assumed its sexual nature, but the joke transpired that the woman had only agreed to wash the man's underwear.[211] One chauvinistic assumption compounded another. Despite the revolutionary emancipation edicts of the government, patriarchal society clearly endured as women were sent home from the front on account of their 'VD-spreading' and there is even an account – apocryphal, perhaps – of the anarchist Durruti executing women who defied this order and returned to the front.[212] Underlying the spread of VD was the massive growth in prostitution produced by the war. Soldiers from both sides frequented brothels, and traditional attitudes towards this industry endured on both sides, too. By the end of the war in 1940, amid the direst poverty for the defeated side, there were as many as 200,000 prostitutes working either in brothels or independently.[213]

Food and morale

Problems with supplying sufficient food to combatant and civilian populations faced both sides in both civil wars. A nationwide subsistence crisis struck in the middle of the first war in 1837 as a combination of war depredations and the 'natural' cycle of poor harvests. Even before then, localized food crises impaired civil–military relations in combat areas. The vital first war harvest of late-summer 1834 posed massive problems to government forces trying to police the Basque and Navarrese countryside. Predicting Carlist depredations and ensuing discontent among their ranks, commissaries in September organized soldiers to gather in as much of the local harvest as possible and to defend granaries.[214] The theft of wheat by Carlist irregulars had been a growing problem throughout 1834. Horses in front-line areas were requisitioned as a safeguard by the Cristino forces, but this measure only compounded the logistical problems of agriculture.[215] Government conscription was concentrated in the September–October period once the harvest was collected in order to free hands for the army. Yet, conversely, rebel volunteering peaked during the harvest months precisely because of opportunities to pillage agriculture 'in the name of the king'.

Harvests in 1834 and 1835 were good, but thereafter the expansion of rebel activity diminished food production and transportation, both reaching a nadir in 1837. Harvest failures and occasional famines were part of the 'natural' cycle of Spain's rural economy until the 1860s. But the hunger of the Carlist War was exacerbated by the distortion to food production caused by mass mobilization and the frequent cases of depredations caused in large part by the inadequate government commissariat. The 'asentista' system of paying private contractors to supply the Army of the North was both expensive and inadequate, for in operating as a form of 'cash-and-carry', goods paid for at source had then to run the gauntlet of banditry and wastage which meant that supplies seldom arrived at the front in their entirety. The private contractor system had been a common feature of European warfare since the end of the sixteenth century.[216] David Parrott's findings concerning the 'business of war' in Early Modern Europe has argued that officers with monetary interests supplying their forces created a 'virtuous cycle' of military effectiveness based on an enlightened interest in the wellbeing of their men and a more offensive attitude against the resources of the enemy.[217] But as civilian sutlers began to take a leading role from the eighteenth century, the direct interest diverged and, in the case of government contractors in 1830s Spain, we see no link between asentistas and military effectiveness. For one thing, the unprecedented degree of militarization in 1830s Spain tested this system beyond its limits. The exterior lines and rebel raids afflicting government forces in the Basque country created a food crisis here in short order. As early as June 1835, and despite a recent good harvest, the government ordered the militia to surrender all its food and arms stocks to the regular army.[218]

Unlike the Basque rebels who benefitted from interior lines, government forces were at the mercy of long-distance contractors. The August 1836 La Granja revolution was partly caused by a strike by contractors who refused to fulfil their engagements until they received outstanding payments.[219] Three months later, when the starving Army of the Centre launched its offensive against Carlist-held Cantavieja, the calculations of its captain-general, Evaristo San Miguel, were driven by the need to feed his troops in a poverty-stricken countryside facing the onset of the dire regional winter. Cantavieja's Carlist garrison surrendered the town after a few days of resistance, but the occupying troops faced disappointment. The rebels had run down the food stocks and what little had remained appeared to have been pillaged by an advance party of government officers who then sold it at inflated prices. Hundreds of liberated Cristino prisoners were left to starve.[220] Even though Espartero was better at asserting discipline over his Army of the North, his forces faced the same subsistence crisis. By February 1837 Bilbao's food stores had recovered to their pre-siege levels, but both civil and military authorities laid claim to their control. Eventually Espartero won control of the food on the condition that he drew upon stocks directly, without recourse to the contractors. Espartero's prestige meant that Liberal local governments trusted him with contracts more than the revolutionary government in Madrid. Provincial authorities in Santander, faced by a growing rebel grip on their hinterland, undertook to arrange supplies only through him directly and not through the Madrid government.[221]

No such arrangement was reached in the area of operations of the Army of the Centre, where the hunger year of 1837 saw both government and rebel troops competing with each other to extract the most foodstuffs from the population. Rations and cash were demanded of communities, receipts often being refused to municipalities on spurious grounds. Civilians faced all manner of privations. During July 1837 some 500 government troops garrisoning Teruel managed to obtain a grossly excessive bread ration. Goods which troops looted from civilians were sold on or back at inflated prices in order to line the pockets of officers, and government conscripts from wine-producing areas demanded wine of villages where it was almost unknown.[222] The subsistence crisis of 1837 linked the battlefronts and home fronts in suffering. A newspaper correspondent from rural Córdoba province complained of the misery induced by the failed harvest and the increased burden of public sinecures produced by the revolution.[223]

The Spanish Civil War, like the Greek and Yugoslav civil wars of the 1940s, showed that the side which controlled the wheat-producing regions would win.[224] In the First Carlist War, the wheat-producing lands of Andalucía accounted for 25 per cent of Spanish bread in normal times[225] and were generally in government hands throughout. Yet, with the exception of the irregular war zones of Old Castile and the east, government civilians in the 1830s generally ate better than government soldiers. In the 1930s, by contrast, the home front starved while government soldiers enjoyed better (but not plentiful) nutrition thanks to their relatively higher pay and closeness to an improved transport infrastructure, even when the contingencies of battle made precarious the final leg of a supply journey from a road or a railway bridgehead. A British intelligence report in April 1937 observed that government soldiers were not yet suffering the privations of civilians.[226] By contrast, soldiers and civilians alike by the middle of the Carlist War were suffering in the combat zones of rural Castile, Aragón and Catalonia owing to disturbed harvests and markets. Sieges drove refugees from the countryside, burdening hungry urban areas and reducing agricultural output. Even after the rebel siege of San Sebastián was lifted in May 1836, Carlists in the surrounding countryside intimidated returning 'enemy' peasants, impairing the harvest.[227] In summer 1836, a Catalan deputy reported from Lérida that 'two harvests have been lost already, and the July harvest will fall prey to the faction ... and there are 300 villages which have not had bread for three months'.[228]

Wheat-producing areas were generally in rebel hands in the 1930s, however, creating food shortages in the government zone which grew in the face of territorial loss compressing refugees onto a diminishing agricultural output.[229] A crisis ensued in the government zone as civilians weakened physically and psychologically on the repetitive and diminishing diet of rice, lentils and chickpeas. Studies of the Allied blockade of the German Empire have shown the marked link between malnutrition and defeatism.[230] By December 1938 the per capita daily calorie intake in Madrid had dwindled to 770. The only malnutrition-related disease which was not prevalent was scurvy, owing to the open road to the orange groves of Valencia. Cats disappeared from the streets of Barcelona and authorities advised each flat to keep at least one chicken on its balcony.[231] As Michael Seidman has shown, 'individualist' behaviour endured behind the façade of solidarity during the anarchist-inspired socialization and collectivization of agriculture during 1936–37.[232] 'Individualist' behaviour in food production amounted to hoarding, shirking and bartering, depleting supplies to the refugee-filled government cities and compounding the structural deficiencies faced by a government which at the outset had lost control of the Castilian bread-basket. As soon as May 1937, shortages had become persistent enough to warrant their role in propaganda supporting counter-revolution. *El Sol* claimed, 'A single command will eliminate bread queues in Madrid by allowing authorities to respond to the needs of the people.'[233] The communist press campaigned for increased production at all costs, condemning uncultivated land as sabotage.[234] Fraternization events were 'organized' between Popular Army units and olive workers in Aragón with the aim of maximizing the first harvest of 1938 'because olive exports worth seventy million pesetas in foreign currency will buy arms with which to vanquish the invaders'.[235]

Food shortages shaped black humour and propaganda as a coping measure for communities at war. The subsistence crisis of 1837 across northern Spain was caused by the requisitioning of both government and rebel forces. Horses and draught animals were slaughtered for food in acts of direst necessity by Castilian villagers warding off starvation.[236] Outright starvation faced communities under direct siege. The governor defending Morella (Valencia) on 10 December 1837 wrote to the besieging Carlists that four months of blockade had exhausted his city's food supply, so the defenders would now begin eating known Carlist families. Cabrera, delighted for once at not being cast as the villain, replied vowing reprisals against Liberal families, but they would stop short of cannibalism.[237] Neither man could have known that just as they exchanged black propaganda, government prisoners-of-war captured at the August 1837 Battle of Herrera (Zaragoza) had actually begun eating the dead bodies of their starved comrades.[238]

By autumn 1837 Commander-in-Chief Espartero cited depleted food stocks in his rejection of government demands to launch a general offensive. Espartero's pleas for food, money and winter clothing, and his complaints about the extortion of the asentistas, were dismissed as excuses in Madrid. The hunger of garrisons was undoing Espartero's painstaking efforts to restore discipline in the post-revolutionary army. The consequences for the villagers of Northern Spain were dire. Northern Castile had been reduced to virtual famine conditions throughout 1837 as traditional meat sources were pillaged and abandoned. Even oxen were being seized and eaten, as local farmers had nothing else left to be pillaged. A Polish aristocrat was shocked at the damage that four years of rebel insurgency and government counter-insurgency had inflicted on the villages of Guadalajara province:

> You have no idea of the desolation in this country. Villages are so exhausted that they have come up with their own solutions to survive the armed bands. Many municipalities have organised two local governments, one Cristino and the other Carlist. When news arrives of the approach of a Carlist column the Cristino authorities go and hide in the church or other large buildings (which are all fortified now). The priest then steps in to receive the Carlists and to moderate the reprisals and vengeance of the invaders. When the column moves on, the real authorities re-emerge but remain ready to restore the priest the moment danger returns.[239]

Villagers in the enemy zone were made to suffer for the government's subsistence crisis. Zurbano's cavalry raids into the Basque country were the only major offensive operations undertaken over the autumn and winter of 1837. These *chevauchée* raids scorched the earth north of the Ebro, destroying arms stores and foundries. But above all, they rustled cattle, the raiders feeding themselves on enemy stocks.[240]

In the 1930s, food shortages affected only the government zone and were largely systemic in nature (although pillaging added to the misery). The growing defeatism in the government zone was caused by food shortages more than anything else. The war weariness among smallholders forced into collectivization was given a culinary term: they were dubbed 'radishes' (red on the outside, white on the inside).[241] 'Radishes' became the butt of jokes in the immiserated government home front. A man at his wits' end decides to commit suicide by going to an anarchist meeting and giving the Falangist salute. The anarchists jump up and shout, 'Be careful! We are not sure of the doorman!'[242] The immiseration of the government home front provided sincerity to the peace feelers which were stretched out as early as May 1937.

The socialist Besteiro used the occasion of his attendance at King George V's funeral to approach Anthony Eden for mediation, and in the same month the Vatican approached Franco suggesting its own good offices for a negotiated peace.[243] Both Rome's and Churchill's support of a mediated peace was roundly rejected by Franco. He got encouragement (although he hardly needed any) from the Nazi charge d'affaires who reported to Berlin that too much blood and hatred had passed for either of the Two Spains to be reconciled and that Churchill's intervention could be explained by historic British interests in Bilbao.[244]

Black humour grew among the 1830s rebels after the military tide turned against them. Whereas Carlist troops used to march to ballads containing such uplifting verses as 'If Cristina wins, we'll all be brothers; if Carlos wins, we'll all be masters' (*Si vence Cristina, seremos hermanos; si vence Carlos, nosotros los amos*), after 1837 patriotic parlance had become subverted by sarcastic humour. The mediocre aide-de-camp to Carlist Prince Sebastián, Alonso de Cuevillas, was punned by his long-suffering men in the rhyme '*Cuevillas nunca hizo maravillas*' (Cuevillas never made marvels).[245] The popular father of the Carlist cavalry arm, Carlos O'Donnell, had the habit of commenting on military failures with the preamble 'If only!' (*¡Ojalá!*). After he was killed in action in May 1835 term *ojalateros* (the 'if onlys') was used to ridicule shirkers and desk officers in the Carlist home front. Women suffering from the increasing shortages in the blockaded Basque country shouted '¡ojalatero!' at war profiteers, deserters and, unfairly, war-wounded men or other men incapacitated from serving.

As defeatism set in after the failed Royal Expedition of 1837, the peace faction surrounding General Maroto was excoriated as ojalatero by diehards. The question of a compromise peace was anathema in the government zone until 1836 and in the rebel zone until 1837. Two moderado enemies of the 1836 revolution informally approached Don Carlos's court to discuss peace terms, only to be turned away with terms amounting to unconditional surrender.[246] On 19 May 1837, Commander-in-Chief Espartero issued a proclamation to the Basque-Navarrese population, appealing to them to lay down their arms, promising commissions for their officers in a reunified army in return for their recognition of Isabella's throne.[247] But it would take the defeat in September of the Royal Expedition for pervading pessimism to envelop the northern rebels. Even then, government attempts at feelers were cack-handed. José Antonio de Muñagorri was an Alavese arms magnate who, in November 1837, after many months of dithering, finally betrayed the Carlism of his native Verástegui by entering Cristino service. In April 1838 he invaded the Basque country from France at the head of a Basque free corps, proclaiming the peace slogan *paz y fueros* (peace and the fueros). Muñagorri enjoyed the powerful sponsorship of both Britain and France, as well as the mentoring of spymaster Aviraneta. His manifesto confirmed what several other Carlists were thinking, namely that the question of fueros and the reign of Don Carlos were separable. The way was thus laid for a *transacción*, or compromise peace.[248] The reasons why these generous terms were not accepted sooner lie partly with the military incompetence of Muñagorri's force, which quickly became the butt of jokes from both Carlists and Liberals, and partly because the fueros themselves were only part of the motivation behind Basque Carlism. Rather, religious monarchy remained a central factor for the diehard *apostólicos* clinging to Don Carlos, and the Cristino regime was seen as diabolical in these terms.[249]

Muñagorri's manifesto was answered in the 29 May 1838 edition of the official *Boletín de Navarra y Provincias Vascongadas*. It charged that even though it was correct that the population was suffering under Carlist taxation, the suffering they would experience under Liberal occupation would be far worse, as the Cristinos would seek to rebuild their war-ravaged territory by exacting reparations from the Basque country.[250] In the autumn, the royal government tried to bolster morale by holding an extravagant wedding of Don Carlos to Princess María Teresa de Braganza, sister of his first wife (who had died in exile in Portsmouth in 1834). The rebel prime minister Airas Tejeiro, busily editing press coverage, called this marriage the 'latest blow to the Revolution now at the point of succumbing'. But Basques realized that the new queen brought no wealth to the bankrupt Carlist cause, while enemies of Maroto suspected he had worked this union in order to displace Don Carlos (given that Princess María had been formally excluded from the line of succession by the Cristino Cortes in January 1837).[251] The Madrid government sought to exploit the mounting disillusionment in the rebel zone. In March 1839, spymaster Eugenio de Aviraneta circulated some of the most effective propaganda of the entire war. His 'Letter from a Basque farmer to a tinker' was a pun on the shirkers on the Carlist home front (tinker, or '*hojalatero*' was a homonym of 'if only'). Its content urged the Carlist Basques to seek peace instead of being 'stitched up' by theocratic diehards and non-Basque Carlists.[252]

In the 1930s, food was more plentiful in the rebel zone as rebels controlled the Castilian and Andalucían 'bread-baskets' and the harsh suppression of strikes led to the emergence of a coercive producer culture.[253] The complex rebel governor of Seville, Queipo de Llano, a right-wing Republican infamous for his use of radio propaganda, pre-empted the producer culture of Francoism alongside a rebarbative media campaign. Privately, Queipo's rebel allies resented his bloodthirsty radio diatribes but officially they represented his 'Queipogrammes' as 'military eloquence true to the spirit of his native Andalucía'.[254] In fact, he turned Radio Seville into a platform for visceral hate speeches, boasting at how his Moroccans would rape 'red' women and murder their menfolk. This reprehensible propaganda served the dual purpose of intimidating listeners in the government zone and threatening former leftists under his control.

Accompanying Queipo's 'eloquence' was what Michael Seidman has described as an authoritarian political economy of capitalism subjected to the state. Ironically, Queipo's regulation of the Andalucían economy shared many features with Prime Minister Mendizábal's policy in the government zone one hundred years earlier. Mendizábal pioneered similar 'voluntarist' measures in the name of the war effort. Cristino public servants faced similar arrears of pay, and a whole culture of barter and deferred payments arose around their needs,[255] something which would be more sophisticated in the Republican zone of 1936–39. During his first month as prime minister, Mendizábal achieved the remarkable feat of securing donations from grandees and financiers, and government officeholders accepted a 10 per cent cut to their salaries for the duration of the civil war.[256] As finance minister in 1837, Mendizábal imposed a forced loan on the middle and upper classes on onerous terms. Even though the government repaid captive subscribers at 5 per cent interest, it repaid not scarce cash but chits that could only be spent on paying government taxes.[257]

Queipo forced 'patriotic donations' from wealthy residents in the rebel zone, levying a 10 per cent tax on luxury products, decreeing 'single-dish Fridays' in restaurants (when customers would pay for three courses but receive only one) and cowing the vanquished working class with demands for work on subsistence wages. Similar economic efficiency applied to the Nationalist peseta, which gained international confidence and helped the rebels to fuel their war effort on credit. Exports from the Nationalist zones remained steady throughout the war, and were sold exclusively in sought-after foreign currency. By the end of the war in 1939 the Nationalist peseta had lost only about 20 per cent of its value; the Republican peseta, by contrast, had lost nearly 100 per cent of its value. Hence inflation was controlled, not just by international confidence but also by authoritarian interventions into pricing. 'Voluntary donations' to the *Auxilio Social* and other regime proxies also kept the regime liquid, and this 'voluntarism' was sustained as much by propaganda as by terror or the threat of terror. For example, Nationalist newspapers warned Spaniards not to shake the hand of any man or woman sporting a gold wedding ring. Aristocrats with links to the exiled monarchy (grandees) made the biggest and most ostentatious donations.[258]

Queipo imposed a right-wing version of the 'moral economy' including price controls and regulated working conditions, repressing workers but also curtailing some of the abuses of the bourgeoisie. He set maximum repayment terms on 'usurious' interest on loans (5%), and the Bank of Spain norm of 4 per cent became the standard repayment interest rate for farmers borrowing to improve or expand production. In August 1937 the National Wheat Service (*Servicio Nacional del Trigo* or SNT) was set up in Burgos as a bureaucracy to manage a hybrid of anti-capitalist and authoritarian agrarian economy. All of these measures amounted to the privileging of the values of the countryside over those of the town, and with good reason, as the bogeymen of Nationalist propaganda – Jews, emancipated women, reds, Masons – were very much associated with the cities and their corrupted urban values rather than with the 'pure' countryside.[259] The number of Jews in 1930s Spain was negligible: around 1,000 plus around 10,000 in Spanish Morocco.[260] But as in the 1830s the virtual absence of Spanish Jews did not stop the rebels turning anti-Semitism into a propaganda weapon.

In general, foreign observers were more impressed by the apparent 'order' of Nationalist Spain than they were by communist attempts to restore capitalism in the government zone.[261] In October 1937 a pro-rebel British banking agent who toured Queipo's 'fiefdom' of Andalucía was impressed by the authoritarian production ethos in the economy, by how former 'reds' earned redemption for their sins through labour: 'At Seville's old zeppelin aerodrome, much drainage work is in progress by prisoners who receive army food and five pesetas per day under Franco's decree.'[262] Three months earlier, Churchill's friend, the British naval attaché in rebel-held Palma de Mallorca, had made a similar tour in Andalucía. Hillgarth's insight was pithy: 'If order is the secret to winning this war, we have little doubt which side will win.'[263]

Foreign dignitaries mistook subjection and terror in the population for peace and cooperation. Even so, the full logic of Queipo's violent propaganda was moderated by two factors. First, the Spanish Falange provided membership and therefore immunity from persecution for those quick-witted leftists who passed themselves off as frustrated national syndicalists or simply expressed a desire for violence against 'reds'. A foreign observer called these base recruits 'social scrap iron'.[264] 'Respectable' rebels dubbed them the 'FAIlange', punning the anarchist organization (the FAI, or *Federación Anarquista Ibérica*), and even Queipo recognized that the blue shirt of the Falange was really a 'life-jacket' against persecution. As in most civil wars, behind ostensibly ideological motivations there lurked personal enmities, vendettas and local factionalism. However much acts of violence and denunciation were dressed up as political, in reality they were exercised for logical rather than ideological reasons.

The second factor moderating rebel terror was precisely the pressure for production. Even though caciques were far more often persecuting leftists in the rebel zone than shielding them, in Galicia, repression was sometimes modified by the intercession of all-powerful caciques, as their financial interests in exploiting workers ironically placed them in the right. That caciquismo continued, and not just in Galicia, despite the rhetoric of the Falange, may be accounted for in part because the Falange itself saw an influx of new members with apolitical opportunistic motives or former red backgrounds who therefore saw membership as political cover rather than an invitation to join the crusade against the caciques which the 'old shirt' Falangists had long been demanding. The primacy of food even tempered some of the counter-revolutionary terror against reds who had benefited under the Republic. In Nationalist Andalucía and Extremadura, some oxen ploughmen (*yunteros*), whose claims to landownership had been controversially recognised by the pre-war Popular Front, were permitted to stay on the land they 'illegally' occupied until September 1937 precisely in order to bring in the harvest.[265] The 1930s rebels were the best fed, and this in no small way contributed to their victory.

3

Legacy and memory of the Spanish Civil Wars

The Republic should have fought like the Liberals of the First Carlist War. The National Militia bathed itself in glory resisting Carlists at Cenicero, Caspe, Villafranca and Gandesa while freeing up Espartero's field army to campaign for the final victory.[1]

Civil wars do not begin with the declaration of hostilities, nor do they end with their conclusion. Rather they are products of mounting pre-war tension which become violently reshaped in fighting, casting trauma over the post-war 'peace'. In part, this trauma was the product of human agency (the vengeance of the victors) and, in part, it was the product of the circumstances of war (displacement, hunger, mobilization).

Both the legacy and memory of the Spanish Civil Wars embrace diverse levels. The architects of defeat in both civil wars, Generals Rafael Maroto in 1839 and Segismundo Casado in 1939, have been subjected to debate and censure from both sides. The personal blame and attributions of treachery levelled at the leaders of the defeated sides in both wars were strangely convenient, as they caused 'stab-in-the-back' myths to grow. This phenomenon appears to have endured several generations. Until quite recently, historians viewed the actions of the 'Casado coup' of March 1939 in a positive light. The actions of his National Defence Council in ending the war have been viewed as a humanitarian intervention and as a necessary coup against what was suspected to be an imminent communist takeover of the Republic. Such foreign anti-communist historians as Stanley Payne and Burnett Bolloten needed little convincing that Negrín had become a pawn of Stalin. Segismundo Casado's memoirs, published in two parts (straight after the war and again as he was dying in Spain in the 1960s), were generally received positively by the Franco regime precisely because his anti-communism reinforced the victor regime's mission statement.[2] Defeat created an urge for personal recriminations, and what was true after the Spanish Civil War was true one hundred years earlier. Traditionalist historians excoriated Rafael Maroto for conducting a 'shameful' surrender to the government in 1839.[3] Even though Maroto was rehabilitated by the doyen of First Carlist War history, Antonio Pirala, his black legend endured and he ended his career where he had begun it, in obscurity in Spanish America.

Both conflicts submerged Spain in a collective trauma, leaving profound demographical and psychological scars on the population. The human scars were greater than the physical scars, despite the victorious rebels' decision to preserve devastated Belchite (Zaragoza) as a ghost town commemorating the war. The human casualties were greater in proportion to damage to infrastructure than had been the case in the fronts of the Great War. The last redoubt of Carlism in May 1840 was Cabrera's capital Morella (Aragón). Even though half the town had been burnt by government artillery bombardment, such intense physical damage was the localized exception rather than the general rule.[4] One hundred years later, an American Democrat touring post-war Spain was surprised that damage to buildings had not been as great as the human casualties owing to 'the small cannon and bombs used during the Spanish war'.[5] Local memory of civil war accordingly tended to centre on human rather than physical destruction. The repetition of similar ideological wars every two generations led Carlist villagers to conflate local episodes into a continuum. Carlist Viana (Navarra) is a parable of this human trauma. In November 1838 Carlist Balmaseda massacred some thirty-six government soldiers captured outside the walls and Espartero responded with a massacre of his own.[6] During the Second Carlist War in 1874, the town was sacked by Republican forces for siding with the Carlists.[7] In 1936, Carlist Viana, having sided with the locally powerful rebels at the outset, faced less trauma. But the corpse of an anonymous 'spy' dubbed 'El Ruso' was found nearby in the first days. Carlist strongholds of Catalonia became anarchist one hundred years later, but the same small communities faced killing all the same. In 1838 Carlists razed Ripoll to the ground in an act of collective punishment[8]; one hundred years later anarchists meted out collective punishment in reverse in the same small town when thirteen Fascist sympathisers, including priests, were executed by revolutionaries.[9]

The First Carlist War produced as many casualties in proportion to the Spanish population, and perhaps rather more,[10] but the Spanish Civil War produced more enduring terror against the vanquished side. Nationalists and Republicans were divided into the categories of the 'victors' and the 'vanquished', respectively, and no objective Republican memory of the civil war was permitted to emerge. No public space was made available for the memory of the 'vanquished' who were marginalized in society, unable to grieve for their relatives who died in the civil war, many of whom remained in forgotten mass graves.[11] Franco's Nationalist victory in April 1939 confirmed his untrammelled power as head of state, commander-in-chief, head of the single party and, eventually, regent for life. Alfonso remained in exile, abdicating in 1941 and dying shortly afterwards. His successor, Don Juan, immediately clashed with the victorious caudillo, Franco, upon the need for monarchical restoration and that its form should be 'above' party politics and constitutional in nature. Franco, by contrast, condemned the entire 'liberal' and 'constitutional' nature of Alfonsine monarchism and demanded his successor adhere to his Falangist-inflected partisan vision of a 'totalitarian' monarchy, inspired by the example of sixteenth-century Isabella I instead of nineteenth-century Isabella II. Franco's personal monarchical pretensions grew in the wake of Alfonso's death in 1941, one hundred years after Espartero's monarchical pretensions evolved into outright regency in 1841. Ironically, both Espartero and Franco expressed contempt for monarchy. In September 1840, war-hero Espartero sided with revolutionaries in ejecting Queen-Mother María Cristina and making himself regent of Spain the following year. Franco took longer to make himself regent for life, and the constitutional legacy of the First Carlist War was never far from his mind. Franco refused to 'abdicate' in favour of a monarchical restoration, stating that 'as long as I live, I will never be a queen mother' and dismissing the birthright succession claims of Spanish monarchism with reference to the notorious immorality of Isabella II: 'The last man to sleep with Doña Isabel cannot be the father of the King and what comes out of the belly of the Queen must be examined to see if it is suitable.'[12]

The vanquished Republicans were either driven into exile or persecuted. Exile had long been a formative phenomenon for Spanish political elites, even a virtual rite of passage. Whereas some elite exiles found their times abroad to be temporary, others, such as the self-exiled Blanco White in the early nineteenth century or the generation of Spanish Republicans in Mexico, never returned.[13] Liberal exiles who returned from Paris and London to lead Cristino fortunes in the First Carlist War were the famous subject of Vicente Llorens, himself, poignantly, an exiled Republican of the Spanish Civil War.[14] Even though the trials and tribulations of the elites are well documented, very little exists concerning the ordinary exiles who crossed into France in their droves in 1839 and 1939.

To a large degree, this situation arises from politically distorted memory. Both Espartero and Franco used their supreme military powers to block the re-entry of refugees into Spain and to exterminate diehard militants. The condign nature of the peace arose to the letter of Franco's 1939 'Law of Political Responsibilities' and in spite of the more generous concessions of Espartero's 1839 Vergara settlement. The violence of both victorious regimes was dressed up as 'public order' and, more abstractly, by the need to centralize political power, the major difference being the degree to which Franco was both more vindictive and more successful in achieving these aims than Espartero. The chances of 'redemption', to borrow the regime's Catholic slogans, for former leftists rested largely on whether they had embraced Francoism during the war. Even a minimum commitment to the Nationalist cause, or even better, 'new-shirted' membership of the Falange, could be enough either to protect family members from reprisals or even to get commanding officers to overlook previously leftist pasts when it came to writing character references for their men in order to override any earlier blacklisting and secure employment.[15]

Woe to the vanquished after both 1839 and 1939 affected the women associated with the defeated side in similar ways. The emigration of vast numbers of Carlist fighters from the Basque country after 1839 to France and to emigration in Cuba and Latin America left Carlist womenfolk in direst poverty and generally unable to break out of it in an honest fashion. Carlist areas of Spain occupied by the victorious Cristinos remained traditionalist: Carlist women in general had not experienced the independent agency of several Cristino women during the war and prevailing mores prevented women, even destitute mothers and war-widows, from gaining redress by participating in the public sphere. Even worse, the victorious Cristinos remained vindictive in spirit and, as we shall later report, large numbers of male exiles remained in France or overseas, disbelieving the *esparterista* offer of amnesty.[16]

Both wars ended in conditions which did not really feel like peace. Irregular combatants dubbed 'bandits' persisted in remote parts of the countryside, especially in the wake of the first war and in both wars especially in areas adjacent to the Pyrenees. Bandits who had used Carlism as a flag of convenience were violently suppressed first by Espartero's army and later by a new, centralized paramilitary force, the Civil Guard, which was created in 1844 after Espartero had been ousted from power. This force also dissolved the popular 'heroes' of the winning side, the National Militia, although generally without resorting to violence. Thus, unlike after 1939, the newly unified Spanish state of the 1840s asserted itself against both extremes of the recent conflict. To a large extent, popular memory of diehard combatants was distorted by the side on which they had fought. By 1939, the communists had long become the 'aristocracy' of the Popular Army, enjoying the greatest power and privileges, even as the government slid to defeat.[17] The communists thought that the anarchists were akin to the nineteenth-century bandits plaguing Spain, and suppressed them in 1937 in the name of militarization. Even though the government lost the civil war, Spanish communists in exile remained remarkably unreflective, keeping faith with their policy of militarization and, by the 1970s, to a 'policy of national reconciliation', neither of which left any room for memory of irregular guerrilla warfare which seemed like nothing more than a ghost from a bygone era of Spanish history.[18] The anarchist response to defeat was very different. Democratic socialist George Orwell, while the war was still raging, arrived at the same conclusion as the anarchists that war by revolution was correct.[19] Neither communist nor non-communist Republicans really understood how their defeat was ultimately caused by the way the Nationalists had waged war.

To a large degree, the communist hostility towards irregular warfare was justified by its pragmatism. Even though the guerrilla expert, Walter Laqueur, wondered whether the government might have won on the strength of a concerted serious guerrilla effort, this question remains largely hypothetical.[20] The fact that Republican guerrilla activity peaked not during the war but in the months after the rebel victory demonstrates the reactive rather than proactive nature of a defeated side responding to extreme repression. The victorious rebels' pattern of extra-judicial executions (ironically dubbed the *ley de fugas*), marginalization, extortion and revenge killing of fugitives' relatives, cowed the civilian population and had the effect of severely limiting any voluntary assistance offered by villagers to the guerrillas.[21] The violent repression matched and even exceeded Espartero's punishment of Carlist 'wrongdoing' after 1839. The US journalist Thomas Hamilton noted in late-1939 that 'the road between Oviedo and León was too dangerous to travel at night. Finally, a brigade of Moors hunted them down. In the province of Pontevedra there were still more, and the provincial military governor finally had to issue a proclamation guaranteeing them against arrest if they would come down peacefully. It was a bitter blow to this honourable man that Franco had them killed or imprisoned all the same.'[22]

The violent repression after 1939 exceeded that of the government forces after 1839. Defeated Carlist officers were allowed by the Convention of Vergara to keep their swords, ranks and pay, as long as they swore to serve the Queen rather than the Pretender. In reality a generation of pardoned Carlists stagnated in their careers, being passed over for promotion by vindictive liberals. Yet the rank-and-file of the rebel army fared worst. They faced the grim choice to serve in appalling conditions of the reunified army or to be sent home without the right to any pension or, thanks to the economic devastation wrought on the rebel heartlands, much chance of a livelihood. The armaments foundries which had served the rebels were barred from contracts for the peacetime army, the customs frontier was shifted from the Ebro to the Pyrenees, punishing Carlist Navarra and Alava and rewarding Liberal Bilbao and San Sebastián. Throughout 1841 the newspapers related a surge in emigration from the northern ports to Cuba and the former colonies, as unhappy men and sometimes entire families chose exile, even indentured labour abroad, rather than remain as the vanquished of Liberal Spain.[23]

The victory celebrations of 1839 and 1939 could not have been more different. News of the Treaty of Vergara reached different parts of Spain according to the pace of horse/mule transport. Spontaneous celebrations, banquets and dances broke out in Madrid and all provincial capitals.

Many of these were prompted by town halls, but the enthusiasm soon swept celebration out of official hands, especially in Madrid where two weeks of festivities reigned. The Ateneo, restricted by its mission statement of solemnity, organized a donation for the war-wounded in hospitals. Donations were organized elsewhere for widows and wounded, and even some prisoners were rewarded with double rations.[24] News of the peace took days to reach other European capitals and the official note from the US secretary of state expressing his 'joy on behalf of the United States to learn of the end of the war in Spain' did not reach Madrid until six weeks later.[25] By this time the heady celebrations of August already seemed hollow due to Cabrera's refusal to recognise the Treaty and the subsequent continuation of the war in the east.

Franco on 1 April 1939, like Cabrera throughout the spring of 1840, was bedridden with flu brought on by exhaustion. Franco's peace, in contrast to 1839, met no popular enthusiasm in Spain, not even from Franco himself who issued the tersest telegram. Even though news flashed around the world now in minutes, only Franco's backers greeted the news. The nature of Franco's settlement was harsher than Espartero's. He kept more than a quarter of a million Republicans in a state of abject misery. As terror slackened from the late 1940s into mere repression, even pardoned prisoners faced vigilance by the state, controls on their movements and wide-ranging discrimination in terms of jobs and housing.[26]

Unlike after 1939, the victorious regime of 1839 had neither the means nor will to indoctrinate the population with a rigid narrative of the recent war. Because the 1840 settlement did not produce memories that were coerced by the victorious liberal state, veterans and victims expressed their experiences in eclectic ways: widows guarding their martyred menfolk's memory, cherishing images of Espartero as the people's war hero, hanging veterans' militia uniforms in a pride of place. All of these were more likely to be chosen by individuals or communities (unlike after 1939) and were therefore more likely to be accepted. Above all, the National Militia, flush with victory, enabled the triumph of the town-hall revolution of 1840, which raised Espartero to the regency. Even when Espartero turned against the revolution, veterans continued to lay public claim to their victory. When radical militia veterans presided over the 1841 exhumation of the massacred victims of the 1835 Carlist atrocity at Rubielos, they did so not just to remember these martyrs to liberty, but also to reaffirm the claim of the citizenry-in-arms to a stake in Spain's liberal future.[27]

A dynamic peace

Thanks to the morality of certain governments, rioting in Spain seems to have become a job like any other. We have no idea why it does not attract a state subsidy.[28]

Unlike Espartero, who had to ride the tiger of leftist grievances, Franco's regime managed to keep its rightist social support relatively united to withstand the resurgence of working-class protest. The two men shared some things in common and some major differences. Espartero has been largely forgotten. Francoists sidelined him for his liberalism, regionalists for his centralism and democrats for his authoritarianism.[29] Franco, by contrast, has been loathed and even loved by some, but has certainly not been forgotten.

Espartero's demise could hardly have been foreseen in the context of his hero status in 1840. Not only had he defeated the Carlists, but he had also captained the progresista revolution of September 1840 which defeated the moderado attempt to suppress the autonomy of town halls. Espartero even sent the queen-regent into exile after she committed herself against the popular cause. Hopes rose on the back of the elaborate peace celebrations. The well-travelled poet, Jacinto de Salas y Quiroga, championed a petition to the provisional government which demanded that 'this time the revolution should not be made by the many for the benefit of the few'.[30] Republican newspapers organized petitions demanding the redistribution of national property to veterans of the winning side and the institution of universal suffrage.[31] The Republican deputy Lorenzo Calvo y Mateo signed the manifesto on behalf of the 'Spanish nation', and demanded an end to the 'illegal' sale of *bienes nacionales*, which 'have been alienated without any public benefit' and should instead be handed over to 'the worthy defenders of liberty, both veterans and militiamen, as reward for their heroic community spirit'.[32]

But behind this 'peace dividend' revolution more prosaic forms of revolution were becoming visible. In Jaén, local progresistas tried to divert attention away from the issue of *reparto* by raising a crowd which chased the prefect out of town.[33] In a similar vein, when the prefect of Salamanca prevaricated over whether to resist or join the revolution, he marked himself out as a convenient target, and was thus forced to flee town in order to escape being lynched.[34] The main Madrid junta which had organized the town-hall revolution was dissolved with indecent haste. Two weeks later, the Republican newspaper *El Huracán* defiantly headlined with the demand for sales of disentailed lands to be halted.[35] By early October 1840, *El Huracán* complained of more backsliding on the revolution as militia veterans were demobilized across Spain as if they were mere lackeys.[36] Even so, General Espartero, the 'son of the people', retained enough political support to achieve in May 1841 the remarkable feat of becoming regent of Spain, less than two years after his civil-war victory, whereas Franco took eight years to manoeuvre himself into the same title. Espartero's politics were perhaps more mediocre than Franco's. 'Let the National Will be fulfilled!' (¡cúmplase la voluntad nacional!) was his abiding aphorism. In practice, this did not amount to much, for while the regent left progresista oligarchs to manage their politics, he had ears only for his inner clique of fellow ayacuchos, several of whom he rewarded with high office and lucrative monopolies while the rank-and-file of the army were left hungry and penniless.[37]

Unlike Franco, who ruled by the Grace of God rather than the will of the people, Espartero's fate was intimately linked to liberal public opinion. His fate was sealed by the popular leftist backlash in late 1841 following the regent's 'ungrateful' response to the defeat of a moderado coup attempt (the exiled court's October 1841 sponsorship of moderado military risings in Pamplona, Vitoria and even the Royal Palace in Madrid). Even though both progresistas and Republicans united in defence of the regime, thus aiding esparterista officers in their crushing of the rebellions, the response of the regime to this mobilization has been epitomized in the historiography as rank ingratitude.[38]

The rest of his subsequent regency was beset by rising support for republicanism and disaffection in the army. The unsatisfactory state of popular opinion, combined with the surfeit of wartime arms, meant that it was only a matter of time before the veterans turned against Espartero. One indignant war veteran complained: 'Was not the *pronunciamiento* of 1840 as heroic as that of 1835? Was it not as glorious as 1820? Did it not complete the revolution of 1836? We deserve admiration!'[39] Unlike General Franco, who made sure to starve his people rather than his army, General Espartero had neither the will nor the means to keep Spain as a military colony. In 1842, one progresista reflected on his party's growing animosity towards the Duke of Victory: '60,000 well-paid troops would be better than 140,000 in rags.'[40] Crucially, Espartero's fate was sealed by violent working-class revolution in Barcelona.

Red Barcelona, the industrial city which had been an inspiration to wartime radicals and diabolical to the Carlists, would now topple the Duke of Victory from power.[41] The spark came on the night of 13 November 1842, when a member of the *Tejedores* textile union defied soldiers posted at Barcelona's city gates who had wanted to search him. His arrest provoked some Republicans to take to the streets, whereupon these too were arrested. Now hundreds of armed militiamen and youths took to the streets to demand their release. Even though the army temporized by moving the prisoners to a militia barracks, this concession came too late, and the army was forced to pull out of the city, whereupon Barcelona was in rebellion for twenty days.[42] The first two days of the rising saw the militia come to the aid of the Republicans, as barricades were erected all over the city and some five hundred soldiers were killed in protracted skirmishes, insurgent casualties being considerably less. Even though troops in Montjuich at first held out, they had no supplies and were forced by sheer hunger to quit the city. However, with 'order' now restored by the revolutionary authorities, things started to go wrong. For the insurgent junta hoisted into power as president one Juan Manuel Carsy, an adventurous embezzler who had escaped prison in 1835, made for exile, and then returned to Catalonia after 1840 in order to ingratiate himself with a Republican rank-and-file eager to accept his credentials (Carsy probably reinvented himself as a political, rather than criminal, fugitive). If the movement thus seemed contaminated from the start, the junta nonetheless produced a popular programme: a multiple regency, Constituent Cortes and, most importantly, protection for national industry.[43]

Even if the streets of Barcelona were now in insurgent hands, only fraternal risings elsewhere in Spain could impose this programme on the government. Yet ongoing censorship of Republican newspapers in Spain prevented any risings, while even if some towns elsewhere in Catalonia rebelled, these proved too weak to withstand the government onslaught which ayacucho General Van Halen would now orchestrate. In the meantime, for two weeks Barcelona was steeped in a 'pork-barrel' revolution as the junta revived the militia, thereby providing wages for workers laid off by the free-trade crisis. Yet the relentless motto of the junta, 'union and constancy', proved ephemeral, as the wealthy classes, fearing that social revolution was afoot, dispatched agents provocateurs in an attempt to incite to mutiny the troops who had joined the rebellion. In fact, open class war was forestalled, as Van Halen marched a government army on the city, retook Montjuich and subjected the city to a bombardment which lasted thirty-six hours. While several militiamen stood their ground, the French Consulate brokered a deal which allowed for Carsy's escape to France in return for power being handed over to a conservative junta comprising the Bishop of Barcelona and several wealthy merchants and industrialists. This new junta received the entry into the city of government troops. An onerous tribute was imposed on the municipality and some 239 militiamen who had not fled their barricades were arrested and subjected to courts martial. While the Carsy junta was safely in exile, the rank-and-file were thus abandoned to their fate. The luckier ones were conscripted into carrying out reconstruction work on the hated Montjuich fortress. Thirteen of the insurgents were executed. Around half of these were former Carlist regulars, who were thus shot for being treacherous twice over.[44] The crackdown of 1842 had also fatally undermined *progresismo*. When Barcelona erupted again the following year, progresista elites would turn on the regent. In doing so they fell into the hands of the moderado counter-revolution. But they also secured the downfall of Espartero.

Given this context, it is hardly surprising that new radical forces were emerging; first and foremost, republicanism. Republicanism was organized both formally and clandestinely, or to put it another way, in both elections and secret societies. Regarding the former, Republicans triumphed in December 1841 municipal elections at Seville, Huelva, Valencia, San Sebastián, Teruel, Cádiz and, especially, Barcelona.[45] Adopting the 'social republic' model of *El Huracán* as a loose manifesto, Republican mayors often adopted 'pork-barrel' policies of reducing taxes for their electors, exempting them from the perennial burden of conscription, and taxing those who voted against them.[46] Espartero's suppression of the Republican press in October 1841 had the effect of channelling agitation towards secret societies. In 1842 a well-connected secret society called Confederation of Spanish Regenerators decried how the 'glorious revolutionary actions of September 1840 and October 1841 have served only to place on the absolute throne an arrogant and hypocritical soldier'.[47]

The Regenerators condemned both Espartero and the free trade policy foisted upon him by his wartime allies. Their manifesto, unlike all those of other secret societies during the recent war, was unequivocally democratic and republican, while its social liberalism advanced beyond subsidy of poorer members to the Anglophobic demand for 'protection for national industry'. Thus the British want to 'turn Iberia into a new India, have no principles beyond their own egotism, and want to keep us poor and ignorant so that we might work for them as slaves'.[48] In this invective the Regenerators were answering the main socio-economic grievance which ignited Barcelona's popular radicalism in 1842: Espartero's agreement to a British loan in return for the abolition of import tariffs on cotton imports. Even though free trade would have legally let in cheaper Lancashire cotton, thereby solving a major part of the contraband crisis in one fell swoop, the loss of the formally protected internal market would have spelt disaster for the Catalan industry, which on a level playing field could not have competed with the British.

Barcelona had been subdued but it erupted again in coordination with the moderado counter-revolution of 1843–44 led by General Narváez. He could command more than just the rank-and-file loyalties he had earned as commander of the Reserve Army; he could also be assured that the exiled *camarilla* of María Cristina was ready to bribe soldiers to desert the hero of 1840, or reward them with politically expedient promotions. For despite a renewed rising in Barcelona during the summer of 1843, it was fundamentally the army which swept Espartero from power. In this regard, it is important to show how the aftermath of the Carlist War left soldiers seething with discontent. Tangibly speaking, Spain was now awash with arms as the esparterista regime dared not demobilize the army fully, while even those soldiers and militia who were disbanded often concealed their muskets. Popular frustration rankled not just at the absence of reparto, but also at the legalism bestowed on property rights. The villages of Barajas el Melo and Huete (Cuenca) in 1842 were in conflict about customary rights to graze and forage. Huete imprisoned 'trespassers' from Barajas el Melo, and it took the intervention of the powerful local man, Fermín Caballero, editor of the radical *Eco del Comercio*, to secure the release of the foragers. The defeated mayor of Huete reminded Caballero that customary rights were 'a hangover from the time of absolutism to which one cannot go back'.[49]

In fact, 1843 and 1844 were witness to a culmination of events which saw no real popular defence of Espartero's regime. Former supporters defected to the moderado counter-revolution. One of Espartero's last desperate acts was to convene a government led by the radical progresista, Joaquín María

López, who, though bowing to army pressure by formally approving states of siege against insurgent juntas, nonetheless was eased out of office by the bulk of his own party which cynically tried to curry favour with Narváez.[50] López's replacement was the erstwhile street radical of the Triennium, Salustiano de Olózaga, who, though now shorn of his youthful idealism, yet maintained a modicum of decency which made him vulnerable in these cynical times. In brief, Olózaga was forced to resign amid a fallacious scandal that he had forced the hand of the young queen, the very symbol of liberty during the war, for the dissolution of the Cortes.[51] Olózaga was replaced by González Bravo, editor of the wartime democratic newspaper *El Guirigay*. González's credentials were a cover for the moderado 'dirty work' of dissolving the juntas which had risen against Espartero. Some of these, like the junta at Alicante, were repressed only after great bloodshed. Soon afterwards, González was sacked and replaced as prime minister by Espartero's great rival, General Narváez. The year before, on 30 July 1843, Espartero took ship at Cádiz for a British exile, thereby leaving Narváez the master of Spanish politics. He was banned from returning to Spain on pain of execution until an amnesty was passed in 1847.

In most respects the moderado counter-revolution of 1844 undid the plebeian gains of the First Carlist War. The National Militia was dissolved, as were the popularly elected town halls to which this force answered. From 1844 a new paramilitary force, the centralized Civil Guard, held sway. Sales of Church property were scaled back as part of the gradual *détente* with the Holy See, and in 1845 a new Constitution was proclaimed very much in the moderado image. A generation of veterans retained their social networks even though their poverty barred them from participating in the 'respectable' politics of the bourgeois era. Yet the country was exhausted and Spain lost its pivotal role in the European balance of power. The Revolutions of 1848 passed Spain by, just like the Second World War after 1939. The Marqués de Viluma, one of the most reactionary moderados, summed up the post-war era: 'Spain in 1846 is very different from 1836. The country is tired of revolts, abhors revolutions, and has suffered harsh disappointments.'[52] A foreign traveller visiting Spain in the wake of Espartero's fall commented on the ex-regent's role in this weariness:

> In the sliding scale of foiled ambition, which popular characters would do well to study, he fell from idolatry to enthusiasm, from enthusiasm to attachment, from attachment to respect, from respect to indifference, from indifference to contempt, from contempt to hatred, and from hatred he fell into the sea![53]

Whereas Espartero had sought to liberalize Spanish trade relations with Britain, Franco imposed a siege economy on a ravaged country. Francoist historian, Ricardo de la Cierva, claimed that autarky was a product of circumstance, namely the embargo placed on normal international trade during the Second World War.[54] More recently, however, historians have stressed that the ideological ascendancy of Falangism in the 1940s made an extreme autarkic economy inevitable regardless of the World War.[55] What is clear is that the extreme nutritional and material deprivation of 'Franco's peace' was a factor in the regime's survival. Unlike Franco, Espartero never attained complete domination of politics in the wake of his victory. Franco's grip on power rested on his army, but the emotional appeal of victory over the 'Anti-Spain' was of negligible interest compared to the material advantages offered to the winning side in a devastated economy. The army presided over an empire of corruption that extended to the dictator himself, as officers profited from black-market goods, brothels, smuggling and the abuse of scarce transport.[56] Similar corruption characterized Espartero's regime, as ayacucho cronies were awarded monopolies. Miguel Ors, a wealthy friend of the regent, in 1841 bought a monopoly to run the coast guard of the entire south coast, enriching himself even more with bribes from smugglers in the process.[57] Espartero's late-night card games in smoke-filled rooms became notorious for the jovial abandon with which the war-hero granted contracts to his favourites. Similarly, Franco spent his maturing years approving deals during rounds of golf and hunting trips with cronies. But the Duke of Victory did not enjoy a cowed population unwilling to protest. After 1939, however, even Catholic supporters of Franco were depressed at the state of Spain. José Taboada, Catholic leader of the clandestine fifth column in Madrid, emerged to face liberation and disappointment: 'I came to realise that the title "Crusade" was unfitting given the moral disaster ... the slightest disagreement was shouted down as "red" ... the masses were stripped of all spirituality and condemned to respond only to their basest material needs.'[58]

The vanquished half of Spain became outcasts in their own country, as Republican war-wounded, widows and dependents were denied pensions. Years of harsh imprisonment faced reds who were discovered to have even the remotest public relationship with the vanquished Popular Front parties. Public officeholders were dismissed to be replaced by sinecurists linked to the winning side.[59] Nationalist families could mourn their dead but Republicans could not. Remaining members of General Miaja's family in Oviedo were snubbed by a neighbouring family that had previously been on good terms, all because the neighbours had lost a son on the Nationalist side during the Battle of Teruel.[60] The food shortage degenerated into outright famine in 1942, a famine whose victims were almost exclusively Republicans. The gaols were full of political prisoners until the late-1940s and the working classes were forced by subsistence wages to shoulder the slow economic recovery. Even the Asturian miners, who had almost toppled governments in 1917 and 1934, could not shake the grip of the state. Their strike of 1962 was successfully met by force, the ageing Franco rebutting speculation that he was contemplating relinquishing power, reminding critics that his entire mandate rested on his victory against the 'Anti-Spain' in 1939.[61] None of this longevity compared with Espartero's plight after 1840. Espartero could expect no deference to his 1839 victory when he used force against the Barcelona radicals of 1842 and 1843. The left, after all, had won the Carlist War, and Carlist War veterans manning the working-class barricades on the Ramblas could hardly be termed the 'Anti-Spain'; indeed, Espartero himself better fitted that bill on account of his free-trade treaty.

Francoist army loyalty meant that the regime was unwound only after the dictator's death, in stark contrast to army relations after the First Carlist War when Espartero could not rely on army support for his dictatorship. As so much of Franco's victory was owed to the intervention of Hitler and Mussolini, his feat of remaining in power after the Second World War compares even more favourably. Espartero retained after 1840 the close support of Britain, the only global power, which supported Spain in an 1841 waterways dispute with Portugal,[62] yet Espartero lacked any compelling progressive vision equal to Franco's conservative – and rebarbative – vision of Spain. The unconditional surrender of the Republic and the systematic persecution of the vanquished created a binary memory of victors and vanquished, held in place by a dictatorship sworn to remove every trace of the victorious liberal constitutionalism of the first civil war. The degree of cultural repression exceeded anything imposed by the Cristinos after 1840. Even postage stamps, which traditionally bore neutral or positive images, after 1939 bore triumphalist iconography, an egregiousness which the victors of the nineteenth-century Carlist Wars had never shown.[63]

The defeated side in both civil wars was obliged to forge new bonds in exile with forces against which it had been opposed during the war. The clash and contradictions of ideology were evident at various intervals over the hundred years separating the Spanish Civil Wars. 'Montemolinista' Carlists, in despair at the scale of the defeat and repression of 1839, joined in a tactical alliance with Spanish Republicans in the 1840s. The abdication of Don Carlos was followed by the 'succession' of his son, Carlos Luis, whose manifesto of 1845 promised to heal the wounds of civil war by recognizing only Spaniards and no political parties: 'I will neither destroy all that the revolution had erected nor revive all that it destroyed.'[64] But the Carlist rising Montemolín unleashed had negligible Republican support and paled in comparison with the 1830s. The 1846–48 'War of the Early Risers', sometimes called a Second Carlist War, was confined almost entirely to rural Catalonia (where it is known as the 'Guerra dels Matiners'). Carlist guerrilla bands exploited the misery imposed by failed harvests. The burning of land-sale registers and invoices, combined with some resurgent 'social banditry' in the Serranía de Ronda, certainly showed some of the Carlist appeal of the 1830s. But General Narváez's disciplined regulars conducted a successful counter-insurgency, and the Republican efforts leading up to 1848 proved a damp squib.[65] Certainly, the defeated side managed a greater military effort during 1846–48 than the Spanish communist maquisards managed during their 1944 invasion of the Pyrenees. By early 1946 it was clear that the anti-Franco guerrilla campaign had failed.[66] For all the international intervention in both civil wars, the victorious regimes were safe from external aggression. This feature is all the more remarkable given that each war was shaped not just by the intervention of other powers, but also by crucial military and cultural factors in Spain's imperial adventures.

PART TWO

The international aspect of the Spanish Civil Wars

4

Imperial origins of the
Spanish Civil Wars

*My years in Africa live within me with indescribable force. There
was born the possibility of rescuing a great Spain. There was
founded the idea which today redeems us. Without Africa, I cannot
explain myself to myself or to my comrades-in-arms.*[1]

GENERAL FRANCO, 1938

Spanish monarchism entered a century of crisis as a result of the death of
Ferdinand VII in 1833. Of all the monarchs between 1833 and 1931, only
Alfonso XII ended his reign 'naturally', dying in 1885 of tuberculosis at
the age of twenty-seven. None of the Carlist pretenders sat on the throne,
and all other monarchs – María Cristina (1840), Regent Espartero (1843),
Isabel II (1868), Amadeo I (1873) and Alfonso XIII (1931) – were forced
to abdicate the throne due to the unworkable constitutional legacy of the
First Carlist War. This crisis reshaped a country which before Ferdinand VII
had traditionally been one of the most monarchical of European polities.
Empire and Catholicism were consubstantial with monarchy, Spaniards
have never executed their king, and in 1808 the abduction by Napoleon of
King Ferdinand was the casus belli for a national war.

The pre-war crises of Kings Ferdinand VII and Alfonso XIII were thus
bound to have profound consequences. The kings' personalities showed
differences: Ferdinand was vindictive, timid and mediocre, whereas Alfonso
was virile, militaristic and flamboyant. These differences may be attributed
to their births. Unlike Ferdinand, Alfonso was born a sovereign owing to the

death some months before of his father, whereas Ferdinand in his formative years battled against a royal favourite. As a consequence, Ferdinand was psychologically incapable for the rest of his reign of promoting too far any favourite. Ministers of both kings complained about their royal masters' cleverness for intrigue in personal audiences designed to undermine collective policy-making. This cleverness was not matched by much intellectual curiosity. Neither Ferdinand nor Alfonso read a book from cover to cover. Alfonso's first presidency of a cabinet meeting in 1902 set the disastrous tone for the rest of his majority when he prevented his ministers from reducing openings in the Spanish officer corps which was notoriously overstaffed with political appointees. His words of comfort to the rampaging army garrison in Barcelona in 1905 helped to stifle liberal opposition to the disastrous Law of Jurisdictions the following year. Alfonso repeated his contempt for civilian authority with his encouragement of the army mutinies of 1917. Most disastrously, his personal intervention in the counter-insurgency campaign in Morocco helped to lead General Silvestre into the deathtrap at Annual in 1921, resulting in the massacre of 10,000 Spanish soldiers.[2] Both Ferdinand and Alfonso also delegitimized themselves with their unpopular support for pre-war strongmen (Calomarde and Primo de Rivera), who for various reasons pleased neither militant sides of the Two Spains.

The impact of Ferdinand's failure was felt immediately after his death in 1833, in the form of a fugitive Carlist court declaring war on the 'illegitimate' regency of the royal widow and daughter in power in Madrid. Even though the First Carlist War would turn into much more than a war of succession, the dynastic dispute was its main trigger. The impact was felt eventually after Alfonso's forced exile in 1931, following five years of a republic. Opposition to the Republic was more heterogeneous than Carlist opposition to Cristino liberalism had been, and for this reason, full-blown civil war did not start until 1936. Whereas the 1830s saw a contest between two visions of monarchy, the 1930s saw monarchism as only one part – albeit, perhaps, the most natural part – of the right-wing alliance opposed to the Republic.

Both civil wars were products of lost imperial wars. In the first case, the Patriot Spanish victory in the Peninsular War in 1814 was marred by physical and financial devastation and a growing pro-independence insurgency in the American empire. The Spanish–American independence wars of 1810–25 provided economic and military causes for the First Carlist War. All Cristino commanders-in-chief of the Army of the North, except Marcelino Oráa, were connected to the American wars either through the direct combat of themselves or their close families or through the help Spanish–American agents had given to Spanish liberal conspiracies.[3] Of the thirty-one changes of war minister on the government side during the First Carlist War, on twelve occasions the office was filled by veterans of the Spanish–American independence wars, most of whom had served in Peru, the last bastion of American royalism to have fallen.[4]

The final diplomatic separation of Spain from mainland America came in the wake of the French invasion of 1823. British foreign secretary Canning, who had refused backing for the counterrevolutionary invasion, suspected France might try to turn Spain into a junior partner in French-dominated Europe like a century earlier. Thus Britain, which already had ample commercial interests in doing so, finally recognized the independence of Spanish America. Canning determined that 'even if France ends up controlling Spain, it will have to be a Spain minus its Americas'.[5] The de facto independence of mainland Spanish America following the 1824 Battle of Ayacucho bequeathed a depression in Spanish state finances which would not be overcome until the emergency wartime measures of Prime Minister Mendizábal. Whereas the economic impact of the second lost colonial war of 1898 was comparatively modest, its intellectual and cultural impact was profound. 'Regenerationism' prepared the ground for the overhaul of the constitutional system in place since the first civil war. The most powerful Regenerationists were right-wing authoritarians who used the 1898 defeat to construct a new imperial identity and ultimately in 1936 to retro-colonize Spain itself. Sugar-rich Cuba was the fulcrum of Spain's diminished nineteenth-century empire. The architect of late-nineteenth-century conservatism, Cánovas del Castillo, called Cuba 'Spain's Alsace-Lorraine'.[6] The Spanish empire's defeat in the Spanish–American War was blamed by repatriated army officers on the Spanish Liberals. Rightist officers attributed imperial defeat to the incompetence of the Liberal government, and to the treachery of Catalanism and socialism. An unholy trinity of liberalism, socialism and separatism emerged as the internal enemy in the minds of an officer corps buoyed up with the ersatz imperial mission in Spanish Morocco, a protectorate created in 1912 and 'pacified' by Primo de Rivera in 1927.

The loss of the greater part of the American empire in the early nineteenth century convinced Carlists of the illegitimacy of the liberal revolution. Yet despite its geographical vastness, the impact of this loss has not been studied in anything like as much detail as that of 1898.[7] Yet right-wing responses showed similarities. Ferdinand VII was convinced that the constitutional revolution of 1812 was 'the work of the machinations of those who desired to separate the Americas from the metropolis'.[8] The inability of the Spanish monarchy either to suppress the independence movements or to adapt to their outcomes has polarized historical debate. The neo-traditionalist 'Navarra school' saw 1814 as a fork in the road from which two irreconcilable visions of reform emerged among elites: 'renovation' versus 'innovation'. The Renovators were traditionalists who had signed the anti-liberal Manifesto of the 'Persians' whereas the Innovators were the Liberals expelled from their first spell in office.[9] In 'Restoration' Europe as a whole, these years witnessed great experimentation in political ideology, to the extent that Lucy Riall and David Laven have questioned the usefulness of such overarching terms as 'Progress' and 'Reaction'.[10] In Spain this experimentation was at its greatest because of persistent wars and ensuing economic crisis. The royalist insurgents of 1821–23 anticipated the Carlists not just in their violent rejection of constitutional rule but also in their unfocused resentment at economic decline. Even though the counter-revolution of 1823 tried to restore much of the old order, this was not entirely possible, and still less was it desired by the rural insurgents who had hailed God and the Faith alongside 'renovating' demands for access to the land and ownership of the harvest. Historians struggle to find vivas uttered in defence of feudalism and the tithe, however much liberals painted the rebels as priest-ridden dupes.[11] Equally, 'innovating' liberals in power between 1810–14, 1820–23 and after 1833 presided over unstable regimes which failed to achieve the contemporary shibboleth of 'liberty properly understood' (*libertad bien entendida*). Leftist liberals undermined state power with demands for local autonomy and property and tax reforms. Ultimately both ministerial and radical liberals were beholden to army officers they did not trust. The failure of the royalist armies in America confirmed liberals in their belief that regular war was not only ethically suspect but also ineffective unless imbued with a popular dimension.

Imperial failure in the Disaster of 1898 also influenced the crisis that led to renewed civil war. Spanish isolation and defeat in the war with the United States produced an unfocused revanchism in the Spanish army, for whom post-1898 separatism in Catalonia and expansionism in Morocco provided an explosive interaction. A new right emerged which seemed to offer Spain's traditional oligarchy the chance to re-launch Spain's imperial mission by modernizing its political structure and dismantling the corrupt liberal legacy of caciques. Joaquín Costa, a man whose radical politics at the end of the nineteenth century stood above the left versus right divide of the dynastic parties, was responsible for coining the term 'Regenerationism'. His ideas inspired the most prolific politician of the new right, Antonio Maura. Maura was a radical conservative from a liberal background. His ideas of 'revolution from above' aimed to overthrow the time-serving oligarchies of the *turno pacífico* parties and their caciques, using the prestige of the monarch and what he called the 'neutral masses', including the powerful Catholic middle classes, in order to do so. Maura opposed colonial expansion in Morocco and, unlike most conservatives, was a Francophile during the First World War. Despite this the effect of both Morocco and the First World War were plain to see in the Spanish Civil War. In office several times, his most concentrated attempts at reform came during his tenure lasting from January 1907 until October 1909. But in attempting to smash caciquismo Maura had to forge alliances with the powerful rightist – and cacique – Ricardo de la Cierva.

As Alejandro Quiroga has observed with regard to the rise of the new right, the post-1898 climate changed the discourse and social scope of Spanish nationalism. Ideologically, both the traditionalist and the liberal canons were reformulated. The former became increasingly martial, clerical, pan-Hispanic and anti-liberal, and developed a deep hostility towards peripheral nationalism and the organized working class. Political parties, intellectuals, the armed forces, conservative newspapers, and a plethora of organizations generally related to the Church, constructed a new Spanish nationalism in an imagined siege situation. The fact that these groups were unable to come together into a single party should not lead us to assume the absence of a Spanish political nationalism in the years that preceded Primo's dictatorship. Indeed most of the ideas that would eventually constitute the official ultra-nationalist discourse of the *primorriverista* regime were first formulated during the last years of the Restoration.[12] In particular, the 1917 army juntas crisis pitted the two tribes of the Spanish army in a contest which largely anticipated the war of 1936. The bureaucratic *peninsulares* (officers based in Spain whose promotion depended on length of service) saw their strike broken by the africanistas (Moroccan-based officers who won promotion on the battlefield). The most important man of the latter category was Francisco Franco. Franco spent ten years in Morocco, showing what his native *regulares* called 'baraka' (guts), and was remarkably wounded only once in a decade of campaigning during which he became Spain's youngest general (aged thirty-three).[13] During March 1917 Franco was posted to strike-torn Asturias where he got engaged to Carmen Polo.

Franco's rise to prominence was accompanied by the cultural and political growth of the 'new Right', which ultimately culminated in the dictatorship of Primo de Rivera in 1923. The bourgeoisie had increasingly been drawn to the idea of rule by an 'iron surgeon'. Proto-fascist agitation had been growing since 1898, focusing its appeal and support on the army, monarchy and (National) Catholicism. The Regenerationist 'Maura Youth' were accompanied by Catholic groups trying to re-evangelize society: in 1909 the ACNP (*Asociación Nacional de Propgandistas*) was formed and in 1917 the Social Catholic economic model was advanced in an interclass union of smallholders and large landowners aimed at halting the advance of the left in the countryside, the CNCA (*Confederación Nacional Católica Agraria*). Unlike during most of the nineteenth century, when Catholicism had stood apart from liberal nation-building, twentieth-century Spanish Catholicism became an agent in 'nationalizing Spaniards'. But the working class and the regionalist middle classes had their own ideas, and the gap between the 'official' and 'real' Spain grew to its greatest extent with the Primo de Rivera coup.[14]

The pan-Hispanism which had been growing in the wake of 1898 inspired Primo's imperial mission as traditionalists mobilized myths of 'heroic' Spanish colonialism to advocate a forward policy in Morocco and to reconstruct a sort of 'moral empire' over Spanish-speaking republics in the Americas. For all of Primo's enthusiasm, the Madrid legation of Revolutionary Mexico in the 1920s was in fact a haven for Spaniards opposed to his regime.[15] This 'spiritual expansion' had been in train before Primo seized power, and was associated with the ideologue of the Carlist movement, Vázquez de Mella, whose 1915 book, *El Ideal de España*, came out at the same time as Juderías's *La Leyenda Negra*, the latter defending a conspiratorial thesis of the outside world having undermined Spanish influence. In 1918 the Maura government made 12 October the 'Day of the Race' in honour of Columbus's 'discovery' of America. This came at the peak of a 'monumentalist' fever mirroring France and Germany, but unlike the 'Bismarck statues' of the Kaiserreich, Spanish heroes were immortalized in granite and marble, including heroines: Agustina de Aragón was honoured with a statue in Zaragoza in 1908 with Catholic overtones.[16] The Church at the turn of the twentieth century contained much rank-and-file that sympathized with the Carlist movement. A 'moderate' Catholic party (Unión Católica) had joined the Conservative Party in 1883. This inspired an anti-liberal Integrist movement which flourished until the 'accidentalist' Pope Leo XIII applied pressure to dissolve it in the early 1900s.[17]

Pan-Hispanism targeted not just the former empire but also separatism within Spain. Primo's coup was preceded by the 10 September 1923 meeting of Catalan, Basque and Galician nationalists in Barcelona who 'insulted' the army and the fatherland with cheers for the Rif rebels; the following day, the coup happened.[18] Thirteen years later some of the same officers were involved in the coup which produced the Spanish Civil War. Such was the hatred for separatism among the rebels that even Basque and Catalan religious were suspect. Once state clericalism fell into abeyance in the wake of the Republic of 1931, the minority Social Catholic and regionalist trend among Basque and Catalan clergy became more evident. When Nationalist refugees from Catalonia and the Basque country fled Republican Spain in 1936, they were frequently received with suspicion in Castile.[19] The inverse had been true in the 1830s, when 'Castilian' refugees (non-Basque Carlists) escaped to the Basque country.

The legacy of pan-Hispanism bestowed a great irony on 1936. The rebels' 'Reconquest' of Spain was launched not from the north of Spain, as according to eighth-century legend of Covadonga, nor even solely from Catholic Navarra as in 1833, but from Muslim Africa, the springboard of the medieval Islamic conquest of Christian Iberia. The Spanish presence in northern Morocco had expanded and been formalized by the 1906 Treaty of Algeciras, and the Protectorate quickly became a focus for class warfare in Spain itself when in 1909 the Spanish government called up conscripts in Barcelona to defend threatened mining interests against Moroccan rebellion. The response of anarchists and radicals was the 'Tragic Week' of revolution and government counter-revolution whose features were a microcosm of the 1930s war. Before the advent of the Protectorate, Spanish colonial interests in Morocco had centred on the centuries-long possession of garrison towns, mainly Ceuta, Tetuán and Melilla, as well as islands (Alhucemas, Perejil) looming closely off the African coast. The Spanish African enclaves played a significant role in the First Carlist War. The garrisons were populated by Carlist prisoners, some of whom were granted limited freedom in return for bearing arms against the forces of Emir Abd-el Kadr, whose protracted campaign against the French on occasion threatened Spanish outposts. The Spanish counter-revolution of 1837 transported to Alhucemas, Ceuta and Melilla hundreds of left-wing radicals active in the press and militia the following year. A defiant progresista press campaign made heroes out of these transportees, and in a development even worse for the moderado government, publicised the successes of Carlists and exaltados, supposedly unlikely bedfellows, in overwhelming government guards and seizing control of fortified centres.[20] The need for punitive expeditions sometimes placed the government in an embarrassing diplomatic predicament. The Carlist rebellion at the garrison-colony at Alhucemas in March 1839 caused a diplomatic crisis as the French warship stationed off Málaga refused to join Cristino and British warships in a punitive expedition, its captain citing French 'neutrality' in the Spanish civil war. The Cristino ambassador to France, Count Miraflores, complained, the French captain was replaced, and orders were issued by the incoming (and pro-interventionist) French premier, Thiers, that French vessels should forthwith abide by the Quadruple Alliance.[21]

A century later found Franco–Spanish cooperation united against the mutual enemy of Moroccan nationalism. The 1920s Spanish dictator, Primo de Rivera, allowed himself to be persuaded by his africanista army to reconquer the Protectorate which had been all but lost as a consequence of the 1921 defeat at Annual. His 1924 Rifean offensive led to a decisive victory in 1925 following an amphibious landing at Alhucemas Bay. The Moroccan nationalists, whom 1830s Spaniards orientalized as 'barbaric' Moors, were still demonized as barbaric one hundred years later. But right-wing paranoia amongst the africanistas now suspected an 'Islamic–Bolshevist' military threat to Spain's major colony. Primo's victory thus produced adulations comparing him to great military leaders, even to Napoleon.[22] Primo's conservative authoritarianism was in many ways shared by his French counter-insurgent opposite number, Marshal Pétain, in the larger French part of Morocco. Primo de Rivera encouraged adulations of the Frenchman, and indeed, Pétain was idolized by Spaniards who called him the 'saviour of his fatherland', and 'the Messiah who carries the sun of justice in his right hand in order to illuminate the beloved Spanish soil'.[23] Franco–Spanish collaboration in twentieth-century North Africa was more consistent than in the 1830s, when the March 1839 crisis symbolized the real fractures in Franco–Spanish relations.

Primo's reconquest turned Spanish Morocco into the biggest training-ground for the best part of the Spanish army, the regulares and their Moroccan mercenaries. The Spanish Civil War socialist Arturo Barea had spent his youth doing his military service in the Protectorate and was impressed with how the authoritarian right-wing culture of the army thrived alongside a multi-religious environment, in which a barracks sporting an altar at Xauen was flanked by a mosque on one side and a synagogue on the other: 'It was as if Medieval Spain had been reborn and lay before my eyes.'[24] The most important non-Spanish force under Franco's command were the Moors. Although the Moorish recruits were brutalized and exploited by africanistas, Seidman has recently shown Franco's policy in the Protectorate to have been far more sophisticated, a form of multiculturalism *avant la lettre*, complete with cultural understanding and religious accommodation.[25] The Nationalists' control of Morocco also gave them the advantage of training large units together, giving officers and men time to create cohesion and trust, vital assets in war.[26] Franco admitted in a 1938 interview that his African experience had taught him everything about his 'mission' to rescue Spain.[27]

The political repercussions of colonial wars on domestic politics has been observed in other European countries, yet until the research of Sebastian Balfour, comparatively few studies had been done in respect of Spanish Morocco, even though its impact was greater on Spain than other colonial wars were on other European metropoles, and the fighting was probably the most savage of all.[28] The terror that the imperial army inflicted on Spanish reds after July 1936 formed what Paul Preston has called an 'investment in terror' which yielded the victors such long-term dividend of apathy, fear and trauma among the defeated populace.[29] The Spanish–American context of the First Carlist War is also clearly marked yet little studied.[30] Both sides in the 1830s civil war were led by imperial veterans of the lost American wars, and both were brutalized by their experiences accordingly. Imperial controversies overshadowed subsequent civil wars in Spain itself. The Ayacucho clan learnt a contempt for civilian politicians during the 1830s and in 1839 made peace over the heads of their respective governments. Equally, the 1930s Africanist officers drew a sinister lesson about civilian politics. Also, both the brutalizing effects of the war in Spanish America and later conflict in Morocco dictated many of the tactics of insurgent army officers and men.

The first civil war was a product of the political collapse of the worldwide Spanish monarchy. For a long time, historians blamed the intransigence of Spanish absolutism for the dissolution of the worldwide Spanish monarchy. But Carlists in the 1830s bitterly protested the 'usurping' government's recognition of Spanish American independence. Even though the formal reconquest of the Americas was both a military and diplomatic impossibility after 1836, the American question continued to shape the traditionalist world view in a manner obvious to contemporaries. US annexationist interests towards Cuba were stirred for the first time by the Carlist War. Former president John Quincy Adams declared that 'Spain is locked in a cruel civil war and cannot protect Cuba. Either the island will join with the USA or it will come under the protection of British seapower.'[31] When Captain-General Tacón placed Cuba's coasts under blockade in response to General Lorenzo's revolt, the US government protested strongly.[32] Madrid's rule on the island had to contend not just with liberal revolts but also with the machinations of the Carlists, including the pro-rebel Archbishop of Cuba (who was expelled) and agents charged with stoking up sedition in the colony. The war-winning potential of Cuban turmoil were obvious. The slave plantations of Cuba were vital to the government war effort, accounting for some 15 per cent of state revenue. The booming 1830s sugar price and the advent of steam-powered technology created ideal conditions for a resurgence in Spain's slavery empire, strengthening resistance to abolitionism, despite the vocal minority of left-wing abolitionists in the 1836–37 revolutionary Cortes.[33]

The Spanish–American war of 1898, which removed Spain's last vestiges of empire in the Americas, was partly caused by the fear of a Carlist rebellion in the event of bloodless surrender to Yankee imperialism.[34] A best-selling novelist embedded Carlist revanchism into his 1902 novel *Sarita the Carlist*, whose protagonists identify Spain's propensity to civil war as stemming from 'unsettled relations with America'.[35] The imperialist image of Spain barely shifted in Latin America until the Spanish Civil War recast the country as a battleground between democracy and authoritarianism. The Mexican academic, Andrés Iduarte, saw the Republic's fight as the democratic redemption of Latin America's colonial 'stepmotherland': 'Death to the *gachupines* (Spanish imperialists) and long live the true Spaniards!'[36]

The 'true Spaniards' had never really been estranged. The divorce between America and the Peninsula was hardly pre-ordained. The American juntas of 1808 sprang up in the name of Ferdinand VII, and even though both Spain and its former American territories eventually separated from one another, the newly independent nations remained linked by a common Hispanic culture, religion, demographics and constitutional heritage.[37] Anticlericalism in both Spain and her former Americas created the diplomatic and ideological conditions for the First Carlist War. From 1831, the very conservative Pope Gregory XVI managed to displease both Spanish Liberals and Carlists by re-opening de facto if not yet de jure ecclesiastical relations with the Latin American states, a process which gradually led to the filling of bishops' sees which had been vacant because of the unresolved question of the rights of appointment associated with the now defunct *patronato real*. Mexico was the wealthiest of Spain's former dominions. Repeated royalist attempts during the 1820s to recapture Mexico for the Spanish Crown had centred on invasion forces from Cuba and an influential Spanish minority of merchants and priests within Mexico itself. The Mexican authorities issued a series of expulsion orders for resident Spaniards, culminating in 1833 with the expulsion of the entire Spanish regular clergy from Mexico.[38] Repatriated clerics were doubly confirmed in their hostility to liberal revolution, and it was no wonder that clerics provided decisive moral leadership to Carlists after 1833, not least because they were typically the only educated men in regular contact with villagers in the Carlist Basque country.[39] When Spain's radical–liberal revolution of 1835–36 recognized the Spanish American republics, the Carlist press called this the perverse consequence of illegitimate revolution in Spain itself.[40]

Spanish Liberals, by contrast, drew a very different conclusion from the loss of America. In the wake of Spain's counter-revolution of 1823 and defeat in Peru the following year, one of the leading liberal exiles, Alvaro Flórez Estrada, had abandoned hopes to reunite the Hispanic world via the Constitution of 1812, and instead urged that efforts be concentrated on resurrecting liberal revolution inside Spain. The exiles' leader, Peninsular War hero Francisco Espoz y Mina, accepted this strategy. Whereas in 1817 he had condemned the emancipation mission to Mexico of his adoptive nephew, Xavier Mina, after 1823 Espoz actively explored opportunities to enlist Latin American support for the Spanish exiles. When Espoz met a Mexican representative in London, he agreed that Spain should recognize Latin American independence on mutually beneficial terms and that the best path towards this would be for the Spanish–Americans to help the exiles with money in order to fund renewed liberal revolution in Spain. In the event, the Mexican government gave fraternal blessings but no money.[41]

In lieu of money the Spanish Liberals turned their military and political experiences in Spanish America to good effect. Repatriated Spanish Liberals were quick to apply their American experiences to the First Carlist War. The struggle between independents and royalists quickly evolved into guerrilla warfare par excellence as sparse demographic and economic resources prohibited the maintenance of large regular armies. Whereas the ayacuchos learnt counter-insurgency tactics in America which they later applied against Carlists, civilian returnees from American independence wars also shaped Carlist War politics. Eugenio de Aviraneta and Ramón Ceruti had been bitter enemies in 1820s Mexico. Both men were Liberals, but whereas it had taken Aviraneta his participation in the last Spanish invasion of Mexico (the Barradas expedition of 1829) to realize the futility of reuniting the empire, Ceruti, the Spanish refugee of 1823, had turned himself into a Mexican federalist and anti-Spanish nativist soon after setting foot in the Americas. Both men later exercised public roles during the Carlist War, Ceruti in a series of regional governorships, Aviraneta as the chief espionage and counter-espionage leader of the Cristino war effort. Even though Cristino Spain finally recognized Mexican independence in 1836, post-imperial patriotism limited Ceruti's career in Spain once news spread of his history of distasteful nativist activities in Mexico.[42]

Even though the 1830s liberal revolution set in train the eventual recognition by Spain of the independence of its former colonies on the Spanish–American mainland, the brutality of the independence wars marked Spanish veterans with an instinctive anti-*criollismo*. The British ambassador promoting reconciliation discovered ironically that 'it is among Liberals that the greatest suspicion toward the independence of the former colonies is to be found'.[43] Part of this attitude lay in the belief of peninsulares that Spanish rule had been beneficial to the indigenous Americans and that the historical example of miscegenation proved the 'softness' of Spain's empire when compared to the overbearing British.[44] This belief survived into the 1930s war when the pro-Nationalist historian Jesús Casariego asserted that the sixteenth-century Catholic monarchy protected the rights of the American indigenous whereas 'Anglo-Saxon imperialists exterminated whole races even while they preached the philanthropic principles of liberalism'.[45]

Once Spanish Liberals accepted the loss of America, there was nothing left to divide them from their Latin American counterparts. Liberals on both sides of the Hispanic Atlantic shared hostility to the immense corporate power of the Catholic Church. The breakthrough of radical liberalism in newly independent Mexico was accompanied by the new state's first exercise in anticlericalism. The secularizing measures of the Gómez Farías administration during 1832–35 pre-empted those of the Cristino Liberals in Spain itself after 1835. Clerical opposition in both successor states showed remarkable similarities. Once the cholera pandemic reached Mexico in 1832, conservatives called the malady 'divine punishment'.[46] In the same manner, Spanish clerics spoke of the cholera as a 'plague of wickedness for Spain's sins'.[47] But whereas the Gómez Farías administration had to fight only a brief (albeit bloody) civil war against clerical opposition in Mexico, in Spain the contest was lengthier and bloodier. The reason for this was in part because the Carlists, too, had learnt military and moral tactics from the loss of America.

Both civil wars were won by officers whose experience was forged fighting lost causes of Spanish imperialism. In the 1830s civil war, these were 'Ayacuchos' (so named after the place of definitive defeat in 1824 of Spanish imperialism on the Spanish–American mainland); in the 1930s civil war these were 'africanistas' (so named for their experience fighting in Spain's post-1898 replacement empire in Morocco). Both types were brutalized by their colonial fighting and brutal in the way they applied this to the 'enemy within' in the civil wars. As a consequence, both types also developed a charismatic high-handedness towards civilian constituted authority. A prosopographical study of both groups shows how their imperial combat experiences shaped their views independently of the causes and institutions for which they fought. In 1839, ayacuchos who were leading both opposing armies in the civil war made peace over the heads of their respective governments. In the 1930s, africanistas were almost entirely on one side of the struggle, the victorious Nationalist side. The victors of the civil wars, Ayacucho Generalísimo Espartero and africanista Generalísimo Franco, both drew admiration from their soldiers for their demonstrations of physical bravery in colonial campaigns.[48] The civil wars found them with armies under their command which differed in terms of their quality. Whereas an obituary remarked that Espartero 'managed to defeat a good army with a bad one', the same could not be said of Franco (who admittedly faced an opponent of similar size).[49] The men are also similar in the way that they crowned their victories by making themselves regent of Spain. Just as Napoleon had used his army to control France's destiny, so did Espartero in 1840 and, with greater effect, Franco in 1939. This plebeian assumption of monarchical power points to a wider crisis of legitimate monarchy at both key stages in Spanish history. Franco's powers exceeded any Spanish ruler since Ferdinand VII, the king whose death triggered the First Carlist War.[50] Even though Franco's fellow officers correctly predicted that their leader, as a true africanista, would never willingly relinquish power,[51] they failed to dislodge him. Unlike Espartero, Franco managed to cling onto dictatorial powers until his natural death.

The imperial origins of the civil wars also include such intangibles as the use of language. Modern Spanish expressions are littered with unflattering orientalisms born of imperialism. Spanish expressions orientalized colonial cultures pejoratively. Catholics dubbed unbaptized children 'Moors' in reference to the conflict between Muslims and Christians in Medieval Spain.[52] Arch-Catholics (Integristas) of the 1930s dubbed lapsed Catholics 'mestizos'.[53] The celebrated 'Great Man' writer of the early twentieth century, Pío Baroja, called Latin America the 'stupid continent'; certainly the indigenous of the ex-Spanish empire in the New World supplied the Spaniards with a stereotype of stupidity that was reflected in the common phrase *hacer el indio*, or 'to pass for an idiot'.[54] There was nothing novel in a European context for Spanish culture to orientalize colonial cultures in a pejorative manner. But what was different in Spain was that racial slurs did not just describe discourse but also violence. After the Castilblanco incident of December 1931 (the group lynching by villagers of a trigger-happy Civil Guard detachment), the Civil Guard director, General Sanjurjo, compared the villagers to Riffian rebels. The Moderate Socialist leader of the Asturian Miners' Union remembered the 'African hatred' unleashed by government forces against insurgent miners in October 1934.[55] Racial slurs were also common in the 1830s conflict: Carlists were dubbed 'caribes' (indigenous Caribbeans), although Carlist dubbing of Liberals as blacks ('negros') related to their 'black souls'. The term 'negro' took on a different meaning in the 1930s, however. 'Negro' became shorthand for 'fascist', and 'red' became a term of endearment. Government officer cadets were instructed that whereas 'black' represented fascism, 'red' (*rojo*) represented 'life and the Republic'.[56]

The 1830s military strategy was informed by first-hand experience of imperial wars in Latin America. In an indirect fashion, Latin America retained its importance even for the 1930s rebel campaign. Many German advisers to the Nationalists learnt Spanish far better than the Soviet advisers on the government side because of their activities advising South American armies during the era of the Weimar Republic.[57] But the Latin American origins of the First Carlist War were far more direct. Leading generals like Valdés, Canterac, Rodil, Serna and Camba had fought 'pauper's wars' in Spanish America where the underdeveloped infrastructure and patchy population did not permit the operation of large or even medium-sized armies. Spanish America was guerrilla country par excellence, where taboos of plunder and other outrages were more relaxed than in Europe. The greatest pitched battle of the Spanish–American Independence Wars gave the First Carlist War clique its name. The 1824 Battle of Ayacucho (Peru) fielded only 15,000 combatants on both sides. The small-scale irregular warfare in the Americas prepared the Ayacuchos for successful campaigning against Carlists. Gerónimo Valdés pacified Catalonia in 1834, having adopted counter-insurgency tactics he had learned in Peru. American experience had also taught returned officers to understand the complexities of discipline, morale and primary group cohesion among their men.[58]

These imperial lessons were not confined to Spanish participants in the First Carlist War. The apologist for slavery, George Dawson Flinter, was an Irish-born British Army officer posted to the Caribbean during 1810–19. Ingratiating himself with the cause of royalism in Spanish America, Flinter returned to Europe in 1819 in a bid to frustrate Bolivarian attempts to recruit British and Irish mercenaries for the cause of American independence. Returning to Venezuela as a naturalized Spaniard, Flinter married into Creole royalist plantocracy, but the victory of the Bolivarians persuaded him to retreat in 1829 to Puerto Rico, an island which along with Cuba was the last bastion of Spanish royalism in the Americas. After publishing an apologia in defence of the 'humane' system of slavery Spain defiantly administered in the Carribbean, civil war in his adopted home country allowed Flinter to achieve one of his long-term aims of obtaining a colonelcy in the government army. After an uneventful two years in Extremadura, Flinter in 1836 was promoted to lead a new force of counter-insurgents in New Castile whom the rebels dubbed *peseteros* ('money-whores'), on account of the rather desperate motivations and attire of Flinter's men. But Flinter applied his first-hand knowledge of the American wars to good effect, organizing a counter-insurgency which achieved more successes against local terrain and conditions than the garrison-bound government militia.[59]

In other instances, imperial veterans applied the wrong military lessons of empire. The last rebel offensive against Madrid was led in March 1937 by Mussolini's *Corpo Truppe Volontarie* at the Battle of Guadalajara. Initial gains led the Italians to abandon all normal precautions, as if the campaign was set to be a walkover like their 1935 invasion of Ethiopia. Franz Borkenau reported: 'After their initial successes the Italians lost all control over themselves. Drunk with the glory of their easy victories in Ethiopia … they dropped every precaution … denuding their flanks, grouping reinforcements on the main roads, drawing their staffs very near the advancing front line. According to all rules of reasonable warfare, it was madness.'[60] The Italians were checked and then pushed back to their starting lines in no small measure thanks to that rarest of phenomena in the Spanish Civil War, a devastating government air strike against an enemy column.[61]

If Ethiopia had taught the Italians to be arrogant, at the other extreme, the war against Spanish–American independence had taught the Cristino

General Ramón Rodil to be overcautious. Rodil had distinguished himself in his dogged defence of the Peruvian port of Callao, the last South American bastion of royalism to fall in 1826. Rodil's American experience had suited him well during his four-month command of the Army of the North in 1834. Copying the brutally effective counter-insurgency of Spanish America, Rodil burned crops, executed Carlist mayors and evicted families thought to have sheltered rebels.[62] But as minister of war presiding over the defence of Madrid in 1836, Rodil was much criticized for applying Callao-style tactics. His refusal to mount mobile counter-insurgency operations against the Gómez expedition, and his resort to a defence in depth, seemed a grossly inappropriate answer to an invasion by a few thousand Carlists. Worse, Rodil's bombastic rhetoric of liberal defence did not translate into reinforcement of sensitive targets. The famous mercury mines of Almadén (Ciudad Real) had been leased in 1835 to the Rothschild bank by a Spanish government desperate for finance. Gómez's capture of Almadén in October 1836 led to the capture of Flinter and the resignation of Rodil amid much national and international controversy. Flinter managed to escape captivity but would end up taking his own life in 1838. The disgraced General Rodil fled to Portugal ahead of demands from the revolutionary Cortes for an example to be made of his 'treachery'.[63] Ambassador Villiers never forgave Rodil for the damage he did to British interests. Villiers needed little convincing that Rodil's sulky Lisbon manifestoes were a cover for a march on Madrid comprising prisoners and disgraced members of the Royal Guard whom Gómez had defeated on the approaches to the capital.[64] In the end, Rodil did not march, and Villiers's side won the civil war, thanks largely to the military skill of the most famous ayacucho, Baldomero Espartero, commander-in-chief from 1837, and thanks to unrelenting British military aid. But the outcome had long been in the balance, and not just because of Spain's own imperial legacy, but also because Spain in the 1830s – and again in the 1930s – was a battleground of international power politics.

5

World wars in miniature

Foreigners intervened in the Seven Years War (1833–40) just as they are doing now. France and England clamoured to aid the liberal, democratic regime then. They gave that regime all manner of assistance. They organised the first International Brigades who came to fight us on land while the English fleet bombarded our lines around Bilbao and supplied that besieged city ... We Carlists stood alone, for liberalism pervaded Europe and not even the good-natured Chancellor Metternich was able to drive out the scourge of Freemasonry and corrupted materialist rationalism ... Now National Spain has counted from the first day of our Crusade with the sympathy and inspiration of the Nazis and Fascists. They understand why we fight. But back then we stood quite alone.[1]

Historically, European civil wars had always been to varying degrees international. The Thirty Years War (1618–48) was both a devastating civil war for Germany and an international struggle of European states bent on weakening Habsburg power. The 1640 revolt of the Portuguese and Catalans against Castilian rule could be classed as both national war and Iberian Civil War, and the overlapping nature of civil and international war was even plainer during the War of Spanish Succession (1701–14). But in the wake of the trauma of the Napoleonic and Great Wars, the diplomatic consensus condemned wars unless they were 'defensive' in nature. Both the Vienna settlement of 1815 and the League of Nations settlement of 1919 envisaged the collective security of strong states which would make formal military intervention in other countries' affairs a last resort. In reality, these hopes had decidedly limited outcomes. As Lawrence Freedman has observed, the attempts in both 1815 and 1919 to establish international consensus following the defeat of a dominant ideology foundered as soon as 'new ideological faultlines opened up'.[2] This rendered conditional the principle of non-intervention in internal affairs. In the words of Paul Schroeder, 'for purposes of international politics, the term "restoration" simply does not fit the Vienna settlement at all'.[3] Spain was an ideological fault line in both epochs which showed that nothing was really restored or settled.

Hugh Thomas referred to the Spanish Civil War as a world war in miniature, and Romero Salvadó called it a 'great distorting mirror' for international conflict. The international participation in the Spanish Civil War is so well known as to have become almost folklore. The international dimension to the First Carlist War, by contrast, is known only to specialists. The 1830s war was in many ways a mirror opposite of the 1930s: the liberal powers of Progress intervened while the powers of Reaction were constrained into honouring Non-Intervention. The cause of Liberty prevailed in large part thanks to the support of the Liberal Atlantic, unlike in the 1930s. The 1930s international brigaders were lauded as heroes of the last great cause; their counterparts a hundred years earlier, by contrast, were vilified, for complex reasons, partly related to the unheroic success of their home government's foreign policies. Both civil wars have attracted writers identifying with the losing side. This state of affairs also pertains to foreign scholarship, particularly in the case of the 1930s war. The defeat of legitimacy in the 1830s and then of democracy in the 1930s energized indignant foreign writers and in the process reaffirmed the degree to which foreign intervention shaped each civil war. Whereas 1930s democratic powers observed 'Non-Intervention' to the detriment of the progressive side, Europe's Fascist powers provided full support to the Nationalists short of a formal alliance. This aspect is crucial because both civil wars were won by the side with the greatest foreign intervention. The 1930s war therefore deserves comparison with the lesser-known international impact of the 1830s war.

Any analysis of international intervention in Spain must begin with an overview of the fateful 1930s. Romero Salvadó's concise analysis of the European powers' respective approaches to the Spanish Civil War offers us a pithy synthesis from the point of view of supporters of the Republic: the United Kingdom was bad, France paralysed, Germany evil, Italy and Portugal evil but generous, the USSR pragmatic, and Mexico good but ineffective. The moral and ideological motives behind international history scholarship for long clouded detailed study of the actual extent and impact of foreign intervention. But Gerald Howson's revisionist account from 1999 dispelled the Nationalist myth that the Republicans received far more foreign intervention than Franco. In fact, the Anglo–American arms embargo was so effective that Republican agents had to turn to the vagaries

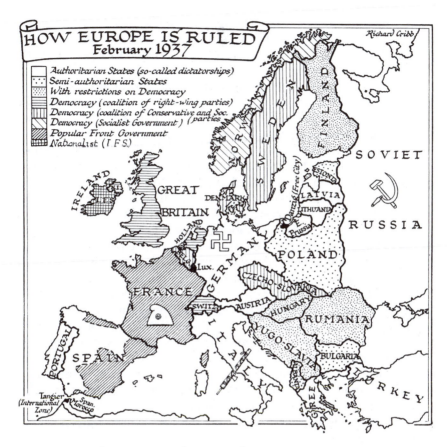

FIGURE 5.1 *The uniqueness of Spain's civil war in 1930s Europe (Getty Images).*

of the international illegal arms market, and even the gold reserves delivered to the Soviets paid for little better than junk. Given that the Republic had to compensate with foreign purchases for its technical inferiority in July 1936, Howson argued that the arms embargo was the decisive cause of the Republic's defeat.[4] But Howson's thesis fails to account for the Spanish context in which the arms were used. International commentators were aware of the Republic's poor war effort: General Gamelin in 1938 knew any formal French arms supplies would end up having little effect due to Republican inepitude.[5]

Debates about international intervention in the Spanish Civil War reflect the scholarly consensus that Spain was pivotal in the European Civil War. Yet Spain, of course, was a belligerent in neither the First nor the Second World Wars. By contrast, Spain in the 1830s had experienced two generations of almost uninterrupted war, beginning with Napoleon and ending with the Spanish–American wars which would not formally end until

1836. Moreover, 1930s commentators were at the very least ambivalent about the war's international cause. Those who saw the hand of Hitler or Stalin were themselves policy-makers and protagonists playing to the international gallery of public opinion, impressed by the danger that Spain's war might unleash a global conflagration. In this spirit, foreign side-takers were reluctant to describe Spain's conflict as the civil war it really was. The anti-appeasement Member of Parliament Katharine Atholl stressed foreign fascists' role in Spain's 'so-called "civil War"'.[6] Foreign volunteers accepted that a 'people's war' was being waged in Spain against fascism. A British communist charged that 'Spaniards were the first people to stand up to Hitler and Mussolini'.[7] Canadian medical volunteer Norman Bethune thought, 'If we don't stop them (the fascists) in Spain, they'll turn the world into a slaughterhouse.'[8] Long-serving British Brigade volunteer Walter Gregory wrote home that 'We are facing Moorish infantry, German machine-gunners and aeroplanes, Italian tanks. Oh yes, we also have a few Spanish fascists.'[9] The American folk-singer and activist Pete Seeger began his foreword to a study of American volunteers in stark terms: 'The Spanish Civil War ended in 1939, but it will go down in history as the first battle of World War II.'[10] Spanish Republicans also highlighted the international nature of the war in order to protest Western democracies' Non-Intervention. In 1940, the anarchist Abad de Santillán attributed the recent defeat of the Republic to three factors: government centralization against Catalonia, the democracies' Non-Intervention policy and Stalin's treachery, namely two-thirds international.[11] The onset of the Second World War five months after the end of the Spanish Civil War vindicated progressive voices from Spain and the world which protested that the struggle against 'fascism' should have been a concerted effort.

But this narrative puts the teleological cart before the contingent horse. There *were* civil wars in Europe which had international origins – the Yugoslav and Greek civil wars of the 1940s – but the Spanish Civil War was not among them, however quick foreign powers were to plot beforehand and to intervene once the civil war had broken out.[12] While no foreigner present in Spain in 1936 could have been oblivious to the global extremes of fascism and communism, only a highly selective reading of their writings can reveal the hand of Hitler and Stalin throughout, and with good reason. Mussolini was frustrated by his subordination to Franco's strategy of attritional warfare which denied his forces in Spain the opportunity for a dynamic victory consistent with Fascist propaganda.[13] The Nazi charge d'affaires to Nationalist Spain showed repeated frustration at Franco's failure to tow the ideological line. In January 1937, Faupel complained of Franco's 'coolness' towards the Falange and his 'warming' towards the Carlists, a significant report given the dictator's exile of the independent-minded Carlist leader Fal Conde only a month earlier.[14] In April 1937 Franco merged all right-wing parties into a single 'Movement', and it appeared that the modern Falange enjoyed precedence over the Carlists, Alfonsists and Catholics. But two months later a Nazi press correspondent complained that fascism remained a paper tiger, and that Franco's regime 'had not done very much ... in fact a return to the bad old days of monarchy is likely'.[15] The irredeemably Spanish nature of the civil war was also obvious to the main foreign backer of the government side. Payne argues that Soviet intervention was bent on Stalinizing Spain in the event of a government victory,[16] but the rebel victory deprives us of the last word on this issue. What does seem clear, however, is that such a totalitarian outcome in 1936 was hard for anyone to imagine. Even La Pasionaria doubted the prospect of a Stalinist state, citing the absence of a communist monopoly over the media and the prevalence of the rival, and distinctly Hispanic, anarchist movement.

In fact, observers of Spain's 1930s crisis found it hard to step out of the shadow of the Two Spains. A 1938 Carlist newspaper dedicated a full-page spread comparing the military feats of the *requetés* of 1837 with 1937: 'From 1833 to 1938 Carlists fight in the vanguard to save the fatherland.'[17] 1930s historians wrote that the issues at stake in the Spanish Civil War were 'fundamentally the same as one hundred years ago', the only difference being that Carlists were no longer alone in opposing liberalism. We do not need to call the 1930s war a 'Carlist war' in order to observe its similarities.[18] A 1930s American liberal historian identified the nascent Second Republic as the latest victory of modern Spain against its nemesis, the unbridled power of clerical monarchy of the era of Don Carlos.[19] The celebrated Hispanist Gerald Brenan saw the 'purest' Hispanic extremes of Carlism and anarchism as the real militancies of the Spanish Civil War.[20] George Steer listened to a member of the Basque government in 1937 explain the 'Spanish' nature of the war afflicting his homeland: 'Carlists who lose their faith become Anarchists immediately, and as they are Spaniards, they fight each other: let them.' Basque nationalism, by contrast, was a version of an international idea, consistent with the outward-looking Basque country.[21] Young Carlists fighting anarchists in 1930s Seville complained of the myopia of their enemy: 'If the Syndicalists only believed in God, they would be Traditionalists for life.'[22]

Not just 1930s historians made links to the 1830s. For all the nightmares of impending world war, foreign protagonists in Spain's 1930s war actually went to remarkable lengths to compare the country's plight with historical rather than contemporary events. When news of the military coup reached Paris, the first response of the Popular Front prime minister Leon Blum was to dismiss the news as yet another idiosyncratically Spanish *pronunciamiento*.[23] Once the coup failed and civil war ensued, a British Conservative Member of Parliament saw the Spanish Civil War as the product of tension quintessentially Spanish, calling it a 'Third Carlist War'.[24] *The Times* even complained that the Spanish atrocities of 1936 lacked the 'grandeur' of those of the 1830s.[25] Unwittingly, foreign powers also reacted to Spain in the 1930s in similar ways to the 1830s. The left-leaning Great Powers supporting the government sides reached similar emotional

conclusions. British diplomats in the 1830s spoke of defending the cause
of 'humanity' and even lobbied the pro-Carlist powers of Austria, Prussia
and Russia to condemn rebel atrocities.[26] Stalin used the same language of
'defending humanity' in an article he penned for *El Mundo Obrero* in 1936,
and repeated the same message in *Izvestia* in the Soviet Union itself.[27]

Foreigners present in Spain often jumped to conclusions about the
Spanish propensity to violence. In 1835 an Anglo-Irish recruiter of the
British auxiliaries described the violence of the Carlists as a product of
'poverty and priestcraft'.[28] Edward Costello thereby both projected his own
Protestant prejudice and asserted the customary Spanish propensity to civil
war. The Hungarian communist Arthur Koestler appreciated the conflict of
1936 as a successor to the Carlist Wars, and condemned the undiminished
power of clericalism in all Spanish conflicts.[29] Amid the atrocities and
counter-atrocities of 1937, the Austrian sociologist Franz Borkenau referred
to more than a century of conflict when he remarked that 'it is not so much
an anarchist as a Spanish habit to massacre one's enemies wholesale'.[30] Even
when foreign observers refrained from insulting their host culture, they
still kept the nineteenth century as a point of reference. In the summer of
1939 an American visitor lamented how the destruction had destroyed the
moveable wealth accumulated since the Carlist Wars.[31]

Given the seamless links between the nineteenth and twentieth centuries
imagined by foreign observers, we should also compare the international
context of the Spanish Civil Wars, especially the role reversal of Europe's
Great Powers. In the First Carlist War, the progressive Cristino side was
supported diplomatically, financially and militarily by the Liberal Atlantic
powers, Britain, France and Portugal, as well as benevolent diplomatic
manoeuvres in the Americas. The Carlist side, by contrast, failed to obtain
similar intervention from the sympathetic Absolute powers of Austria,
Prussia, Russia and the Italian states. Even though Chancellor Metternich
despised Spain's liberal regime, judging that 'liberalism made no sense
in Spain' for the Spanish character is 'incapable of nuance',[32] he never
challenged Anglo–French hegemony in Spain by either recognizing Don
Carlos or openly challenging the Quadruple Alliance blockade. Whereas the
liberal powers, especially Britain, had a vested interest in the triumph of
property reform and constitutionalism in Spain, the opposite was the case
in the Spanish Civil War. The ogre of Bolshevism led the policy-makers of
the same liberal powers of the 1830s privately to welcome the suppression
of a workers' revolution in Western Europe, even if the price for this
counter-revolution was Nazi and Fascist intervention. This about-turn in
progressive Western policy towards Spain's civil wars has not been analysed
comparatively. The rich international nature of the First Carlist War remains
massively understated in contrast to the more famous example one hundred
years later.[33] This mismatch can be attributed in part to the differing balance
of forces. Whereas government forces maintained the upper hand for at least
a year after the start of the first civil war in 1833, the summer of 1936 found

both sides tragically evenly balanced, which made international intervention immediately attractive for both sides.[34]

Of all the world powers, special consideration should be made of the role of Britain, as during both Spanish wars this country was the leading Western power, possessing the greatest actual or potential global power. Both Spanish civil wars occurred during post-war lows in the British Army establishment, as the nineteenth-century nadir of 87,993 men was reached in 1838 during the first war. In the latter war, rearmament only seriously took off from 1938. In addition, in neither war did British governments consider using land forces as an instrument of policy on the continent, notwithstanding Lord Palmerston's liberal use of naval 'gunboat policy' and the Chamberlain government's begrudging commitment to deploy an expeditionary force in the event of war with Germany.[35] That said, the major disparity in British involvement did not relate to land forces: even during the 1830s no British soldiers were deployed on the ground in Spain, only British volunteers for the Spanish government and, in moments of acute crisis (such as during the Carlists' rout of British and Cristino forces at Oriamendi in 1837), Royal Marines.

The major difference concerns arms deliveries. In the 1930s, British-led Non-Intervention ensured that the arms embargo penalized the Spanish government: Eden's 'leaky dam' leaked foreign weapons disproportionately into rebel hands.[36] In the 1830s, by contrast, British naval supremacy managed not only to intercept most seaborne attempts to arm the rebels but also to meet the lion's share of government arms requirements. In the wake of the La Granja revolution, the beleaguered Calatrava government ordered an emergency levy of 50,000 men for which the British government obligingly delivered on credit 100,000 muskets and offered to use its naval supremacy to land the arms on different points of the Spanish coast in proportion to need.[37] This flexible disembarkation of arms resolved a crisis surrounding the first major arms shipments. By the end of March 1835, the Tower of London had accumulated 22,000 muskets, 3,000 rifles and 4,000 swords,[38] all of which were dispatched to the port of Lisbon, where they were joined by further shipments of smaller quantity, until by the end of October some 50,000 firearms had arrived at Lisbon.[39] But their onward transportation to Spain was delayed by the sensitivity of elections in Portugal and revolution in Spain. When the arms finally began to reach Badajoz in December 1835, they did so in penny-packets owing to the shortage of draught animals. Even then, some baggage trains were delayed and reduced further by desertions. By February, matters had become so bad that the Cristino minister to Portugal proposed to Prime Minister Mendizábal that all future arms shipments proceed as far as possible into Spain on the River Tagus so that they might be unloaded at a river jetty in the charge of a mutually agreed official.[40] No relief came from Portugal itself either. In September 1835 a Spanish request for 10,000 obsolescent muskets from the Lisbon armoury was turned down on the grounds that

Portugal itself needed the arms in order to play its role in the Quadruple Alliance and to equip its Guardia Nacional.[41] British seaborne deliveries throughout the war to San Sebastián, Bilbao, Barcelona, Valencia and Málaga transformed the supply situation for the Spanish government and contrasted with the situation of the Peninsular War when Wellington had relied on Lisbon as the entrepôt for Allied supplies.

In fact, British sea power in 1836 played a decisive role analogous to the Nazi airlift of 1936. The Anglo–Cristino naval supremacy of the 1830s stood in stark contrast to the inability of the government navy in 1936 which, German intelligence was glad to report, had been rendered ineffective because of the elimination of its trained officers at the hands of the crew.[42] One hundred years earlier, the picture was very different. British vessels bolstered the Cristino navy, transporting troops and supplies, ensuring government control of coastal areas and diminishing the ability of Carlists to obtain seaborne foreign aid. During the 1836 rebel siege of San Sebastián, General Córdova was confident that the city could not fall because British steamships could borrow reinforcements from Bilbao and get them safely to San Sebastián in a matter of hours.[43] As early as spring 1834 the Spanish government had declared the entire northern coastline to be in a state of blockade, thereby reserving for itself and its allies the right to turn away neutral ships aiding the rebels. Since the sixteenth century, the main problem facing belligerent naval forces had been stopping neutral ships carrying cargoes for an enemy. The 1812 US declaration of war against Britain had been motivated by British interference with 'neutral rights', and a similar crisis threatened to emerge in respect of Spain. In November 1836 the State Department instructed the US minister to Madrid to protest the northern blockade as 'the United States cannot acknowledge the legality of any blockade which is not confined to particular designated ports, each having stationed before it a force competent to sustain the blockade, nor the legality of any capture for breach of blockade, unless the vessel captured has attempted to enter a blockaded port after having been previously warned off.'[44] But as the rebels captured no major ports, the formality of blockade could hardly be tested. In the end, the inability of the Quadruple Alliance to police the whole coastline all the time, combined with the sane refusal of most blockade-runners to make for remote rebel-held coastlines, stopped Spain's war escalating into a naval confrontation between rival powers.

Cristino naval domination was all the more remarkable given the decrepit state of the government navy in 1833, a shadow of its imperial heyday. The situation was improved by the British donation in 1834 of two state-of-the-art steamships which performed an essential transport role in amphibious operations throughout the war, and continued to be captained by the British in Cristino service. Government naval supremacy contrasted markedly with the balance of sea forces one hundred years later. Even though ratings killed some 70 per cent of their officers aboard government ships in July 1936, thereby saving most capital ships from falling into rebel hands,[45] subsequent naval operations betrayed little of the proactive strategy of the 1830s. Throughout the Spanish Civil War the government navy distinguished itself only in protecting vital Soviet supply convoys in the Mediterranean, and both the extent and impact of direct Soviet naval intervention on the government side paled in comparison to the British one hundred years earlier when no aircraft, submarines or mines existed to impair their efforts.[46]

Even though enough Soviet relief convoys arrived in order to stave off the Spanish government's defeat, there was never enough to ensure victory either. In lieu of material superiority, more might have been expected of Soviet technical expertise. As the Republic re-established its war academies (Escuelas Populares de Guerra), Soviet advisers became ever-more important for technical training, although the mutual linguistic incomprehension (Spanish and Soviet advisers wrote back to the USSR requesting more advisers with a mutual foreign language, presumably French) meant that many key areas of instruction, like tank-driving, were done by mime.[47] Despite the initial tactical advantages gained on the battlefield by the first deployments of T-26 tanks, government troops suffered decreasing Soviet interest in their development. Ironically, both the USSR and Nazi Germany approached the Spanish Civil War in 1936 with virtually identical doctrines of armoured warfare. Secret joint training exercises held in Kazan by officers from the Red Army and the Weimar Republic's Reichswehr had led both states to conclude that 'deep penetration' by tanks, a synergy of mechanization and mass, was the key to modern offensive warfare. Whereas Condor Legion experimentation in Spain strengthened German belief in this doctrine, the inefficient use of Soviet material by the Republicans persuaded the Soviets that tanks should be demoted to support roles in offensive warfare.[48] No serious revival in the tank's fortunes was possible, as even though the war academies were standardized in January 1939 with tactical instruction including armoured warfare, by then the war was almost over. This tardiness summed up the problems with the Republican Army. Political patronage and rivalry impaired military effectiveness much more than was the case in the Nationalist zone. In particular, the Republican army lacked an adequate cadre of junior officers and NCOs which distinguished the Nationalist war effort.[49]

The British in the 1830s, by contrast, provided durable naval supremacy to the government side. In addition to their permanent stationing after 1835 of a Royal Navy squadron at Pasaia (Guipúzcoa) and extended stationing at such major ports as Málaga, Barcelona and Valencia, the British also supplied the officers for the two British steamships gifted to the Spanish service and which were renamed *Reina Gobernadora* and *Isabel II*. From March 1836 Royal Navy vessels began transporting government troops across the entire northern front from Galicia to the French border.[50] In May 1836 the same Royal Navy remit was extended to Spain's eastern coast and Britain effectively controlled Spain's naval strategy.[51] Lord John Hay, commander of the Pasaia squadron, was challenged by Admiral Ribera to replace the British officers with their Spanish allies. Hay, who had repeatedly complained of Ribera's 'lack of cooperation' in accepting British leadership of naval operations, protested to the Spanish government. Prime Minister Istúriz conceded his every point and Ribera was forced to resign.[52]

The 1830s British naval presence in the Bay of Biscay and the Mediterranean remained substantial enough to dissuade foreign intervention in the Carlists' favour and to bolster Cristino authorities, whereas in the 1930s government-held coasts in the Mediterranean were perversely entrusted to the German and Italian contingents of the Non-Intervention blockade. Lacking a northern fleet condemned the Carlists to failure in the 1830s. Their first attempt to conquer Bilbao in 1835 was based on the desire to gain international recognition, indeed a large loan was pledged from the Netherlands in the event of the city's fall.[53] But their lack of a navy prevented the Carlists from interfering with government reinforcements. Carlist domination from 1838 of the area of the Ebro estuary allowed the construction for the first time of a dedicated Carlist coastal flotilla, although this came too late to alter the course of the war.[54] On the key northern front the Cristinos after 1837 enjoyed naval supremacy, backed by the British Navy, and efficient steamship communications. By contrast, the British naval presence in the 1930s worked to the advantage of the rebels. The diplomatic subterfuge surrounding the Non-Intervention agreement meant that German submarines operated unmolested from Pasaia – the British base of the 1830s – and the Royal Navy patrols in the Bay of Biscay effectively blockaded Bilbao, diminishing its ability to resist rebel attack.[55]

In the first war rebel hopes for international help were not entirely sabotaged in the Bay of Biscay. From 1835 the rebels controlled large stretches of the Spanish border with France, which eased the passage of supplies and international agents. On 20 January 1837 the French government issued an order prohibiting any export of foodstuffs from departments bordering Carlist Spain. This order was generally ignored, but not to the extent where it was a complete paper tiger, distress and frustration being caused to border communities and both formal and informal forms of commerce. Meanwhile, Carlist financial agents in European capitals put up a plan to raise 20 million *pesos fuertes* on international markets to be repaid at 5 per cent interest and in its entirety after eight years of either Don Carlos entering Madrid or his being recognized as king. This attempt replaced the earlier 'Ouvrard loan', which was stillborn.[56] What all of this amounted to was nothing more than the half-measures and inadequacies of individual aid and volunteering and, at best, strong diplomatic representations in favour of the Carlist cause. In 1837 Carlist agents were received politely in the courts of Italy, central and eastern Europe, but they were not given much help.

Similarities in international intervention

The extreme examples of interference in both post-war settlements can be seen in civil wars, in both cases in Spain. Despite the forbidding diplomatic environment, the question of foreign intervention on the side of the left in civil wars became ethically justified for the first time in the 1830s owing to John Stuart Mill's *Spanish Essay* (1837). The British government had intervened on the side of the anti-revolutionary *chouannerie* in France two generations earlier, but Palmerston's intervention on the side of the revolution in Spain marked a new departure. Mill's moralistic and intellectual defence of this policy and of the motives of individual volunteers pre-empted the galaxy of studies dedicated to the International Brigades one hundred years later.

Their motives appear surprisingly similar in both conflicts. Whereas the prevailing image of the International Brigade volunteers is heroic and selfless – the 'Last Great Cause' so cherished by such communist propaganda organs as Bill Rust's *Britons in Spain* – in fact international volunteers had an eclectic range of motives (unemployment, adventure, flight, ideological commitment), and responses from wives, girlfriends and families ranged from understanding to despair.[57] Foreign volunteers for both sides in the 1930s were drawn to Spain's war by prosaic motives. Bill Alexander argued that the British battalions joined for regular meals. Pro-rebel foreigners were allowed to join the elite Spanish Legion where the 'pay and food were infinitely better than for the rebels' regular army'.[58]

In some contexts group politicization produced group volunteering. Communist mobilization in the 1930s South Wales mining districts produced over one hundred Brigade volunteers, whereas the Durham coalfield, where communism was weak, produced far fewer.[59] In other words, the 1930s volunteers shared the eclectic motivations of their predecessors one hundred years earlier. Certainly, the ideologically committed Brigade volunteers were convinced that Republican Spain was undergoing a 'people's war'.[60] And unlike the auxiliaries of the 1830s, the Brigaders were vindicated soon afterwards by the onset of the Second World War, which bestowed on their veterans more prestige than that afforded to their forbears. Yet in other respects the experiences of both sets of volunteers show similarities. Contemporary sources attest to the tendency of international fighters to seek release from boredom and neglect in Spain's cheap and plentiful wine. The Dutch poet and international brigadesman Jef Last in October 1936 was fighting close to Madrid and yet spent uncomfortable hours hungry at the trenches when rebel shelling targeted the field kitchen. Eventually his sergeant crawled on his belly to bring back wine and grapes, and told his men: 'If you drink much on an empty stomach, you can't shoot straight any more.'[61] Alcohol consumption was generally forbidden in advance positions, which came as a cultural shock to Northern Europeans.[62] In both wars the demoralization and disaffection of foreign soldiers would be expressed in drunken disorderliness. In January 1837 drunken British and Portuguese auxiliaries assaulted people and property in a tavern in Santander.[63]

Both wars cast international volunteers as decisive in the defence of key cities, in Bilbao and Madrid, respectively, and, therefore also in the strategic stalemate of both wars, namely, the rebel obsession with conquering Bilbao in the 1830s and the Republican obsession with defending Madrid after 1936.[64] The British air attaché commented, 'The Madrid defenders are obsessed by the saying "They shall not pass". Yet they fail to realise that it is necessary to advance in order to win the war.'[65] Even though international volunteers comprised only 5 per cent of Madrid's defence during November 1936,[66] proportionately fewer than the foreigners present in the 1830s sieges of Bilbao, they were rewarded with the lion's share of the acclaim for the defensive victory. Similarities also extend to Spain as a seat of civil wars within a civil war. The Battle of Barbastro in June 1837 pitted Germans on opposing sides against each other in combat, as the Carlists had formed their own Foreign Legion comprising German-speaking defectors from the French Foreign Legion. One hundred years later, a similar fratricidal tragedy occurred at Brunete, albeit between émigré German International Brigade members and Nazi German interventionists.[67]

Beyond the Quadruple Alliance of 1834 intellectuals were energized by the question of intervention in Spain's civil war. The Greek revolution of the early 1820s provided a highly iconic precedent for foreign volunteers, and by the 1830s two young liberal internationalists, Giuseppe Mazzini and John Stuart Mill, were using Spain's conflict to help formulate their doctrines of interventionism. Both men arrived at similar conclusions, that foreign intervention in a civil war could not be justified when no similar intervention was underway in favour of the other side (to do so would imply that the Spanish people were unworthy of liberty). But intervention could be justified if the forces of tyranny were doing the same, and both men appreciated the very real material help being extended from Absolutist Europe to the Carlist side even if this help stopped short of open war with Liberal Europe. The result was the presence of Mazzinian volunteers fighting on the government side in Catalonia in 1837, just as these volunteers had fought, and would continue to fight, in several liberal revolutions across Europe. The same year saw John Stuart Mill collaborate with the Spanish exile, José María Blanco White, in publishing the first serious theoretical defence in favour of armed intervention in the civil wars of other nations. Mill's *Essay on the Spanish Question* (1837) is almost forgotten. The mere mention of intervention in Spain evokes the International Brigades, not least because the Brigades defied what in retrospect appeared a pusillanimous Anglo–French policy of collective security and Appeasement.

John Stuart Mill advanced practical as well as moral reasons to support the Liberal cause, seeing the medieval fueros of the Carlist Basque country as obstructions to economic progress. His support for their political extension beyond the Basque country was a cunning ploy to dress them up as respect for traditionalism even while they would thus become politically meaningless. John Stuart Mill is the last great nineteenth-century British philosopher to have been subjected to academic study with regard to his influence in Spain. Even though we now possess an adequate study of his economic and, especially, political impact,[68] little account has been taken of his 1837 *Spanish Essay*. Although Mill agreed that non-intervention in other countries' affairs was a sound principle, it only worked when all powers respected it. Yet Austria and Russia had proved their own interventionism in Italy and Poland, respectively, and Mill believed that Quadruple Alliance intervention promised to bring the brutal Spanish war to a speedy end. Mill also rejected notions of Basque privileges (fueros) being popular: Bilbao was opposed to them and their existence propagated administrative corruption and smuggling.[69]

Yet even the British establishment was divided in its stand. British Tories were either neutral or pro-Carlist in sympathies, and the newspaper of official note, *The Times*, argued that the Quadruple Alliance was in itself an affront to non-intervention.[70] Wellington abhorred the Quadruple Alliance for its overturning of the Quintuple Alliance at the heart of the Vienna Settlement and for exporting dangerous liberalism. Tory Carlism was steeped in the romanticism emanating from Disraeli's 'Young England', a group of Eton and Oxford aristocrats wedded to 'lost causes' of nobility, feudalism and anti-capitalism. Spanish Carlists indulged European romantics' support for their cause. Don Carlos himself throughout 1835–36 led an itinerant royal court which relocated to seven different towns in Navarra over the course of the year in order to bolster the morale of the Basque peasants and to frustrate Cristino plans to conduct offensives against the centre of Carlist power. On 12 September 1836 Don Carlos embarked upon a tour of his Basque kingdom, and made a point of including the entire Carlist-held section of the border with France. The official *Gaceta de Navarra* reported melancholic Spanish exiles hailing the king from the other side of the Bidasoa. They were joined by cheering French legitimists and by spectators from further afield. Among these spectators was the young Englishwoman, Marianne Richards, who from 1845 would be Cabrera's wife.[71]

The peak in influence of the Tory 'Young Englanders' ranged between the 1832 franchise act and the 1846 abolition of the Corn Laws. In foreign affairs, their pro-Carlism was a perfect example of support for a lost cause, and this inflected their general assault on utilitarianism advocated by Mill.[72] Great hopes were cherished that the Duke of Wellington, hero of the Peninsular War, would declare his support for the Carlists, and both Liberal and Carlist historians since have held that he was pro-Carlist in thought if not in deed.[73] Carlists were crestfallen at Wellington's public approval of Espartero's victorious military operations in 1839. Tory opinion, best expressed through the *Morning Post*, usually favoured the Carlists, but much of this sentiment came from a peculiarly personal antipathy to Lacy Evans,

the radical member of Parliament and commander of British auxiliaries
who had insulted the most prestigious part of the military establishment,
the Horse Guards. Even though Wellington's humanitarian intervention via
Lord Eliot amounted to something of a moral victory for the Carlists (in
recognizing them as equal combatants), Wellington remained persistently
non-interventionist and exasperated at the improvident Spanish and their
war.[74] Serving as Tory prime minister for a few months in early 1835,
Wellington honoured the Quadruple Alliance out of a sense of propriety
rather than conviction.

France, the other Great Power signatory to the Quadruple Alliance, was
as bitterly divided by the First Carlist War as by the Spanish Civil War.
France's constitutional monarch privately held Don Carlos's dynastic claim
to be stronger than Princess Isabella's, which deprived a divided political
establishment of an honest broker and also appeared not to win King Louis-
Philippe much support abroad for his regime of 1830.[75] Other European
monarchs, such as William IV in Liberal Britain to the Absolutist Tsar of
Russia, were cold towards Louis-Philippe, seeing him as a bourgeois upstart
and traitor to Charles X.[76] Within France itself an unbowed legitimist
movement remained strong in the south-western departments closest to
Spain. The doyen of French legitimism, Viscount Chateaubriand (1768–
1848), relished the Carlist insurgency as proof that 'Spain will save itself
through its old laws, its aristocratic classes, its foral institutions, and above
all through its religious spirit'.[77] Spain was the most cited country in the
French press between 1833 and 1840, ahead of Britain and the German and
Italian states.[78] Legitimist France gave Carlist Spain its first distinguished
volunteer. Septuagenarian Penne de Villemur had fought against the French
Revolution and for the Spanish Patriots against Napoleon. On 27 February
1834 he escaped from a failed Carlist rising at Zaragoza and survived to
see Don Carlos make him minister of war and president of the junta of
Navarra.[79]

Spain's war was a national security crisis for the July Monarchy. For
reasons of external and internal instability, France in fact grew ever more
minimalist in its support for the Quadruple Alliance, especially in the wake of
the La Granja revolution. Local frontier forces' actions sometimes obscured
lukewarm official policy. General Harispe, who commanded covering forces
along the border, was prepared to go beyond the precepts of his government
by cooperating with Espartero to throttle Carlist communications along the
border.[80] Local actions like these mitigated the increasing coolness of French
foreign policy towards the Cristino side.

The French government, which had been openly pro-Cristino at the
signing of the Quadruple Alliance in April 1834, was more reticent at the
signing of its additional articles on 18 August 1834 (basically, the right
of the Spanish government to recruit auxiliaries abroad), had grown even
cooler by the time of the September 1835 revolution, and had become
virtually neutral by the time of the La Granja revolution in August the

following year. Swings in France's Spain policy were reflected in border relations. In October 1835 French observation forces promised the Carlists not to permit any more Cristino refugees to assemble on the French border and also promised that no more armed Cristino exiles expelled from border forts would be allowed to find sanctuary in France. Carlist Spain was gaining international recognition de facto if not de jure.[81] The following year, in an attempted rapprochement with Austria, the French government even suspended their embargo on supplies passing into Spain to aid the Carlists.[82] Amid the September 1835 revolution of the juntas, the French king's words of assurance to General Fernández de Córdova that France would remain 'neutral' were words of alarm for a Cristino establishment expecting much better than 'neutrality' from a Great Power signatory to the Quadruple Alliance.[83]

The omens were not good. Even before the August 1836 revolution, the Francophile moderado prime minister, Javier de Istúriz, had had no success pleading for a French army to intervene in northern Spain against the Carlists. King Louis-Philippe, never more than lukewarm to Isabella's cause, had strategic reasons to resile from the Quadruple Alliance. French Interior Minister Adolphe Thiers saw his promotion in 1836 to the offices of foreign and prime minister rescinded as soon as he tried to advance his plan to create a 20,000-strong 'Army of Observation' near the Spanish border at Pau. Just as in the 1930s, Spain's war polarized France more than it did Britain. Republicanism remained a significant constituency in the French army until 1836, and despite the liberalizing legacy of the 1830 revolution, mooted reforms to create mobile National Guard units and even a large army reserve had never left the drawing board for fears of their revolutionary potential.[84] The spectacle of Spain's revolutionary militia horrified the king who sacked Thiers and dissolved the Pau reinforcement depot. The king and Thiers had been at odds for several reasons, but news of La Granja was the last straw. An admirer rebuked Thiers for having to resign over 'that hateful Spain'.[85] The dissolution at Pau ended any chance of formal French intervention, especially as Thiers's defeat was accompanied by a pledge not to expand the Legion which France had already deployed in Spain.[86] Virtual French neutrality condemned neighbouring Catalonia to a long war at best. In vain, Catalan Cortes deputy, Castell, pleaded that intervention was a moral necessity: 'If the family of my neighbour is affected by thieves and assassins they have a right to my assistance and it is my duty to afford it.'[87] With more coolness, the Spanish government appealed to both Britain and France to 'overlook' the excesses of the 1836 revolution, and to commit a large land army against the 'exhausted' Carlist Basque country which was 'desirous of peace'. Formal French intervention would free up the government army to suppress irregular rebel bands as well as the hothead revolutionaries which so vexed Paris and which 'thrive on the war'.[88]

Notwithstanding, a non-interventionist French ambassador was appointed to Madrid whose first act was to insist that French auxiliaries be 'quarantined' away from the 'contagion' of the revolutionary Spanish government soldiers. France's diplomatic position remained delicate, even if the internal threat of Duchess Berry's legitimism had clearly passed, as had the influence of French legitimist Bourmont in Portugal, and even though Europe's Absolutist Powers were grudgingly beginning to accept the July Monarchy as a force for stability in France. Thiers's successor, the conservative Louis-Molé, was convinced that 'no *cordon sanitaire* could prevent the Spanish revolution from spreading to France'.[89] Molé categorically stated that France would *never* intervene in the Spanish war, and this resounding *jamais* set the tone for French foreign policy until March 1839, when a centre-left administration under Thiers once more came to power.[90] Thus the French Foreign Legion was denied reinforcements, and the last French auxiliaires fighting in Catalonia were withdrawn in December 1838,[91] one hundred years almost to the day before the last International Brigades were withdrawn from Spain. In October 1938 La Pasionaria gave a rousing farewell speech to the International Brigades marching out of Barcelona, thanking the volunteers who 'gave us everything: their youth and their maturity, their science and their experience, their blood and their lives, their hopes and their aspirations, and they asked us for nothing at all.'[92] One hundred years earlier, by contrast, the French auxiliaries crossed the frontier without fanfare and without the French government even requesting reasons for their dissolution.[93] In December 1837 all British auxiliaries, barring some cavalry and artillery, were withdrawn from Spain. Both Spanish and British authorities tried to keep the circumstances of their departure quiet, because the men had rioted at outstanding pay arrears. Eventually direct British intervention embarked the men, but their pay arrears remained outstanding for as long as two decades in some cases.[94]

The August 1836 revolution presented the government with a diplomatic crisis as great as one hundred years later. The Russian foreign minister Karl Robert Nesselrode since the start of the Carlist War had isolated Spain's government envoy to St Petersburg, rejecting all his entreaties for an audience and placing his movements and correspondence under police surveillance. By contrast Spain's rebel 'legate', de Paez, enjoyed full diplomatic privileges, short of recognition, and in the month following La Granja, Tsar Nicholas I himself pressed Metternich and Prussia for a joint formal recognition of Carlist Spain.[95] In September, Prime Minister Calatrava expelled the pro-Carlist Austrian, Sardinian and Neapolitan *charges d'affaires*.[96] By November the last remaining diplomatic agent still in Madrid, representing a power that did not recognize the government, left the capital. The Dutch charge d'affaires, Baron van Grovestins, was according to Villiers a 'decided Carlist who must not be allowed to linger on the border with Spain'.[97]

One hundred years later, the Popular Front government in France in 1936 was equally regarded in suspicion by both Europe's remaining democracies

FIGURE 5.2 *French Foreign Legion attacking a rebel rampart (Courtesy of Museo Zumalakarregi).*

and the Fascist powers. As a result, French involvement in both civil wars took on a heightened sense of self-preservation (legitimist and Radical plots in the 1830s; rightist and Fascist plots in the 1930s). In both wars, French foreign policy found itself subordinate to a senior partner, Britain. Matters were surely not helped by the Tory attitudes in Britain of Castlereagh, Wellington and King William IV that most of Europe was not 'ready' for liberalism.[98] Tory attitudes one hundred years later had evolved but remained on the same lines: Europe was at least as equally at risk from Bolshevism as from Fascism. The polarization of opinion in France and Portugal, added to the reserve shown by the pro-Carlist powers, left the field free for Britain to intervene at will.

Yet, while the Royal Navy played a decisive role, both British and foreign auxiliaries were largely supplementary in their military effectiveness, in the sense that the war would probably have followed the same pattern even if no foreign volunteers had been present on land. Mill defended the volunteers from the excoriation heaped upon them in the Tory–Carlist press: 'If General Evans be a mercenary for accepting pay from Queen Isabella, what name must be given to George III, paying blood-money and head-money to margraves and landgraves for the hire of their subjects?'[99] Villiers had no time for such grandstanding, dubbing Evans a 'conceited incapable coxcomb of no real merit'.[100] Indeed, it would not be unreasonable to synthesize Mill's and Villiers's contrasting views of Evans, seeing as the Member of Parliament for Westminster was motivated both by international liberalism and glory. Frustrated by the reluctance of serving officers to join his Legion (to the extent that he even offered volunteers automatic promotion to the next rank if they joined), Evans was obliged to recruit 'gentlemanly' volunteers.[101] A caucus of Evans's personal friends occupied commanding posts, leading to accusations of cronyism in parallel to those levelled against Espartero's ayacuchos.[102] The relative inactivity of the British Army and its wars in the 1820s and 1830s drew men such as Evans to serve in Spain, allowing auxiliary officers to gain promotion and cut a dash in the name of international liberal ideals.[103] Edward Costello failed to flourish in his father's business but discovered his elan recruiting for the Legion throughout Ireland.[104] Thirty per cent of the Legion's troops were recruited in Ireland.[105] If service in Spain could thus appeal to officers, most British ranks enlisted out of poverty (in much the same way as the Brigaders one hundred years later).[106] Colonel Shaw led the recruitment drive in Scotland and found proletarianized handloom weavers to comprise most of his volunteers.[107] As in earlier European wars, British volunteers in the 1830s came disproportionately from rural, especially Highland, Scotland, where poverty and a martial tradition of feudalism made overseas service a better alternative for men of military age than in England.

The British 'superpower' status in both wars obliged the rebels to treat British combatants falling into their captivity with special consideration. Juan Bautista Erro became the Carlist prime minister in April 1836 after having spent a year in Gibraltar and London as a refugee from Cristino captivity. Erro soon repaid the kindness of his British hosts by agreeing to mitigate the harsh Durango decree in the case of Crown forces (Royal Navy and Marines) operating on the Spanish coastline.[108] One hundred years later, Franco's rebels proved far less likely to execute captured British International Brigade volunteers than those of other nationalities.[109] But the Carlist War made Spain a dangerous place for foreigners in general, as danger did not exclusively come from rebel soldiers. On 13 July 1835 three British crewmen from a steamship docked at Bilbao were lured by three Basque women beyond the government lines where they were seized and executed.[110] Actual auxiliaries faced the reprisals not just of their Carlist captors, but also sometimes of enraged villagers who sometimes lynched straggling auxiliaries in reprisal for the indiscriminate torching of houses committed by retreating British and government troops at Andoain in September 1837.[111]

The Spanish government's perennial financial crisis was worsened by the enlistment of foreign auxiliaires. From the summer of 1835, the annual cost of maintaining the government regular army amounted to 600,000 reales and that of the auxiliaries 100,000 reales. This made the auxiliaries relatively more expensive, and for little appreciable gain. Few auxiliaries could match the performance of Spanish soldiers in the signature mountain warfare in the northern front. For much of the war, the British Legion proved unable to fight outside of the environs of San Sebastián and Vitoria, even though it acquitted itself well in fortification work at Treviño and Peñacerrada.[112]

Whereas French, Belgian and Portuguese auxiliaires tended to be more seasoned on account of their recent action in Portugal and North Africa, they, like the British, suffered from an unholy trinity of irregular pay, equivocal political support from their home governments and a propensity to alienate Spanish allies and civilians. The French government washed its hands of its defection-prone Foreign Legion. Even before the French reached Spain, the Legion had acquired a reputation for ill-discipline and opportunism during its service in the Portuguese civil war. In the summer of 1834, at the French barracks in Lisbon, the legionaries' complaints about their officers' corruption and use of excessive corporal punishment boiled over into an armed standoff. Even though the riot was quelled, some 440 legionaries were returned to Le Havre at the first opportunity. Upon arrival, the Spanish liaison officer reported, all of the legionaries took ship to the pro-Carlist Netherlands in order to join the service of the Pretender.[113]

Arrears in pay, more than any ideological affiliation, explain the repeated instances of defecting auxiliaries. The pay issue vexed responsible authorities. Villiers feared that the British auxiliaries billeted in San Sebastián might start 'helping themselves' if their arrears of pay were not met. The Spanish government pleaded irregular bookkeeping by the British and the financial paralysis caused by the Gómez Expedition which 'had halted the proceeds of the forced loan to Madrid and encouraged local Committees of Armament and Defence to help themselves in the confusion'.[114] On 3 July 1837 a part of the British Legion at Hernani rebelled over severe arrears of pay. A British auxiliary, one 'Owen', seconded to a Portuguese battalion, was executed after he had organized a mutiny over pay which threatened the life of its colonel.[115] The Regiment of Oporto Grenadiers and their cavalry section (the Chasseurs) suffered from a troublesome reputation in the eyes of the Spanish authorities, something which persisted after the war in the wake of Carminati's rebellion in 1841. In March 1836 some 133 Oporto Grenadiers and seven accompanying women mutinied on board the *San Nicolás* and set sail for the Carlist-held coastline.[116] Six months later scandal shook Barcelona when an Oporto cavalry colonel eloped to France with a local lady. Authorities ransacked Colonel Urbanski's apartment and imprisoned his batman, the British *pedrista* veteran John Bromley who was held for three months with 'the lowest criminals', which 'caused a lively sense of indignation in the officers and crews of his Britannic Majesty's forces cooperating on the coast of the Mediterranean'.[117]

Of all the foreign auxiliaries fighting for Liberal Spain, the Portuguese came from a country whose politics most resembled the war in Spain. The rebel Gómez expedition of 1836 originally intended to reach the border with Carlist-friendly northern Portugal, Carlist commander-in-chief Bruno de Villareal seeing internationalization as a way to break the stranglehold of theocrats reluctant to expand the war effort beyond the Basque country. Villareal therefore launched Gómez westwards towards Galicia at the head of five battalions and 200 cavalry and Don Carlos gave the force instructions to turn Galicia into a new zone of operations akin to Cabrera's zone in Aragón.[118] Both government demoralization in Galicia and the presence across the border in Northern Portugal of defiant *miguelista* bands combined to promise an international legitimist enclave. Gómez's expedition could not deliver on this objective, because the government counter-insurgency was close on the invaders' heels and obliged the Carlists to make a virtue out of a necessity and to march through the rest of Spain.[119] The Gómez Expedition was thus a disappointment from an international point of view. Only a handful of miguelistas joined the Carlists on campaign, which was an indictment of the ideological appeal for volunteering, considering that about half of the Portuguese Legion dispatched to aid the Spanish government comprised pardoned miguelistas. Nevertheless, the Galicia–Portuguese border remained a hotbed of Carlist–miguelista local activities. Two-and-a-half years after Gómez left Galicia, the government prefect of Pontevedra complained of the cross-border 'Junta of Monção' which extorted villages on both sides of the border and attracted Galician draftees into its ranks.[120]

One hundred years later, the balance of Portuguese involvement was reversed formally in the rebels' favour. Yet miseries of service continued to characterize the Portuguese volunteers for Franco, as they had for Isabella II: the Portuguese were poorly treated and rated by their Nationalist allies. Some 8,000 Portuguese volunteered for Franco in the 'Viriarto' battalion, the same number as did for the Cristinos one hundred years earlier (i.e. relative to population, far fewer Portuguese fought in their neighbour's civil war during the 1930s). But some aspects looked similar: the Carlist–miguelista network of the 1830s breathed life afresh as Carlist agents from Spain recruited Portuguese in the same areas of northern Portugal in 1936.[121] And in both wars Portugal was polarized by the 'madhouse' next door, albeit for diametrically opposed reasons. The Salazar regime had objected to Spanish support for democratic dissidents since 1931 and had to face a pro-Republican naval mutiny at Oporto in September 1936, and therefore supported Franco for its own domestic security.[122]

Although few rank-and-file foreigners in the Spanish Civil War appear to have been much bothered about the romantic appeal of volunteering, the same could not be said of their leaders. The British communist leader Harry Pollitt urged the poet Stephen Spender to become a communist and to die fighting in Spain because 'we need a Byron in our movement'.[123] Lacy Evans displayed a Byronesque quest for honour that would have seemed incomprehensible either to his downtrodden auxiliaries or to the anti-fascist ranks one hundred years later. Evans breezily interfered in Spanish domestic politics almost as much as any Spanish general, and like Spanish generals had a keen eye for his political advantage, the only difference being that his primary concern was his radical Westminster constituency which had elected him member of Parliament. Evans, became notorious among the Carlists when he motioned the British Parliament to declare Don Carlos 'outside civilisation' ('*fuera de la civilización*'), just as it had done to Napoleon in 1815.[124] Other officers mixed subjective motives of adventurism and careerism with the objective of confronting Carlism which represented not just a repressive, clerical Spain but also a threat to Liberal Europe. For the French foreign legionary Joseph Tański service in Spain was a stepping stone to redeeming the liberty of his Polish homeland. Tański displayed a sophisticated liberalism which was not articulated by most auxiliaries, criticizing the Constitution of 1812, which motivated the revolutionaries of 1835–36 but remaining decidedly constitutional all the same.[125] The prominence of highly educated and literate memoirs has obscured the views of rank-and-file volunteers, especially in the first conflict. Suffice to say that in the 1830s most foreign auxiliaries were driven by material want to volunteer, in common with patterns of enlistment in that era. In the 1930s, the same un-romantic material want motivated many volunteers, but one major difference concerned their homelands. Unlike the 1830s auxiliaries who went to Spain with the blessing of the Quadruple Alliance governments, all International Brigade volunteers had to arrive in Republican Spain clandestinely owing to the Non-Intervention agreement. Even more striking is the fact that most Brigade volunteers were either themselves political émigrés from such totalitarian regimes as Italy and Nazi Germany or were the immediate descendants of émigrés who had fled persecution.[126]

In both wars, the formal 'Non-Intervention' adhered to by Europe's Great Powers was in fact a smokescreen for massive informal, indirect or plausibly deniable intervention. The only difference was that this phenomenon worked in favour of the progressive side in the 1830s but against it in the 1930s. Lord Palmerston, the Whig architect of Liberal interventionism in the Carlist War, was already a controversial figure because of his late-night parties, his unconcealed mistress, as well as his reputation as a discourteous and reluctant debater. His personality and politics clashed with those of the Duke of Wellington, the statesman generally considered to be an unassailable authority on Spanish affairs, who admonished that the Spaniards should be left to decide matters themselves (an attitude which was often misread in Cristino Spain as Wellington's pro-Carlism). As much as Palmerston was pro-interventionist, he realized that getting the British regular army involved would be impossible.[127] Winning the British radicals' support on the only world event where he backed leftist revolution up to the hilt, Palmerston was nonetheless at once both generous and stringent in his dealings with Cristino Spain. On the one hand, he encouraged Cristino recruitment of British auxiliaries, while on the other, he rejected all Cristino pleas for British government loans.[128] Britain's ambassador Villiers, for his part, pressed for concessions for British commerce in a manner which may have been consistent with Britain's breakneck rush to free trade in the 1830s and 1840s but which also reignited the Perfidious Albion theme that never left Spanish politics.[129]

From the very beginning of the war, Palmerston instructed Villiers to 'protect British interests'.[130] Villiers certainly demonstrated a level of arrogance consistent with a hegemonic power. As negotiations to ease the entry of British imports stalled over the summer of 1835, Villiers scoffed at Toreno's rejoinder that the Cortes must first take time to examine proposals: 'I am too well acquainted with the mode of doing business in this country to be satisfied with any such excuse.'[131] Yet the British hegemony over government policy never produced the same explosive incidents as in the case of the Soviet hegemony one hundred years later. Villiers may have conducted angry debates with a series of Spanish prime ministers, but none would be as provoked as Prime Minister Largo Caballero during his infamous March 1937 rebuff of the Soviet ambassador. Cristino governments knew that France could barely be counted upon as an ally, and so Villiers's arrogance needed to be suffered in order to keep vital British military aid flowing.

This aid was vital during the second Carlist siege of Bilbao, an event which had global repercussions. From summer 1836 rebel control of the Nervión estuary had cut off the British and French consuls at Bilbao, as their boats on the Nervión were intercepted. Throughout 1836 Anglo–French attention was fixed on the ever more vigorous Carlist siege of the Basque seaports. The Royal Navy became proactively hostile, opening fire without provocation on the Carlists at the coast, who were trying to strengthen their siege of Bilbao by interdicting the movements of Cristino reinforcements. Mid-April saw Evans lead his British volunteers by leaving Vitoria for an attack against the rebel siege lines outside San Sebastián. His offensive, beginning on 22 April 1836, succeeded in evicting the rebels from their main siege lines and in repelling counterattacks. The supporting fire of the Royal Navy was decisive in this local success, and the British victory is significant not only because of its international nature but also because its propaganda value eased a government crisis between the radical ministry of Mendizábal and Commander-in-Chief Fernández de Córdova who had been summoned to attend a council of war in the capital.[132]

The main focus of international attention over 1836–37 was the Carlists' second siege of Bilbao. Espartero's relief of the city over the Christmas of 1836 – the acclaimed Battle of Luchana – turned Bilbao into a heroic cause célèbre, matching Madrid one hundred years later. Even before Espartero's liberation, the stoicism of *bilbaíno* civilians under enemy fire had attracted world attention, in much the same way that their stoicism under Franco's bombs one hundred year later impressed foreign journalists and observers.[133] On 6 January 1837, the queen-regent hosted six public dances in Madrid in order to raise funds for the orphans and widows of Cristinos fallen in Bilbao, and a subscription opened to strike a commemorative medallion abroad. Ten points of thanks were granted by the Crown on behalf of the liberal nation. The National Militia, the British and Espartero were all explicitly thanked, Bilbao was granted the title 'Invicta' and its local government 'Excelencia', the Order of San Fernando was bestowed upon the militia and army units that had defended the city, the defensive victory was turned into the official motto of local militiamen and Espartero himself was made Count Luchana. Sunday, 5 February 1837, was declared a nationwide day of thanksgiving marked by Masses and bell-ringing in churches across the country. A Cortes motion was passed promising to indemnify Bilbao's burghers for their war damage, and a victory monument was ordered to be constructed in Madrid.[134]

International interest was excited by the British auxiliaries and regulars who contributed to the victory. Even the Duke of Wellington – a British statesman whom the Carlists thought to be backing their side – praised Espartero's operations.[135] In part, international interest was military in nature. After Luchana, several lower-ranking British officers proposed defensive measures, such as the major in the Royal Engineers, William Reid, who proposed that the Spaniards may both safeguard Bilbao and use it as a flank to strangle Carlist communications with Asturias by erecting nothing less than a version of the Torres Vedras Lines, which Wellington had seen constructed around Lisbon in 1810.[136]

But the greatest international interest in the government victory was not military but propagandistic in nature. Subscriptions to aid the victims of the siege were opened in January and February 1837 in London, Paris, Lisbon, Oporto, Hamburg, Gibraltar and Bayonne. £782 and five shillings were raised from sixty-nine individuals in London (including twenty-six resident Spaniards) and several companies, the most generous being £50 from the General Steamboat Navigation Company. £1,275 and 16 shillings were raised in Gibraltar. In Paris the vast majority of the 133 subscribers fixed their donations at 20 francs, a notable exception being the anonymous 'español' who managed only five. From Portugal came 243,320 reis, a quarter from Oporto (itself a city traumatized by recent sieges) and the rest from the capital. Given the hostile diplomatic environment in Germany, comparatively little money came from Hamburg and virtually all the subscribers had Spanish names.[137] The fact that international donations were led by prominent Liberals both Spanish and foreign suggests an active fundraising effort on a similar pattern to the various trades union, charity and political party donations raised across the world in aid of Republican Spain in the 1930s.

In at least one case, a large public donation served as a diplomatic gambit concerning Spanish America. Prime Minister Mendizábal had used the pretext of the closure of the Cortes in early 1836 to delay the final step towards recognizing the Mexican republic, and had shown irritation at British pressure to this end, defying Villiers that Latin America was a 'family affair'.[138] When the Calatrava administration finally implemented recognition during the siege of Bilbao, the Mexican plenipotentiary responded with a donation of 20,000 reales for the Bilbao relief fund.[139] The cause of Spanish liberty produced Mexican recognition of the erstwhile motherland that would last a century until Franco's victory in 1939. There would be no further expulsions of Spaniards from Mexico and no more attempts to liberate Spain's valuable sugar colony of Cuba, vital for funding the war effort against the Carlists. In February 1843 the Spanish minister to Mexico organized a subscription directed at Spanish residents and sympathetic Mexicans to raise money to donate a warship to the 'home country ... so mutilated by its cruel and fratricidal war'. By November 15,068 pesos had been raised and a junta was convened to present the warship to Spain.[140]

The successes of Mexico–Spain relations would contrast with the surprisingly lacklustre Mexican public relations during the Spanish Civil War. Although Bilbao was largely fed by Mexican chickpeas during the siege of spring 1937 (a variation of the miracle 'Biscay cod' of the 1836 siege),[141] thereafter practical aid to the Republic failed to keep pace with the left-wing rhetoric of the Mexican government. Certainly, Mexico defended the Spanish Republic at the League of Nations, Octavio Paz attended the July 1937 Anti-Fascist Writers' Conference and President Lázaro Cárdenas agreed to welcome Republican refugees in the event of a Spanish government defeat.[142] But none of these activities much helped the actual government war effort. The Cárdenas regime's un-Catholic policy of aiding the Spanish Republic was unpopular in Mexico itself. Cristero leader, Aurelio Acevedo, expressed the views of Mexico's provincial middle-class Catholics when he ridiculed Octavio Paz's pretensions, attacked the 'hypocrisy' of interfering with aid to the Spanish rebels, and praised the rebel General Mola for his Christian soldiery and his revival of traditional Carlist values in a modern form. As early as September 1936, Acevedo began distributing propaganda for the rebels: 'Under the scourge of the same enemy, Mother Spain and her son Mexico are trying to save themselves from the monster which wants to destroy us: COMMUNISM. The cause is sacred. Let us throw off our yoke. ¡Viva Cristo Rey!'[143] Once Mexico became a channel for US exports to Republican Spain, Acevedo fumed: 'The Americans are hypocrites, sending war material via Mexico to help the reds in Spain, all the while appearing neutral and innocent, and making Mexico look like the guilty party.'[144] Nor was Mexico the only ex-colony where public opinion was on the side of the rebels. In the Philippines, which had not been Spanish since 1898, public opinion in these deeply Catholic islands was mostly in favour of the Nationalist side in Spain's war.[145]

Official Mexico backed the Spanish government, whereas real Mexico sided with the rebels. The behaviour of Mexico's ambassador in Barcelona amid the war-weariness of January 1938 betrayed little of the idealism or generosity of official propaganda. Twenty-seven-year-old Alejandro Gómez Mangada had to fight off accusations of sexual impropriety and blamed his failure to attend a ceremony renaming a street in Gerona as 'Mexico–Russia' on the lack of an embassy car.[146] The Spanish Republic took very seriously its twentieth anniversary celebrations of the Russian Revolution and the ambassador's *demarche* was a source of embarrassment. Certainly, after the Republic's defeat, the Cárdenas government made good on its promise of asylum by appointing Gilberto Bosques as ambassador to France (later Consul to Vichy France) where he acted as a sort of 'Mexican Schindler' in managing to conduct to safety in Mexico thousands of Spanish Republicans and Jews. But unlike in the 1840s, the attitude in the 1940s of the very community which might have been expected to welcome the refugees, the established Spanish 'colony', was decidedly pro-rebel. Mexico's wealthy Spanish colony was disproportionately Basque in origin, and yet it generally refused to donate to the refugees, even though the first contingent of these arriving in June 1937 comprised Basque children escaping Bilbao. President Cárdenas repeated the spirit of 1837 when he praised the children as 'the sons and daughters of the Basque soldiers who defended Bilbao'.[147] Despite this official welcome, the actual experiences of the refugee children were mixed, ranging from full integration into Mexican life to alienation sometimes caused by emotional and sexual abuse in remote schools.[148]

Bilbao thus triggered international involvement in both civil wars. The contribution of the Royal Navy and Marines to the 1836 government victory at Bilbao emboldened British military involvement in the rest of Spain. Not for the last time Britain intervened militarily using amphibious forces. The following year Royal Navy vessels transported Cristino troops under Borso di Carminati's command in the Army of the Centre from Vinaroz to Valencia, thereby reinforcing the Cristino offensive against Chiva. The British alliance also served as a bulwark to counter-revolution, just like the long arm of Stalin one hundred years later. In spring 1837 Admiral Parker disembarked Royal Marines in Barcelona who freed up Cristino army units to impose martial law in the city.[149] Two working-class National Militia battalions (known as the 'Sappers' and the 'Overalls') were disarmed and an inflammatory newspaper editor executed. There were no more riots in Barcelona for the rest of 1837 as street politics were subsumed into the competing bribery networks of the Moderate and Progressive parties, under the watchful eye of armed militia in the streets and British vessels off the coast.[150]

The British contribution to the government victory persisted even after the Treaty of Vergara ended the war on its main front. The Treaty of Vergara doomed the rebels to international isolation from their erstwhile supporters in the rest of Europe. Cabrera's last hope hinged on a six million real loan his agents had raised with the Gower banking house in London in late 1839. These funds paid for 20,000 Belgian-manufactured rifles, which were transported on a British vessel destined to land them on Carlist-held coastline in the Levante. Intelligence reports set off a flurry of diplomatic activity in Brussels and London, and both capitals in early

January 1840 placed a ban on all arms sales to Spain. In the event, the ship and its precious cargo sailed before the ban.[151] Quite how the rebels planned to land this ostentatious cargo remains a mystery, although Carlist control of some points in the Ebro estuary suggests the likeliest planned destination. But the Royal Navy intercepted the ship in the Mediterranean before it could land its cargo, and handed over the weapons to government authorities in Barcelona. This action more than any other demonstrated the decisive international effects of foreign intervention, for the weapons were detailed to arm a 22,000-strong march on Madrid in the summer of 1840. Whether Cabrera could have stormed the capital seems highly unlikely, but such an arms boost would at least have prolonged rebel resistance beyond June 1840.[152]

The volunteering tradition one hundred years later

Given this tradition of international intervention, foreign interest in 1936 was hardly viewing fallow ground. Spaniards as well as foreigners viewed the Spanish Civil War as a repeat of the Carlist Wars. International volunteers found themselves fighting over the same ground. The heroic Cristino defence of Gandesa became legendary in nineteenth-century Spain, nor was it entirely forgotten after 1936. Episodes of heroic resistance, like that of Gandesa against Cabrera in May 1837, when women and the elderly joined in the defence, or Caspe, which was a repeated battleground between Carlists and liberals,[153] were remembered by anarchists such as Abad de Santillán as an inspiring defence of liberty.[154] Gandesa became notorious during the Spanish Civil War, too, as British International Brigaders suffered some of their worst casualties in its defence against Franco's eastern offensive in 1938, and Caspe was the location of a desperate last stand by the XV International Brigade during the Nationalist offensive of April 1938, one hundred years after the town had been burnt to ashes in the fighting of the First Carlist War.[155] Pro-rebel foreign observers liked to exaggerate the intervention of foreign foes: the *Daily Mail* correspondent Harold Cardozo grotesquely estimated that there were as many as 60,000 foreign reds in Spain by the end of 1936.[156] Such hyperbole added a xenophobic strand to Spanish conservatism, which remembered France and Britain as historical enemies. At the height of the First Carlist War, the rebel general Eguía made promises to 'exterminate all Englishmen at least as far as London'.[157] But the ostentatious xenophobic strand was by no means limited to actual Carlists. This attitude became explicit as Spanish opinion divided during the 'war of words' regarding Spanish neutrality in the First World War. The pro-Entente intellectuals and regionalists were accused by the pro-Central Powers, *germánofilos,* of choosing Europe over Spain.[158]

Despite the avowed Spanishness of Carlism, it would draw international acolytes in 1936 just as it had one hundred years earlier. Many foreigners were fascinated by the pre-war mobilization of the Carlists of Navarra. The centenary of Zumalacárregui's death was turned into a campaign to impose discipline, martial values and obedience, in preparation for a renewed Carlist War.[159] Peter Kemp, who was 'too conservative for the Cambridge University Conservative association', was inspired by the historical example of Zumalacárregui to volunteer in 1936 for the Carlists. Kemp's friend, the British *Daily Mail* correspondent Cardozo, toured the rebel zone wearing the historical red beret of the Carlists.[160]

The emotional appeal of the 1830s was used not just by the 1930s generation but also in the political afterlife of Carlist War veterans themselves. The post-war result by 1840 was the fusion of demands for political and social rights in Spain and elsewhere in Europe (Barcelona's rising in 1842, Chartism, the 1848 revolutions). This situation stood in stark contrast to the European situation one hundred years later. The First World War had left a legacy of pacifism and international socialism, while the European legacy of the Second World War was no longer revolutionary, the continent being split between Stalinism, social democracy, Christian democracy and authoritarian regimes. The picture of the 1830s pitting romantic volunteers for the Liberals against Ultramontane knights-errant for the Carlists was modernized into a 'Last Great Cause' one hundred years later. The 1930s international fight was a fight of émigrés, as most volunteers were either refugees from authoritarian regimes or were the first generation of immigrants with a similar persecuted background. They presided over the transformation of left-wing pacifism. Pacifism, so dominant in European intellectual circles in the wake of the Great War, in 1936 was virtually interchangeable with anti-fascism; by 1938, however, pacifism and anti-fascism had become intractable opposites. The British poet Julian Bell wrote shortly before his death at Brunete in July 1937 that pacifism now meant submission to fascism.[161] Socialist anti-militarism at once both supported pacifism and justified the use of violence in self-defence.[162] The war in Spain thus appeared wholly defensive.

Carlists during the 1830s and Nationalists during the 1930s talked of foreign volunteers for the other side as scum. The French legitimist press condemned the 1830s foreign auxiliaries as 'bandits collected in the taverns of London and the alleyways of Paris and Brussels'.[163] Over a century later, Francoist historians pointed to the 'first International Brigades' as evidence of the 'foreignness' of liberalism, imposed by force on an unwilling population.[164] Nineteenth-century liberal writers who celebrated the auxiliaries' 'altruism' were largely forgotten.[165] In the 1930s the Nationalist press returned to the excoriating language of the 1830s. The main difference concerned anti-Semitism. Whereas the 1830s Carlists adopted what may be termed Christian, or traditional, anti-Semitism, especially during the revolutionary premiership of Mendizábal, the right's anti-Semitism during the 1930s was much more insidious and arraigned along 'scientific' principles. The International Brigades were described as 'dirty, smelly foreigners with monstrous faces'.[166] They met congenial company according to the 1939 Francoist novel *Heroismo oscuro* ('Hidden Heroism'), which depicted the Republicans of Madrid as 'gorillas, sub-humans' and 'a people who are evil to the marrow'.[167] The propaganda of the rebels' most formidable ally, Nazi Germany, dubbed the volunteers for the Republic the 'International Criminal Brigade'.[168] In retaliation, the Republican side tried its best to match such hyperbole in its propaganda claim that its struggle against 'fascism' was ultimately resistance to 'foreign' fascism directed from Rome and Berlin.[169]

The vituperation of volunteers for liberty in the 1830s and 1930s was countered by an opposing extreme of romantic representation. In fact, the motives of volunteers were mixed, and their biographies after Spain were not usually happy and comfortable. After the Liberal victory of 1839, Spanish diplomats abroad were swamped by demands for back-pay by veterans of the foreign auxiliary legions. As late as 1859, complaints reached the legation in Lisbon relating to outstanding payments owed to veterans. The Regiments of Oporto Chasseurs and Grenadiers appear to have suffered the longest arrears in pay. The grenadiers were forcibly dissolved in October 1841 in response to the rebellion of their commander, Borso di Carminati, against Espartero's regime. For two decades, Spanish authorities refused to honour the grenadiers' arrears on the grounds that the veterans had not submitted the correct paperwork.[170] Bad blood existed between the grenadiers and the Spanish government, but the same could not be said of the British veterans who also faced lengthy arrears. As late as 1855, the British legation in Madrid was kept busy relaying to the Spanish government appeals from veterans' families in Britain. On irate letter exclaimed, 'Some of the claims are for sums of 400 and 250 reales and it really seems incomprehensible that the Government of her Catholick Majesty should submit to being damned for such paltry amounts.'[171]

Of course, one hundred years later, foreign volunteers often had far worse privations to face than poverty. Yet the post-war lives of the 1830s auxiliaries remain unexplored, despite their apparent political significance. Felix Lichnowsky's armed service with the Carlists helped to target him for assassination by German revolutionaries in 1848. British auxiliary Alexander Somerville became a leading Chartist who once managed to calm a radical crowd in Nottingham with allusions to Spanish violence, proving the need for peaceful change. In his old age Somerville and other Chartists regretted the return of another Carlist revolt in the 1870s and cherished hopes for the success of the Spanish Federal Republic of 1873.[172] After 1945, by contrast, no oblivion enveloped the International Brigade veterans. A cult of international heroes was cultivated in respect to the Spanish Civil War, especially in the socialist states of Eastern Europe. Yet there were of course countless individual tragedies which did not fit the heroic narrative. The onset of the Second World War made the veterans' plight even more dangerous than it had been in the last century. Even during the war, the brutality of totalitarianism claimed foreign victims. The Independent Labour Party volunteer Bob Smillie was killed by his own side after the May 1937 counter-revolution, probably because the communist-dominated authorities believed that he was an anti-communist of considerable standing.[173] Western European volunteers had to contend with the Nazi takeover of their homelands in 1940. US veterans faced suspicion during the McCarthy era.

Other volunteers were their own worst enemies. Herbert George Rowlands (alias Roland Miller) served on the government side in Spain and then in the British Merchant Navy. When his ship was sunk in June 1940 and he was captured, Miller was interned in Germany where, in June 1944, he joined the pro-Nazi British Free Corps. Court-martialled after the Second World War by the British, the 'criminal, cunning and persistent liar' was found at the same time to have been 'ferociously anti-Hitler' even though he had a German girlfriend. This baffling testimony resulted in his sentence of two years' hard labour.[174] Adventurous desperados could be found in the 1930s just as in the 1830s. Yet the role of international volunteers in the 1830s has been virtually lost to history, as has Mill's defence of them. The International Brigade volunteers have suffered no such oblivion. In 1996, some sixty years after the start of the Spanish Civil War, the government of post-Francoist Spain awarded honorary Spanish citizenship to International Brigade veterans. No honour was extended to the first generation of international volunteers of the 1830s, whose lives and plight were lost to history.

6

Woe to the vanquished

There is another, personal aspect to the international history of the Spanish Civil Wars which bears comparison. Geography compelled France to become the main destination for both wartime and post-war refugees from both conflicts. The French border was no stranger to war in both conflicts. During the 1830s the proximity of the French border to fighting on the northern front shaped a diverse range of human, commercial, military and diplomatic factors. In the 1930s civil war French border settlements would get caught in the crossfire, especially in the early days of battle raging in Navarra: French Behobie near Hendaye was raked by crossfire during the Nationalist assault on Irún and authorities imposed a virtual curfew on its residents, just as when Spanish fire raked Behobie in the 1830s and 1870s Carlist Wars.[1] During the First Carlist War the protracted nature of military operations close to the French frontier regularly drew spectators, not least because the port of San Sebastián was always bursting at the seams with Anglo–French shipping.

During the First Carlist War, remote Pyrenean passes into France became the haunt of Carlist officers fleeing government counter-insurgency operations. The Carlist junta of Catalonia in 1838 took refuge across the border in protest at the actions of its own captain-general. In late January 1837 Ramón Cabrera interned himself on the French side of the border in order to heal his wounds and flee a counter-insurgency operation.[2] But the real story of cross-border movements concerns not the distinguished, but the ordinary Spaniards forced to flee. Some seeking refuge were soldiers, even officers, especially after 1839 when a large contingent of the Carlist army refused to accept the Vergara settlement. Often they fled in the company of their families, and sometimes families and even individuals fled the war without any military claims at all.

Being the only Great Power bordering Spain, including the most conflictive regions of Spain in both civil wars, it was no surprise that France faced the greatest challenges dealing with refugees and militants crossing its border. During both the 1830s and 1930s wars the French government had to reconcile a willingness to accommodate Spanish border-crossers with the limitations of financial resources. Even though in March 1834 the National Assembly proclaimed the border départements out of bounds to Spanish exiles, it also voted some 4 million francs to aid the 5,500 refugees in France at that time, which amounted to the first ever refugee policy conducted by a parliamentary regime in history. Refugees were assigned to fixed localities (*assignation à residence*) where they were obliged to report regularly to the gendarmes and prohibited from travelling without permission. Absconders forfeited their subsidy and were referred to the Interior Ministry.[3] The financial burden and polarized French views about Spain's war in the 1830s anticipated the controversy of the 1930s. A radical deputy compared the paucity of French old-age pensions (some 50 francs per month) with the 'generosity' shown to Spanish refugees, which could be as high as 150 francs per month in the case of young children. The right-wing press lobbied for the repatriation of Spanish refugee children for financial and family reasons. Thus, in October 1937, the National Assembly decreed that all Spaniards 'who are not able to assure themselves of their sustenance would be returned to their country'.[4] By the winter of 1937 the cost of sustaining the 45,000-strong group of Spanish exiles had risen to 1 million francs per day, and one-third of these recipients were children, many of whom were unaccompanied.[5] Monetary values are difficult to compare with the First Carlist War but the 1 million francs per day was likely to be relatively greater than the 16,000 francs per day cost to the French government of supporting the 30,000 Carlist refugees at the height of the influx of 1840.[6] Realizing the impracticality of repatriating vulnerable refugees to a warzone, the French government relaxed its decree in the case of refugees living with private families or earning their own living, and conceded that children supported privately or through trade-union efforts would also remain in France.[7]

Even though the polarized ideology of the 1930s made France anxious about its security, the presence of refugees in the 1830s actually presented a greater security threat. In both wars the French government tried to limit refugee numbers close to the border, repeatedly ordering local authorities to disperse Spanish nationals deeper into France. Bayonne was the centre of Cristino and Carlist espionage in the first war and Biarritz performed a similar role in the 1930s.[8] France's south-western border départements were bastions of legitimism and had proved remarkably friendly to Carlist exiles. Presbyteries and chateaux lent shelter, money and even arms for the cause of God and King in the country next door. Emmanuel Tronco has shown that French pro-Carlism was expressed in four forms: morally (propaganda), charitably (refugees), financially and materially (weapons), and militantly (volunteering for the Pretender).[9] Despite the shock of the 1832 legitimist rising by the Duchesse de Berry, the French police remained less than fully effective at interdicting this cross-border support network linking Spanish Carlists with French 'Carlists' (supporters of the exiled Charles X), much to the chagrin of the Spanish government. The 1930s Spanish refugees were citizens of a friendly government, but those of the 1830s were either potentially hostile rebels or unwelcome deserters from the Spanish government army. It was with relief that the French government greeted Don Carlos's order over the winter of 1837–38 for displaced Carlists in France to return to the rebel-held areas of Spain.[10] Appeals by the rebels were also made one hundred years later, but as these targeted friendly Republican exiles, they were greeted with consternation in France. From May 1937 British and French vessels began evacuating Basque families fleeing the rebel advance.[11] Two months after the rebel capture of Bilbao, Franco launched a public appeal for the repatriation of all Basque children refugees abroad, and this apparently humanitarian gesture was supported by the Vatican emissary to France, Monsignor Hildebrand Antoniutti.[12] Many did return while the war was still raging, especially women and children whose male heads of household were still thought to be in Spain. But many more remained out of fear or out of a desire for independence or freedom.

The plight of wartime refugees in both conflicts was eclipsed by the mass emigrations of 1839 and especially 1939. Around 27,000 refugees crossed into France after 1839, and they found themselves caught between the Scylla of an increasingly hostile host government and the Charybdis of a vindictive post-war government in Spain. The French state was determined to prevent them from collecting near the border, and still more collaborating with legitimist plots inside France, so fifteen depots were hastily established in different locations to receive them.[13] At first only some 6,000 internees were reckoned with, the number of militants who had refused to swear to the Vergara Accord. But four-and-a-half times this number in fact reached France over 1839–40. Authorities tried to keep Carlists away from the border with Spain, but also away from sensitive areas in France like the restive Vendée. As Cabrera's refugees swelled the influx in June 1840, there were calls in the National Assembly to enlist the vanquished fighters in the French Foreign Legion, and as numbers remained high by 1842, the French government even offered refugees 100 francs in return for emigrating to Latin America. With the war in Spain over, defeated Carlists met an increasingly hostile reception in France. In June 1841 a government circular confirmed that the fourteen departments closest to Spain remained out of bounds to Carlists, and this prohibition was extended in 1843 to France's twelve western departments, where diehard legitimism, Paris feared, might be boosted by Spanish Carlists.[14] The last restrictions on Carlists' movements would not be removed until the end of the Second Empire in 1870. Even though restrictions slackened in practice before they were removed by law, Spanish exiles suffered from informal discrimination owing to contemporary stereotypes, reinforced by the Carlist War, that their nationality was lazy, fanatical and violent.[15]

But the real tragedy facing Carlist exiles after 1839 relates to the vindictive attitude of the triumphant Liberal regime in Spain. The influx of refugees into France after the Vergara settlement alarmed Spanish diplomatic agents who saw them as a national security threat for two reasons. The rebels in the east had not yet been subdued. The government was in no mood to distinguish between the 6,000 genuine Carlist diehards from Navarra and Alava who had rejected the Vergara settlement, and the many more innocent defeated militants and civilians driven by fear and destitution into France. In October the consul at Bayonne urged Madrid to exercise the utmost pressure on the French for internment as 'Carlists (in the border regions) can be heard shouting "Death to the *negros*! Death to the tyrants! Long live the Basque country! Long live *los fueros netos*!"'.[16] Two weeks later the anguished consul reported that 'of the 3,577 Carlists interned in Bayonne, 2,323 have already returned to Spain, although more than 200 have been arrested for turning out to be deserters from our own army'.[17] As winter swept south-western France in 1839 the Spanish consul at Bordeaux explained the complexity of the refugee crisis:

> The greatest number of those remaining in France will not return to Spain because they are utterly destitute, others because letters from their party inside Spain spread fear of our reprisals, and others cannot be granted amnesty because they refuse point-blank to swear allegiance to the queen. For these reasons I advise our embassy that it is impossible to know whether exiles returning to Spain are innocent.[18]

Generalísimo Espartero in 1839, like Franco in 1939, was worried that his victory might be undone by armed exiles returning: 'Let us nip this evil in the bud by soliciting the French government to intern all Carlists at liberty in that kingdom, and to imprison them at least one hundred leagues from our frontier.'[19] Espartero's pressure resulted in a decree banning the issuance to refugees of passports by Spanish consuls in France. On 21 September the Spanish government decreed that no refugees whatsoever would be allowed to return to their homes in the chief war zones of Navarra, Catalonia, Aragón or Valencia, and that even those applying to return to homes elsewhere in Spain would need to produce at Spanish consulates in France testimonies of their good conduct.[20] Miraflores, Spanish ambassador to Paris, hoped that Madrid's own hard line combined with the anti-Carlist 'movement' government in office since May 1839 might result in effective collaboration against the refugees.[21] But in fact the French government was conducting its own policy with Spanish refugees. Even though soldiers arriving with family dependants were distributed to an archipelago of depots that sprang up across south-western France, little attempt was made to detain individual men of military age trying to cross into Spain. Even though Espartero condemned the 'the refugees amassed on our border who invade us each day ... and who want to prolong our misery', the French government countered that many of the men were in fact deserters from the government army.[22] In May 1839 Molé was replaced as prime minister by Marshal Soult of the pro-interventionist 'movement' party, but the French government continued to disappoint Spanish hopes of secure internment of exiles. Soult complained to ambassador Miraflores of the 'terrible burden of Carlists in France', especially of the 14,000 who followed the Pretender into exile after the Vergara surrender, and advised that only a complete amnesty and a commitment to preserve the fueros would avert a humanitarian catastrophe from unfolding.[23] The victorious Cristinos, by contrast, just like the rebels of 1939, saw no reason to 'reopen the civil war' by allowing the refugees back, and felt no compunction to ease the plight of a government that had repeatedly shown its bad faith to the victorious side of the Spanish Civil Wars. They still had their hands full with a desertion crisis within Spain, which showed no sign of abating even with the onset of peace. In August 1840, two months into the 'peace', the prefect of Cáceres (Extremadura) decreed collective punishment in the form of fines against family members who refused to aid authorities in recapturing deserters.[24] In any case, Ambassador Miraflores responded to Soult's pleas icily, accusing the French of having permitted the build-up of rebel arms on the frontier with Catalonia.[25]

Long into the 1840s and 1940s, refugees from the losing side found themselves stranded abroad and barred from returning to Spain. Defeated Republican refugees in 1939 fled in droves across the border into France. Bourg-Madame was one of several concentration camps that persisted into the Vichy era (other camps being Le Vernet, Gurs and Bram). The neglect and, later, designed brutality inflicted on red prisoners under Nazi pressure and then outright occupation,[26] contrasted with Bourg-Madame's role during the First Carlist War as a repeated zone of violation for Carlists rather than Liberals passing along the 'neutral road' between Puigcerdà and the Spanish exclave of Llívia.[27]

The details of individual refugees reveal the tragedy of exile. Carlist refugee José Esteban y Baltasar of Montalbán (Teruel) in September 1840 applied for leave to return from France, having secured eyewitness testimonies that he had been forcibly abducted by the rebels on campaign, and promising to swear allegiance to the Constitution. The Paris embassy rejected his petition because 'if an exception were made in this case, exceptions would have to be made for others offering the same stories'.[28] Carlist soldier, Bernabé Santibáñez, fled to Portugal after the peace, leaving his family in Extremadura utterly destitute. By the end of 1841 he managed the remarkable feat of an interview with Portugal's Marshal Saldanha, who was moved to issue him a passport to return to Cáceres. But once Santibáñez entered Spanish territory, the prefect of Cáceres had him arrested all the same. Santibáñez was imprisoned for 'common crimes' rather than 'political crimes' pardonable by the Vergara Treaty. Espartero's 'general amnesty' of 30 August 1841 could not apply because not only had Captain Santibáñez waged war outside the region covered by the Eliot Treaty, but he had escaped capture when his comrades ambushed his government militia captors and spirited him across the border. Santibáñez languished in prison and his family faced the reprisals of the victorious liberal state.[29] Others renounced their Carlism and swore allegiance to Isabella II in the hope of amnesty, only to face the reprisals of fellow diehards. Marcos Carrero pleaded that he was a 'Castillian in all the glory of its meaning', but in May 1840 remained interned with his wife at Limoges, even though 'many months have passed since I swore allegiance to the Constitution'. Carrero's 'treason' was detested by his fellow internees and his wife had frequently had to intervene to stop violence. The wife protested that her family in Villacarlos de Campos (Valencia) had been ruined by the absence of the male breadwinner, and her appeal for amnesty was approved.[30]

In November 1840, pressure had reached such a degree that the Espartero regime set up an advisory commission concerning the fate of exiles and prisoners.[31] Espartero, anticipating the language of Franco one hundred years later, reiterated that the Vergara settlement only absolved rebels of 'political' crimes, and not of 'common' crimes. In practice, this hard line barred thousands of exiles from returning on often specious grounds. Over the winter of 1840–41 the wife of exiled captain Francisco Jáuregui pleaded for her husband's return to Catalonia, promising his willingness to swear to the Constitution, only to be disappointed by demands for 'guarantors to present Jáuregui's case at the local (esparterista) authorities'.[32] Meanwhile, known wrongdoers were sometimes amnestied. Francisco Grau had led a rebel faction in Catalonia, which was hated by villagers in its path for its extortion of money and provisions in the name of the king. Once Grau started publicly flogging municipal leaders, the Carlist high command intervened by demoting Grau to a minor role. In 1840 Grau escaped vengeance by following other Carlist exiles into France.[33] But in August 1841 he secured testimonies on his behalf by the young Catalan Cortes deputy, Juan Prim, and was permitted to return home to his native Reus, perhaps in recognition of the damage his tyranny had done to the rebel cause.[34]

Far fewer Carlist exiles reached Britain compared to France, but even the Spanish legation in London was unable to cope with applications for amnesty. The legation made sure to refuse passports to notorious figures, such as Segismundo Puigbó, a veteran of the Royalist in addition to the Carlist War, whose petition to return to Catalonia was rejected on security grounds.[35] But by April 1843 the legation complained that it could no longer cope with the numbers and threatened to issue passports to all ex-Carlists.[36] In January 1844 numbers petitioning the London legation were still high, and after a meeting at Abbeville with the Spanish ambassador to France, the legate wrote to Madrid protesting yet another instruction to deny passports in the wake of renewed instability in Spain following the fall of Regent

Espartero: 'The terms of the Vergara Treaty would seem still to apply ... and the unhappy émigrés lack all recourse for living, knowledge of English, and even lack access to compatriots who might help them.'[37]

The privations and even terror that faced the 40,000 or so refugees after 1839 cannot be compared with the terror facing a large proportion of the ten times as many refugees who fled the collapse of the Republic one hundred years later. Collective memory of Franco's terror is particularly marked in the Basque Country, seat of the global notoriety of Guernica. This can be explained by the unambiguous repression of autonomy in the defeated provinces of Guipúzcoa and Vizcaya, the persistence of Francoist martial law in these provinces alongside an explicit repression of the Basque cultural identity, and fourth, the contingent factor that the collapse of Catalonia early in 1939 drove some 500,000 refugees into exile in France, and a large proportion of these (between 100,000 and 150,000) were Basques displaced from their homeland.[38]

Francoist legislation against the two coastal Basque provinces meant a prolonged state of war for many, due to a campaign of cultural repression, political persecution and ethnic discrimination with the Basque identity being stigmatized as counter-Spanish.[39] The Basque memory of the conflict combined with the short-lived autonomy that many Basques saw snatched away from them almost certainly bred anger and resentment amongst many, not just with the resultant far-right regime, but also with their unwanted inclusion in the affairs of Spain. In reality, physical destruction in the Basque region was less than what was inflicted on other regions of Spain, and immediate repression was also at a lower level due to the humane interventions of the Basque Church and even of some victorious Carlists following the Church lead.[40] Fewer than 25,000 were killed by Nationalist forces in the Basque Country, most of these meeting their fate in the 'two-month terror' that followed the fall of Bilbao.[41] Horrific though they figures are, they are not exceptional when compared to the rest of Spain. Nor are they horrific when compared with the killing of the Carlist War. The refugee figures, however, are much greater than the numbers after 1839, which describes a greater degree of terror and real or threatened persecution. But we cannot ultimately discern whether the milder repression of the vanquished in 1839 was the result of a 'gentler' victorious regime or merely the benign result of a more backward state with less power to terrorize and coerce.

Conclusions

A myth emerged from the defeated side in both conflicts that defeat was the product of being 'stabbed in the back'. Thus Maroto's 1839 coup and 'shameful' peace left Navarra and Alava undefeated on the battlefield. Similarly, the communist coup of 1937 and suppression of the 'people in arms' was held in anarchist and libertarian quarters to have made Franco's victory possible. These myths were consoling for the losers in both wars, who refused to acknowledge that they had been outnumbered in the 1830s and outfought in the 1930s. Certainly, both civil wars appear to fly in the face of the adage that history is written by the winners. The collective memory of the 1833–40 conflict remains very much weighted towards the defeated Carlist side, whereas leftist historians were sidetracked by the liberal revolution of the 1830s and tended to overlook the complexities of the remarkable liberal military victory. Similarly, several historians of the Spanish Civil War have marvelled how the history of that conflict has been far more sympathetic to the defeated Republicans.[1]

The first conclusion to draw is military in nature. This comparison of the two Spanish Civil Wars demonstrates that technological advances in warfare did not equate to a brutalization of conflict. In both wars atrocities were much more the product of 'primitive' conflict at close quarters: massacres of both civilians and combatants tended to be the product of timeless, indeed pre-modern, motives and to be conducted within easy range of sight between perpetrators and victims. The rapes, murders and public humiliations could easily have been chapters out of the European Wars of Religion. In the First Carlist War the preponderance of irregular warfare and the lack of any breakthrough in modern military technology beyond steamships guaranteed such 'pre-modern' atrocities. Even though the technological potential for 'mass' atrocities one hundred years later was immensely greater, the nature of atrocity proved remarkably similar. The iconic (and therefore distorting) cultural impact of Guernica is the exception that proves the rule. Thus, in spite of the exogenous showcasing of modern weaponry by Nazis and Fascists, the intimate nature of killing in the 1930s retained more of a nineteenth-century nature than a superficial glance at modern weaponry would imply. These findings support thematic studies in military history, which have revised simplistic master narratives of modernized weaponry being equated with an intensification or totalization of warfare.[2]

Similarly, even though Spain in the 1930s possessed much more developed economic and military infrastructure, both civil wars witnessed similar degrees of militarization. The unprecedented 1835 government levy of 100,000 men would have equated to almost 250,000 in proportion to the 1935 population. The million or so men under arms in 1838 proportionately compare to the rather more than two million under arms in 1938. Indeed, by some measures, 'people's war' was even more developed in the 1830s. Military historians identify three types of people's war: guerrilla warfare, war with militia armies and war with conscript armies.[3] All three pertained to the 1830s, but only the latter two to the 1930s.

Of the two major differences, the first concerns the political trajectory of each conflict. The 1830s war produced Spain's first modern politics out of an absolutist state, establishing a constitutional legacy that was severed by the Spanish Civil War. Although both the Patriots' Cortes of Cádiz of 1810–14 and the Liberals of 1820–23 had ruptured the absolutist tradition, it took the 1830s civil war to create a liberal–constitutional legacy that lasted (despite some hiatus) until the Spanish Civil War. The struggle for constitutional liberty was won in the 1830s but lost one hundred years later. Whereas the 1830s conflict bestowed a legacy of modern political participation and representation, the 1930s conflict ended it, not only because of the victory in 1939 of the side committed to eradicating Spain's liberal tradition, but also because of illiberal responses by Republicans themselves. This comparative aspect thus links Spain's (and Europe's) romantic era of liberal revolution with the eclipse of interwar European liberalism, offering a new perspective for Mark Mazower's thesis concerning the brutalization of European politics. It demonstrates the importance of civil war in creating and overturning political systems and allegiances.

Whereas Franco's victory closed off democracy in Spain for two generations, the praetorian liberal state which triumphed in the First Carlist War could never quite put the genie of radicalism back in its bottle. The suppression of the militia in 1844 did not remove it as a moral force. Disbanded veterans retained their own networks which sprang into life during later revolutions. The working-class barricades of Barcelona of 1842 and 1843 were manned by Carlist War veterans. Other veterans militated against the iniquities of the liberal property revolution and the poor conditions of the post-war army. Political demands grew for the disentailed land to be awarded to Carlist War veterans. At the end of the war, the radical poet and godfather of Spanish romanticism, Espronceda, joined with the Republican journalist, Victor Pruneda, in demanding the reparto of disentailed lands among the people.[4] The land question achieved mass political consciousness as a consequence of the First Carlist War and it was closed by the victory of counter-revolution one hundred years later.

Both wars had ironic legacies in terms of their religious impact. Mendizábal's disentailment of religious properties did not bestow upon Spain the wish of the Liberal party for a Catholic and yet laic Spain. The Church lost most of its landed property as a consequence of the 1830s war, and the lowest point in relations between the liberal regime and the Holy See was reached a year after the ending of hostilities, in 1841, when the Vatican attacked Espartero's attempts to extend disentailment to parish property in words which amounted to a declaration of war.[5] Yet Narváez's ousting from power of Espartero in 1843 set in train a gradual process of *détente* between church and state. Liberal newspapers in 1840 complained about former Carlist parishes in the north relapsing into bad old ways, as priests used moral pressure to oblige villagers to pay the 'true tenth', despite the abolition of tithes. The formerly Carlist strongholds in rural Guipúzcoa persisted in this practice until at least as late as 1846.[6] The victorious liberal regime itself softened its stance towards the Church in the wake of the 1843 moderado counter-revolution. In 1848 Narváez dispatched Spanish troops to help defend Rome from Italian revolutionaries and by 1851 a Concordat was agreed. Even though the Vatican accepted the loss of its landed property in Spain, it was effectively free to regain all its former power, and arguably more besides, via an 1857 monopoly granted in education and via newer investments in more lucrative urban properties. The material recovery in the Church's position was accompanied by the reconciliation of Catholics with the Spanish nation, owing to the 'Neo-Catholic' philosophies espoused in the 1840s by Jaime Balmés and Donoso Cortes. Sor Patricinio, the Carlist stigmatic of the 1830s, became Queen Isabella II's most intimate confidant. Thus was set in train the process towards the very 'National Catholicism' which motivated the rebels of 1936. In most of Spain, beyond the medieval smallholdings of Navarra, the Basque provinces and Old Castile, this was very much a Catholicism of the wealthy, of the landowner rather than the day-labourer, of the factory owner rather than the machinist. The anticlericalism which gripped the working classes from the last third of the nineteenth century was the logical consequence. Even so, the National Catholicism of 1936 was powerful enough to unite Franco's right-wing factions and to attract support from the majority of the world's Catholics, which was much more than Don Carlos had achieved one hundred years earlier.

The second irony lies with the victory of the rebels in 1939. The victory of Franco's Nationalists allowed the Spanish Church to return to the levels of power and advantage that it had not enjoyed since the eve of the First Carlist War.[7] Despite the victorious doctrine of 'National Catholicism', regime attempts to 'rechristianize' Spaniards were a failure, especially among the anticlerical working classes, not least because supposedly religious redemption was so transparently political. It was the tragedy of Spanish Catholicism that, in allying itself so closely with the civil war victors, it effectively abandoned its pastoral task among the vanquished.[8] In fact, Spain grew ever more aconfessional and secular in its everyday culture, and this process accelerated on the back of the economic boom of the 1960s. Mass attendance fell to figures comparable with 'Catholic' – and democratic – Italy, and by the early 1970s they had fallen far behind democratic Ireland.[9] Mammon dictated a new consumer culture which raised Spanish living standards by 1970 almost on par with those of Northern Europe. Only misfits such as Carlists yearned for a return to a spiritual instead of a materialistic Spain. The Spanish Civil War was in many respects the last of a cycle of nineteenth-century civil wars whose political and international ramifications resembled the First Carlist War more than any other. Happily, the transition to democracy since General Franco's death appears to have been consolidated. Despite such anti-democratic challenges as the Francoist army then and Eurozone deflation now, renewed civil war in Spain is unthinkable.

NOTES

Acknowledgements

1 Disclaimer: I made every effort to contact the copyright holder (Archivo Municipal de Málaga).

Introduction

1 Francisco J. Romero Salvadó, *The Spanish Civil War: Origins, Course and Outcomes* (London, 2005), p. 100.
2 H. Graham, 'The Spanish Civil War', *The Historical Journal* 30(4) (1987), pp. 989–993, p. 989.
3 Jordi Canal, Preface, in Emmanuel Tronco, *Les carlistes espagnols dans l'Ouest de la France, 1833–1883* (Rennes, 2010), p. 10.
4 Claud Cockburn, *In Time of Trouble* (London, 1956), p. 252.
5 Antonio Gómez López-Quiñones, *La guerra persistente* (Madrid, 2006), p. 12. Examples of 'normalization' studies include Guy Thomson, *The Birth of Modern Politics in Spain* (Basingstoke, 2009); David Ringrose, *Spain, Europe, and the 'Spanish Miracle', 1700–1900* (Cambridge, 1996); Isabel Burdiel, *La política en el reinado de Isabel II* (Madrid, 1998); *Economía, sociedad, política y cultura en la España de Isabel II*, ed. Gonzalo Anes Alvarez de Castrillón (Madrid, 2004); Manuel Santirso Rodríguez, *Progreso y libertad: España en la Europa liberal, 1830–1870* (Madrid, 2008)
6 The most recent examples include Alejandro Quiroga and Miguel Angel del Arco (eds), *Right-Wing Spain in the Civil War Era: Soldiers of God and Apostles of the Fatherland, 1914–45* (London, 2012); and Helen Graham, *The War and Its Shadow: Spain's Civil War in Europe's Long Twentieth Century* (Sussex, 2012).
7 Michael Jabara Carley, 'Caught in a Cleft Stick: Soviet Diplomacy and the Spanish Civil War', in Gaynor Johnson (ed.), *The International Context of the Spanish Civil War* (Cambridge, 2009), pp. 155–156.
8 E.g. Enrique Moradiellos García, *La perfidia de Albión: el gobierno británico y la guerra civil española* (Madrid, 1996); Gerald Howson, *Arms for Spain* (London, 1998); Graham, *The War and Its Shadow*.
9 The relegation of Spain to the historical margins endured, even among eminent scholars, until quite recently. As late as 2004 a major book of world history barely mentioned Spain and Spanish America at all in the 'long' nineteenth century (Christopher Bayley, *Birth of the Modern World, 1780–1914: Global Connections and Comparisons* (London, 2004)).

10 Eric Hobsbawm's 'dual revolution' thesis discovered an economic revolution in Britain during 1789–1848 and a political revolution in France during the same period (Eric Hobsbawm, *The Age of Revolution, 1789–1848* (London, 1962)).

11 Blackbourn and Eley, *The Peculiarities of German History*; Edward Crankshaw, *The Shadow of the Winter Palace* (London, 1976).

12 Mayer, *Persistence of the Old Regime*.

13 Alexis de Tocqueville, *The Old Regime and the French Revolution*, trans. Stuart Gilbert (New York, 1955), p. x.

14 Adrian Shubert, *A Social History of Modern Spain*, p. 2.

15 Walther L. Bernecker, *España entre tradición y modernidad: política, economía y sociedad (siglos XIX y XX)* (Madrid, 1999), pp. 57–58; José María Cuenca Toribio, *La iglesia española ante la revolución liberal* (Madrid, 1971).

16 Carlos Marichal, *Spain, 1834–1844: A New Society* (London, 1977), pp. 207–210.

17 Graham, *The War and its Shadow*, pp. 3, 26–27.

18 Marek Jan Chodakiewicz and John Radzilowski (eds), *Spanish Carlism and Polish Nationalism: The Borderlands of Europe in the 19th and 20th Centuries* (Charlottesville, 2003).

19 Michael Seidman, *The Victorious Counterrevolution* (Wisconsin, 2011).

20 Stanley G. Payne, *Civil War in Europe, 1905–1949* (Cambridge, 2011); Philip B. Minehan, *Civil War and World War in Europe: Spain, Yugoslavia and Greece, 1936–1949* (New York, 2006).

21 E.g. Susan Graysel, *Women and Identities at War*; Winter and Louis-Robert, *Capital Cities at War*; Baldoli, *Forgotten Blitzes*.

22 Eve La Haye, *War Crimes in Internal Armed Conflicts* (Cambridge, 2010), pp. 1–2.

23 Stathis N. Kalyvas, 'Civil Wars', ch. 18, in Carles Boix and Susan C. Stokes (eds), *The Oxford Handbook of Comparative Politics* (Oxford, 2007), pp. 416–422.

24 Theda Skocpol and Margaret Somers, 'The Uses of Comparative History in Macrosocial Enquiry', *Comparative Studies in Society and History* 22 (1980), pp. 174–97, 193–194.

25 An excellent discussion of these problems in relation to comparisons of Nazism and Stalinism can be found in Ian Kershaw and Moshe Lewin (eds), *Stalinism and Nazism: Dictatorships in Common* (Cambridge, 1998), pp. 1–25.

26 Thomas Welskopp, 'Vergleichende Geschichte', *European History Online* (EGO) (3 December 2010), 1–8 (Accessed 25 August 2014).

27 Jürgen Kocka and Heinz-Gerhard Haupt, 'Comparisons and Beyond: Traditions, Scope and Perspectives of Comparative History', in Heinz-Gerhard Haupt and Jürgen Kocka (eds), *Comparative and Transnational History: Central European Approaches and New Perspectives* (New York; Oxford, 2009), pp. 16–17.

28 Julián Marías, *España ante la historia y ante sí misma (1898–1936)* (Madrid, 1996), p. 30.

29 Nigel Townson, 'A Land Apart?' in Townson (ed.), *Is Spain Different?* (Sussex, 2015), pp. 6–7.

30 Luis Garrido Muro, 'El Nuevo Cid. Espartero, María Cristina y el primero liberalismo español (1834–1840)' (Unpublished PhD thesis, Universidad de Cantabria, 2012), pp. 53–54.

31 Cited in Raymond Carr, *The Republic and Civil War in Spain* (London, 1971), p. 38.
32 Jaime del Burgo, *El valle perdido* (Madrid, 1942).
33 Tomás Borras, *Oscuro heroismo* (Seville, 1939), p. 23.
34 Paloma Aguilar Fernández, *Políticas de la memoria y memorias de la política* (Alianza Editorial, 2008), pp. 136–137.
35 E.g. Federico Suárez, Jose-Luis Commellas García, Alfonso Bullón de Mendoza.
36 E.g. Melchor Ferrer, *Historia del tradicionalismo*; Oyarzun, *El carlismo*.
37 E.g. Modesto Lafuente, *Historia de España.*
38 For an example of the second charge, see Book review, Alejandro Quiroga, Manuel Alvarez Tardío and Fernando del Rey Reguillo, eds, *The Spanish Second Republic Revisited: From Democratic Hopes to Civil War (1931–1936)* (Brighton, 2011), in *European History Quarterly* 43(3) (2013), pp. 519–597.
39 Stanley Payne, *The Franco Regime, 1946–1975* (Wisconsin, 2011), p. 210.
40 William Rust, *Britons in Spain* (London, 1939), pp. 1–2.
41 José Alvarez Junco, *Mater Dolorosa* (Madrid, 2001), pp. 145–46; Xosé-Manoel Núñez Seixas, 'Nations in Arms against the Invader: On Nationalist Discourses during the Spanish Civil War', in Chris Ealham and Michael Richards (eds), *The Splintering of Spain: Cultural History and the Spanish Civil War, 1936–1939* (Cambridge, 2005), pp. 47–50.
42 Lluís Roura i Aulinas, 'Hi hagué algun protocatalanisme politic a Cadis?' *L'Avenç*, no. 113 (1988), pp. 32–37; Ronald Fraser, *Las dos guerras de España* (Madrid, 2012). For a contrary view, see Angel Smith, *The Origins of Modern Catalanism, 1770–1898* (Basingstoke, 2014).
43 Ronald Fraser, *Dos guerras de España* (Madrid, 2012). The other comparative study is by M. Chamorro Martínez, *1808–1936: dos situaciones históricas concordantes* (Madrid, 1974). Chamorro argued that both the Peninsular War Patriots and the Spanish Republicans failed to wage war effectively.
44 The oppressive academic culture of Franco's Spain did not permit the production of critical works such as the American Gabriel Jackson's *Spanish Second Republic and Civil War* (New York, 1965), Raymond Carr's highly readable and de-romanticized *Spain, 1808–1939* (Oxford, 1966), and Hugh Thomas's exhaustive and unusually objective *Spanish Civil War* (London, 1962).
45 E.g. Julio Aróstegui, Jordi Canal and Eduardo González Calleja, *El carlismo y las guerra carlistas: hechos, hombres e ideas* (Madrid, 2003).
46 Martin Blinkhorn, *Carlism in Crisis, 1931–1939* (Oxford, 1975).
47 John Keegan, *Face of Battle* (London, 1976), p. 30.
48 Carolyn P. Boyd, 'The Military and Politics, 1808–1874', in José Alvarez Junco and Adrian Shubert (eds), *Spanish History Since 1808* (London, 2000), p. 72.
49 *The Manchester Guardian*, 11 April 1904.
50 Antonio Manuel Moral Roncal, '1868 en la memoria carlista de 1931: dos revoluciones anticlericales y un paralelo', *Hispania Sacra*, LIX (119) (2007), 337–361.
51 Moral Roncal, '1868 en la memoria carlista de 1931', p. 357.
52 Coro Rubio, *Revolución y tradición: el país vasco*, 93–126.
53 Ludger Mees, 'Politics, Economy, or Culture? The Rise and Development of Basque Nationalism in the Light of Social Movement Theory', *TS* 33 (2004), p. 314.

54 Manuel Alvarez Tardío and Roberto Villa García, *El precio de la exclusión: la política durante la Segunda República* (Madrid, 2010), p. 44.

55 Pan-Montojo, 'Mendizábal'; Burdiel and Ledesma, *Liberales, agitadores*.

56 Carlos Navajas Zubeldia, *Leales y rebeldes: la tragedia de los militares republicanos* (Madrid, 2011), pp. 85–86.

57 Buckley, *The Life and Death of the Spanish Second Republic*, p. 19.

58 Esdaile, 'Enlightened Absolutism versus Theocracy in the Spanish Restoration, 1814–1850', in David Laven and Lucy Riall (eds), *Napoleon's Legacy: Problems of Government in Restoration Europe* (Oxford, 2000), 65–82.

59 Martin Blinkhorn, *Carlism and Crisis* (Oxford, 1975), pp. 145–162; Frances Lannon, *Privilege, Persecution and Prophecy: The Catholic Church in Spain 1875–1975* (Oxford, 1987), p. 170.

60 Manuel Aznar, *Historia militar de la guerra de España* (Madrid, 1940), pp. 11–12, 113.

61 José M. Sánchez, *The Spanish Civil War as a Religious Tragedy* (Notre Dame, 1987), p. 148.

62 Frances Lannon, 'The Church's Crusade against the Republic', in Preston (ed.), *Revolution and War in Spain, 1931–39*, pp. 35–36.

63 Alpert, *Republican Army*, p. 29.

64 Blinkhorn, *Carlism and Crisis*, pp. 2–40.

65 Blinkhorn, *Carlism and Crisis*, pp. 20–30.

66 Hilari Raguer, *Gunpowder and Incense* (London, 2007), pp. 39–49.

67 Blinkhorn, *Carlism and Crisis in Spain*, pp. 163–182.

68 Douglas W. Foard, 'The Forgotten Falangist: Ernesto Giménez Caballero', *Journal of Contemporary History*, 10(1) (Jan. 1975), p. 11.

69 *El pensamiento navarro*, Pamplona, 8 May 1938, p. 23 (Jesús Casariego, 'Liberalismo, Marxismo y "Frente Popular").

70 Alice L. Lascelles and J. M. Alberich (eds), *Sir Vincent Kennett-Barrington: Letters from the Carlist War (1874–1876)* (Exeter, 1987), pp. 32–35.

71 Javier Ugarte Tellería, *La nueva Covadonga insurgente: orígenes sociales y culturales de la sublevación de 1936 en Navarra y el País Vasco* (Madrid, 1998), pp. 160–163, 250, 268–269.

72 Fraser, *Blood of Spain*, p. 53.

73 Barrington, *Letters from the Carlist War*, p. 45.

74 Harold Cardozo, *March of a Nation*, p. 83.

75 Javier Ugarte Tellería, *La nueva Covadonga insurgente: orígenes sociales y culturales de la sublevación de 1936 en Navarra y el País Vasco* (Madrid, 1998), pp. 408–409.

76 Jeremy MacClancy, *The Decline of Carlism* (University of Nevada Press, 2000), p. 25.

77 William Bollaert, *The Wars of Succession of Portugal and Spain, from 1826 to 1840* (London, 1870), Vol. II, pp. 11–19; Eric Christiansen, *Origins of Military Power* (Oxford, 1967), p. 45.

78 Rogelio Pérez Olivares, *Héroes de España: Excmo. Sr. D. Emilio Mola Vidal* (Madrid, 1937), p. 23.

79 Julián Casanova, *The Spanish Republic and Civil War* (Cambridge, 2010), pp. 10–11.

80 R. Smith, *The Day of the Liberals in Spain*, pp. 77–83, 100.

81 Jackson, *Spanish Second Republic and Civil War*, p. 28.
82 Casanova, *Spanish Republic*, p. 12.
83 R. Smith, *The Day of the Liberals in Spain*, pp. 75–85.
84 Stanley Payne, *The Spanish Civil War* (Cambridge, 2012), p. 8.
85 Ricardo de la Cierva.
86 Shlomo Ben-Ami.
87 Stanley Payne, *Spain's First Democracy* (Wisconsin, 1993), pp. 105–106.
88 Jaime Elías Torras, *La guerra de los Agraviados* (Barcelona, 1967), xi–xii.
89 Payne, *Spanish Civil War*.
90 Elías Torras, *La guerra de los Agraviados*; George Esenwein and Adrian Shubert, *Spain at War: The Spanish Civil War in Context, 1931–1939* (London, 1995), pp. 83–87.
91 Luis Arranz Notario, 'Libertad y democracia en la España contemporánea: (a propósito de El camino a la democracia en España. 1931 y 1978)', *Cuadernos de pensamiento politico (FAES)*, no. 9 (2006), pp. 233–234; Pío Moa, *Los mitos de la guerra civil* (La Esfera, 2004); Stanley G. Payne, *The Spanish Civil War* (Cambridge, 2012), pp. 37–63.
92 Angel Viñas, 'Playing with History and Hiding Treason: Colonel Casado's Untrustworthy Memoirs and the End of the Spanish Civil War', *Bulletin of Spanish Studies*, 91(1–2) (2014), 295–323.
93 José Ruiz de Luzuriaga, *La contra-gaceta de la Gaceta de Madrid del 7 de abril de 1833* (Bordeaux, 1833), xxviii.
94 Frances Lannon, *Privilege, Persecution and Prophecy* (Oxford, 1987), p. 187.

Part One

1 A. H. N., II-C, Sección Histórica, Carlistas, 1833–34, 2841: October 1833 handbill extract from Pretender's 'Manifesto of Abrantes'.
2 Cited in Ronald Fraser, *Blood of Spain* (London, 1979), p. 61.

Chapter 1

1 Stathis N. Kalyvas, 'Civil Wars', in Carles Boix and Susan C. Stokes (eds), *The Oxford Handbook of Comparative Politics* (Oxford, 2007), p. 427.
2 Wayne H. Bowen and José E. Alvarez, *A Military History of Modern Spain: From the Napoleonic Era to the International War on Terror* (Westport, 2007), p. 2.
3 Antoine Henri Jomini, *Descripción analítica de las combinaciones más importantes de la guerra* (Madrid, 1833).
4 *Eco del Comercio*, 3 April 1837.
5 Alpert, *Republican Army*, p. 194; Preston, *Franco*, pp. 10–11.
6 Preston, *Franco*, pp. 59–60.
7 Stanley G. Payne, 'Political Violence during the Spanish Second Republic', *Journal of Contemporary History*, 25(2/3) (May–June 1990), pp. 269–288.
8 Pedro Pegenaute, *Represión política en el reinado de Fernando VII: las comisiones militares (1824–1825)* (Pamplona, 1974), pp. 1–23.

9 Michael Alpert, 'Soldiers, Politics and War', p. 206; Payne, *Military and Politics*, p. 276; Raymond Carr, *The Spanish Tragedy: The Civil War in Perspective* (London, 1972), p. 35.

10 Cited in Javier Fernández Sebastián and Juan Francisco Fuentes (eds), *Diccionario político y social del siglo XIX español* (Madrid, 2002), p. 7.

11 Antony Beevor, *The Battle for Spain: The Spanish Civil War, 1936–1939* (London, 2006), p. 49.

12 Seidman, 'The Spanish Civil War', in Nigel Townson (ed.), *Is Spain Different?* (Sussex, 2015), p. 128.

13 James Matthews, *Reluctant Warriors* (Oxford, 2012), pp. 24–25.

14 T.N.A., Long Papers, bundle 715, T 1/4243: 1 June 1835 letters from Spanish ambassador Alava to Foreign Office.

15 P. Risco, *Zumalacárregui en campaña*, p. 74.

16 Francisco J. Romero Salvadó, *The Spanish Civil War: Origins, Course and Outcomes* (London, 2005), pp. 66–98.

17 Pirala, *Guerra civil*, II, pp. 202–206.

18 T.N.A., F.O. 72/457 George Villiers, doc. 2: 2 January 1836 letter from Villiers to Palmerston detailing Cristino strength.

19 J, Semprún, *Del Hacho al Pirineo* (Madrid, 2004), p. 311, also cited in Matthews, *Reluctant Warriors*, p. 218.

20 Aznar, *Historia militar* (1940), p. 74.

21 T.N.A., HW 22/2, 6C 1056, 'Air Employment', report no. 44 (July 1937): British air attaché assessment of aerial warfare in Spain.

22 Alpert, *Republican Army*, pp. 56–58.

23 Charles Frederick Henningsen, *The Most Striking Events of a Twelvemonth's Campaign with Zumalacárregui in Navarre and the Basque Provinces* (London, 1836), p. 81.

24 Pirala, *Guerra civil*, V, p. 292.

25 T.N.A., FO 72/463 George Villiers, Doc. 298: 19 November 1836 letter from George Villiers in Madrid to Lord Palmerston.

26 Pirala, *Guerra civil*, III, pp. 228–231.

27 *El pensamiento navarro*, Pamplona, 8 May 1938.

28 Joaquín García-Morato, *Guerra en el aire* (Madrid, 1940), pp. 38–39.

29 George Steer, *The Tree of Gernika: A Field Study of Modern War* (London, 1938), pp. 21, 44–45.

30 T.N.A., GFM 33 6B/298/1822, 4305H, E0779687/8: 28 December 1936 letter from ambassador Faupel at Salamanca to Auswärtiges Amt in Berlin.

31 Aznar, *Historia militar*, p. 131.

32 Geoffrey McNeill-Moss, *The Epic of the Alcázar: A History of the Siege of the Toledo Alcázar* (London, 1937), pp. 65–66.

33 Pirala, *Guerra civil*, IV, pp. 67–71.

34 Preston, *Franco*, p. 172.

35 Córdova, *Memorias*, Vol. II, pp. 134–142.

36 T.N.A., FO 72/459 George Villiers, Doc. 149: 18 June 1836 letter from Villiers to Palmerston.

37 Córdova, *Memorias*, Vol. I, pp. 348–352; 401–405, Vol. II, pp. 55–75.

38 Roger Bullen, 'France and the Problem of Intervention in Spain, 1834–1836', *Historical Journal*, 20(2) (1977), pp. 363–393, p. 385; Pirala, *Guerra civil*, II, pp. 473–475.

39   T.N.A., FO/72/459, Doc. 91: 17 April 1836 letter from Villiers to Palmerston concerning fraught meeting between Rayneval and Mendizábal.

40   David Boyd Haycock, *I Am Spain*, p. 38.

41   Tom Wintringham, *English Captain*, p. 37.

42   Gerald Howson, *Arms for Spain: The Untold Story of the Spanish Civil War* (London, 1998).

43   Robert M Ripperger, 'The Development of the French Artillery for the Offensive, 1890–1914', *Journal of Military History*, 59(4) (1995).

44   Marcel Acier (ed.), *From Spanish Trenches: Recent Letters from Spain* (New York, 1937), p. 123.

45   Peter Kemp, *Mine Were of Trouble* (London, 1958) p. 151.

46   Kemp, *Mine Were of Trouble*, pp. 70–71.

47   Michael Howard, *War in European History* (Oxford, 2009), p. 57.

48   Carlos Dembowski, *Dos años en España durante la guerra civil, 1838–40* (Madrid, 2008), p. 42.

49   Mary Vincent, *Spain, 1833–2002: People and State* (Oxford, 2002), p. 148; Barbie Zelizer, *About to Die: How News Images Move the Public* (Oxford, 2010), pp. 177–178.

50   Pedro Corral, *Desertores: la Guerra Civil que nadie quiere contar* (Barcelona, 2006), p. 82.

51   Lichnowsky, *Erinnerungen*, vol. 2, p. 134; Jaime del Burgo, *Historia de la primera guerra carlista*, pp. 212–213.

52   Preston, *Franco*, p. 175.

53   Preston, *Franco*, p 236.

54   T.N.A., HW 22/2, 6C 1056, doc. 13: 7 April 1937 report from British air attaché.

55   Antony Beevor, *The Battle for Spain*, p. 119; Vaill, *Hotel Florida*, p. 49.

56   Preston, *Franco*, p. 200.

57   George Orwell, *Homage to Catalonia* (London, 1989), p. 44.

58   Preston, *¡Comrades! Portraits from the Spanish Civil War* (London, 2000), pp. 288–289.

59   Esmond Romilly, *Boadilla* (London, 1971), p. 145.

60   Kemp, *Mine Were of Trouble*, p. 76.

61   T.N.A., FO 72/459 George Villiers, 31 May 1836 letter from Villiers to Palmerston detailing naval rocket bombardment of Pasaia; Pirala, *Guerra civil*, I, pp. 570–73.

62   T.N.A., FO 72/463 George Villiers, Doc. 309: 22 November 1836 letter from George Villiers to Lord Palmerston concerning Carlist efforts against Bilbao.

63   A.H.N., Estado, 8755, en territorio navarro: September and October 1834 letters from government commanders to Viceroy.

64   Antony Beevor, *The Battle for Spain*, p. 125.

65   T.N.A., FO 72/463 George Villiers, unnumbered (after doc. 327): 17 December 1836 letter from Villiers to Palmerston counselling rejection of Angel de la Liva's balloon project.

66   George Steer, *Tree of Gernika*, pp. 176–177.

67   T.N.A., HW 22/2, 6C 1056, 'Air Employment', Report no. 41, 'war weariness' (21–28 June 1937): British air attaché interview with George Steer.

68   Alaric Searle, 'The German Military Contribution to the Spanish Civil War, 1936–1939', in Gaynor Johnson (ed.), *The International Context of the Spanish Civil War* (Cambridge, 2009), pp. 138–139.

69 Acier, *From Spanish Trenches*, p. 73.
70 James Matthews, *Reluctant Warriors* (Oxford, 2012), pp. 19–21.
71 Sebastian Balfour, *Deadly Embrace* (Oxford, 2002), p. 214.
72 Arturo Barea, *La forja de un rebelde*, p. 641.
73 Walter Laquer, *Guerrilla Warfare: A Historical and Critical Study* (New Jersey, 1997), p. 52.
74 Mary Vincent, 'The Keys to the Kingdom: Religious Violence in the Spanish Civil War', in Michael Richards and Chris Ealham (eds), *The Splintering of Spain: New Historiographical Perspectives on the Spanish Civil War* (Cambridge, 2005), pp. 68–89.
75 Cited in Raymond Carr, *The Spanish Second Republic and Civil War* (London, 1971), p. 142.
76 A.H.N., Estado, 8755: En territorio navarro: 23 September 1834 letter from Comandante of Puente la Reina to Viceroy.
77 Lawrence, *Spain's First Carlist War*, p. 78.
78 Pirala, *Guerra civil*, III, pp. 30–46.
79 *Gaceta Oficial*, 15 April 1836; *Eco del Comercio*, 26 March 1836.
80 Barea, *La forja*, p. 644; Acier, *From Spanish Trenches* (1937), p. 81.
81 Joaquín García-Morato, *Guerra en el aire* (Madrid, 1940), pp. 46–47.
82 T.N.A., German Foreign Ministry (GFM), 33 6B/298/1822, E 077972/73, Vermerk, 19 April 1937 and E 077984, 27 April 1937: reports from Salamanca from Nazi ambassador Faupel.
83 Rafael Miralles, *Memorias de un comandante rojo* (Madrid, 1975), pp. 68–75.
84 Hugh Thomas, *Spanish Civil War* (London, 1986), p. 543.
85 Stathis N. Kalyvas, *The Logic of Violence in Civil Wars* (Cambridge, 2006), pp. 8–9.
86 Ruiz Vilaplana, *Burgos Justice: A Year's Experience of Nationalist Spain* (London, 1938), pp. 96–97.
87 Pirala, *Guerra civil*, II, pp. 327–329; Oyarzun, *Historia del carlismo*, p. 148.
88 Pirala, *Guerra civil*, II, pp. 256–260, 545–565.
89 Francisco Cabello, Francisco Santa Cruz and Ramón María Temprado, *Historia de la guerra última en Aragón y Valencia* (Madrid, 1845), I, p. 108.
90 T.N.A., F.O. 72/459, George Villiers, doc. 137: 29 May 1836 letter from Villiers to Palmerston detailing the expansion of Carlist operations.
91 Rafael M. de Labra, *El Ateneo de Madrid, sus orígenes, desenvolvimiento, representación y porvenir* (Madrid, 1878), p. 51; Abad de Santillán, *Por qué perdimos la guerra* (Buenos Aires, 1940), pp. 75–76; Hugh Thomas, *The Spanish Civil War* (London, 1986), pp. 311, 653.
92 Harold Cardozo, *The March of a Nation: My Year of Spain's Civil War* (London, 1937), p. 18.
93 José María Taboada Lago, *Por una España mejor* (Madrid, 1976), pp. 160–161.
94 Bullón de Mendoza, *Primera guerra carlista*, p. 278.
95 Ricardo de la Cierva, 'The Nationalist Army', in Raymond Carr (ed.), *The Republic and the Civil War in Spain* (London, 1971), p. 199.
96 Rafael Abella, *Julio 1936: Dos Españas frente a frente* (Barcelona, 1981), p. 133.

97 A.M.M., Recortes de la Prensa mercantil: 7 March 1837 concession by town hall to honour Espoz's ashes.

98 *La Vanguardia*, 24 November 1936.

99 Orwell, *Homage to Catalonia*, pp. 98–99.

100 Pirala, *Guerra civil*, IV, pp. 381–388; Bullón de Mendoza, *Primera guerra carlista*, pp. 640–641.

101 John Keegan, *The Face of Battle* (London, 1976), p. 107.

102 Vilaplana, *Burgos Justice*, pp. 64–65.

103 *Eco del Comercio*, 26 January 1836 (suplemento); 9 February 1836.

104 Acier, *From Spanish Trenches*, p. 57.

105 Steer, *Tree of Gernika*, p. 174.

106 Cabello, Santa Cruz and Temprado, *Historia de la guerra última*, II, p. 226.

107 Beevor, *The Battle for Spain*, p. 86.

108 Seidman, *Victorious Counterrrevolution*, pp. 29–37.

109 Hilari Raguer, *Gunpowder and Incense*, p. 116.

110 Graham, *The Spanish Republic at War*, p. 103.

111 Balfour, *Deadly Embrace*, pp. 83, 112.

112 Paul Preston, *Spanish Holocaust* (London, 2012), p. 141.

113 William Rust, *Britons in Spain* (London, 1939), pp. 77–78.

114 Anthony Oberschall, 'The Manipulation of Ethnicity: From Ethnic Cooperation to Violence and War in Yugoslavia', *Ethnic and Racial Studies*, 23(6) (2000), 982–1001.

115 Paul Preston, *The Spanish Holocaust* (London, 2012), pp. 335–340.

116 Chris Ealham, 'Anarchism and Illegality in Barcelona, 1931–37', *Contemporary European History*, IV(2) (July 1995), pp. 149–150.

117 Seidman, *Victorious Counterrrevolution*, p. 128.

118 Similar instances of rebel strength in areas lacking in support can be seen in other civil wars, such as Nicaraguan Sandinistas and Confederacy guerrillas in the Appalachians, Ozarks and Cumberlands (Stathis N. Kalyvas, 'Civil Wars', in Carles Boix and Susan C. Stokes (eds), *The Oxford Handbook of Comparative Politics* (Oxford, 2007), pp. 421–427).

119 Gómez López-Quiñones, *La guerra persistente*, pp. 235–237; Rod Kedward, 'Maquis and the Culture of the Outlaw', in Rod Kedward and Roger Austin (eds), *Vichy France and the Resistance. Culture and Ideology* (London, 1985), p. 234.

120 Adrian Shubert, *A Social History of Modern Spain* (London, 1990), p. 76.

121 Pirala, *Guerra civil*, I, p. 117.

122 Coverdale, *Basque Phase of the First Carlist War*, pp. 173–175, 294–308

123 Seidman, *Republic of Egos*, p. 157.

124 Taboada, *Por una España mejor*, p. 176.

125 *Galería militar contemporánea* (Madrid, 1846), I, pp. 217–218.

126 Ruiz Vilaplana, *Burgos Justice: A Year's Experience of Nationalist Spain* (London, 1938), pp. 49–50.

127 Pirala, *Guerra civil*, II, pp. 71–73.

128 Hills, *Battle for Madrid*, pp. 89–91, 100, 280.

129 Stathis N. Kalyvas, 'Warfare in Civil Wars', in Isabelle Duyvesteyn and Jan Angstrom (eds), *Rethinking the Nature of War* (Abingdon, 2005), pp. 88–108.

130 Hugh Thomas, *The Spanish Civil War* (London, 1986), p. 306.

131 Secundino Serrano, *Maquis: Historia de la guerrilla antifranquista* (Madrid, 2001), pp. 42–46; Philip B. Minehan, *Civil War and World War in Europe: Spain, Yugoslavia and Greece, 1936–1949* (New York, 2006), pp. 164–165.

132 Carlos Navajas Zubeldia, *Leales y rebeldes*, p. 158.

133 Juan Rico y Amat, *Historia política y parlamentaria de España* (Madrid, 1861), II, p. 181.

134 Pirala, *Guerra civil*, I, pp. 267–273, 580–84.

135 José Ramón de Urquijo y Goitia, 'Represión y disidencia durante la primera Guerra carlista: la policía carlista', *Hispania: Revista española de historia*, 45(159) (Jan. 1985), pp. 131–186.

136 Capistegui, 'Carlist Identity in Navarra', in Richards and Ealham (eds), *Splintering of Spain*, pp. 182–185.

137 Stanley Payne, *Basque Nationalism* (Reno, 1975), pp. 87–89.

138 Martin Blinkhorn, 'The Basque Ulster: Navarre and the Basque Autonomy Question under the Spanish Second Republic', *The Historical Journal*, 17(3) (1974), pp. 595–613, 602–612.

139 Hilari Raguer, *Gunpowder and Incense: The Catholic Church and the Spanish Civil War* (London, 2007), pp. 15–20.

140 Javier Ugarte Tellería, *La nueva Covadonga insurgente: orígenes sociales y culturales de la sublevación de 1936 en Navarra y el País Vasco* (Madrid, 1998), p. 27.

141 Ronald Fraser, *Blood of Spain* (London, 1981), p. 123.

142 T.N.A.,HW 22/2, 6C 1056, 'Air Employment', No. 7 British Air Staff Intelligence Report.

143 T.N.A.,HW 22/2, 6C 1056, 'Air Employment', No. 12: 12 May 1937 British air attaché report.

144 *The Times*, 28 April 1937.

145 Steer, *Tree of Gernika*, p. 167.

146 Pirala, *Guerra civil*, III, pp. 30–46.

147 Manuel de Irujo, *La Dépêche*, 6 May 1937, cited in Winegate-Pike, *France Divided*, p. 346.

148 June 1998 interview between Jaime del Burgo and historian Manuel Martorell, http://www.eka-partidocarlista.com/delburgo.htm (accessed 7 January 2016).

149 T.N.A., FO 72/443 George Villiers, doc. 108: 10 July 1835 letter from Villiers to Palmerston detailing the response of Don Carlos's court to Zumalacárregui's death.

150 Preston, *Franco*, p. 210.

151 Payne, *Spanish Civil War*, p. 191.

152 UNAM, CESU, Fondo Aurelio R. Acevedo (ARA), Caja 47, Expediente 104, Sección Militante Cristero, Subsección LNDLR, CD y CE, Series: Propaganda, p. 42: 28 November 1937 letter from Cristero leader Aurelio Acevedo paying tribute to Mola.

153 Ruiz Vilaplana, *Burgos Justice: A Year's Experience of Nationalist Spain* (London, 1938), p. 138.

154 Jesús Alonso Carballés, 'La evolución de la memoria de la Guerra Civil en el espacio urbano de Bilbao: una mirada comparativa', *Cahiers de civilisation espagnole contemporaine*, http://ccec.revues.org/3000 (accessed 18 January 2016); DOI: 10.4000/ccec.3000.

155 Bacon, *Six Years in Biscay*, p. 179; Pirala, *Guerra civil*, I, pp. 383–393.

156 Ino Bernard, *Mola: mártir de España* (Madrid, 1938), pp. 154, 242, 301.

157 *El pensamiento navarro*, Pamplona, 8 May 1938, p. 2.

158 Pirala, *Guerra civil*, II, pp. 37–39.

159 Admittedly, the militias on both sides were rapidly regularized into formal military units, especially on the Nationalist side, thereby leading Civil War expert Stathis Kalyvas to remark how exceptional the Spanish Civil War was for relying primarily on conventional warfare (Stathis N. Kalyvas, 'Warfare in Civil Wars', in Isabelle Duyvesteyn and Jan Angstrom (eds) *Rethinking the Nature of War* (Abingdon, 2005), pp. 88–108).

160 Pirala, *Guerra civil*, I, pp. 329–340.

161 *Eco del Comercio*, 3 April 1838.

162 A.H.N., II-C, Sección Histórica, Carlistas, 1833–34, 2841, docs. 50, 57 and 68: 15 July 1834, 19 July 1834 and 23 July 1834 letters from Spanish ambassador to Lisbon to Madrid.

163 A.H.N., Estado, 8146, Asuntos políticos, Guerra civil, Bloqueo de las costas del Norte, 1835 a 1893: 30 June 1835 letter from Captain-General of Cuba, and various documents from Gibraltar to Madrid dated June–December 1835.

164 Matthews, *Reluctant Warriors*, pp. 107–118.

165 Kemp, *Mine Were of Trouble*, p. 73; Matthews, *Reluctant Warriors*, pp. 156–159.

166 Charles Esdaile, *Fighting Napoleon* (Yale, 2004), p. 71.

167 Rafael Abella, *Julio 1936: Dos Españas frente a frente* (Barcelona, 1981), pp. 89–90.

168 Graham, *War and its Shadow*, p. 112.

169 Ruiz Vilaplana, *Burgos Justice: A Year's Experience of Nationalist Spain* (London, 1938), pp. 147–48, 175.

170 Steer, *Tree of Gernika*, pp. 18–19.

171 Rafael Abella, *Julio 1936: Dos Españas frente a frente* (Barcelona, 1981), pp. 111, 149; Frank Pitcairn, *Reporter in Spain*, pp. 44–45.

172 Jordi Carulla and Arnau Carulla (eds), *El color de la guerra* (Barcelona, 2000), p. 80.

173 A.H.N., II-C, Sección Histórica, Carlistas, 1833–34, 2841: 29 July 1834 letter from Madrid to Cristino minister in Lisbon; *Eco del Comercio*, 8 July 1834.

174 Ruiz Vilaplana, *Burgos Justice: A Year's Experience of Nationalist Spain* (London, 1938), pp. 64–66.

175 McNeill-Moss, *The Epic of the Alcázar*, p. 170.

176 Harold Cardozo, *The March of a Nation: My Year of Spain's Civil War* (London, 1937), pp. 193–194.

177 Fernando Díaz-Plaja, *La vida cotidiana en la España de la guerra civil* (Madrid, 1994), p. 51.

178 Corral, *Desertores*, p. 35.

179 12 September 1835 letter from Balmaseda to Jerez, reproduced at http://www.balmasedahistoria.com/08_fuentes.html (accessed 9 September 2014).

180 T.N.A., George Villiers, FO 72/443, No. 132: 9 August 1835 letter from George Villiers at San Ildefonso to Lord Palmerston.

181 T.N.A., George Villiers, FO 72/457, No. 12: 16 January 1836 letter from Villiers to Palmerston.

182 Pirala, *Guerra civil*, IV, pp. 550–552.

202 NOTES

183 Mariano José de Larra, 'Fígaro de vuelta: carta a su amigo residente en París', (Madrid, 2 January 1836), reproduced at http://www.biblioteca.org.ar/libros/131236.pdf.

184 T.N.A., F.O., 72/457, George Villiers, doc. 8: 10 January 1836 letter from Villiers to Lord Palmerston.

185 T.N.A., F.O., 72/457 George Villiers, doc. 28: 8 February 1836 letter from Villiers to Palmerston.

186 Fernando Rodríguez Miaja, *Testimonios y remembranzas* (México DF, 2013), pp. 50–53.

187 Rust, *Britons in Spain*, pp. 174–180.

188 Arthur Koestler, *Spanish Testament*, pp. 35–36.

189 Julio Prada Rodríguez, 'Las milicias de segunda línea en la retaguardia franquista. El caso de Galicia', *Cuadernos de Historia Contemporánea*, 33 (2011), 255–273.

190 Seidman, *Victorious Counterrevolution*, pp. 162–68; Matthews, *Reluctant Warriors*, pp. 119–124.

191 Rafael Valdés, SJ, *Un capellán, héroe de la Legión*, P. Fernando Huidobro SI (Sal Terrae, Santander, 1938), p. 28.

192 Matthews, *Reluctant Warriors*, pp. 45–46, 124; Alpert, *Republican Army*, pp. 186–194.

193 *Avance: Diario Socialista de Asturias*, 1 June 1937.

194 Taboada, *Por una España mejor*, p. 113.

195 Alpert, *Republican Army*, pp. 158, 168–173; Matthews, *Reluctant Warriors*, p. 39.

196 Alpert, *Republican Army*, pp. 181, 201.

197 Burnett Bolloten, *Spanish Revolution* (North Carolina, 1979), pp. 256–257.

198 Pirala, *Guerra civil*, II, pp. 221–228.

199 Pirala, *Guerra civil*, IV, pp. 483–484.

200 Bowen and Alvarez, *A Military History of Modern Spain*, p. 23.

201 A.M.S.S., Actas del Ayuntamiento (Libro 328), p. 46: 26 November 1835 decree; Pirala, *Guerra civil*, II, pp. 247–250.

202 *Gaceta extraordinaria de Madrid*, 9 May 1836; *Gaceta de Madrid*, 15 May 1836.

203 T.N.A., FO/72/459, George Villiers, doc. 140: 4 Jun 1836 letter from Villiers to Palmerston.

204 Edward Spiers, *Radical General: Sir George de Lacy Evans, 1787–1870* (Manchester, 1983), p. 70.

205 Bullen, 'France and Intervention in Spain', p. 385; Pirala, *Guerra civil*, II, pp. 473–475.

206 Manuel Martínez Martín, *Revolución liberal y cambio agrario en la Alta Andalucía* (Granada, 1995).

207 A.H.N., *Diversos (Gobierno y Político)*, leg. 167, doc. 82, dated 01.04.1839.

208 A.H.N., *Diversos (Títulos y Familias)*, leg. 3601, dated 28.08.1839 and 29.08.1839.

209 A.H.N., *Diversos (Títulos y Familias)*, leg. 3601.

210 A.H.N., *Diversos (Títulos y Familias)*, leg. 2544, Docs. 253–298.

211 Pirala, *Guerra civil*, IV, pp. 541–546.

212 Raúl Martín Arranz, 'Espartero: figuras de legitimidad', in José Alvarez Junco, *Populismo, caudillaje y discurso demagógico* (Madrid, 1987), pp. 102–127.

213 Ted Allen and Sydney Gordon, *The Scalpel and the Sword: The Story of Doctor Norman Bethune* (Boston, 1952), p. 113.

214 Lawrence, *Spain's First Carlist War*, pp. 50–51.

215 Jaime del Burgo, *Historia de la primera guerra carlista* (Pamplona, 1981), pp. 186–187, 235–237, 240–241.

216 Burke Honan, *Court and Camp of Don Carlos*, p. 389.

217 T.N.A., F.O. 72/458 George Villiers: Doc. 55 12 March 1836 letter from George Villiers in Madrid to Lord Palmerston in London concerning the pernicious travels of Michael Burke Honan.

218 T.N.A., F.O. 72/457 George Villiers: Doc. 17 25 January 1836 letter from Villiers to Lord Palmerston concerning Mendizábal's actions.

219 Bolloten, *Spanish Civil War*, pp. 45–56.

220 Taboada, *Por una España mejor*, pp. 108–110.

221 *Frente Rojo*, 6 May 1937; *ABC*, 22 May 1937.

222 T.N.A., HW 22/2, 6C 1056, report 68 (3rd – 16th January 1938) 'Assistance to both sides': 18 January 1938 British air attaché's report.

223 Pirala, *Guerra civil*, V, 35–36.

224 T.N.A., F.O. 72/443 George Villiers: Doc. 117 31 July 1835 letter from Villiers to Lord Palmerston concerning vice-consul's plight; T.N.A., F.O. 72/463 George Villiers, Doc. 303: 28 November 1836 letter from Villiers to Palmerston concerning consul at Santoña.

225 T.N.A., F.O. 72/457 George Villiers: Doc. 16 24 January 1836 letter from Villiers to Lord Palmerston concerning violence in Barcelona.

226 *Eco del Comercio*, 3 May 1837.

Chapter 2

1 *Solidaridad Obrera*, 26 August 1936, no. 1362 (p. 2).

2 Jackson, *Spanish Second Republic and Civil War*, pp. 44–46.

3 Jesús Millán, 'Una reconsideración del carlismo', *Ayer*, 29 (1998), pp. 91–107.

4 Alvaro Gómez Becerra, *Observaciones sobre el estado del poder judicial en España* (Madrid, 1839), pp. 26–35.

5 Moreno Alonso, *Blanco White*, pp. 470–596.

6 Manuel Alvarez Tardío and Roberto Villa García, *El precio de la exclusión* (Madrid, 2010), pp. 56, 83.

7 Carolyn P. Boyd, ' "Responsibilities' and the Spanish Second Republic, 1931–6', *European History Quarterly*, XIV(2) (April, 1984), pp. 151–182.

8 Ronald Fraser, *Blood of Spain* (1979), p. 517.

9 Rogelio Pérez Olivares, *Heroes de España: Excmo. Sr. D. Emilio Mola Vidal* (Madrid, 1937), p. 18.

10 Sheelagh Ellwood, *Spanish Fascism in the Franco Era* (London, 1987), p. 8.

11 David Porter, *Vision on Fire: Emma Goldman and the Spanish Revolution* (London, 2007), pp. 229–230.

12 Miaja, *Testimonios y remembranzas*, p. 39.

13 Bolloten, *Spanish Civil War*, pp. 46–56; Preston, *Franco*, p. 149.

14 George Esenwein, 'The Spanish Civil War', in José Alvarez Junco and Adrian Shubert (eds), *Spanish History Since 1808* (London, 2000), p. 238.

15 Beevor, *The Battle for Spain*, p. 62.
16 Edward Malefakis, *Agrarian Reform in Spain: Origins of the Civil War* (New Haven, 1971), p. 396.
17 Savadó, *Twentieth-Century Spain*, p. 72; Gabriel Jackson, 'The Azaña Regime in Perspective', *The American Historical Review*, 64 (1959), p. 293.
18 Fernando del Rey Reguillo and Manuel Tardío Alvarez, *Spanish Second Republic Revisited* (Sussex, 2012), p. 11.
19 Blinkhorn, *Spain in Conflict*, p. 65.
20 Jackson, *Spanish Second Republic and Civil War*, p. 117.
21 Cayetano Barraquer y Roviralta, *Los religiosos en Cataluña durante la primera mitad del siglo XIX*, 4 vols. (Barcelona, 1915), II, p. 387.
22 T.N.A., FO 72/458 George Villiers, Doc. 92: 17 April 1836 translation from Villiers to Palmerston of Cortes intervention of Catalan deputy Castell.
23 *El Español*, 19 August 1836.
24 A.M.M., 3/183, *Anales*, 12 August 1836.
25 *Eco del Comercio*, 6 November 1839.
26 A.H.N., Consejos, leg. 12232, Doc. 5: 15 November 1839 report by judge of first instance of Orgiva into disturbances of 24 October 1839.
27 The neo-traditionalist Francisco Asín, contrary to Pirala's opinion, found Caspe to be very Carlist, as some 300 of its menfolk left the town throughout the conflict to join Cabrera (cited in Bullón de Mendoza, *Primera guerra carlista*, p. 679).
28 *Eco del Comercio*, 11 July 1835; Pirala, *Guerra civil*, II, pp. 66–69. Cabrera's ruthlessness may have been inspired by the behaviour of Caspe's Cristino priest, Fray Crisóstomo, who had led some of the Zaragoza anticlerical massacres in April 1835 (Bullón de Mendoza, *Primera guerra carlista*, p. 780). The priesthood in the First Carlist War showed greater heterogeneity in its politics than in the Spanish Civil War.
29 T.N.A., F.O./72/458, Doc. 61, 19 March 1836 letter from George Villiers in Madrid to Lord Palmerston in London relating O'Lawlor's complaints; T.N.A., F.O./72/459, Doc. 109, 2 May 1836 letter from George Villiers in Madrid to Lord Palmerston in London relating Captain-General Quiroga's visit to Soto de Roma. The Wellington estate was untouched by 1930s pre-war expropriations and the outbreak of hostilities in 1936 found Íllora under rebel control. Even though some estate lands were sold to local colonists in 1941, the Wellington estate is still known locally as the 'Granadine Gibraltar' (*El País*, 30 May 2010).
30 A.H.N., Consejos, leg. 12232, Doc. 9: 11 September 1839 letter to Audiencia Territorial de Granada concerning events of 7 September 1839 in Ohanes.
31 Carlos Navajas Zubeldia, *Leales y rebeldes: la tragedia de los militares republicanos* (Madrid, 2011), p. 155.
32 T.N.A., FO/72/461 George Villiers, docs. 235 and 237: 17 September 1836 and 21 September 1836 letters from Villiers to Palmerston concerning persecution of émigrés.
33 T.N.A., F.O. 72/462 George Villiers, doc. 294: 12 November 1836 letter from Villiers to Palmerston detailing recent Cortes debates.
34 T.N.A., F.O. 72/462 George Villiers, doc. 296: 12 November 1836 letter from Villiers to Palmerston detailing recent Cortes debates.
35 Georges Sorel, *Reflections on Violence* (New York, 1941), p. 53.
36 Michael Seidman, *Republic of Egos* (Wisconsin, 2002), p. 27.

37 Boyd Haycock, *I Am Spain*, pp. 86–87.
38 George Esenwein and Adrian Shubert, *Spain at War: The Spanish Civil War in Context, 1931–1939* (London, 1995), pp. 130–133.
39 Jackson, *Spanish Republic and Civil War*, p. 276.
40 Rafael Abella, *Julio 1936: Dos Españas frente a frente* (Barcelona, 1981), p. 130; Seidman, *Republic of Egos* (Wisconsin, 2002), pp. 35–38; Xosé-Manoel Núñez, 'New Interpretations of the Spanish Civil War', *Contemporary European History*, 12(4) (November, 2004), p. 524.
41 Cited in Esenwein and Shubert, *Spain at War*, p. 115.
42 Payne, *Basque Nationalism*, pp.181–2; Payne, 'Catalan and Basque Nationalism', *Journal of Contemporary History*, 6 (1971), pp. 15–51, 46–47.
43 Payne, *Basque Nationalism*, pp.181–82; Beevor, *The Battle for Spain*, p. 104.
44 E.g. Joseph Augustín Chaho, *Voyage en Navarre pendant l'insurrection des Basques (1830–1835* (Paris, 1836).
45 T.N.A., F.O. 72/444 George Villiers, doc. 143: 5 September 1835 letter from Villiers to Palmerston explaining desire in Catalonia to restore the old kingdom of Aragón; Isabel Burdiel, *Política de los notables*, pp. 200–211.
46 T.N.A., F.O. 72/444 George Villiers, doc. 153: 27 September 1835 letter from Villiers to Palmerston.
47 Angel Smith, *The Origins of Catalan Nationalism, 1770–1898* (Basingstoke, 2014), pp. 36–38, 52–53.
48 Stanley Payne, 'Political Violence during the Spanish Second Republic', *JCH*, 25(2/3) (May–June 1990), pp. 269–288, 272.
49 Lawrence, *Spain's First Carlist War*, p. 89.
50 Alfonso García Tejero, *Historia político-administrativa de Mendizábal* (Madrid, 1858), vol. 1, p. 152.
51 T.N.A., FO 72/443 George Villiers, doc. 136: 18 August 1835 letter from Villiers to Palmerston.
52 T.N.A., F.O./72/462, George Villiers, doc. 254: 13 October 1836 letter from Villiers to Palmerston detailing the state of revolutionary politics.
53 T.N.A., F.O./72/462, George Villiers, doc. 255: 15 October 1836 letter from Villiers to Palmerston detailing the state of revolutionary politics.
54 Artola-Gallego, *Partidos y programas*, pp. 228–229.
55 T.N.A., F.O./72/462, George Villiers, doc. 263: 23 October 1836 letter from Villiers to Palmerston counselling rejection of Mendizábal's scheme to drawn a British loan to be repaid by Spanish and imperial customs revenues.
56 A.H.N., Estado, 1815, Convenio de Vergara: Real Decreto of 20 June 1837 plus 22 July 1837 note from Justice Ministry concerning Carlism and crime.
57 *Diario de Sevilla*, 13 December 1837, no. 3245.
58 Carlos Marichal, *Spain (1834–1844): A New Society* (London, 1977), pp. 139–40.
59 Miguel Angel Esteban Navarro, *La formación del pensamiento político y social del radicalismo español (1834–1874)* (Zaragoza, 1995), pp. 103–105; Trías and Elorza, *Federalismo*, pp. 80–82.
60 Pirala, *Guerra civil*, IV, pp. 328–335.
61 T.N.A., F.O. 72/458 George Villiers: Doc. 68: 26 March 1836 letter from George Villiers in Madrid to Lord Palmerston in London concerning meeting with Colonel Alba.

62 Julius Ruiz, *The Red Terror*, p. 74.

63 Julian Casanova, *The Spanish Republic and Civil War* (Cambridge, 2010), p. 258.

64 George Orwell, *Homage to Catalonia* (London, 2000), p. 107.

65 García Oliver radio message to CNT members 4 May 1937, in George R. Esenwein, *The Spanish Civil War: A Modern Tragedy* (New York, 2005), p. 193.

66 Friends of Durruti Handbill distributed 5 May 1937, in Augustin Guillamon, *The Friends of Durruti Group: 1937–1939* (Edinburgh, 1996), p. 50.

67 Helen Graham, '"Against the State": A Genealogy of the Barcelona May Days (1937)', *European History Quarterly*, 29 (1999), pp. 485–541.

68 Letter from Lois Orr to her family on 11–12 May 1937, in Gerd-Rainer Horn (ed.), *Letters from Barcelona: An American Woman in Revolution and Civil War* (Basingstoke, 2009), p. 161.

69 George Esenwein, Review of Payne, *AHR* (June 2005), pp. 876–878.

70 Borkenau, *Spanish Cockpit*, p. 132.

71 Preston, *Franco*, pp. 208–209.

72 James Matthews, *Reluctant Warriors* (Oxford, 2012), pp. 30–31.

73 Pirala, *Guerra civil*, V, pp. 125–128.

74 Jesús Cruz, 'De cortejadas a ángeles del hogar. Algunas reflexiones sobre la posición de la mujer en la elite madrileña, 1750–1850', in Alain Saint-Saëns (ed.), *Historia silenciada de la mujer: La mujer española desde la época medieval hasta la contemporánea* (Madrid, 1996), p. 140.

75 Mary Vincent, '"The Keys of the Kingdom": Religious Violence in the Spanish Civil War, July–August 1936', in Chris Ealham and Michael Richards (eds), *The Splintering of Spain: Cultural History and the Spanish Civil War, 1936–1939* (Cambridge, 2005), pp. 68–92.

76 Helen Graham, 'Women and Social Change', in Helen Graham and Jo Labanyi (eds), *Spanish Cultural Studies: An Introduction* (Oxford, 1995), p. 101.

77 Brian D. Bunk, *Ghosts of Passion* (Durham, 2006), p. 89.

78 *Gaceta Oficial*, 10 June 1836.

79 Frank Pitcairn, *Reporter in Spain*, p. 37.

80 Bullón de Mendoza, *Primera guerra carlista*, p. 77.

81 Julius Ruiz, *The 'Red Terror' and the Spanish Civil War: Revolutionary Violence in Madrid* (Cambridge, 2014), p. 21.

82 Graham, 'Women and Social Change', p. 101.

83 Graham, 'Women and Social Change', pp. 107–109, 135.

84 Shirley Mangini, 'Memories of Resistance: Women Activists from the Spanish Civil War', *Signs*, 17(2) (1991), 171.

85 Mary Nash, 'Women in War: *Milicianas* and Armed Combat in Revolutionary Spain, 1936–1939', *The International History Review*, 15(2) (1993), 270, 273; Ronald Fraser, *Blood of Spain: An Oral History of the Spanish Civil War* (London, 1994), p. 286; Frances Lannon, 'Women and Images of Women in the Spanish Civil War', *Transactions of the Royal Historical Society*, 6(1) (1991), 221.

86 Helen Graham, *The Spanish Civil War: A Short Introduction* (Oxford, 2005), pp. 55–56.

87 Mary Nash, *Rojas: las mujeres republicanas en la Guerra Civil* (Madrid, 1999), p. 97.

88   Lannon, 'Women and Images of Women in the Spanish Civil War', p. 222.

89   Acier, *From Spanish Trenches*, p. 84.

90   Fraser, *Blood of Spain*, p. 309.

91   *El pensamiento navarro*, 8 May 1938, p. 20 ('Hospital Alfonso Carlos').

92   María Rosa Urraca Pastor, *Así empezamos. Memorias de una enfermera* (Bilbao, 1940), pp. 39–40.

93   *El Genio de la Libertad*, no. 49, 19 May 1840.

94   *Boletín del Ejército Real de Aragón, Valencia y Murcia*, 17 January 1838, cited in Antonio Caridad Salvador, 'Las mujeres durante la primera guerra carlista (1833–1840)', *Memoria y Civilización*, Anuario de Historia (2011), Vol. 14, 175–199, 175.

95   Peter Janke, *Mendizábal y la instauración de la monarquía constitucional en España (1790–1853)* (Madrid, 1974), p. 232.

96   Antonio Caridad Salvador, 'Las mujeres durante la primera guerra carlista (1833–1840)' in *Memoria y Civilización*, Anuario de Historia, 14 (2011), 175–199.

97   Wilhelm Baron von Rahden, *Cabrera. Erinnerungen aus dem spanischen Bürgerkriege* (Frankfurt-am-Main, 1840), pp. 464–465.

98   Pirala, *Guerra civil*, III, pp. 30–46.

99   Alexander Somerville, *History of the British Legion and War in Spain* (London, 1839), pp. 196–197.

100 Pirala, *Guerra civil*, II, p. 453. For the Carlist message to enemy women, see Lawrence, *Spain's First Carlist War*, p. 155.

101 *Gaceta Oficial*, 1 March 1836. The female *urbanas* are discussed both by the Liberal doyen, Antonio Pirala, and by the official Carlist press on repeated occasions (*Gaceta Oficial*, 4 March 1836; 26 April 1836).

102 Pirala, *Guerra civil*, II, p. 467; *Gaceta Oficial*, 26 April 1836.

103 A.H.N., Estado, 8755, en territorio navarro: 4 October 1834 letter from Comiasario Regio de Navarra to Madrid.

104 Pirala, *Guerra civil*, IV, 614–615.

105 Holt, *Carlist Wars*, p. 219.

106 Régis Debray and Max Gallo (eds), *Santiago Carrillo: Dialogue on Spain* (London, 1976), pp. 101–102.

107 Borkenau, *Spanish Cockpit*, pp. 120–121.

108 Lannon, *Privilege and Prophecy* (1987), p. 31.

109 Manuel Revuelta González, *La exclaustración (1833–40)* (Madrid, 1976), pp. 494–502.

110 Pirala, *Guerra civil*, IV, pp. 467–471.

111 Fernando Molina, 'The Reign of Christ over the Nation: The Basque question in the Second Republic, 1931–1936', *National Identities*, 13(1) (2011), 17–33, 21.

112 Coverdale, *Basque Phase of the First Carlist War*, 3–10; Coro Rubio Pobes, *Revolución y tradición: el país vasco ante la revolución liberal y la construcción del estado liberal, 1808–1868* (Madrid, 1996); Coro Rubio Pobes, 'Que fue del oasis foral? (Sobre el estallido de la Segunda Guerra Carlista en el País Vasco)', *Ayer*, 38 (2000), 65–89.

113 UNAM, CESU, Fondo Aurelio R. Acevedo (ARA), Rollo 3, Caja 4, Expedientes 14–17, Sección Militante Cristero, Subsección LNDLR, CD y CE, Series: Propaganda, Exp. 14, 2–5: declarations of Cruz Lete.

114 Blinkhorn, *Carlism and Crisis*, p. 51.
115 Harold Cardozo, *March of a Nation* (London, 1937), pp. 64–65.
116 Michael Alpert, *A New International History of the Spanish Civil War* (Basingstoke, 1994), p. 92; Preston, *Franco*, pp. 219–220.
117 Frances Lannon, *Privilege, Prophecy* (1987), pp. 22–24.
118 Lichnowsky, *Erinnerungen*, Vol. 2, p. 134; Jaime del Burgo, *Historia de la primera guerra carlista*, pp. 212–213.
119 Rafael Abella, *Julio 1936: Dos Españas frente a frente* (Barcelona, 1981), p. 144.
120 Ruiz Vilaplana, *Burgos Justice: A Year's Experience of Nationalist Spain* (London, 1938), pp. 48–49.
121 Hilari Raguer, *Gunpowder and Incense: The Catholic Church and the Spanish Civil War* (London, 2007), pp. 92–102, 309–325; Seidman, *Victorious Counterrevolution*.
122 Townson, 'Anticlericalism and Secularization: A European Exception?', in Townson (ed.), *Is Spain Different?* (Sussex, 2015), pp. 72–79.
123 Antonio Moliner, 'La conflicitividad social', *Trienio* (May 2000), p. 84; 'La España de finales del siglo XVIII y la crisis de 1808', in Moliner (ed.), *La Guerra de la Independencia en España (1808–1814)* (Barcelona, 2007), p. 46.
124 Conde de Toreno, *Historia del levantamiento, guerra y revolución de España*, (Madrid, 1953), p. 447.
125 B.U.Z., Faustino Casamayor archive: 13 April 1817 diary entry detailing Archbishop of Zaragoza's condemnation.
126 Gil Novales, *Sociedades Patrióticas*, pp. 574–577.
127 A.H.N., Estado, leg. 217-2, No. 24: May 1826 Barcelona police report.
128 H. Raguer, *Gunpowder and Incense* (2013), pp. 13–17.
129 Nigel Townson, 'Anticlericalism and Secularization: A European Exception?' in Townson (ed.), *Is Spain Different?* p. 75.
130 Shlomo Ben-Ami, 'The Republican Take-Over: Prelude to Inevitable Catastrophe?' in Paul Preston, *Revolution and War in Spain* (London, 1984), p. 22.
131 R. Smith, *The Day of the Liberals in Spain*, pp. 88–95.
132 Payne, 'Political Violence', pp. 272–273.
133 Cited in Alvarez Tardío and Villa García, *El precio de la exclusión*, p. 173.
134 R. Smith, *The Day of the Liberals in Spain*, p. 90.
135 *Gaceta Oficial*, 22 April 1836; 26 April 1836.
136 *Gaceta de Madrid*, 29 July 1835.
137 Anes Alvarez de Castrillón, *Economía, sociedad, política*, pp. 61–63.
138 Cuenca, *Iglesia española*, pp. 29–65.
139 *Eco del Comercio*, 28 October 1836; Tejero, *Historia político-administrativa de Mendizábal*, p. 283.
140 Sheelagh Ellwood, *The Spanish Civil War* (Oxford, 1991), p. 16.
141 *Eco del Comercio*, 2 January 1836; Pirala, *Guerra civil*, II, pp. 252–254.
142 *Gaceta Oficial*, 24 November 1835; 27 November 1835.
143 Lawrence, *Spain's First Carlist War*, p. 105.
144 Taboada, *Por una España mejor*, p. 89.
145 Pirala, *Guerra civil*, IV, pp. 588–606, 742–751.

146 José María Cuenca Toribio, *La iglesia española ante la revolución liberal* (Madrid, 1971).

147 Pirala, *Guerra civil*, III, pp. 30–46.

148 Pirala, *Guerra civil*, IV, pp. 472–478.

149 T.N.A., FO/72/758, Docs. 96 and 101: 18 April 1836 and 23 April 1836 letters from George Villiers in Madrid to Lord Palmerston concerning recent debates in the upper chamber.

150 Pirala, *Guerra civil*, II, pp. 149–150; *Eco del Comercio*, 6 November 1835.

151 Georges Bernanos, *Los grandes cementerios bajo la luna* (Siglo Veinte, 1964), pp. 94–98.

152 *Gaceta Oficial*, 8 December 1835; 31 May 1836; Pirala, *Guerra civil*, II, pp. 339–346.

153 Francisco Foz, *Mis memorias: andanzas de un veterinario rural (1818–1896)* (Madrid, 2013), pp. 36–38.

154 A.M.M., 3/183, *Anales*: 7, 8 and 17 September 1836 reports.

155 Luis Garrido Muro, 'El Nuevo Cid. Espartero, María Cristina y el primero liberalismo español (1834–1840)' (Unpublished PhD thesis, Universidad de Cantabria, 2012), pp. 62–65.

156 The 'slavery' suffered by villagers at the hands of the Galician Church radicalized the liberal priest of the Peninsular War, Juan Antonio Posse (cited in Richard Herr (ed.), *Memorias del cura liberal don Juan Antonio Posse con su discurso sobre la Constitución de 1812* (Madrid, 1984), pp. 260–261).

157 Artola (ed.), *Memorias de Espoz y Mina*, II, p. 338.

158 Pirala, *Guerra civil*, V, pp. 123–124.

159 T.N.A., FO 72/458, George Villiers, Doc. 86: 9 April 1836 letter from Villiers to Palmerston concerning 6 April 1836 Cortes intervention of Conde de las Navas.

160 T.N.A., FO 72/463, George Villiers, Doc. 321: 10 December 1836 letter from Villiers to Palmerston detailing his recent audience with Prime Minister Calatrava.

161 Córdova, *Memorias*, Vol. I, p. 356.

162 José Miguel Quesada González, 'El reservismo militar en España' (Doctoral thesis, Instituto Universitario General Gutiérrez Mellado, 2013), pp. 107–108.

163 Secundino Serrano, *Maquis: historia de la guerrilla antifranquista* (Madrid, 2001), p. 33.

164 Córdova, *Memorias*, Vol. II, pp. 37–53.

165 Alexander Somerville, *History of the British Legion in Spain*, pp. 51, 215.

166 Acier, *From Spanish Trenches*, p. 141.

167 Javier Ugarte Tellería, *La nueva Covadonga insurgente: orígenes sociales y culturales de la sublevación de 1936 en Navarra y el País Vasco* (Madrid, 1998), pp. 206–208.

168 Pirala, *Guerra civil*, II, pp. 503–505.

169 A.H.N., Estado, 8755, en territorio navarro: 10 July 1834 letter from the Viceroy to the Cristino commander of Puente la Reina approving Rafael Elisabet's request.

170 T.N.A., FO 72/462 George Villiers, Doc. 289: 12 November 1836 letter from Villiers to Palmerston detailing his complaint to Prime Minister Calatrava; T.N.A., FO 72/463 George Villiers, Doc. 274: 10 December 1836 letter from

NOTES

Villiers to Palmerston detailing Calatrava's agreement to exempt British
subjects from billeting.

171 Pirala, *Guerra civil*, IV, pp. 420–424.
172 Robert Stradling, *Your Children Will Be Next: Bombing and Propaganda in the Spanish Civil War, 1936–39* (Cardiff, 2008), p. 13.
173 Alicia Alted Vigil, 'Las consecuencias de la Guerra Civil española en los niños de la República: de la dispersión al exilio', *Espacio, Tiempo y Forma*, Serie V, Historia Contemporánea, 9 (1996), 207–228, 213.
174 Luis Bazal, *¡Ay de los vencidos!* (Paris, 1966), p. 122.
175 Fernando Rodríguez Miaja, *Testimonios y remembranzas: mis recuerdos de los últimos meses de la guerra de España (1936–1939)* (Colegio de México, 2013), pp. 182–185.
176 Fernando Díaz-Plaja, *La vida cotidiana* (Madrid, 1994), p. 74.
177 *Eco del Comercio*, 2 February 1836.
178 A.H.N., Estado, 8755: en territorio navarro: 20 May 1834 letter from Viceroy to Comandante of Punete la Reina.
179 A.H.N., Estado, 8755/32: en territorio navarro, No. 1: José Briol Mayál renders hospital accounts for August 1834 to Viceroy.
180 A.H.N., Estado, 8146, Asuntos políticos, Guerra civil, Bloqueo de la costas del norte, 1835 á 1839, Doc. 343: undated letter from consul at Bayonne to government.
181 T.N.A., FO 72/459 George Villiers, doc. 149: 18 June 1836 letter from Villiers to Palmerston detailing intelligence from Commander-in-Chief Córdova.
182 Pirala, *Guerra civil*, III, pp. 616–620.
183 A.H.N., Estado, 8755: en territorio navarro: 6 June 1840 complaint by Comandancia Nacional de Fitero.
184 T.N.A., FO 72/457 George Villiers, doc. 12: 16 January 1836 letter from Villiers to Palmerston.
185 George Borrow, *The Bible in Spain* (London, 1839), pp. 236–37.
186 August von Goeben, *Vier Jahre in Spanien: Die Carlisten, ihre Erhebung, ihr Kampf und ihr Untergang* (Hannover, 1841), pp. 245–247.
187 William Walton, *A Reply to the Anglo-Cristino Pamphlet, Entitled the Policy of England towards Spain* (London, 1837), p. 129.
188 Acier, *From Spanish Trenches*, pp.12–13.
189 Kemp, *Mine Were of Trouble*, pp. 6–7, 141.
190 George Orwell, *Homage to Catalonia*, pp. 140–144.
191 García Ferrandis X. and A. J. Munayco Sánchez, 'La evolución de la Sanidad Militar en Valencia durante la Guerra Civil Española (1936–1939), *Sanidad Militar*, 67(4) (2011), 383–389; Nicholas Coni, *Medicine and Warfare: Spain, 1936–1939* (London, 2008), p. 106.
192 Nicholas Coni, *Medicine and Warfare: Spain, 1936–1939*, p. 23.
193 Matthews, *Reluctant Warriors*, pp. 134–135.
194 Bullón de Mendoza, *Primera guerra carlista*, pp. 256–277.
195 Alpert, *Republican Army*, p. 167; Thomas, *Spanish Civil War*, pp. 550–551.
196 Mark Lawrence, 'Poachers Turned Gamekeepers: A Study of the Guerrilla Phenomenon in Spain, 1808–1840', *Small Wars and Insurgencies*, 25(4) (2014), pp. 843–857, p. 851.
197 T.N.A., Long papers, bundle 715, T/4243, doc. 14362: 18 July 1835 request from Mr Backhouse at Foreign Office.

198 Rutherford Alcock, *Notes on the Medical History and Statistics of the British Legion* (London, 1838), pp. 4–7.

199 Charles Shaw, *Personal Memoirs and Correspondence of Colonel Charles Shaw, K.C.T.S., &c, of the Portuguese Service and late Brigadier-General, in the British Auxiliary Legion of Spain; Comprising a Narrative of the War for Constitutional Liberty in Portugal and Spain, from its Commencement in 1831 to the Dissolution of the British Legion in 1837* (London 1837), 2 vols., II, p. 494.

200 Shaw, *Personal Memoirs,* II, pp. 528–529.

201 Jason Gurney, *Crusade in Spain* (London, 1974), p. 114.

202 Pirala, *Guerra civil*, IV, pp. 67–71.

203 Bollaert, *Wars of Succession*, p. 142.

204 Tom Buchanan, *The Impact of the Spanish Civil War on Britain: War, Loss and Memory* (Brighton, 2007), pp. 43–65; Nicholas Coni, *Medicine and Warfare: Spain, 1936–1939* (London, 2008), p. 30.

205 Kemp, *Mine Were of Trouble*, p. 197.

206 Pirala, *Guerra civil*, II, pp. 483–486.

207 A.H.C.B., *Política y Representaciones*, 1836, 1D. IV-111: 27 May 1836 report from Captain-General to civil authorities.

208 Buckley, *Life and Death of the Spanish Republic*, p. 227.

209 Pedro Corral, *Desertores* (Barcelona, 2006), pp. 69–70.

210 Alpert, *Republican Army*, pp. 162–165; Matthews, *Reluctant Warriors*, p. 156.

211 Rust, *Britons in Spain*, pp. 99, 163

212 Díaz-Plaja, *La vida cotidiana*, p. 216; Alpert, *Republican Army*, pp. 165–167.

213 Matthews, *Reluctant Warriors*, pp. 131–133.

214 A.H.N., Estado, 8755, en territorio navarro: 12 September 1834 letter from Count Almides de Toledo, divisional commander, to Viceroy of Navarra.

215 A.H.N., Estado, 8755, en territorio navarro, doc. 40: 21 May 1834 letter from Viceroy to commander of Puente la Reina.

216 Geoffrey Parker, *The Military Revolution: Military Innovation and the Rise of the West, 1500–1800* (Cambridge, 1996), p. 64.

217 David Parrott, *The Business of War* (Cambridge, 2012).

218 A.H.N., Estado, 8755: En territorio navarro: 13 June 1835 order from Viceroy to Milicia Urbana.

219 T.N.A., F.O. 72/461 George Villiers, doc. 215: 31 August 1836 letter from Villiers to Palmerston detailing privations of the government army.

220 T.N.A., F.O. 72/462 George Villiers, doc. 287: 31 October 1836 letter from Villiers to Palmerston detailing operations of the Army of the Centre; Pirala, *Guerra civil*, III, pp. 158–160.

221 Pirala, *Guerra civil*, IV, pp. 10–17.

222 Pirala, *Guerra civil*, IV, pp. 392–395.

223 *Eco del Comercio*, 9 June 1837.

224 Minehan, *Civil War and World War in Europe*, p. 34.

225 Charles Esdaile, *Outpost of Empire* (Oklahoma, 2012), p. 52.

226 T.N.A., HW 22/2, 6C 1056, doc. B2 6: 7 April 1937 British air attaché report from Madrid.

227 T.N.A., FO 72/459 George Villiers: 31 May 1836 details from a letter from
     General Evans sent to Palmerston describing recent Carlist execution of
     returning peasant.
228 T.N.A., FO 72/458 George Villiers, Doc. 92: 17 April 1836 letter from Villiers
     to Palmerston concerning recent Cortes debates.
229 Steer, *Tree of Gernika*, pp. 90–91.
230 Avner Offer, *The First World War: An Agrarian Interpretation*
     (Oxford, 1989).
231 Nicholas Coni, *Medicine and Warfare: Spain, 1936–1939* (London, 2008),
     p. 84; Díaz-Plaja, *La vida cotidiana*, p. 185.
232 Seidman, *Republic of Egos*.
233 *El Sol*, 5 May 1937.
234 *Frente Rojo*, 6 May 1937.
235 *Comisariado: División 25*, January 1938.
236 Marques de Miraflores, *Memorias del reinado de Isabel II* (Madrid, 1964),
     Vol. I, p. 118.
237 Pirala, *Guerra civil*, IV, pp. 402–407.
238 For the traumatic details of the starvation facing Cristino captives under
     Cabrera's control in 1837 and 1838, see Lawrence, *Spain's First Carlist War*,
     pp. 171–173.
239 Carlos Dembowski, *Dos años en España durante la guerra civil, 1838–40*
     (Madrid, 2008), p. 40.
240 Pirala, *Guerra civil*, IV, pp. 298–302.
241 T.N.A., HW 22/2, 6C 1056,'Assistance to both sides', Report no. 44 (July
     1937): British air attaché report on demoralization.
242 T.N.A., HW 22/2, 6C 1056,'Assistance to both sides', Report no. 59 (25–31
     October 1937): British air attaché report on demoralization.
243 Preston, *Franco*, pp. 276–277.
244 T.N.A., GFM 33 6B/298/1822, E 077986, 11 May 1937 and 23 May 1937
     letters from charge d'affaires, Wilhelm Faupel, to Auswärtiges Amt in Berlin.
245 Pirala, *Guerra civil*, IV, pp. 161–166.
246 Lawrence, *Spain's First Carlist War*, p. 168.
247 Pirala, *Guerra civil*, IV, pp. 72–75; Oyarzun, *Historia del carlismo*, p. 133.
248 Canal, *El carlismo*, p. 104.
249 Coverdale, *Basque Phase of the First Carlist War*, pp. 3–10. Coverdale's
     emphasis on religion and worldview as motivating factors for Carlism
     mirrored a shift in Spanish historiography which until the 1980s
     overemphasized the fueros as mobilizing factors for Carlism (Rubio Pobes,
     País vasco ante la revolución liberal; Rubio Pobes, 'Que fue del oasis foral?',
     pp. 65–89).
250 Pirala, *Guerra civil*, V, pp. 183–184.
251 Pirala, *Guerra civil*, IV, pp. 619–622.
252 Eugenio de Aviraneta, *Memoria dirigida al gobierno español sobre los planes
     y operaciones puestos en ejecución para aniquilar la rebelión en las provincias
     del norte de España* (Madrid, 1844), pp. 111–113.
253 Díaz-Plaja, *La vida cotidiana*, p. 207.
254 Rogelio Pérez Olivares, *Héroes de España: Excmo. Sr. D. Queipo de Llano*
     (Madrid, 1937), p. 32.

255 Luis Garrido Muro, 'El Nuevo Cid. Espartero, María Cristina y el primero liberalismo español (1834–1840) (Unpublished PhD thesis, Universidad de Cantabria, 2012), pp. 68–69.

256 T.N.A., FO 72/457 George Villiers, doc. 163: 15 October 1835 letter from Villiers to Palmerston.

257 Janke, *Mendizábal*, pp. 133–37.

258 Díaz-Plaja, *La vida cotidiana*, pp. 168–72; Seidman, *Victorious Counterrrevolution*, pp. 93–120.

259 T.N.A., HW 22/2, 6C 1056, 'Assistance to both sides', Report 53 (13-19th September 1937): British air attaché reports; Seidman, *Victorious Counterrevolution*, pp. 83–91, 125–126.

260 Othen, *Franco's International Brigades*, p. 228.

261 *Avance: Diario Socialista de Asturias*, 2 June 1937.

262 T.N.A., HW 22/2, 6C 1056, Assistance to both sides: Late-October 1937 report of recent visit to rebel-held Spain.

263 T.N.A., HW 22/2, 6C 1056, Assistance to both sides, report 53: Letter from Commander Hillgarth relating recent tour (August–September 1937) in rebel-held Spain.

264 George Steer, *Tree of Gernika*, p. 37.

265 Seidman, *Victorious Counterrrevolution*, pp. 29–37, 82.

Chapter 3

1 Diego Abad de Santillán, *Por qué perdimos la guerra* (Buenos Aires, 1940), pp. 165–166.

2 Yet Casado's lies have been made plain by more recent academic studies which have shown his delusional sense of self-importance and quest for the political limelight. It is remarkable how long Casado's benevolent legend persisted. In fact, the second most important officer in the Republican zone, General José Miaja Menant, has been labelled as the opportunist, 'simple', geographically loyal and vain in accepting leadership of Casado's council (Angel Viñas, 'Playing with History and Hiding Treason: Colonel Casado's Untrustworthy Memoirs and the End of the Spanish Civil War', *Bulletin of Spanish Studies*, 91(1–2) (2014), 295–323; Alpert, *Republican Army*, pp. 100–106). The recent memoirs published by his nephew are a strident rejection of these representations, and recent scholarship points the finger towards Casado (Fernando Rodríguez Miaja, *Testimonios y Remembranzas: mis recuerdos de los últimos meses de la guerra en España (1936–1939)* (Colegio de México, 2013), pp. 56–58, 68–70, 156–58).

3 Oyarzun, *El carlismo*; Jaime del Burgo, *Primera guerra carlista*.

4 *Eco de Aragón* (suplemento), 29 May 1840.

5 Thomas J. Hamilton, *Appeasement's Child: The Franco Regime in Spain* (New York, 1943), p. 25.

6 *Eco del Comercio*, 27 March 1839; Pirala, *Guerra civil*, IV, pp. 588–606, 742–751.

7 Alice L. Lascelles and J. M. Alberich (eds), *Sir Vincent Kennett-Barrington: Letters from the Carlist War (1874–1876)* (Exeter, 1987), pp. 34–35.

8   Lawrence, *Spain's First Carlist War*, p. 214.

9   John Langdon-Davies, *Behind the Spanish Barricades*, pp. 100–106.

10 Figures suggesting at least an equivalence may be found in Juan Pablo
    Fusi and Jordi Palafox, *España: 1808–1936: El desafío de la modernidad*
    (Madrid, 1997), p. 41; Alfonso Bullón de Mendoza, *La primera guerra carlista*
    (Madrid, 1992).

11 A. Cenarro, 'Memory Beyond the Public Sphere: The Francoist Repression
    Remembered in Aragon', *History and Memory*, 14 (2002), p. 167.

12 Paul Preston, *Juan Carlos: A People's King* (London, 2004), pp. 25–27.

13 Moreno Alonso, *Blanco White*.

14 Vicente Llorens, *Liberales y románticos. Una emigración española en
    Inglaterra (1823–1834)* (1954).

15 Matthews, *Reluctant Warriors*, pp. 144–148.

16 Antonio Caridad Salvador, 'Las mujeres durante la primera guerra carlista
    (1833–1840)', pp. 175–199; Jean-Luc Marais, 'Les carlistes espagnols dans
    l'Ouest de la France, 1833–1883', *Annales de Bretagne et des Pays de l'Ouest*
    [Online], http://abpo.revues.org/2222 (accessed 8 September 2014).

17 Carlos Navajas Zubeldia, *Leales y rebeldes: la tragedia de los mlitares
    republicanos* (Madrid, 2011), p. 153.

18 Secundino Serrano, *Maquis. Historia de la guerrilla antifranquista* (Madrid,
    2001), pp. 13–22.

19 Orwell, *Homage to Catalonia*.

20 Walter Laquer, *Guerrilla Warfare: A Historical and Critical Study* (New Jersey,
    1997), p. 197.

21 Secundino Serrano, *Maquis: Historia de la guerrilla antifranquista* (Madrid,
    2001), pp. 34–38.

22 Thomas Hamilton, *Appeasement's Child*, pp. 45–46.

23 *Eco del Comercio*, 12 February 1841; 3 March 1841; 12 March 1841; 17
    March 1841; 26 March 1841; Coro Rubio, *Revolución y tradición: el país
    vasco*, pp. 93–126.

24 Luis Garrido Muro, 'El Nuevo Cid. Espartero, María Cristina y el primero
    liberalismo español (1834–1840)' (Unpublished PhD thesis, Universidad de
    Cantabria, 2012), pp. 14–25.

25 A.H.N., Correspondencia Embajadas y Legaciones, E.E.U.U., 1834–35, 1465,
    doc. 4: 12 October 1839 note from Secretary of State to Spanish minister in
    New York.

26 Graham, *War and its Shadow*, p. 112.

27 Rújula (ed.), *Historia de la guerra última*, LX.

28 *El Correo Nacional*, 15 December 1840.

29 Adrian Shubert, 'Baldomero Espartero, 1793–1879: del ídolo al olvido',
    in Isabel Burdiel and Manuel Ledesma (eds), *Liberales, agitadores y
    conspiradores* (Madrid, 2000), pp. 190–198.

30 *Eco del Comercio*, 25 August 1840; 5 September 1840; 7 September 1840.

31 *El Huracán*, 18 June 1840; 26 June 1840; 27 June 1840; 29 June 1840; 7
    July 1840.

32 *El Huracán*, 5 September 1840.

33 A.H.N., Diversos (*Gobierno y Política*), leg. 167, Docs. 32, 40: 8 September
    1840 account by *jefe político* of Jaén, Muñoz, of events of 7 September 1840;

11 September 1840 account by José Manuel Arenas, commander of 2nd battalion of Volunteers of Granada, of *prounciamiento* of previous day.

34 *El Huracán*, 8 September 1840.

35 *El Huracán*, 23 September 1840.

36 *El Huracán*, 27 October 1840.

37 Nemesio de Pombo, *Situación de España a fines del año 1842* (Madrid, 1843), p. 25.

38 Marichal, *Spain (1834–1844)*, p. 167; Espadas Burgos, *Espartero: un candidato al trono*, p. 78; Cepeda Gómez, *Ejército español*, pp. 222–236; Eiras Roel, *Partido demócrata*, pp. 102–106.

39 *Eco del Comercio*, 30 August 1841.

40 Nemesio Pombo, *España a fines de 1842*, p. 25.

41 Eiras Roel, *Partido demócrata*, pp. 102–112.

42 Ibid., pp. 117–118.

43 *The Times*, 25 November 1842; 28 November 1842; 3 December 1842.

44 *The Times*, 3 December 1842; 22 December 1842; 17 October 1843; Maluquer de Motes claims Carsy escaped the city on the pretext of rallying armed émigrés, who, of course, did not exist (Maluquer de Motes, *Socialismo*, pp. 275–284).

45 Eiras Roel, *Partido demócrata*, pp. 102–106.

46 José A. Piqueras and Manuel Chust (eds), *Republicanos y repúblicas en España* (Madrid, 1996), pp. 100–105; Peyrou, *Republicanismo popular*, pp. 77–78; Marichal, *Spain (1834–1844)* pp. 169–172.

47 A.G.P., Caja 28/32, no. 1, Reinados, Ferdinand VII, 27: 1842 government report concerning 'Society of Regenerators'.

48 A.G.P., Caja 28/32, No. 1, Reinados, FVII, 27: undated police transcription of the manifesto of the Sociedad de Regeneradores Españoles.

49 R.A.H., 9/4714, Papeles de Fermín Caballero (Papeles inéditos, II, 1830–1845): pp. 237–240 transcriptions of 17 December 1842–5 January 1843 correspondence between Caballero and mayor Manuel Azesita.

50 Moliner, *Revolución burguesa*, p. 255.

51 Gracia Gómez, *Olózaga*, pp. 155–165.

52 Cited in Comellas, *Moderados en el poder*, pp. 51–52.

53 T. M. Hughes, *Spain in 1845* (London, 1845), I, pp. 15–16.

54 Ricardo de la Cierva, *Historia del franquismo* (Barcelona, 1975), p. 133.

55 Quiroga and Angel del Arco, *Right-wing Spain*, p. 161.

56 Peter Day, *Franco's Friends: How British Intelligence Helped Bring Franco to Power in Spain* (London, 2012), p. 200.

57 Marichal, *Spain (1834–1844)*, pp. 162–165.

58 Taboada, *Por una España mejor* (1977), p. 159.

59 Paloma Aguilar, *Políticas de la memoria*, p. 102; Filipe Ribeiro de Meneses, *Franco and the Spanish Civil War* (London, 2001), pp. 120–122.

60 Miaja, *Testimonios y remembranzas*, p. 189.

61 Paul Preston, *Franco* (London, 1995), p. 702.

62 J. A. Gallego, J. R. Urquijo and M. Espadas, 'La España de Espartero', *Cuadernos*, historia, 16(118) (1985), p. 4.

63 Paloma Aguilar Fernández, *Políticas de la memoria y memorias de la política* (Alianza Editorial, 20008), p. 84.

64 A.H.N., II-C, Sección Histórica, Carlistas, 1835–1850, 2842, No. 22: Manifesto from Carlos Luis proclaimed at Bourges on 23 May 1845 and inserted in correspondence from Spanish Embassy at Paris dated 31 May 1845.
65 *Eco del Comercio*, 16 March 1847; Josep Carles Clemente, *Las guerras carlistas* (Barcelona, 1982), pp. 155–157.
66 Bowen and Alvarez, *Military History of Modern Spain*, p. 16.

Chapter 4

1   Preston, *Franco*, p. 16.
2   Henry Buckley, *The Life and Death of the Spanish Republic: A Witness to the Spanish Civil War* (London, 2013), pp. 50–62.
3   Pirala, *Guerra civil*, II, pp. 175–179; Córdova, *Memorias*, Vol. I, pp. 126–128.
4   For a list of names and their chronologies, see Christiansen, *Origins of Military Power*, pp. 168–169.
5   Agustín de Argüelles, *1820 á 1824: reseña histórica*, pp. 182–186;
6   Sebastian Balfour, *The End of the Spanish Empire, 1898–1923* (Oxford, 1997), p. 7.
7   Brian Hamnett, 'Spain and Portugal and the Loss of Their Continental American Territories in the 1820s: An Examination of the Issues', *European History Quarterly*, 41(3) (July 2011), pp. 397–412, p. 408.
8   Gabriel Paquette, 'The Dissolution of the Spanish Atlantic Monarchy', in *Historical Journal*, 52(1) (2009), pp. 175–212, p. 199. Paquete's historiographical review provides an excellent summary of recent scholarship criticizing early nineteenth-century Spanish Liberalism's failure to offer the American empire any fair representation or even autonomy in the liberal project. This recent trend breaks with the orthodox tendency to blame absolutism, and Ferdinand himself, for the dissolution of the American empire.
9   Federico Suárez Verdeguer, *La crisis política del antiguo régimen en España (1808–1840)* (Madrid, 1950); Jaime E. Rodríguez O., '*We Are Now the True Spaniards*': Sovereignty, Revolution, Independence, and the Emergence of the Federal Republic of Mexico, 1808–1824 (Stanford, 2012), p. 236.
10 Lucy Riall and David Laven (eds), *Napoleon's Legacy* (London, 2000).
11 Jaime Torras, *Liberalismo y rebeldía campesina (1820–23)* (Barcelona, 1976), pp. 7–31.
12 Quiroga, *Making Spaniards*, p. 30.
13 Ellwood, *Franco*, pp. 18–19.
14 Quiroga, *Making Spaniards*, pp. 21–23, 30–31.
15 Julio del Vayo, *The Last Optimist* (London, 1950), p. 214.
16 Quiroga, *Making Spaniards*, pp. 24–29.
17 Francisco L. Romero and Angel Smith, 'The Agony of Spanish Liberalism and the Origins of Dictatorship: A European Framework', in Francisco J. Romero and Angel Smith (eds), *The Agony of Spanish Liberalism: From Revolution to Dictatorship, 1913–23* (Basingstoke, 2010), p. 9.
18 Quiroga, *Making Spaniards*, p. 20.
19 Hilari Raguer, *Gunpowder and Incense*, pp. 41–42, 118.
20 *El Eco del Comericio*, 8 July 1838; 12 July 1838; 13 July 1838; 15 July 1838; 22 July 1838; 28 July 1838; 14 March 1839.

21 Marques de Miraflores, *Memorias del reinado de Isabel II* (Madrid, 1964), Vol. I, pp. 151–154.

22 Quiroga, *Making Spaniards*, pp. 39–42.

23 Shlomo Ben-Ami, *Fascism from Above: Dictatorship of Primo de Rivera in Spain, 1923–30* (Oxford, 1973), pp. 165–166.

24 Arturo Barea, *La forja*, p. 344.

25 Seidman, *Victorious Counterrevolution*, pp. 37–47.

26 Matthews, *Reluctant Warriors*, p. 50.

27 Preston, *Franco*, p. 16.

28 Sebastian Balfour, 'The Making of an Interventionist Army, 1898–1923', in Francisco J. Romero and Angel Smith (eds), *The Agony of Spanish Liberalism: From Revolution to Dictatorship, 1913–23* (Basingstoke, 2010), pp. 255–258.

29 Paul Preston, *Spanish Holocaust* (London, 2012), p. 471.

30 J. H. Parry, for example, made only brief mention of this link in his magisterial *Spanish Seaborne Empire* (London, 1966), p. 362.

31 A.H.N., Correspondencia Embajadas y Legaciones, E.E.U.U., 1834–35, 1465, Doc. 80: Muy reservado report date 18 November 1836 from Calderón de la Barca to Madrid.

32 A.H.N., Correspondencia Embajadas y Legaciones, E.E.U.U., 1834–35, 1465, Doc. 81: 25 November 1836 protest from Department of State to Spanish minister in Washington.

33 Josep M. Fradera and Christopher Schmidt-Nowara (eds), *Slavery and Anti-Slavery in Spain's Atlantic Empire* (New York, 2013), pp. 234–235.

34 Thomas Hamilton, *Appeasement's Child*, p. 57.

35 Arthur W. Marchmont, *Sarita the Carlist* (1902), p. 15.

36 Andrés Iduarte, *En el fuego de España* (México DF, 1982), pp. 105–112.

37 Jaime E. Rodríguez O., 'We are now the True Spaniards', pp. 344–345.

38 Harold Sims, *The Expulsion of Mexico's Spaniards*, p. 217.

39 Jaume Torras, 'Peasant Counter-revolution?' *Journal of Peasant Studies*, 5(1) (1977), 66–78; John Coverdale, *Basque Phase* (Princeton, 1984), p. 21.

40 Lawrence, *Spain's First Carlist War*, p. 132.

41 Miguel Artola (ed.), *Memorias del general Don Francisco Espoz y Mina* (Madrid, 1962), Vol. II, p. 122.

42 Mark Lawrence, 'Playing the Man, Not the Ball: Ramón Ceruti and Transatlantic Careerism in Mexico's First Federal Republic and Spain's Liberal Revolution', *Bulletin of Spanish Studies*, forthcoming, DOI: 10.1080/14753820.2016.1172835.

43 T.N.A., FO 72/444, George Villiers, Doc. 165: 21 October 1835 letter from Villiers to Palmerston concerning fraught diplomatic negotiations.

44 Christopher Schmidt-Nowara, 'La España ultramarina: Colonialism and Nation-Building in Nineteenth-Century Spain', *European History Quarterly*, 34(2) (April 2004), pp. 191–214, 209.

45 *El pensamiento navarro*, Pamplona, 8 May 1938, p. 23 (Jesús Casariego on 'Liberalismo, Marxismo y "Frente Popular"').

46 Will Fowler, 'Valentín Gómez Farías: Perceptions of Radicalism in Independent Mexico, 1821–1847', *Bulletin of Latin American Research*, 15(1) (1996), 39–62, p. 45.

47 Lawrence, *Spain's First Carlist War*.

48 Preston, *Franco*, p. 35.

49 J. W. Parker and Sons, 'Espartero', *Saturday Review of Politics, Literature and Art*, 47(1211) (11 January 1879), p. 32.
50 Stanley Payne, *Politics and the Military in Modern Spain* (Stanford, 1967), p. 25.
51 Helen Graham, *The Spanish Civil War: A Very Short Introduction* (Oxford, 2005), p. 71
52 Neil MacMaster, *Spanish Fighters: An Oral History of Civil War and Exile* (Basingstoke, 1990), p. 44.
53 Hilari Raguer, *Gunpowder and Incense*, p. 20.
54 Andrés Iduarte, *En el fuego de España* (México DF, 1982), pp. 30–31.
55 Paul Preston, *The Coming of the Spanish Civil War: Reform, Reaction and Revolution in The Second Republic* (London, 1994), pp. 16, 95.
56 José María Gárate Córdoba, *Tenientes en campaña: la improvisación de oficiales en la guerra del 36* (Madrid, 1976), p. 84.
57 Alpert, *Republican Army*, pp. 151–156.
58 Natalia Sobrevilla, 'From Europe to the Americas and Back: Becoming los Ayacuchos', *European History Quarterly*, 41(3) (2011), pp. 472–488.
59 Christopher Schmidt-Nowara, 'Continental Origins of Insular Proslavery: George Dawson Flinter in Curaçao, Venezuela, Britain and Puerto Rico, 1810s-1830s', *Almanack*, no. 8 (28 November 2014); Pirala, *Guerra civil*, III, pp. 172–179. The Carlist press regularly derided all government soldiers as 'peseteros'.
60 Borkenau, *Spanish Cockpit*, p. 267.
61 Coverdale, *Italian Intervention in the Spanish Civil War*, pp. 230–247.
62 Christiansen, *Origins of Military Power*, pp. 63–66.
63 Pirala, *Guerra civil*, III, pp. 270–275.
64 T.N.A., F.O. 72/463 George Villiers, doc. 297: 19 November 1836 letter from Villiers to Palmerston detailing operations of the Army of the Centre.

Chapter 5

1 *El pensamiento navarro*, 8 May 1938, p. 8 ('La Comunión Tradicionalista').
2 Cited in Jo Fox and David Welch, 'Justifying War: Propaganda, Politics and the Modern Age' in David Welch and Jo Fox (eds), *Justifying War: Propaganda, Politics and the Modern Age* (Basingstoke, 2012), pp. 11–12.
3 Paul W. Schroeder, *The Transformation of European Politics, 1763–1848* (Oxford, 1984), xii.
4 Gerald Howson, *Arms for Spain* (London, 1998).
5 Michael Alpert, *A New International History of the Spanish Civil War* (Basingstoke, 1994), p. 155.
6 Arthur Koestler, *Spanish Testament*, p. 7.
7 William Rust, *Britons in Spain* (London, 1939), p. 19.
8 Ted Allen and Sydney Gordon, *The Scalpel and the Sword: The Story of Doctor Norman Bethune* (Boston, 1952), p. 107.
9 Cited in William Rust, *Britons in Spain* (London, 1939), p. 135.
10 Pete Seeger, Foreword to Harry Fisher, *Comrades: Tales of a Brigadista in the Spanish Civil War* (Lincoln, 1997), ix.

11 Diego Abad de Santillán, *Por qué perdimos la guerra* (Buenos Aires, 1940), pp. 10–11.

12 Philip B. Minehan, *Civil War and World War in Europe: Spain, Yugoslavia and Greece, 1936–1949* (New York, 2006), pp. 47, 86–87.

13 John Coverdale, *Italian Intervention in the Spanish Civil War* (Princeton, 1975).

14 T.N.A., GFM 33 68/298/1822, E 077972/73: 18 January 1937 letter from Faupel at Salamanca to Auswärtiges Amt in Berlin.

15 T.N.A., HW 22/2, 6C 1056, report 42 (copy no. 17), 'Assistance to both sides', 29 June 1837–4 July 1937: British air attaché's report of the opinion of von Goss, German correspondent at Salamanca.

16 Stanley Payne, *The Spanish Civil War, the Soviet Union and Communism* (Yale, 2004).

17 *El pensamiento navarro*, Pamplona, 8 May 1938, p. 18 ('Los de antes y los de ahora').

18 Alexander Parker, 'Carlism in the Spanish Civil War', *Irish Quarterly Review*, 26(13) (1937), p. 394.

19 Joseph McCabe, *Spain in Revolt, 1814–1931* (New York, 1932), pp. 64–65.

20 Gerald Brenan, *The Spanish Labyrinth* (London, 1943).

21 Steer, *Tree of Gernika*, pp. 343–344.

22 Blinkhorn, *Carlism and Crisis in Spain, 1931–39*, p. 174.

23 Anthony Adamthwaite, 'The Spanish Civil War Revisited: The French Connection', in Gaynor Johnson (ed.), *The International Context of the Spanish Civil War* (Cambridge, 2009), pp. 10–11.

24 Buchanan, *The Impact of the Spanish Civil War on Britain*, p. 18.

25 Tom Buchanan, *Britain and the Spanish Civil War* (Cambridge, 1997), p. 12.

26 A.H.N., II-C, Sección Histórica, Carlistas, 1835–1850, 2842: 22 January 1839 letter translated from the British legation in Madrid.

27 Amanda Vaill, *Hotel Florida* (New York, 2014), p. 68; Michael Jabara Carley, 'Caught in a Cleft Stick: Soviet Diplomacy and the Spanish Civil War', in *The International Context of the Spanish Civil War* (Cambridge, 2009), p. 162.

28 Edward Costello, *Adventures of a Soldier* (London, 1841), p. 227.

29 Arthur Koestler, *Spanish Testament*, p. 46.

30 Franz Borkenau, *The Spanish Cockpit*, p. 76.

31 Thomas J. Hamilton, *Appeasement's Child*, pp. 35–36.

32 Romeo Mateo, 'The Civil Wars of the Nineteenth Century', in Townson (ed.), *Is Spain Different?* p. 49.

33 Even the leading Spanish authority on the First Carlist War devoted only thirty-five pages out 650 (6% of his study) of his monograph to the international intervention (Alfonso Bullón de Mendoza, *La primera guerra carlista* (Madrid, 1992), pp. 403–438).

34 Hugh Thomas, *Spanish Civil War* (London, 1986), p. 333.

35 Peter Burroughs, 'An Unreformed Army? 1815–1868', in David G. Chandler and Ian Beckett (eds), *The Oxford History of the British Army* (Oxford, 2003), pp. 163–164; Brian Bond, 'The Army between the Two World Wars 1918–1939', in Chandler and Beckett (eds), *British Army*, p. 256.

36 Gerald Howson, *Arms for Spain* (London, 1998).

37   T.N.A., FO 72/462 George Villiers, doc. 285: 5 November 1836 letter from
     Villiers to Palmerston relaying Prime Minister Calatrava's gratitude.
38   T.N.A., Long Papers, bundle 715, T 1/4243: 25 May 1835 Foreign
     Office letter from Mr. Backhouse relating General Alava's notification to
     Palmerston.
39   A.H.N., II-C, Sección Histórica, Carlistas, 1835–1850, 2842: 15 October 1835
     letter from Ignacio Sabat of Cristino legation in London to Pérez de Castro at
     Cristino legation in Lisbon.
40   A.H.N., II-C, Sección Histórica, Carlistas, 1835–1850, 2842: 24 October
     1835, 14 November 1835, 4 December 1835, 10 December 1835, 10 February
     1836 and 23 February 1836 letters from Pérez de Castro, Cristino legate at
     Lisbon, to Prime Minister Mendizábal.
41   A.H.N., II-C, Sección Histórica, Carlistas, 1835–1850, 2842, doc. 369: 23
     September 1835 letter from Pérez de Castro, Cristino legate at Lisbon, to
     Madrid government.
42   T.N.A., GFM 33 6B/298/1822, E077992: 18 May 1937 letter from Faupel at
     Salamanca to Auswätiges Amt (Berlin).
43   T.N.A., FO/72/459 George Villiers, Doc. 146: 12 June 1836 letter from Villiers
     to Palmerston.
44   A.H.N., Correspondencia Embajadas y Legaciones, E.E.U.U., 1834–35, 1465,
     doc. 81: 25 November 1836 letter from Washington to Madrid.
45   Bolloten, Spanish Civil War, 46–80.
46   Hugh Thomas, Spanish Civil War (London, 1986), p. 549.
47   Alpert, Republican Army, pp. 151–156.
48   Mary Habeck, Storm of Steel: The Development of Armor Doctrine in
     Germany and the Soviet Union, 1919–1939 (Ithaca, 2014), pp. 248–274.
49   Alpert, Republican Army, pp. 151–156.
50   T.N.A., FO 72/458 George Villiers, doc. 82: 9 April 1836 letter from
     Villiers to Palmerston concerning unruliness of raw Spanish conscripts
     aboard ships.
51   T.N.A., FO/72/459 George Villiers, Doc. 111: 5 May 1836 letter from Villiers
     to Palmerston concerning expansion of Captain Hyde Parker's mission.
52   T.N.A., FO 72/460 George Villiers, doc. 163: 2 July 1836 letter from Villiers
     to Palmerston detailing Lord Hay's complaints.
53   T.N.A., FO 72/443 George Villiers, doc. 108: 10 July 1835 letter from Villiers
     to Palmerston.
54   Pirala, Guerra civil, V, pp. 44–48.
55   Steer, Tree of Gernika, pp. 142, 196–198.
56   Pirala, Guerra civil, IV, 459–461.
57   Buchanan, The Impact of the Spanish Civil War on Britain, pp. 131–139.
58   Kemp, Mine Were of Trouble, p. 116.
59   Hwyel Francis, 'Welsh Miners and the Spanish Civil War', Journal of
     Contemporary History, V(3) (July 1970), pp. 177–191, 182–187.
60   David Boyd Hancock, I Am Spain, p. 72.
61   Acier, From Spanish Trenches, p. 38.
62   Acier, From Spanish Trenches, p. 46.
63   El Constitucional, 12 January 1837; 12 January 1837.
64   Hills, Battle for Madrid, p. 51.

65 T.N.A., HW 22/2, 6C 1056, doc. B2 6: 7 April 1937 British air attaché report from Madrid.

66 Francisco J. Romero Salvadó, *The Spanish Civil War: Origins, Course and Outcomes* (London, 2005), pp. 66–98.

67 Alfred Kantorowicz, *Spanisches Kriegstagesbuch* (Berlin, 1966), pp. 430–432.

68 Estrella Trincado and José-Luis Ramos, 'John Stuart Mill and Nineteenth-Century Spain', *Journal of the History of Economic Thought*, 33(4) (December 2011), pp. 507–526.

69 José Luis Ramos Gorostiza and Estrella Trincado, 'John Stuart Mill on Spain', *Journal des Economistes et des Etudes Humaines*, 18(2) (2012), Article 1, pp. 5–8.

70 *The Times*, 30 September 1836.

71 Pirala, *Guerra civil*, II, pp. 545–565; http://cabrerayelmaestrazgocarlista. blogspot.mx/2009/09/el-diario-de-marianne-richards.html (accessed 22 August 2014).

72 Luis Garrido Muro, 'El Nuevo Cid. Espartero, María Cristina y el primero liberalismo español (1834–1840)' (Unpublished PhD thesis, Universidad de Cantabria, 2012), pp. 50–53.

73 Melgar, *Pequeña historia*, pp. 44–45; Pirala, *Guerra civil*, IV, pp. 461–466.

74 C. K. Webster, *The Foreign Policy of Palmerston, 1830–41* (London, 1951), Vol. I, p. 429.

75 Córdova, *Memorias*, Vol. I, pp. 296–297.

76 Luis Garrido Muro, 'El Nuevo Cid. Espartero, María Cristina y el primero liberalismo español (1834–1840)' (Unpublished PhD thesis, Universidad de Cantabria, 2012), pp. 77–78.

77 Cited in Emmanuel Tronco, *Les carlistes espagnols dans l'Ouest de la France, 1833–1883* (Rennes, 2010), p. 59.

78 Tronco, *Les carlistes espagnols*, p. 58.

79 Pirala, *Guerra civil*, III, pp. 441–444.

80 Pirala, *Guerra civil*, IV, pp. 58–67.

81 Pirala, *Guerra civil*, II, p. 280.

82 Bullen, 'France and Non-Intervention', pp. 383–86.

83 T.N.A., 72/444 George Villiers, doc. 149: 15 September 1835 letter from Villiers to Palmerston.

84 Paddy Griffith, *Military Thought in the French Army, 1815–51* (Manchester, 1989), pp. 10–14.

85 Robin Harris, *Talleyrand: Betrayer and Saviour of France* (London, 2007), p. 307.

86 T.N.A., FO/72/461 George Villiers, doc. 239: 21 September 1836 letter from Villiers to Palmerston concerning French policy.

87 T.N.A., FO 72/458 George Villiers, Doc. 92: 17 April 1836 letter from Villiers to Palmerston concerning recent Cortes debates.

88 T.N.A., FO 72/461 George Villiers, Doc. 213: 31 August 1836 letter from Villiers to Palmerston concerning Spanish government pleas.

89 T.N.A., FO 72/462 George Villiers, Doc. 261: 15 October 1836 letter from Villiers to Palmerston detailing hard-line policy of the French government in the wake of the La Granja revolution.

90 Marques de Miraflores, *Memorias del reinado de Isabel II* (Madrid, 1964), Vol. I, pp. 97–101, 114–115, 151–154.

91 A.H.N., II-C, Sección Histórica, Carlistas, 1835–1850, 2842: 7 January 1839 letter from Spanish ambassador to Paris, Miraflores, to Ministry of War; Jean-Charles Jauffret, 'La division de Légion étrangère du général Bernelle, 1835–1838', in *Légion étrangère 1831–1981*, Revue historique des armées (1981), pp. 51–72.

92 Cited in Francisco Guzmán Vega, *La última carta* (Palibro, 2011), pp. 166–167.

93 A.H.N., II-C, Sección Histórica, Carlistas, 1835–1850, 2842, doc. 108: 28 December 1838 letter from Spanish ambassador to Paris, Miraflores, to Spanish government.

94 Pirala, *Guerra civil*, IV, pp. 427–431, 519.

95 A.H.N., Correspondencia Embajadas y Legaciones, H-1720, Russia (1834–60), Doc. 37: 24 August 1834 letter from Cristino interim envoy at St Petersburg to Ministerio de Estado (Madrid); Lawrence, *Spain's First Carlist War*, p. 132.

96 T.N.A., FO 72/461 George Villiers, Doc. 243: 24 September 1836 letter from Villiers to Palmerston.

97 T.N.A., FO 72/463 George Villiers, Doc. 305: 28 November 1836 letter from Villiers to Palmerston.

98 Luis Garrido Muro, 'El Nuevo Cid. Espartero, María Cristina y el primero liberalismo español (1834–1840)' (Unpublished PhD thesis, Universidad de Cantabria, 2012), p. 76.

99 John Stuart Mill, 'The Spanish Question' (1837), in John M. Robson (ed.), *The Collected Works of John Stuart Mill, Vol XXXI* (Toronto, 1989), http://oll.libertyfund.org/?option=com_staticxt&staticfile=show.php %3Ftitle=238&chapter=53611&layout=html&Itemid=27 (accessed 4 December 2013).

100 Edgar Holt, *Carlist Wars*, p. 129.

101 Evans, *Memoranda of the Contest*, p. 26.

102 Duncan, *English in Spain*, p. 42.

103 Martin Robson, 'Strangers, Mercenaries, Heretics, Scoffers, Polluters: Volunteering for the British Auxiliary Legion in Spain, 1835', in Nir Arielli and Bruce Collins (eds), *Transnational Soldiers: Foreign Military Enlistment in the Modern Era* (London, 2013), p. 189.

104 Edward Costello, *Adventures of a Soldier* (London, 1841), pp. 1–10.

105 Webster, *Palmerston*, p. 428.

106 Francis Duncan, *The English in Spain*, p. 11.

107 Charles Shaw, *Personal Memoirs and Correspondence*, II, pp. 411–413; Alexander Somerville, *British Legion*, p. 6.

108 Bell Stephens, *The Basque Provinces*, I, pp. 130–31.

109 William Rust, *Britons in Spain* (1939), pp. 63, 67.

110 T.N.A., FO 72/443 George Villiers, doc. 122: 1 August 1835 letter from Villiers to Palmerston; *Eco del Comercio*, 28 July 1835.

111 Pirala, *Guerra civil*, IV, pp. 256–261.

112 Pirala, *Guerra civil*, II, pp. 238–240.

113 A.H.N., II-C, Sección Histórica, Carlistas, 1833–34, 2841: 17 September 1834 letter from Spanish minister to Lisbon, Evaristo Pérez de Castro, to Madrid.

114 T.N.A., FO 72/463 George Villiers, doc. 320: 8 December 1836 letter from Villiers to Palmerston detailing the auxiliaries' plight and Finance Minister Mendizábal's response.

115 *Eco del Comercio*, 21 June 1838.

116 A.H.N., Estado, 5448, no. 105: Circunstancias en que se halla el carlista indultado (legajo 2). 4 April 1836 letter from Prime Minister Mendizábal to Naval Ministry.

117 T.N.A., FO 72/463 George Villiers, Doc. 318: 3 December 1836 letter from Villiers to Palmerston explaining Bromley's case.

118 *Gaceta Oficial*, 20 May 1836.

119 Pirala, *Guerra civil*, II, pp. 514–521.

120 A.H.N., Estado, 5448, no. 105: Circunstancias en que se halla el carlista indultado (legajo 2): 23 March 1839 letter from prefect of Pontevedra concerning cross-border Carlism of Sarmiento and Quiroga.

121 Othen, *Franco's International Brigades*, pp. 88–89, 258–259.

122 Alpert, *A New International History*, p. 55.

123 Hugh Thomas, *The Spanish Civil War* (London, 1986), p. 491.

124 Pirala, *Guerra civil*, II, pp. 483–486.

125 *Joseph Tański: el informe Tański y la guerra civil carlista de 1833–1840* (Traducción, notas y studios complemetarios de Manuel Santirso) (April 2011), p. 29.

126 Helen Graham, *The War and its Shadow* (2012), pp. 76–78.

127 Webster, *Lord Palmerston*, p. 428.

128 Jasper Ridley, *Lord Palmerston* (London, 1970), pp. 269–284.

129 Mark Lawrence, 'Peninsularity and Patriotism: Spanish and British Approaches to the Peninsular War, 1808–14', *Historical Research*, 85 (2012), pp. 453–468.

130 T.N.A., FO 72/406 September 1833 letter from Palmerston to George Villiers.

131 T.N.A., FO 72/444, Doc. 144, 8 September 1835 letter from George Villiers to Lord Palmerston.

132 Pirala, *Guerra civil*, II, pp. 475–483, 503–505.

133 T.N.A., HW 22/2, 6C 1056, doc. B2 6: 7 April 1937 British air attaché report that civilian morale remains high in Bilbao and is adapting to aerial bombing; Pirala, *Guerra civil*, II, pp. 28–31.

134 A.H.N., Estado, 8146, Asuntos politicos, Guerra civil, Bloqueo de las costas del norte, 1835 a 1839: Reports from Palace and Finance Ministry, 7th and 3rd January 1837, respectively.

135 Pirala, *Guerra civil*, V, pp. 398.

136 Pirala, *Guerra civil*, III, pp. 607–610, 620–630.

137 A.H.N., Estado, 8146, Asuntos politicos, Guerra civil, Bloqueo de las costas del norte, 1835 a 1839, docs. 10, 20, 98, 107, 138 and 615: letters from Cristino representatves in Bayonne, Paris, London, Lisbon and Gibraltar respectively detailing subscriptions raised between January and March 1837.

138 T.N.A., F.O. 72/457, George Villiers, No. 46: 27 February 1836 letter from George Villiers to Lord Palmerston detailing frustration of Mexican envoy Santa María and Venezuelan General Soublette.

139 A.H.N., Estado, 8146, Asuntos politicos, Guerra civil, Bloqueo de las costas del norte, 1835 a 1839, 3 January 1837 letter to Calatrava from Ministerio de Hacienda.

140 A.H.N., Correspondencia Embajadas y Legaciones, Méjico, 1839–1844, 1647: 15 February 1843 letter from Spanish minister to Mexico, Francisco

Preto y Neto, to Madrid and despatched no. 6, dated 12 November 1843 from the same.

141 Steer, *Tree of Gernika*, pp. 86–87.

142 Juan Simeón Vidarte, *Todos fuimos culpables: testimonio de un socialista español* (México, 1973), pp. 750–795.

143 UNAM, CESU, Fondo Aurelio R. Acevedo (ARA), Caja 47, Expediente 17, Sección Militante Cristero, Subsección LNDLR, CD y CE, Series: Propaganda, doc. 28: September 1936 Cristero pamphlet written by Aurelio Acevedo.

144 UNAM, CESU, Fondo Aurelio R. Acevedo (ARA), Caja 47, Expediente 17, Sección Militante Cristero, Subsección LNDLR, CD y CE, Series: Propaganda, doc. 41: 1 April 1938 pamphlet written by Aurelio Acevedo entitled 'Orientaciones (Dios y mi derecho)'.

145 Othen, *Franco's International Brigades*, pp. 207–208.

146 UNAM, CESU, 1938, fotocopia, primera copia, Libro 4, Gilberto Bosques, Fondo reservado: 22 January 1938 letter from Consul Gómez Mangada to Mexican Foreign Minister Gilberto Bosques.

147 Dorothy Legaretta, 'Basque Refugee Children as Expatriates: Political Catalysts in Europe and America', in William A. Douglass (ed.), *Basque Politics: A Case-Study in Ethnic Nationalism* (University of Nevada Press, 1986), p. 193.

148 Dorothy Legaretta, *The Guernica Generation: Basque Refugee Children of the Spanish Civil War* (University of Nevada Press, 1985), pp. 190–196; Patricia W. Fagen, *Exiles and Citizens: Spanish Republicans in Mexico* (University of Texas Press, 1973), pp. 26–28.

149 Alfonso Bullón de Mendoza, *La primera guerra carlista* (Madrid, 1992), p. 420.

150 Maluquer de Motes, *Socialismo en España (1833–1868)* (Barcelona, 1977), pp. 117–122, 275–284.

151 A.H.N., II-C, Sección Histórica, Carlistas, 1835–1850, 2842, docs. 59, 62 and 88: 7 January and 24 January 1840 letters to Madrid from Spanish minister to Brussels, and 4 January 1840 confidential letter to Madrid from Spanish minister to Lisbon.

152 Pirala, *Guerra civil*, V, p. 539.

153 Pirala, *Guerra civil*, IV, pp. 398–399.

154 Diego Abad de Santillán, *Por qué perdimos la guerra* (Buenos Aires, 1940), pp. 165–166.

155 William Rust, *Britons in Spain* (London, 1939), pp. 117, 142, 151.

156 Cardozo, *March of a Nation*, p. 184.

157 *Eco del Comercio*, 9 February 1836; 16 May 1836; 22 May 1836 (suplemento).

158 Francisco J. Romero Salvadó, *Spain 1914–1918: Between War amd Revolution* (London, 1999), p. 13.

159 Blinkhorn, *Carlism in Crisis*, p. 218.

160 Kemp, *Mine Were of Trouble*, pp. 8–12, 33.

161 Boyd Haycock, *I Am Spain*, pp. 267–268.

162 Gómez López-Quiñones, *La guerra persistente*, p. 105.

163 Cited in Tronco, *Les carlistes espagnols*, p. 62.

164 Melgar, *Pequeña historia*, pp. 93–98; Oyarzun, *Historia del carlismo*, p. 18; *Gaceta Oficial*, 24 May 1836; 5 July 1836; 20 September 1836.

165 Cabello, Santa Cruz and Temprado, *Historia de la guerra última*, II, p. 308.

166 Xosé-Manoel Núñez Seixas, 'Nations in Arms against the Invader: On Nationalist Discourses during the Spanish Civil War', in Chris Ealham and Michael Richards (eds), *The Splintering of Spain: Cultural History and the Spanish Civil War, 1936–1939* (Cambridge, 2005), pp. 57–58.

167 Tomás Borrás, *Oscuro Heroismo* (Seville, 1939), p. 23.

168 Alaric Searle, 'The German Military Contribution to the Spanish Civil War, 1936–1939' in Gaynor Johnson (ed.), *The International Context of the Spanish Civil War* (Cambridge, 2009), p. 133.

169 Xosé-Manoel Núñez Seixas, 'Nations in Arms against the Invader', p. 52.

170 A.H.N., II-C, Sección Histórica, Guerra civil, Legión Portuguesa, 2853 (Ministerio Asuntos Exteriores): 1852, 10 February 1852 letter from Portuguese legation in Madrid to Marqués de Miraflores; No. 23: 29 November 1855 letter from Ministerio de Estado (Madrid) to Lisbon.

171 A.H.N., II-C, Sección Histórica, Guerra civil, Legión Portuguesa, 2853 (Ministerio Asuntos Exteriores): 24 August 1855 letter from British legation to Spanish government.

172 Owen Ashton, *W. E. Adams – Chartist, Radical and Journalist: An Honour to the Fourth Estate* (Whitley Bay, 1991), p. 124.

173 Buchanan, *The Impact of the Spanish Civil War on Britain*, p. 107.

174 T.N.A., KV 2/625: case against Herbert George Rowlands (alias Roland Miller) of Ranelagh Road, Westminster.

Chapter 6

1 George Steer, *Tree of Gernika*, pp. 24, 48–50; and Alice L. Lascelles and J. M. Alberich (eds), *Sir Vincent Kennett-Barrington: Letters from the Carlist War (1874–1876)* (Exeter, 1987), pp. 34–35.

2 Pirala, *Guerra civil*, IV, pp. 372–377.

3 Tronco, *Les carlistes espagnols*, pp. 127–131.

4 Louis Stein, *Beyond Death and Exile: The Spanish Republicans in France, 1939–1955* (Harvard, 1979), p. 11.

5 Stein, *Beyond Death and Exile*, p. 15.

6 Tronco, *Les carlistes espagnols*, p. 179.

7 Stein, *Beyond Death and Exile*, p. 15.

8 A.M.S.S., Actas del Ayuntamiento (Libro 328), Acta 73, 5 January 1836 and Acta 75, 8 January 1836: correspondence from Madrid and mayor of St. Jean de Luz; David Winegate Pike, *France Divided: The French and the Civil War in Spain* (Sussex, 2011), pp. 140–142.

9 Tronco, *Les carlistes espagnols*, p. 69.

10 Tronco, *Les carlistes espagnols*, p. 135.

11 *El Sol*, 5 May 1937.

12 Tara Zahra, *The Lost Children: Reconstructing Europe's Families After World War II* (Harvard, 2011), pp. 52–53.

13   At Amiens, Maçon, Cahors, Vendome, Angouleme, Espinal, Arras, Pau, Tours, Montpellier, Burdeos, Limoges, Perigueux, Langres, Chaumont and Clermont-Ferrand. Don Carlos was assigned a court in exile in Bourges, and in 1840 Cabrera and his staff were interned in Lille.

14   Tronco, *Les carlistes espagnols*, pp. 136–138, 183–196, 204–210.

15   Jean-Luc Marais, 'Les carlistes espagnols dans l'Ouest de la France, 1833–1883', *Annales de Bretagne et des Pays de l'Ouest* (online), http://abpo.revues.org/2222 (accessed 8 September 2013).

16   A.H.N., Estado, 8119: Emigrados, Doc. 257: 28 October 1839 letter from Bayonne Consul to Spanish government.

17   A.H.N., Estado, 8119: Emigrados, Doc. 272: 11 November 1839 confidential despatch from Bayonne Consult to Gamboa.

18   A.H.N., Estado, 8119: Emigrados, Doc. 274: 22 December 1839 letter from Consul at Bourdeau to Prime Minister in Madrid.

19   A.H.N., Estado, 8119: Emigrados: 28 December 1839 letter from Espartero to Spanish government.

20   A.H.N., Estado, 8119: Emigrados: 21 September 1839 decree from Council of Ministers.

21   A.H.N., Estado, 8119: Emigrados, Doc. 544: 1 November 1839 letter from ambassador Miraflores to Spanish government.

22   A.H.N., Estado, 8119: Emigrados: 27 December 1839 letter from Prime Minister to embassy in Paris and consulates in Bourdeau, Bayonne and Perpignan urging resistance to French diplomatic pressure; A.H.N., Estado, 8119: Emigrados: 3 January 1840 letter from Ministry of War.

23   A.H.N., II-C, Sección Histórica, Carlistas, 1835–1850, 2842 (contd.), (No. 1, corresponde al 16a 756): 26 September 1839 letter from Ambassador Miraflores in Paris to Madrid.

24   *Boletín Oficial de Cáceres*, 15 August 1840, no. 55.

25   A.H.N., II-C, Sección Histórica, Carlistas, 1835–1850, 2842 (contd.): 7 October 1839 letter from Spanish consul at Perpignan to Miraflores in Paris.

26   Helen Graham, *The War and its Shadow: Spain's Civil War in Europe's Long Twentieth Century* (Sussex, 2012), p. 18.

27   Peter Sahlins, *Boundaries: The Making of France and Spain in the Pyrenees* (Berkeley, 1989), pp. 208–209.

28   A.H.N., Estado, 1815: Convenio de Vergara, doc. 70: 29 September 1840 letter from ambassador Miraflores to Madrid.

29   A.H.N., Estado, 5448, no. 105: Circunstancias en que se halla el carlista indultado (legajo 2): 13 January 1842 letter from prefect of Cáceres to Espartero and 6 February 1842 letter from Grace and Justice Minister to Espartero.

30   A.H.N., Estado, 1815: Convenio de Vergara, Doc. 192: 15 May 1840 letter from Ambassador Miraflores to Madrid.

31   A.H.N., Estado, 1815: Convenio de Vergara: 7 November 1840 letter from Ministro de Gracia to Ministerio del Estado.

32   A.H.N., Estado, 1815: Convenio de Vergara: 3 February 1841 letter from Ministro de Guerra to Ministerio del Estado.

33   Pirala, *Guerra civil*, II, pp. 47–50.

34   A.H.N.,Estado, 1815: Convenio de Vergara: 8 August 1841 letter from Spanish consul at Cette to Ministerio del Estado.

35 *Gaceta de Madrid*, 24 July 1822; A.H.N., Estado, 1815: Convenio de Vergara, Doc. 279: 28 March 1843 letter from Spanish legation in London to Ministerio del Estado.

36 A.H.N., Estado, 1815: Convenio de Vergara, Doc. 310: 13 April 1843 letter from Spanish legation in London to Ministerio del Estado.

37 A.H.N., Estado, 1815: Convenio de Vergara: 30 January 1844 letter from Spanish legation in London to Ministerio del Estado.

38 Paloma Aguilar, 'The Memory of the Civil War in the Transition to Democracy: The Peculiarity of the Basque Case', *West European Politics*, 21 (1998), pp. 5–25; Cameron Watson, *Basque Nationalism and Political Violence* (Reno, 2007), pp. 167–174.

39 Cameron Watson, *Basque Nationalism and Political Violence* (Reno, 2007), pp. 167–174.

40 Aguilar, 'The Memory of the Civil War in the Transition to Democracy', p. 21; Watson, *Basque Nationalism*, p.172.

41 Watson, *Basque Nationalism*, p.148.

Conclusions

1 Ruth MacKay, 'History on the Line. The Good Fight and Good History: The Spanish Civil War', *History Workshop Journal*, 70(1) (2010), pp. 199–206; Tim Rees, 'Visions of the Vanquished: Recent Work on the Spanish Civil War', *European History Quarterly*, 23 (1993), pp. 571–582.

2 E.g., Roger Chickering, 'Total War: The Use and Abuse of a Concept', in Manfred F. Boemke, Roger Chickering and Stig Förster (eds), *Anticipating Total War: The German and American Experiences, 1971-1914* (Cambridge, 1999).

3 Stig Förster and Jörg Nagler (eds), *On the Road to Total War* (Cambridge, 2002), p. 6.

4 Eiras Roel, *El Partido Demócrata* (Madrid, 1962), pp. 84–89.

5 William C. Atkinson, *A History of Spain and Portugal* (London, 1960), p. 282.

6 *Eco del Comercio*, 8 September 1840; Maluquer de Motes, *Socialismo*, pp. 32–33.

7 William Callahan, 'The Spanish Church: Change and Continuity', in Nigel Townson (ed.), *Spain Transformed: The Late Franco Dictatorship, 1959–1975* (Basingstoke, 2007), p. 183.

8 Vincent, *Catholicism and Second Republic*, p. 259.

9 Nigel Townson, 'Anticlericalism and Secularization: A European exception?' in Townson (ed.), *Is Spain Different?* (Sussex, 2015), pp. 92–96.

GLOSSARY OF RELEVANT GROUPINGS AND ACTORS

Acevedo, Aurelio (1900–68): Mexican Cristero leader during the Second Cristero War (1934–38). Acevedo opposed the Mexican government's support for the Spanish Republic.

Africanista: term describing a clique of authoritarian army officers who dominated right-wing politics during the Spanish Civil War.

Aguirre, José Antonio (1903–60): professional footballer, PNV leader and president (*lendakari*) of the autonomous Basque government of 1936–37.

Auxiliary Legions: volunteers dispatched by Britain, France and Portugal to fight in the service of the Spanish government against the Carlists in Spain (1835–38).

Ayacucho: term describing a clique of authoritarian army officers who dominated liberal politics during the First Carlist War.

bienes nacionales: 'national property', or noble, ecclesiastical and common lands nationalized by Spanish governments for the purpose of auction throughout the late-eighteenth and nineteenth centuries.

Borrow, George (1803–81) British travel writer whose *Bible in Spain* (1843) recounted his experiences in Spain during the First Carlist War.

Cacique: pejorative term for regional political bosses whose power was greatest during the Restoration monarchy of 1876–31.

Calomarde, Francico Tadeo (1773–1842): last absolutist prime minister before the First Carlist War.

Carlism: reactionary political movement originating in the 1820s, defeated in the First Carlist War but victorious as part of General Franco's right-wing coalition in the Spanish Civil War.

Casado, Segismundo (1893–1968):   Commander-in-chief of the government Army of the Centre who in March 1939 mounted a coup which ended the Civil War.

Confederación Nacional Católico-Agraria (CEDA):   The Spanish Confederation of Autonomous Rightists Groups; the largest political organization of the legalist right during the Second Republic.

Confederación Nacional del Trabajo (CNT):   anarcho-syndicalist trade union founded in 1910.

Corpo Truppe Volontarie (CTV):   50,000 troops sent by Fascist Italy to fight on the side of the rebels in the Spanish Civil War.

Durruti, Buenaventura (1896–36):   revolutionary anarchist who led the first militia column (Durruti Column) on the Aragón front. After being killed in action, Durruti achieved near-legendary status in the government zone.

Eliot Treaty: British-brokered humanitarian treaty signed by both warring sides in April 1835 allowing for the lives of captured regular soldiers to be spared in the Basque-Navarra front of operations.

Evans, George de Lacy (1787–1870):   Commander of the British auxiliaries during 1835–37 and radical Member of Parliament for the constituency of Westminster.

Exaltado: left-wing liberal movement of 1820–36

Federación Anarquista Ibérica (FAI):   the insurrectionary vanguard of the anarchist movement.

Fal Conde, Manuel (1894–1975):   Carlist leader who opposed Franco's attempt to unify the right under his command. Refusing to renounce his desire to reinstitute

Fernández de Córdova, General Luis (1798–1840):

a traditional monarchy, Fal Conde was forced into exile during the Spanish Civil War.

moderado commander-in-chief of the government Army of the North during 1835–36, who exiled himself in France as a consequence of the La Granja revolution.

Falange Española Tradicionalista de las Juntas de Ofensiva Nacional-Sindicalista (FET/JONS):

the unified Nationalist party created by Franco's decree in 1937.

Franco, General Francisco (1892–1975):

military commander of the Canary Islands at the beginning of the Spanish Civil War, leader of the July rebellion in Spanish Morocco and director of the rebels from October 1936 until the end of the Spanish Civil War. Franco was head of the Spanish state from 1939 until his death in 1975.

Ibárurri, Dolores (1895–1989):

better known as 'La Pasionaria', an iconic communist activist and a secretary-general of the PCE during 1942–60.

International Brigade:

communist-organized international volunteers fighting on the side of the Spanish Republic during 1936–38.

Iron Ring (*cinturón*):

a defensive line hurriedly constructed around Bilbao by the Basque government during 1936–37 which was betrayed from within at the height of the successful Nationalist offensive against the Basque country in the summer of 1937.

Largo Caballero, Francisco (1869–1946):

a moderate socialist for most of his life, Largo Caballero became a revolutionary during 1934–36. More pragmatic during his tenure as prime minister and war minister (1936–37), he was forced to resign these offices during the communist-led counter-revolution of May 1937.

Margarita: member of the Carlist women's movement during the Spanish Civil War.

Mendizábal, Juan Alvarez (1790–1853): *Exaltado* prime minster during 1835–36 and progresista finance minister during 1836–37.

Miaja, General José (1878–1956): government general who directed the defence of Madrid during the Spanish Civil War and in March 1939 supported the Casado coup which organized the surrender of the Republic to the rebels.

Moderado: conservative liberal movement of 1820–68.

Mola, General Emilio (1887–1937): military governor of Pamplona (Navarra) and director of the July 1936 rebel conspiracy. He was killed in a plane crash in June 1937.

Miguelistas: supporters of Dom Miguel, pretender to the Portuguese throne, defeated in 1834; the Portuguese equivalent of Spanish Carlists.

Muñagorri, José Antonio de (1794–1841): Basque arms magnate who in November 1837 launched a movement supported by the Madrid government for a compromise peace based on the exile of Don Carlos and the preservation of Basque autonomy (fueros).

Negrín, Juan (1892–1956): Spanish socialist prime minster of 1937–39 who depended on the power of the communists.

Ojalatero: 'shirker' (or 'if only'). Ironic term of abuse for desk officers and peacemongers in the rebel zone during the First Carlist War.

Oriamendi: the location of a famous Carlist victory over British and government forces near San Sebastián in March 1837. 'Oriamendi' was the name of the Carlist battle-hymn of the Spanish Civil War.

Orwell, George (1903–50): British democratic socialist and foreign volunteer for the government side in the Spanish Civil War.

Pan-Hispanism:	enjoyed some following amongst Latin Americans (such as the Cristeros) who resented the power of the United States. Intellectual current popular with early twentieth-century right-wing thinkers calling for Spain to assert a 'moral empire' over her former colonies.
Partido Comunista de España (PCE):	communist party founded in 1920–21, loyal to Moscow.
Partido Nacionalista Vasco (PNV):	Christian Democrat Basque Nationalist Party.
Partido Obrero de Unificación Marxista (POUM):	small group of left-wing, non-Stalinist communists made famous by George Orwell.
Primo de Rivera, José Antonio (1903–36):	son of Miguel Primo de Rivera, military dictator of Spain during 1923–30, and founder member of the main Spanish fascist party, the Falange. Already a prisoner when war broke out, José Antonio was executed by his government captors on 20 November 1936. After his death, José Antonio acquired near-legendary status in the rebel zone.
Primo de Rivera, Pilar:	sister of Falange leader José Antonio and leader of Falange Women's Section.
Progresista:	left-wing liberal successor (1836–68) to the exaltado movement.
Partido Socialista Obrero Español (PSOE):	Spanish Socialist Workers' Party, founded in 1879.
Quadruple Alliance:	diplomatic alliance signed in April 1834 between the constitutional monarchies of Spain, Portugal, France and the United Kingdom, followed in August 1834 by 'additional articles' permitting the recruitment of foreign volunteers to fight for the Spanish government.
reparto:	'redistribution', or the demand voiced by landless agricultural labourers for ownership of the land. This demand peaked during the property revolutions of the First Carlist and Spanish Civil Wars and

	usually formed part of radical left-wing manifestoes.
Requeté:	Carlist military units first founded at the start of the First Carlist War (1833) and revived for military action at the start of the Spanish Civil War (1936).
Royalist Volunteers:	reactionary paramilitary force of 1823–33 continued by the rebels but disbanded by the government side during the First Carlist War.
Traditionalism:	anti-liberal political movement originating in the 1814 'Manifesto of Persians' calling for the institution of a religious monarchy and strongly (though not exclusively) associated with Carlism.
Turno pacífico (peaceful alternation in power):	corrupt power-sharing operation at work between the 1880s and the First World War in which the two oligarchical parties (Liberals and Conservatives) agreed to take turns in office by using the power of the government and regional caciques to fix the results of elections. Originally dreamt up by Cánovas del Castillo as an answer to the chronic instability of Spanish politics, this system barred any genuinely radical forces from coming to power legally, even after universal male suffrage was introduced in 1890.
Unión General de Trabajadores (UGT):	trade union organization of the Socialist movement.
Villiers, George (1800–70):	influential British ambassador to Spain during the First Carlist War. His power peaked during the revolutionary period of 1835–37.
Women's Section (*Sección Femenina*):	women's section of the Spanish fascist party (Falange).
Zumalacárregui, Tomás de (1788–1835):	Carlism's first warlord and military genius of the First Carlist War.

SOURCES AND BIBLIOGRAPHY

Archives

Archivo General del Palacio, Madrid (AGP)
Arxiu Històric de la Ciutat de Barcelona (AHCB)
Archivo Histórico Nacional, Madrid (AHN)
Archivo Municipal de Málaga (AMM)
Archivo Municipal de San Sebastián (AMSS)
Biblioteca Universitaria de Zaragoza (BUZ)
Real Academia de la Historia, Madrid (RAH)
The National Archives, London (TNA)
Universidad Autónoma de México, Centro de Estudios sobre la Universidad, Mexico City (UNAM, CESU)

Primary sources available in the public domain

http://www.balmasedahistoria.com/08_fuentes.html (accessed 9 September 2014)
http://www.eka-partidocarlista.com/delburgo.htm (accessed 7 January 2016)
Larra, Mariano José de, 'Fígaro de vuelta: carta a su amigo residente en París' (Madrid, 2 January 1836), reproduced in http://www.biblioteca.org.ar/libros/131236.pdf
Richards, Marianne, wife of Ramón Cabrera, diary entries, reproduced at http://cabrerayelmaestrazgocarlista.blogspot.mx/2009/09/el-diario-de-marianne-richards.html (accessed 22 August 2014)

Newspapers/pamphlets

ABC
Avance: Diario Socialista de Asturias
Boletín Oficial de Cáceres
Comisariado: División 25
Diario de Sevilla
Eco de Aragón
Eco del Comercio

El Constitucional
El Correo Nacional
El Español
El Genio de la Libertad
El Huracán
El País
El pensamiento navarro
El Sol
Frente Rojo
Gaceta de Madrid
Gaceta Oficial
Galería militar contemporánea
La Vanguardia
Manchester Guardian
Saturday Review of Politics, Literature and Art
Solidaridad Obrera
The Times

Published primary sources

Abad de Santillán, Diego, *Por qué perdimos la guerra* (Buenos Aires: Imán, 1940).

Acier, Marcel (ed.), *From Spanish Trenches: Recent Letters from Spain* (New York: Modern Age Books, 1937).

Alcock, Rutherford, *Notes on the Medical History and Statistics of the British Legion* (London: John Churchill, 1838).

Allen, Ted and Sydney Gordon, *The Scalpel and the Sword: The Story of Doctor Norman Bethune* (Boston: Little Brown, 1952).

Alvarez del Vayo, Julio, *The Last Optimist* (London: Putnam, 1950).

Argüelles, Agustín de, *1820 á 1824: reseña histórica* (Madrid: A. de sin Martin, 1864).

Artola, Miguel (ed.), *Memorias del general Don Francisco Espoz y Mina* (Madrid: Atlas, 1962), 2 vols.

Aviraneta, Eugenio de, *Memoria dirigida al gobierno español sobre los planes y operaciones puestos en ejecución para aniquilar la rebelión en las provincias del norte de España* (Madrid: Imprinta de D. Narciso Sanchiz, 1844).

Aznar, Manuel, *Historia militar de la guerra de España* (Madrid: IDEA, 1940).

Bacon, John Francis, *Six Years in Biscay, Comprising a Personal Narrative of the Sieges of Bilbao, in June 1835, and Oct. to Dec. 1836* (London: Smith Elder, 1838).

Barea, Arturo, *La forja de un rebelde* (Madrid: Editorial Debate, 2000).

Bazal, Luis, *¡Ay de los vencidos!* (Toulouse: Polygraphe Universel 1966).

Bernard, Ino, *Mola: mártir de España* (Granada: Prieto, 1938).

Bollaert, William, *The Wars of Succession of Portugal and Spain from 1821 to 1840* (London: Forgotten Books, 1870; 2013).

Borkenau, Franz, *The Spanish Cockpit: An Eyewitness Account of the Spanish Civil War* (London: Faber & Faber, 1937).

Borras, Tomás, *Oscuro heroismo* (Seville: Editorial Católica Española, 1939).

Borrow, George, *The Bible in Spain* (London: J. M. Dent, 1839).

Buckley, Henry, *The Life and Death of the Spanish Second Republic* (London: IB Tauris, 1940, 2nd edn, 2013).

Burgo, Jaime del, *El valle perdido* (Madrid: Editorial Navarra, 1942).

Burke Honan, Michael, *The Court and Camp of Don Carlos* (London: John Macrone, 1836).

Cabello, Francisco, Francisco Santa Cruz and Ramón María Temprado, *Historia de la guerra última en Aragón y Valencia* (Madrid: Imprenta del colegio de sordo mudos, 1845), 2 vols.

Cardozo, Harold, *The March of a Nation: My Year of Spain's Civil War* (London: The Right Book Club, 1937).

Chaho, Joseph Augustín, *Voyage en Navarre pendant l'insurrection des Basques (1830–1835)* (Paris: Larrouse, 1836).

Cockburn, Claud, *In Time of Trouble* (London: Hart Davis, 1956).

Costello, Edward, *Adventures of a Soldier* (London: H. Colburn, 1841).

Debray, Régis and Max Gallo (eds), *Santiago Carrillo: Dialogue on Spain* (London: Lawrence & Wishart, 1976).

Dembowski, Carlos, *Dos años en España durante la guerra civil, 1838–40* (Barcelona: Editorial Critica, 2008).

Duncan, Francis, *The English in Spain; or, the Story of the War of Succession between 1834 and 1840* (London: J. Murray, 1877).

Fernández de Córdova, Luis and Fernando Valcarcel, *Mis memorias íntimas* (Madrid: Establecimiento Tipográfico de El Liberal, 1886), 2 vols.

Foz, Francisco, *Mis memorias: andanzas de un veterinario rural (1818–1896)* (Madrid: Institución Fernando el Católico, 2013).

García-Morato, Joaquín, *Guerra en el aire* (Madrid: Editora Nacional, 1940).

García Tejero, Alfonso, *Historia político-administrativa de Mendizábal* (Madrid: Ortigosa, 1858), 2 vols.

Goeben, August von, *Vier Jahre in Spanien: Die Carlisten, ihre Erhebung, ihr Kampf und ihr Untergang* (Hannover: Hahn'sche Hofbuchhandlung, 1841).

Gómez Becerra, Alvaro, *Observaciones sobre el estado del poder judicial en España* (Madrid: imprenta Nacional de Sordo-Mudos, 1839).

Gurney, Jason, *Crusade in Spain* (London: Faber and Faber, 1974).

Hamilton, Thomas J., *Appeasement's Child: The Franco Regime in Spain* (New York: Alfred A. Knopf, 1943).

Henningsen, Charles Frederick, *The Most Striking Events of a Twelvemonth's Campaign with Zumalacárregui in Navarre and the Basque Provinces* (London: John Murray, 1836).

Herr, Richard (ed.), *Memorias del cura liberal don Juan Antonio Posse con su discurso sobre la Constitución de 1812* (Madrid: Centro de Investigaciones Sociológicas, 1984).

Hughes, T. M., *Spain in 1845* (London: H. Colburn, 1845), 2 vols.

Iduarte, Andrés, *En el fuego de España* (México DF: Joaquín Mortiz, 1982).

Jomini, Antoine Henri, *Descripción analítica de las combinaciones más importantes de la guerra* (Madrid: Imprenta Real, 1833).

Joseph Tański: el informe Tański y la guerra civil carlista de 1833–1840 (Traducción, notas y studios complemetarios de Manuel Santirso) (Ministerio de Defensa, April 2011).

Kantorowicz, Alfred, *Spanisches Kriegstagebuch* (Berlin: Aufbau-Verlag, 1966).

Kemp, Peter, *Mine Were of Trouble* (London: Cassell, 1958).

Koestler, Arthur, *Spanish Testament* (London: Victor Gollancz, 1937).

Lacy Evans, George de, *Memoranda of the Contest in Spain* (London: James Ridgway, 1840).

Langdon-Davies, John, *Behind the Spanish Barricades* (London: Martin Secker & Warburg, 1936).

Lascelles, Alice L. and J. M. Alberich (eds), *Sir Vincent Kennett-Barrington: Letters from the Carlist War (1874–1876)* (Exeter: University of Exeter, 1987).

Lichnowsky, Felix, *Erinnerungen aus den Jahren 1837, 1838 und 1839* (Frankfurt-am-Main: Druck und Verlag von Johann David Sauerländer, 1841), 2 vols.

Marchmont, Arthur W., *Sarita the Carlist* (Toronto: McLeod & Allen, 1902).

McNeill-Moss, Geoffrey, *The Epic of the Alcázar: A History of the Siege of the Toledo Alcázar* (London: Rich & Cowan, 1937).

Miaja, Fernando Rodríguez, *Testimonios y remembranzas* (México DF: El Colegio de México, 2013).

Miraflores, Marques de, *Memorias del reinado de Isabel II* (Madrid: Atlas Ediciones, 1964), 2 vols.

Miralles, Rafael, *Memorias de un comandante rojo* (Madrid: Librería Editorial San Martín, 1975).

Orwell, George, *Homage to Catalonia* (London: Penguin, 1989).

Pérez Olivares, Rogelio, *Heroes de España: Excmo. Sr. D. Emilio Mola Vidal* (Avila: Imp. Católica y Enc. Sigirano Díaz, 1937).

Pérez Olivares, Rogelio, *Héroes de España: Excmo. Sr. D. Queipo de Llano* (Avila: Imp. Católica y Enc. Sigirano Díaz, 1937).

Pitcairn, Frank, *Reporter in Spain* (London: Lawrence & Wishart, 1937).

Pombo, Nemesio de, *Situación de España a fines del año 1842* (Madrid, 1843).

Rahden, Wilhelm Baron von, *Cabrera. Erinnerungen aus dem spanischen Bürgerkriege* (Frankfurt-am-Main: Wilmans, 1840).

Romilly, Esmond, *Boadilla* (London: MacDonald, 1971).

Ruiz de Luzuriaga, José, *La contra-gaceta de la Gaceta de Madrid del 7 de abril de 1833* (Bordeaux, 1833).

Ruiz Vilaplana, Antonio, *Burgos Justice: A Year's Experience of Nationalist Spain* (London: Constable, 1938).

Rust, William, *Britons in Spain* (London: Lawrence & Wishart, 1939).

Shaw, Charles, *Personal Memoirs and Correspondence of Colonel Charles Shaw, K.C.T.S., &c, of the Portuguese Service and late Brigadier-General, in the British Auxiliary Legion of Spain; Comprising a Narrative of the War for Constitutional Liberty in Portugal and Spain, from its Commencement in 1831 to the Dissolution of the British Legion in 1837* (London: Henry Colburny, 1837), 2 vols.

Somerville, Alexander, *History of the British Legion and War in Spain* (London: J. H. Starib, 1839).

Steer, George, *The Tree of Gernika: A Field Study of Modern War* (London: Hodder & Stoughton, 1938).

Stephens, Edward Bell, *The Basque Provinces: Their Political State, Scenery, and Inhabitants; with Adventures amongst the Carlists and Christinos* (London: Whittaker, 1837), 2 vols.

Taboada Lago, José María, *Por una España mejor* (Madrid: G. del Toro, 1977).

Toreno, Conde de, *Historia del levantamiento, guerra y revolución de España* (Madrid: Imprenta de Berenguillo, 1953).

Urraca Pastor, María Rosa, *Así empezamos. Memorias de una enfermera* (Bilbao: La Editorial Vizcaína, 1940).

Valdés, Rafael, S. J., *Un capellán, héroe de la Legión: P. Fernando Huidobro, SI* (Sal Terrae, Santander: Sal Terrae, 1938).

Walton, William, *A Reply to the Anglo-Cristino Pamphlet, Entitled the Policy of England towards Spain* (London: J. Hatchard, 1837).

Wintringham, Tom, *English Captain* (London: Faber and Faber, 1939).

Secondary sources

Abella, Rafael, *Julio 1936: Dos Españas frente a frente* (Barcelona: Rustica, 1981).

Aguilar Fernández, Paloma, 'The Memory of the Civil War in the Transition to Democracy: The Peculiarity of the Basque Case', *West European Politics*, 21(4) (1998), 5–25.

Aguilar Fernández, Paloma, *Políticas de la memoria y memorias de la política* (Madrid: Alianza Editorial, 2008).

Alonso Carballés, Jesús, 'La evolución de la memoria de la Guerra Civil en el espacio urbano de Bilbao: una mirada comparativa', *Cahiers de civilisation espagnole contemporaine*, 5 (2009), http://ccec.revues.org/3000; DOI: 10.4000/ccec.3000 (accessed 18 January 2016).

Alpert, Michael, *A New International History of the Spanish Civil War* (Basingstoke: Palgrave Macmillan, 1994).

Alpert, Michael, *The Republican Army in the Spanish Civil War, 1936–1939* (Cambridge: Cambridge University Press, 2013).

Alted Vigil, Alicia, 'Las consecuencias de la Guerra Civil española en los niños de la República: de la dispersion al exilio', *Espacio, Tiempo y Forma*, Serie V, Historia Contemporánea, 9 (1996), 207–228.

Alvarez Junco, José, *Mater Dolorosa: la idea de España en el siglo XIX* (Madrid: Editorial Taurus, 2001).

Alvarez Junco, José, *Populismo, caudillaje y discurso demagógico* (Madrid: Editorial Taurus, 1987).

Alvarez Junco, José and Adrian Shubert (eds), *Spanish History Since 1808* (London: Macmillan, 2000).

Alvarez Tardío, Manuel and Roberto Villa García, *El precio de la exclusión: la política durante la Segunda República* (Madrid: Encuentro, 2010).

Anes Alvarez de Castrillón, Gonzalo (ed.), *Economía, sociedad, política y cultura en la España de Isabel II* (Madrid: Rustica, 2004).

Arielli, Nir and Bruce Collins (eds), *Transnational Soldiers: Foreign Military Enlistment in the Modern Era* (London: Palgrave Macmillan, 2013).

Aróstegui, Julio, Jordi Canal and Eduardo González Calleja, *El carlismo y las guerra carlistas: hechos, hombres e ideas* (Madrid: La Esfera de los Libros, 2003).

Arranz Notario, Luis, 'Libertad y democracia en la España contemporánea: (a propósito de El camino a la democracia en España. 1931 y 1978)', *Cuadernos de pensamiento politico (FAES)*, no. 9 (2006), 227–238.

Artola-Gallego, Miguel, *Partidos y programas politicos, 1808–1936* (Madrid: La Esfera de los Libros, 1974).

Ashton, Owen R., *W. E. Adams – Chartist, Radical and Journalist: An Honour to the Fourth Estate* (Whitley Bay: Bewick Press, 1991).

Atkinson, William C., *A History of Spain and Portugal* (London: Penguin, 1960).

Baldoli, Claudia, *Forgotten Blitzes: France and Italy under Allied Air Attack, 1940–1945* (London: Continuum, 2012).

Balfour, Sebastian, *Deadly Embrace: Morocco and the Road to the Spanish Civil War* (Oxford: Oxford University Press, 2002).

Balfour, Sebastian, *The End of the Spanish Empire, 1898–1923* (Oxford: Oxford University Press, 1997).

Barraquer y Roviralta, Cayetano, *Los religiosos en Cataluña durante la primera mitad del siglo XIX*, 4 vols. (Barcelona: F. J. Altés y Alabart, 1915).

Bayley, Christopher, *Birth of the Modern World, 1780–1914: Global Connections and Comparisons* (London: Blackwell, 2004).

Beevor, Antony, *The Battle for Spain: The Spanish Civil War, 1936–1939* (London: Phoenix, 2006).

Ben-Ami, Shlomo, *Fascism from Above: Dictatorship of Primo de Rivera in Spain, 1923–30* (Oxford: Clarendon Press, 1973).

Ben-Ami, Shlomo, *The Origins of the Second Republic in Spain* (Oxford: Oxford University Press, 1978).

Bernanos, Georges, *Los grandes cementerios bajo la luna* (Buenos Aires: Siglo Veinte, 1964).

Bernecker, Walther L., *España entre tradición y modernidad: política, economía y sociedad (siglos XIX y XX)* (Madrid: *Siglo* Veintiuno, 1999).

Blackbourn, David and Geoff Eley, *The Peculiarities of German History: Bourgeois Society and Politics in Nineteenth-century Germany* (Oxford: Oxford University Press, 1984).

Blinkhorn, Martin, *Carlism in Crisis, 1931–1939* (Cambridge: Cambridge University Press, 1975).

Blinkhorn, Martin, 'The Basque Ulster: Navarre and the Basque Autonomy Question under the Spanish Second Republic', *The Historical Journal*, 17(3) (1974), 595–613.

Boemke, Manfred F., Roger Chickering and Stig Förster (eds), *Anticipating Total War: The German and American Experiences, 1971–1914* (Cambridge: Cambridge University Press, 1999).

Boix, Carles and Susan C. Stokes (eds), *The Oxford Handbook of Comparative Politics* (Oxford: Oxford University Press, 2007).

Bolloten, Burnett, *The Spanish Civil War: Revolution and Counterrevolution* (Chapel Hill: University of North Carolina Press, 1991).

Bolloten, Burnett, *The Spanish Revolution* (Chapel Hill: University of North Carolina Press, 1979).

Bowen, Wayne H. and José E. Alvarez, *A Military History of Modern Spain: From the Napoleonic Era to the International War on Terror* (Westport: Praeger, 2007).

Boyd, Carolyn P., '"Responsibilities" and the Spanish Second Republic, 1931–6', *European History Quarterly*, XIV(2) (April 1984), 151–182.

Boyd Haycock, David, *I Am Spain: The Spanish Civil War and the Foreigners Who Went to Fight Fascism* (London: Old Street, 2012).

Brenan, Gerald, *The Spanish Labyrinth* (London: Cambridge University Press, 1943).

Brett, Edward M., *The British Auxiliary Legion in the First Carlist War: A Forgotten Army* (Dublin: Four Courts, 2005).

Buchanan, Tom, *Britain and the Spanish Civil War* (Cambridge: Cambridge University Press, 1997).

Buchanan, Tom, *The Impact of the Spanish Civil War on Britain: War, Loss and Memory* (Brighton: Sussex Academic Press, 2007).

Bullen, Roger, 'France and the Problem of Intervention in Spain, 1834–1836', *Historical Journal*, 20(2) (1977), 363–393.

Bullón de Mendoza, Alfonso, *La primera guerra carlista* (Madrid: Editorial Actas, 1992).

Bunk, Brian D., *Ghosts of Passion: Martyrdom, Gender and the Origins of the Spanish Civil War* (Durham: Duke University Press, 2006).

Burdiel, Isabel, *La política de los notables: moderados y avanzados durante el régimen del Estatuto Real (1834–1836)* (Valencia: Edicions Alfons el Magnànim, 1987).

Burdiel, Isabel, *La política en el reinado de Isabel II* (Madrid: Marcial Pons, 1998).

Burdiel, Isabel and Manuel Pérez Ledesma, *Liberales, agitadores y conspiradores: biografías heterodoxas del siglo XIX* (Madrid: Espasa-Calpe, 2000).

Burgo, Jaime del, *Para la historia de la primera guerra carlista: comentarios y acotaciones a un manuscrito de la época 1834–1839* (Pamplona: Institucion Principe de Viana, 1981).

Canal, Jordi, *El carlismo* (Madrid: Alianza Editorial, 2004).

Carr, Raymond (ed.), *The Republic and Civil War in Spain* (London: Macmillan, 1971).

Carr, Raymond, *The Spanish Tragedy: The Civil War in Perspective* (London: Weidenfeld and Nicolson, 1972).

Carr, Raymond, *Spain, 1808–1939* (Oxford: Clarendon Press, 1966).

Carulla, Jordi and Arnau Carulla (eds), *El color de la guerra* (Barcelona: Postermill, 2000).

Casanova, Julián, *The Spanish Republic and Civil War, 1931–1939* (Cambridge: Cambridge University Press, 2010).

Cenarro Laguna, Angela, 'Memory Beyond the Public Sphere: The Francoist Repression Remembered in Aragon', *History and Memory*, 14(1/2) (2002), 165–188.

Cepeda Gómez, José, *El ejército español en la política española (1787– 1843): conspiraciones y pronunciamientos en el comienzo de la España liberal* (Madrid: Fundación Universitaria *Española*, 1990).

Chandler, David G. and Ian Beckett (eds), *The Oxford History of the British Army* (Oxford: Oxford University Press, 2003).

Chodakiewicz, Marek Jan and John Radzilowski (eds), *Spanish Carlism and Polish Nationalism: The Borderlands of Europe in the 19th and 20th Centuries* (Charlottesville: Leopolis Press, 2003).

Christiansen, Eric, *The Origins of Military Power in Spain, 1800–1854* (Oxford: Oxford University Press, 1967).

Cierva, Ricardo de la, *Historia de la guerra civil española* (Madrid: San Martin, 1969).

Cierva, Ricardo de la, *Historia del franquismo* (Barcelona: Planeta, 1975).

Clemente, Josep Carles, *El carlismo contra Franco* (Madrid: Flor del Viento, 2003).

Clemente, Josep Carles, *Las guerras carlistas* (Barcelona: Peninsula, 1982).

Comellas García-Llera, José-Luis, *El trienio constitucional* (Madrid: Rialp, 1963).

Comellas-Llera, José Luis, *Los moderados en el poder (1844–54)* (Madrid: CSIC, 1970).

Coni, Nicholas, *Medicine and Warfare: Spain, 1936–1939* (London: Routledge, 2008).

Corral, Pedro, *Desertores: la Guerra Civil que nadie quiere contar* (Barcelona: Random House, 2006).

Coverdale, John F., *Italian Intervention in the Spanish Civil War* (Princeton: Princeton University Press, 1975).

Coverdale, John F., *The Basque Phase of Spain's First Carlist War* (Princeton: Princeton University Press, 1984).

Crankshaw, Edward, *The Shadow of the Winter Palace* (London: Macmillan, 1976).

Cuenca, José Manuel, *La iglesia española ante la revolución liberal* (Madrid: Rialp, 1971).

Day, Peter, *Franco's Friends: How British Intelligence Helped Bring Franco to Power in Spain* (London: Biteback, 2012).

Díaz-Plaja, Fernando, *La vida cotidiana en la España de la guerra civil* (Madrid: EDAF, 1994).

Douglass, William A. (ed.), *Basque Politics: A Case-study in Ethnic Nationalism* (Reno: University of Nevada Press, 1986).

Duyvesteyn, Isabelle and Jan Angstrom (eds) *Rethinking the Nature of War* (Abingdon: Frank Cass, 2005).

Ealham, Chris, 'Anarchism and Illegality in Barcelona, 1931–37', *Contemporary European History*, IV(2) (July 1995), 133–151.

Ealham, Chris and Michael Richards (eds), *The Splintering of Spain: Cultural History and the Spanish Civil War, 1936–1939* (Cambridge: Cambridge University Press, 2005).

Eiras Roel, Antonio, *El partido demócrata español* (Madrid: Rialp, 1961).

Elías Torras, Jaime, *La guerra de los Agraviados* (Barcelona: Universidad de Barcelona, Publicaciones de la Catedra de Historia General de Espana, 1967).

Ellwood, Sheelagh, *Franco: Profiles in Power* (London: Longman, 2000).

Ellwood, Sheelagh, *Spanish Fascism in the Franco Era* (London: Macmillan, 1987).

Ellwood, Sheelagh, *The Spanish Civil War* (Oxford: Blackwell, 1991).

Esdaile, Charles, *Fighting Napoleon: Guerrillas, Bandits and Adventurers in Spain, 1808–1814* (New Haven: Yale University Press, 2004).

Esdaile, Charles, *Outpost of Empire: The Napoleonic Occupation of Andalucía, 1810–1812* (Oklahoma: University of Oklahoma Press, 2012).

Esenwein, George, Book review of Stanley G. Payne, *The Spanish Civil War, Soviet Union and Communism* (New Haven: Yale University Press, 2004) in *The American Historical Review*, 110(3) (June 2005), 876–878.

Esenwein, George R., *The Spanish Civil War: A Modern Tragedy* (New York: Routledge, 2005).

Esenwein, George and Adrian Shubert, *Spain at War: The Spanish Civil War in Context, 1931–1939* (London: Longman, 1995).

Espadas Burgos, Manuel, *Baldomero Espartero: un candidato al trono* (Ciudad Real: Diputación Provincial Ciudad Real, 1984).

Esteban Navarro, Miguel Angel, *La formación del pensamiento político y social del radicalismo español (1834–1874)* (Zaragoza: Universidad de Zaragoza, 1995).

Fagen, Patricia W., *Exiles and Citizens: Spanish Republicans in Mexico* (Austin: University of Texas Press, 1973).

Fernández Sebastián, Javier and Juan Francisco Fuentes (eds), *Diccionario político y social del siglo XIX español* (Madrid: Alianza Editorial, 2002).

Ferrer, Melchor, Domingo Tejera and José F. Acedo, *Historia del tradicionalismo español*, Vols. I–XVIII (Madrid: Ediciones Trajano, 1941–1950).

Fisher, Harry, *Comrades: Tales of a Brigadista in the Spanish Civil War* (Lincoln: University of Nebraska Press, 1997).

Foard, Douglas W., 'The Forgotten Falangist: Ernesto Giménez Caballero', *Journal of Contemporary History*, 10(1) (January 1975), 3–18.

Förster, Stig and Jörg Nagler (eds), *On the Road to Total War* (Cambridge: Cambridge University Press, 2002).

Fowler, Will, 'Valentín Gómez Farías: Perceptions of Radicalism in Independent Mexico, 1821–1847', *Bulletin of Latin American Research*, 15(1) (1996), 39–62.

Fradera, Josep M. and Christopher Schmidt-Nowara (eds), *Slavery and Anti-Slavery in Spain's Atlantic Empire* (New York: Berghahn, 2013).

Francis, Hwyel, 'Welsh Miners and the Spanish Civil War', *Journal of Contemporary History*, V(3) (July 1970), 177–191.

Fraser, Ronald, *Blood of Spain: An Oral History of the Spanish Civil War* (Harmondswoth: Penguin, 1981).

Fraser, Ronald, *Las dos guerras de España* (Barcelona: Critica, 2012).

Fox, Jo and David Welch, *Justifying War: Propaganda, Politics and the Modern Age* (Basingstoke: Palgrave Macmillan, 2012).

Fusi, Juan Pablo and Jordi Palafox, *España: 1808–1936. El desafío de la modernidad* (Madrid, 1997).

Gallego, J. A., J. R. Urquijo and M. Espadas, 'La España de Espartero', *Cuadernos, historia* 16(118) (1985).

Gárate Córdoba, José María, *Tenientes en campaña: la improvisación de oficiales en la guerra del 36* (Madrid: Libreria Editorial San Martín, 1976).

García Ferrandis, X. and A. J. Munayco Sánchez, 'La evolución de la Sanidad Militar en Valencia durante la Guerra Civil Española (1936–1939)', *Sanidad Militar*, 67(4) (2011), 383–389.

Garrido Muro, Luis, 'El Nuevo Cid. Espartero, María Cristina y el primero liberalismo español (1834–1840)' (Unpublished PhD thesis, Universidad de Cantabria, 2012).

Gil Novales, Alberto, *Las sociedades patrióticas (1820–1823)* (Madrid: Editorial Tecnos, 1975).

Gómez López-Quiñones, Antonio, *La guerra persistente* (Madrid: Verbuert Iberoamericana, 2006).

Gómez Urdáñez, Gracia, *Salustiano de Olózaga: élites políticas en el liberalismo español (1805–1843)* (Logroño: Universidad de La Rioja, 2000).

Graham, Helen, '"Against the State": A Genealogy of the Barcelona May Days (1937)', *European History Quarterly*, 29 (1999), 485–541.

Graham, Helen, *The Spanish Civil War: A Short Introduction* (Oxford: Oxford University Press, 2005).

Graham, Helen, 'The Spanish Civil War', *The Historical Journal*, 30(4) (1987), 989–93.

Graham, Helen, *The Spanish Republic at War, 1936–1939* (Cambridge: Cambridge University Press, 2003).

Graham, Helen, *War and its Shadow: Spain's Civil War in Europe's Long Twentieth Century* (Brighton: Sussex Academic Press, 2012).

Graham, Helen and Jo Labanyi (eds), *Spanish Cultural Studies: An Introduction* (Oxford: Oxford University Press, 1995).

Grayzel, Susan R., *Women and Identities at War: Gender, Motherhood and Politics in Britain and France during the First World War* (Chapel Hill: North Carolina University Press, 1999).

Griffith, Paddy, *Military Thought in the French Army, 1815–51* (Manchester: Manchester University Press, 1989).

Guillamon, Augustin, *The Friends of Durruti Group: 1937–1939* (Edinburgh: AK Press, 1996).

Guzmán Vega, Francisco, *La última carta* (Bloomington: Palibrio, 2011).

Habeck, Mary, *Storm of Steel: The Development of Armor Doctrine in Germany and the Soviet Union, 1919–1939* (Ithaca: Cornell University Press, 2014).

Hamnett, Brian, 'Spain and Portugal and the Loss of Their Continental American Territories in the 1820s: An Examination of the Issues', *European History Quarterly*, 41(3) (July 2011), 397–412.

Harris, Robin, *Talleyrand: Betrayer and Saviour of France* (London: John Murray, 2007).

Herr, Richard (ed.), *Memorias del cura liberal don Juan Antonio Posse con su discurso sobre la Constitución de 1812* (Madrid: Centro de Investigaciones Sociologicas, 1984).

Hills, George, *The Battle for Madrid* (London: Vantage, 1976).

Hobsbawm, Eric, *The Age of Revolution, 1789–1848* (London: Weidenfeld & Nicolson, 1962).

Holt, Edgar, *The Carlist Wars in Spain* (London: Putnam, 1967).

Horn, Gerd-Rainer (ed.), *Letters from Barcelona: An American Woman in Revolution and Civil War* (Basingstoke: Palgrave Macmillan, 2009).

Howard, Michael, *War in European History* (Oxford: Oxford University Press, 2009).

Howson, Gerald, *Arms for Spain* (London: John Murray, 1998).

Jackson, Gabriel, 'The Azaña Regime in Perspective', in *The American Historical Review*, 64(2) (January 1959), 282–300.

Jackson, Gabriel, *The Spanish Second Republic and Civil War* (New York: Princeton University Press, 1965).

Janke, Peter, *Mendizábal y la instauración de la monarquía constitucional en España (1790–1853)* (Madrid: Siglo XXI de España Editores, 1974).

Jauffret, Jean-Charles, 'La division de Légion étrangère du général Bernelle, 1835–1838' in *Légion étrangère 1831–1981*, Revue historique des armées (1981), 51–72.

Johnson, Gaynor (ed.), *The International Context of the Spanish Civil War* (Newcastle: Cambridge Scholars Press, 2009).

Kalyvas, Stathis N., *The Logic of Violence in Civil Wars* (Cambridge: Cambridge University Press, 2006).

Kedward, Rod and Roger Austin (eds), *Vichy France and the Resistance. Culture and Ideology* (London: Croom Helm, 1985).

Keegan, John, *The Face of Battle* (London: Jonathan Cape, 1976).

Kershaw, Ian and Moshe Lewin (eds), *Stalinism and Nazism: Dictatorships in Common* (Cambridge: Cambridge University Press, 1998).

Kocka, Jürgen and Heinz-Gerhard Haupt (eds), *Comparative and Transnational History: Central European Approaches and New Perspectives* (New York; Oxford: Bergahn Books, 2009).

Labra, Rafael M. de, *El Ateneo de Madrid, sus orígenes, desenvolvimiento, representación y porvenir* (Madrid: Imprenta de Aurelio J. Alaria, 1878).

Lafuente y Zamalloa, Modesto, *Historia general de España: desde los tiempos más remotos hasta nuestros días*, XX (Madrid: Establecimiento Tipográfico de Mellado, 1890).

La Haye, Eve, *War Crimes in Internal Armed Conflicts* (Cambridge: Cambridge University Press, 2010).

Lannon, Frances, *Privilege, Persecution and Prophecy: The Catholic Church in Spain 1875–1975* (Oxford: Clarendon Press, 1987).

Lannon, Frances, 'Women and Images of Women in the Spanish Civil War', *Transactions of the Royal Historical Society (Sixth Series)*, 1 (December 1991), 213–228.

Laquer, Walter, *Guerrilla Warfare: A Historical and Critical Study* (New Jersey: Transaction, 1997).

Laven, David and Lucy Riall (eds), *Napoleon's Legacy: Problems of Government in Restoration Europe* (Oxford: Berg, 2000).

Lawrence, Mark, 'Peninsularity and Patriotism: Spanish and British Approaches to the Peninsular War, 1808–14', *Historical Research*, 85 (2012), 453–468.

Lawrence, Mark, 'Poachers Turned Gamekeepers: A Study of the Guerrilla Phenomenon in Spain, 1808–1840', *Small Wars and Insurgencies*, 25(4) (2014), 843–857.

Lawrence, Mark, *Spain's First Carlist War, 1833–40* (New York: Palgrave Macmillan, 2014).

Lawrence Tone, John, 'Napoleon's Uncongenial Sea: Guerrilla Warfare in Navarre during the Peninsular War, 1808–1814', *EHQ*, 26 (1996).

Legaretta, Dorothy, *The Guernica Generation: Basque Refugee Children of the Spanish Civil War* (Reno: University of Nevada Press, 1985).

Llorens, Vicente, *Liberales y románticos. Una emigración española en Inglaterra (1823–1834)* (México: El Colegio de México, 1954).

MacClancy, Jeremy, *The Decline of Carlism* (Reno: University of Nevada Press, 2000).

MacKay, Ruth, 'History on the Line. The Good Fight and Good History: The Spanish Civil War', *History Workshop Journal*, 70(1) (2010), 199–206.

MacMaster, Neil, *Spanish Fighters: An Oral History of Civil War and Exile* (Basingstoke: Macmillan, 1990).

Malefakis, Edward, *Agrarian Reform in Spain: Origins of the Civil War* (New Haven: Yale University Press, 1971).

Maluquer de Motes, Jordi, *El socialismo en España (1833–1868)* (Barcelona: Critica, 1977).

Mangini, Shirley, 'Memories of Resistance: Women Activists from the Spanish Civil War', *Signs*, 17(1) (Autumn 1991), 171–186.

Marais, Jean-Luc, 'Les carlistes espagnols dans l'Ouest de la France, 1833–1883', *Annales de Bretagne et des Pays de l'Ouest*, 118(4) (2011), http://abpo.revues.org/2222 (accessed 8 September 2014).

Marichal, Carlos, *Spain, 1834–1844: A New Society* (London: Tamesis, 1977).

Marías, Julián, *España ante la historia y ante sí misma (1898–1936)* (Madrid: S.L.U. Espasa Libros, 1996).

Martínez Martín, Manuel, *Revolución Liberal y Cambio Agrario en la Alta Andalucía* (Granada: Universidad de Granada, 1995).

Matthews, James, *Reluctant Warriors: Republican Popular Army and Nationalist Army Conscripts in the Spanish Civil War, 1936–1939* (Oxford: Oxford University Press, 2012).

Mayer, Arno, *The Persistence of the Old Regime* (London: Croom Helm, 1981).

McCabe, Joseph, *Spain in Revolt, 1814–1931* (New York: D. Appleton, 1932).

Mees, Ludger, 'Politics, Economy, or Culture? The Rise and Development of Basque Nationalism in the Light of Social Movement Theory', *Theory and Society*, 33(3/4) (June–August 2004), 311–331.

Melgar, Francisco, *Pequeña historia de las guerras carlistas* (Madrid: Editorial Gómez, 1958).

Meneses, Filipe Ribeiro de, *Franco and the Spanish Civil War* (London: Routledge, 2001).

Miaja, Fernando Rodríguez, *Testimonios y remembranzas: mis recuerdos de los últimos meses de la guerra de España, 1936–1939* (México DF: El Colegio de México, 2013).

Millán, Jesús, 'Una reconsideración del carlismo', *Ayer*, 29 (1998), 91–107.

Minehan, Philip B., *Civil War and World War in Europe: Spain, Yugoslavia and Greece, 1936–1949* (New York: Palgrave Macmillan, 2006).

Miralles, Rafael, *Memorias de un comandante rojo* (Madrid: San Martin, 1975).

Moa, Pío, *Los mitos de la guerra civil* (Madrid: La Esfera de los Libros, 2004).

Molina, Fernando, 'The Reign of Christ over the Nation: The Basque Question in the Second Republic, 1931–1936', *National Identities*, 13(1) (2011), 17–33.

Moliner Prada, Antonio, 'La conflicitividad social', *Trienio* (May 2000).

Moliner Prada, Antonio (ed.), *La Guerra de la Independencia en España (1808–1814)* (Barcelona: Critica, 2007).

Moliner Prada, Antonio, *Revolución burguesa y movimiento juntero en España: la acción de las juntas a través de la correspondencia diplomática y consular francesa, 1808–1868* (Madrid: Milenio, 1997).

Moradiellos García, Enrique, *La perfidia de Albión: el gobierno británico y la guerra civil española* (Madrid: Siglo XXI, 1996).

Moral Roncal, Antonio Manuel, '1868 en la memoria carlista de 1931: dos revoluciones anticlericales y un paralelo', *Hispania Sacra*, LIX(119) (January–June 2007), 337–361.

Moreno Alonso, Manuel, *Blanco White: la obsesión de España* (Seville: Alfor, 1998).

Nash, Mary, *Rojas: las mujeres republicanas en la Guerra Civil* (Madrid: Taurus, 1999).

Nash, Mary, 'Women in War: *Milicianas* and Armed Combat in Revolutionary Spain, 1936–1939', *The International History Review*, 15(2) (May 1993), 269–282.

Navajas Zubeldia, Carlos, *Leales y rebeldes: la tragedia de los militares republicanos* (Madrid: Síntesis, 2011).

Núñez, Xosé-Manoel, 'New Interpretations of the Spanish Civil War', *Contemporary European History*, 12(4) (November 2004), 517–527.

Oberschall, Anthony, 'The Manipulation of Ethnicity: From Ethnic Cooperation to Violence and War in Yugoslavia', *Ethnic and Racial Studies*, 23(6) (2000), 982–1001.

Offer, Avner, *The First World War: An Agrarian Interpretation* (Oxford: Oxford University Press, 1989).

Othen, Christopher, *Franco's International Brigades: Adventurers, Fascists and Christian Crusaders in the Spanish Civil War* (London: C. Hurst, 2013).

Oyarzun, Román, *Historia del carlismo* (Madrid: MAXTOR, 1965).

Paquette, Gabriel, 'The Dissolution of the Spanish Atlantic Monarchy', *Historical Journal*, 52(1) (2009), 175–212.

Parker, Alexander, 'Carlism in the Spanish Civil War', *Irish Quarterly Review*, 26(103) (1937), 383–398.

Parker, Geoffrey, *The Military Revolution: Military innovation and the Rise of the West, 1500–1800* (Cambridge: Cambridge University Press, 1996).

Parrott, David, *The Business of War* (Cambridge: Cambridge University Press, 2012).

Parry, J. H., *The Spanish Seaborne Empire* (London: Hutchinson, 1966).

Payne, Stanley G., *Basque Nationalism* (Reno: University of Nevada Press, 1975).

Payne, Stanley G., 'Catalan and Basque Nationalism', *Journal of Contemporary History*, 6 (1971), 15–51.

Payne, Stanley G., *Civil War in Europe, 1905–1949* (Cambridge: Cambridge University Press, 2011).

Payne, Stanley G., 'Political Violence during the Spanish Second Republic', *Journal of Contemporary History*, 25(2/3) (May–June 1990), 269–288.

Payne, Stanley G., *Politics and the Military in Modern Spain* (Stanford: Stanford University Press, 1967).

Payne, Stanley G., *Spain's First Democracy: The Second Republic, 1931–1936* (Wisconsin: University of Wisconsin Press, 1993).

Payne, Stanley G., *The Franco Regime, 1946–1975* (Wisconsin: University of Wisconsin Press, 2011).

Payne, Stanley G., *The Spanish Civil War* (Cambridge: Cambridge University Press, 2012).

Pegenaute, Pedro, *Represión política en el reinado de Fernando VII: las comisiones militares (1824–1825)* (Pamplona: Universidad de Navarra, 1974).

Peyrou, Florencia, *El republicanismo popular en España (1840–1843)* (Cádiz: Universidad de Cádiz, 2002).

Piqueras, José A. and Manuel Chust (eds), *Republicanos y repúblicas en España* (Madrid: Siglo Veintiuno, 1996).

Pirala, Antonio, *Historia de la guerra civil y de los partidos liberal y carlista*, 6 vols. (Madrid: Turner/Historia, 1984).

Porter, David, *Vision on Fire: Emma Goldman and the Spanish Revolution* (London: AK Press, 2007).

Prada Rodríguez, Julio, 'Las milicias de segunda línea en la retaguardia franquista. El caso de Galicia', *Cuadernos de Historia Contemporánea*, 33 (2011), 255–273.

Preston, Paul, *¡Comrades! Portraits from the Spanish Civil War* (London: Fontana Books, 2000).

Preston, Paul, *Franco: A Biography* (London: HarperCollins, 1993).

Preston, Paul, *Juan Carlos: A People's King* (London: HarperCollins, 2004).

Preston, Paul (ed.), *Revolution and War in Spain, 1931–39* (London: Methuen, 1984).

Preston, Paul, *Spanish Holocaust: Inquisition and Extermination in Twentieth-Century Spain* (London: HarperCollins, 2012).

Preston, Paul, *The Coming of the Spanish Civil War: Reform, Reaction and Revolution in The Second Republic* (London: Routledge, 1994).

Quesada González, José Miguel, 'El reservismo militar en España' (Doctoral thesis, 2013, Instituto Universitario General Gutiérrez Mellado).

Quiroga, Alejandro, *Making Spaniards: Primo de Rivera and the Nationalization of the Masses, 1923–30* (Basingstoke: Palgrave Macmillan, 2007).

Quiroga, Alejandro and Miguel Angel del Arco (eds), *Right-Wing Spain in the Civil War Era: Soldiers of God and Apostles of the Fatherland, 1914–45* (London: Continuum, 2012).

Quiroga, Alejandro, Book review of Manuel Alvarez Tardío and Fernando del Rey Reguillo, eds, *The Spanish Second Republic Revisited: From Democratic Hopes to Civil War (1931–1936)* (Brighton: Sussex Academic Press, 2011), *European History Quarterly*, 43(3) (2013), 519–597.

Raguer, Hilari, *Gunpowder and Incense: The Catholic Church and the Spanish Civil War* (London: Routledge, 2006).

Ramos Gorostiza, José Luis and Estrella Trincado, 'John Stuart Mill on Spain', *Journal des Economistes et des Etudes Humaines*, 18(2) (2012), Article 1, pp. 5–8.

Rees, Tim, 'Visions of the Vanquished: Recent Work on the Spanish Civil War', *European History Quarterly*, 23 (1993), 571–582.

Revuelta González, Manuel, *La exclaustración (1833–40)* (Madrid: Biblioteca de autores cristianos, 1976).

Riall, Lucy and David Laven (eds), *Napoleon's Legacy: Problems of Government in Restoration Europe* (Oxford: Berg, 2000).

Rico y Amat, Juan, *Historia política y parlamentaria de España (desde los tiempos primitivos hasta nuestros días* (Madrid: Imprenta de las Escuelas Pías, 1861), 2 vols.

Ridley, Jasper, *Lord Palmerston* (London: Constable, 1970).

Ringrose, David, *Spain, Europe, and the 'Spanish Miracle', 1700–1900* (Cambridge: Cambridge University Press, 1996).

Ripperger, Robert M., 'The Development of the French Artillery for the Offensive, 1890–1914', *Journal of Military History*, 59(4) (1995).

Risco, Alberto P., *Zumalacárregui en campaña. Según los documentos conservados por su secretario de estado mayor, don Antonio Zaratiegui* (Madrid: Imp. de Jose Murillo, 1935).

Robson (ed.), John M., *The Collected Works of John Stuart Mill, Vol XXXI* (Toronto: University of Toronto Press, 1989).

Rodríguez O., Jaime E., *'We are now the True Spaniards': Sovereignty, Revolution, Independence, and the Emergence of the Federal Republic of Mexico, 1808–1824* (Stanford: Stanford University Press, 2012).

Roel, Eiras, *El Partido Demócrata* (Madrid: Rialp, 1962).

Romero Salvadó, Francisco J., *The Spanish Civil War: Origins, Course and Outcomes* (London: Palgrave Macmillan, 2005).

Romero Salvadó, Francisco J., *Twentieth-Century Spain: Politics and Society in Spain, 1898–1998* (New York: St Martin's Press, 1999).

Romero Salvadó, Francisco J. and Angel Smith (eds), *The Agony of Spanish Liberalism: From Revolution to Dictatorship, 1913–23* (London: Palgrave Macmillan, 2010).

Roura i Aulinas, Lluís, 'Hi hagué algun protocatalanisme politic a Cadis?', *L'Avenç*, no. 113 (1988), 32–37.

Rubio Pobes, Coro, 'Qué fue del oasis foral? (Sobre el estallido de la Segunda Guerra Carlista en el País Vasco)', *Ayer*, 38 (2000), 65–89.

Rubio Pobes, Coro, *Revolución y tradición: el país vasco ante la revolución liberal y la construcción del estado liberal, 1808–1868* (Madrid: Siglo XXI, 1996).

Rújula, Pedro (ed.), Francisco Cabello, Francisco Santa Cruz and Ramón María Temprado, *Historia de la guerra última en Aragón y Valencia* (Zaragoza: Institución 'Fernando el Católico', 2006), 2 vols.

Ruiz, Julius, *The 'Red Terror' and the Spanish Civil War: Revolutionary Violence in Madrid* (Cambridge: Cambridge University Press, 2014).

Sahlins, Peter, *Boundaries: The Making of France and Spain in the Pyrenees* (Berkeley: University of California Press, 1989).

Saint-Saëns, Alain (ed.), *Historia silenciada de la mujer: La mujer española desde la época medieval hasta la contemporánea* (Madrid: Universidad Complutense, Editorial Complutense, 1996).

Salvador, Antonio Caridad, 'Las mujeres durante la primera guerra carlista (1833–1840)', *Memoria y Civilización*, Anuario de Historia, 14 (2011), 175–199.

Sánchez, José M., *The Spanish Civil War as a Religious Tragedy* (Notre Dame: University of Notre Dame Press, 1987).

Santirso Rodríguez, Manuel, *Progreso y libertad: España en la Europa liberal, 1830–1870* (Barcelona: Ariel, 2008).

Schmidt-Nowara, Christopher, 'Continental Origins of Insular Proslavery: George Dawson Flinter in Curaçao, Venezuela, Britain and Puerto Rico, 1810s–1830s', *Almanack*, no. 8 (28 November 2014).

Schmidt-Nowara, Christopher, 'La España ultramarina: Colonialism and Nation-Building in Nineteenth-Century Spain', *European History Quarterly*, 34(2) (April 2004), 191–214.

Schroeder, Paul W., *The Transformation of European Politics, 1763–1848* (Oxford: Oxford University Press, 1984).

Seidman, Michael, *The Republic of Egos: A Social History of the Spanish Civil War* (Madison: University of Wisconsin Press, 2002).

Seidman, Michael, *The Victorious Counterrevolution: The Nationalist Effort in the Spanish Civil War* (Madison: University of Wisconsin Press, 2011).

Serrano, Secundino, *Maquis: Historia de la guerrilla antifranquista* (Madrid: Temas de Hoy, 2001).

Shubert, Adrian, *A Social History of Modern Spain* (London: Unwin Hyman, 1990).

Sims, Harold, *The Expulsion of Mexico's Spaniards, 1821–1836* (Pittsburgh: University of Pittsburgh Press, 1991).

Skocpol, Theda and Margaret Somers, 'The Uses of Comparative History in Macrosocial Enquiry', in *Comparative Studies in Society and History*, 22 (1980), 174–197.

Smith, Angel, *The Origins of Catalan Nationalism, 1770–1898* (Basingstoke: Palgrave Macmillan, 2014).

Smith, Rhea Marsh, *The Day of the Liberals in Spain* (Philadelphia: University of Pennsylvania Press, 1938).

Sobrevilla, Natalia, 'From Europe to the Americas and Back: Becoming los Ayacuchos', *European History Quarterly*, 41(3) (2011), 472–488.

Sorel, Georges, *Reflections on Violence* (New York: Peter Smith, 1941).

Spiers, Edward, *Radical General: Sir George de Lacy Evans, 1787–1870* (Manchester: Manchester University Press, 1983).

Stein, Louis, *Beyond Death and Exile: The Spanish Republicans in France, 1939–1955* (Cambridge, MA: Harvard University Press, 1979).

Stradling, Robert, *Your Children Will Be Next: Bombing and Propaganda in the Spanish Civil War, 1936–39* (Cardiff: University of Wales Press, 2008).

Suárez Verdeguer, Federico, *La crisis política del antiguo régimen en España (1808–1840)* (Madrid: Rialp, 1950).

Thomas, Hugh, *The Spanish Civil War* (London: Eyre & Spottiswoode, 1962, 1st ed.).

Thomas, Hugh, *The Spanish Civil War* (London: Penguin, 1986, 3rd ed.).

Thomson, Guy, *The Birth of Modern Politics in Spain: Democracy, Association and Revolution, 1854–75* (Basingstoke: Palgrave Macmillan, 2009).

Tocqueville, Alexis de, *The Old Regime and the French Revolution* (New York: Anchor Books, 1955).

Torras, Jaime, *Liberalismo y rebeldía campesina (1820–23)* (Barcelona: Ariel, 1976).

Torras, Jaime, 'Peasant Counter-Revolution?', *Journal of Peasant Studies*, 5(1) (1977), 66–78.

Trías, Juan J. and Antonio Elorza, *Federalismo y reforma social en España (1840–1870)* (Madrid: Seminarios y Ediciones S.A., 1975).

Townson, Nigel (ed.), *Is Spain Different? A Comparative Look at the Nineteenth and Twentieth Centuries* (Brighton: Sussex Academic Press, 2015).

Townson, Nigel (ed.), *Spain Transformed: The Late Franco dictatorship, 1959–1975* (Basingstoke: Palgrave Macmillan, 2007).

Trincado, Estrella and José-Luis Ramos Gorostiza, 'John Stuart Mill and Nineteenth-Century Spain', *Journal of the History of Economic Thought*, 33(4) (December 2011), 507–526.

Tronco, Emmanuel, *Les carlistes espagnols dans l'Ouest de la France, 1833–1883* (Rennes: Presses Universitaires de Rennes, 2010).

Ugarte Tellería, Javier, *La nueva Covadonga insurgente: orígenes sociales y culturales de la sublevación de 1936 en Navarra y el País Vasco* (Madrid: Biblioteca Nueva, 1998).

Urquijo y Goitia, José Ramón de, 'Represión y disidencia durante la primera Guerra carlista: la policía carlista', *Hispania: Revista española de historia*, 45(159) (January 1985), 131–186.

Vaill, Amanda, *Hotel Florida: Truth, Love and Death in the Spanish Civil War* (London: Bloomsbury, 2014).

Vidarte, Juan Simeón, *Todos fuimos culpables: testimonio de un socialista español* (México: Fondo de Cultura Económica, 1973).

Viñas, Angel, 'Playing with History and Hiding Treason: Colonel Casado's Untrustworthy Memoirs and the End of the Spanish Civil War', *Bulletin of Spanish Studies*, 91(1–2) (2014), 295–323.

Vincent, Mary, *Catholicism in the Second Republic: Religion and Politics in Salamanca, 1930–1936* (Oxford: Clarendon, 1996).

Vincent, Mary, *Spain, 1833–2002: People and State* (Oxford: Oxford University Press, 2002).

Watson, Cameron, *Basque Nationalism and Political Violence* (Reno: University of Nevada Press, 2007).

Webster, C. K., *The Foreign Policy of Palmerston, 1830–41* (London: G. Bell, 1951), 2 vols.

Welskopp, Thomas, 'Vergleichende Geschichte', *European History Online* (EGO) (3 December 2010), 1–8.

Winegate-Pike, David, *France Divided: The French and the Civil War in Spain* (Brighton: Sussex Academic Press, 2011).

Winter, Jay and Jean Louis-Robert, *Capital Cities at War: Paris, London, Berlin, 1914–1919* (Cambridge: Cambridge University Press, 2008).

Zahra, Tara, *The Lost Children: Reconstructing Europe's Families After World War II* (Cambridge, MA: Harvard University Press, 2011).

Zelizer, Barbie, *About to Die: How News Images Move the Public* (Oxford: Oxford University Press, 2010).

INDEX